DATE DUE

THE NEWS UNDER RUSSIA'S OLD REGIME

THE NEWS UNDER RUSSIA'S OLD REGIME

THE DEVELOPMENT OF A MASS-CIRCULATION PRESS

Louise McReynolds

PRINCETON UNIVERSITY PRESS   PRINCETON, NEW JERSEY

PN
5274
M38
1991

c. 1

23582558
DLC

3-3-93

Copyright © 1991 by Princeton University Press
Published by Princeton University Press, 41 William Street,
Princeton, New Jersey 08540
In the United Kingdom: Princeton University Press, Oxford

All Rights Reserved

Library of Congress Cataloging-in-Publication Data

McReynolds, Louise, 1952–
The news under Russia's old regime : the development of a mass-
circulation press / Louise McReynolds.
p.   cm.
Includes index.
ISBN 0-691-03180-0
1. Journalism—Soviet Union—History. 2. Russian newspapers—
History. 3. Press—Soviet Union—History. I. Title.
PN5274.M38 1991
077'.09—dc20   91-13671

This book has been composed in Linotron Caledonia

Princeton University Press books are printed on acid-free paper,
and meet the guidelines for permanence and durability of the
Committee on Production Guidelines for Book Longevity of the
Council on Library Resources

Printed in the United States of America by Princeton University Press,
Princeton, New Jersey

10 9 8 7 6 5 4 3 2 1

Contents

List of Illustrations   vii

List of Tables   ix

Acknowledgments   xi

Abbreviations Used in Footnotes and Tables   xiii

Introduction   3

1. The Origins of the Mass-Circulation Press   11

2. The Transition to Commercial Independence, 1863–1876   30

3. The Newspaper from the Boulevard, 1864–1876   52

4. The News Shapes the Medium: War and Assassination, 1876–1881   73

5. The Newspaper in Battle with the "Thick" Journal: Commercialization and Objectivity in the 1880s   97

6. The Grounding of a Public Institution in the 1890s   123

7. The Newspaper Reporter   145

8. The Journalism of Imperialism: The Russo-Japanese War   168

9. Russian Newspapers in Revolution, 1905–1907   198

10. The Newspaper Between Revolution and War, 1907–1914   223

11. The Newspaper in World War and Revolution, 1914–1917   253

Conclusion   282

Appendix A. Numbers, Circulations, and Street Sales of Newspapers   293

Appendix B. Statistics on Punishment by the Censorship   300

Appendix C. Content Analyses of Major Newspapers   305

Index   311

Illustrations

1. A. A. Kraevskii, publisher of *Golos*   31

2. A. S. Suvorin, publisher of *Novoe vremia*   75

3. War correspondent V. I. Nemirovich-Danchenko   88

4. N. I. Pastukhov, publisher of *Moskovskii listok*   101

5. *Moskovskii listok* correspondents   103

6. The *Moskovskii listok* building   108

7. V. M. Doroshevich, the "King of Feuilletonists"   146

8. Reporting star V. A. Giliarovskii   152

9. Sofia Bliuvshtein, pickpocket-heroine "The Golden Arm,"
   imprisoned on Sakhalin Island   165

10. I. D. Sytin, publisher of *Russkoe slovo*   172

11. The *Russkoe slovo* building   174

12. *Russkoe slovo* rolling off the presses   178

13. *Novoe vremia* caricatures of "John Bull" during the Russo-
    Japanese War   189

14. Father Grigorii Gapon's suicide in *Novoe vremia*, 1906   205

15. The staff of *Gazeta kopeika*   229

16. Front-page illustrations in *Gazeta kopeika*   236

17. "Secrets of Magic," typical boulevard newspaper
    illustration   246

Tables

1. Numbers of Newspapers in the Two Capitals 293

2. Periodicals in Russia in 1908 and 1909 294

3. Number of Russian-Language Newspapers 294

4. Daily Street Sales, St. Petersburg, 1867–1880 295

5. Annual Street Sales, St. Petersburg, 1905–1915 296

6. Circulations of St. Petersburg Newspapers 297

7. Circulations of Other St. Petersburg Newspapers in 1905 Only 298

8. Circulations of Moscow Newspapers 299

9. Government Closings of Periodicals, 1865–1904 300

10. Number of Administrative Fines and Warnings Against Newspapers, 1865–1904 300

11. Commerce-Related Punishments by Censors, 1870–1904 301

12. Percentages of Types of Punishment, 1865–1904 301

13. Court Trials of Censorship Cases, According to Articles 1008–22, 1024–38, and 1041–48 of the Criminal Code 302

14. Aggregate Punishments, 1905–1910 303

15. The Administration, the Courts, and Censorship, 1907–1909 304

16. Content Analysis of *Golos* 305

17. Content Analysis of *Peterburgskii listok* 306

18. Content Analysis of *Peterburgskaia gazeta* 306

19. Content Analysis of *Novoe vremia* 307

20. Content Analysis of *Birzhevye vedomosti* 307

21. Content Analysis of *Moskovskii listok* 308

22. Content Analysis of *Russkoe slovo* 308

23. Content Analysis of *Gazeta kopeika* 309

Acknowledgments ────────────────────────────

IN WRITING this monograph, I accumulated a number of personal and professional debts that I am happy to make public. Very special thanks go to Donald J. Raleigh, who demonstrated repeatedly that a best friend can also be a most demanding critic. The quality of my undertaking reflects in no small way his insights and support. This project began as a dissertation under Jeffrey Brooks, and I have profited over the years from his criticisms and suggestions. A number of other friends and colleagues helped me to clarify my ideas. Joan Neuberger took time away from her hooligans to comment on several chapters, and helped me as she shared my fun with tabloid journalism. Beth Bailey and David Farber critiqued the first chapters and helped me to refine aspects of the comparative perspective. Others have read portions of my work at various stages, and I thank Abraham Ascher, Beth Haas, Owen V. Johnson, Thomas Sanders, and Richard Stites for their comments. Of the many Soviet friends and scholars who have shared their lives with me, I owe a special debt to Tania Pavlenko for combining high levels of scholarship with those of friendship. I profited from many discussions with A. V. Blium, and also learned from consultations with B. I. Esin and E. A. Dinershtein. My ideas have also been deeply influenced by James W. Carey's entreaties to consider newspaper journalism as primarily a cultural phenomenon. I alone bear responsibility for the shortcomings of this work.

I cannot imagine completing this enterprise without the unflagging support of my sister Betsy, who showed me so often that families are considerably more than those who have to take you in when you have no place else to go. Although she might balk at taking credit for my sanity, insisting that there is no such animal, she must share in whatever success this book enjoys. Other members of my remarkable family have made their presence felt. I owe a large debt to my father for his intellectual stimulation, and regret that he cannot witness the results of his influence. Happily, my mother can enjoy what she did much to encourage for so many years, especially by rewarding me with blueberry pies. I must also credit my parents with not allowing a television into our home for many years, which drove me to newspapers as a primary source of entertainment, whetting the appetite with which I still devour them. In the same vein, I must acknowledge the inspiration provided by Ben Hecht and Charles MacArthur for *The Front Page*, remade more endearingly by Howard Hawks as *His Girl Friday*.

Friends also came to my rescue. My thoughts could not have gelled without years of stimulating discussions with Les McBee, but I thank him more for the friendship that has never known limitations. Pam Chew, Colleen Barrett Clark, and Katy Roberts combined intellectual insights with personal support, for which I am deeply appreciative.

A number of librarians and Soviet archival personnel made conducting research a pleasure. Pat Polansky at the University of Hawaii aggressively pursued a number of sources. Of all the institutions in which I worked, I am most indebted to the staff of the newspaper reading room at the Library of the Academy of Sciences, and I am grateful for having been able to work there before the collection was devastated by fire in 1988. In Leningrad, I also thank those at the Central State Historical Archive, especially G. A. Ippolitova. In Moscow, I benefited from the efforts of those at the Lenin Library and the Central State Historical Archive of Art and Literature. In Helsinki, the staffs of both the university and the Slavic Collection made two summers there a delight.

Less personal, but no less important, are the institutions that made possible my research and writing. The International Research and Exchanges Board (IREX) funded two critical years in the Soviet Union. I also thank the Fulbright-Hays Committee, the National Endowment for the Humanities, and the University of Hawaii's Research Committee for funding research during the summers. Several excursions to the University of Illinois helped me to organize this project, and I have benefited from support by the excellent staff at the Slavic Library there. A grant from the Social Sciences Research Committee gave me the time to finish writing, for which I am extremely grateful. At Princeton University Press, Gail Ullman graciously and with a keen eye for proper editing helped me to pull it all together, and Annette Theuring smoothed the edges of my prose.

Much of Chapter 7 appeared in different form in my "Imperial Russia's Newspaper Reporters: Profile of a Society in Transition, 1865–1914," in *Slavonic and East European Review* 68, no. 1 (1990).

I dedicate this work to the point at which so much of it began, to my beloved grandparents, George and Lucy McReynolds, who surpassed in reality Norman Rockwell's ideals.

Abbreviations Used in Footnotes and Tables _____

PSZ   Polnoe sobranie zakonov
SPB   St. Petersburg

Periodicals

Bv   *Birzhevye vedomosti*
Gk   *Gazeta kopeika*
Iv   *Istoricheskii vestnik*
Nv   *Novoe vremia*
Ml   *Moskovskii listok*
Mv   *Moskovskie vedomosti*
Pg   *Peterburgskaia gazeta*
Pl   *Peterburgskii listok*
Pv   *Pravitel'stvennyi vestnik*
Rb   *Russkoe bogatstvo*
Rm   *Russkaia mysl'*
Rs   *Russkoe slovo*
Rv   *Russkie vedomosti*

Archives and Archival Terms

GIALO   State Historical Archive, Leningrad District
ROBL   Manuscript Division of the Lenin Library
TsGALI   Central State Archive for Literature and Art
TsGIA   Central State Historical Archive
d., dd.   file(s)
ed. khran.   storage unit
f.   fund
k.   carton
l., ll.   page(s)
op.   index

THE NEWS UNDER RUSSIA'S OLD REGIME

Introduction

THE POLICE in St. Petersburg found themselves in an unusual quandary in 1865. Young men were out in the street hawking newspapers, trying to sell single issues to passersby for a few kopecks. Although it had always been possible to buy single editions in select bookstores and kiosks, publishers customarily distributed their papers through annual subscriptions, delivered by post. One Russian newspaper—appropriately, the commerce-oriented *Birzhevye vedomosti* (*The Stock Market Gazette*)— lauded the street sales as both good business and a welcome sign of Europeanization.[1] Petersburg's police force, however, decided that this unprecedented business of noisily selling papers was disturbing the public peace, so they began to prohibit such sales where traffic might be impeded.[2] The newsboys peddling their wares along Nevskii Prospect, however, were upsetting more than just the civic calm.

This book is about the origins, development, and repercussions of imperial Russia's commercial newspaper industry. It begins with the first publishers' petitions to the tsarist government, and ends abruptly with the Bolsheviks' closing of the newspapers forever in 1917. Chronicling the exploits of editors and publishers, writers and readers, this is an analysis of the forces that combined to change the nature of communication when industrialization began to alter the requirements for it. The history of the mass-circulation press weaves together the variety of components that comprised the daily newspaper: it is at once the story of political, social, cultural, and economic transformation.

The early street vendors illustrated the point of departure for the new style of communications. They showed, for example, that now buyers would be actively pursued, which would give readers increasingly greater say in the newspapers' contents. Moreover, hawking newspapers imparted an urgency to the day's events, accentuating how the press was contributing to the restructuring of concepts of time. Seeking profits, publishers catered to the broadly inclusive tastes of the daily street traffic; in so doing, they challenged the dominance that government and intellectuals had previously enjoyed over print communications. The collection and distribution of reader-oriented information had far-reaching political implications; newspapers opened up what Jürgen Habermas termed the "public sphere," a place where readers could formulate and

---

[1] *Bv*, 22 Dec. 1865, no. 279.

[2] B. I. Esin, "Zapreshchenie roznichnoi prodazhi gazet kak sredstvo ogranichenie svobody pechati," *Vestnik MGU*, journalism series, no. 5 (1967): 71.

institutionalize opinion, and then wield it as a political weapon.[3] The persistence of censorship until the end of Russia's Old Regime at times clouded the effectiveness of the press by keeping certain topics off-limits to editors, but the government did not prevent the expansion of this public sphere because officials paid little attention to its commercial side.

Russia's commercial mass-circulation newspaper industry grew in response to Tsar Alexander II's program of Great Reforms, with which he intended to bring his empire into the modern industrial world after its humiliating defeat in the Crimea in 1855. Russia's peculiar version of the Industrial Revolution, borrowed haphazardly from Western experiences and subsidized in part by Western finance, produced a state capitalism that differed in key respects from Western capitalism.[4] But because commercial news industries had also grown in tandem with industrialization in the West throughout the nineteenth century, the research presented here feeds directly into one of the cardinal historiographical concerns regarding the nature of prerevolutionary Russian society: To what extent was Russia evolving according to socioeconomic and political patterns comparable to those of Western countries?[5] In order to provide a meaningful context in which to explore similarities and differences between Russia and the West, this study contains an important comparative element, measuring the growth of the commercial newspaper industry in Russia against that in the United States, England, and France.[6]

The Russian example, however, provides a significant point of analytical departure. Histories of Western journalism have characteristically focused on the observed connection between increased access to information and the expanding electorate.[7] In the West, redistribution of wealth

[3] Jürgen Habermas, "The Public Sphere: An Encyclopedia Article" (trans. Sara Lennox and Frank Lennox), *New German Critique* 1 (1974): 49–55, and *The Structural Transformation of the Public Sphere: An Inquiry into a Category of Bourgeois Society*, trans. Thomas Burger, with the assistance of Frederick Lawrence (Cambridge, Mass.: MIT Press, 1989).

[4] Tim McDaniel, *Autocracy, Capitalism, and the Revolution in Russia* (Berkeley and Los Angeles: University of California Press, 1988).

[5] Arthur Mendel, "On Interpreting the Fate of Imperial Russia," in Theofanis Stavrou, ed., *Russia under the Last Tsar* (Minneapolis: University of Minnesota Press, 1969), 13–41.

[6] The German press developed much differently from the other Western presses and would have required a different frame for comparison. See Daniel Moran, *Toward the Century of Words: Johan Cotta and the Politics of the Public Realm in Germany, 1795–1832* (Berkeley and Los Angeles: University of California Press, 1990).

[7] James Carey criticized this traditional approach as "whig" because it "wed the doctrine of progress to the idea of history." "The Problem of Journalism History," *Journalism History* 1, no. 1 (1974): 3–5, 27. See also James Curran, "Capitalism and Control of the Press, 1800–1975," in James Curran, Michael Gurevitch, and Janet Woollacott, eds., *Mass Communication and Society* (London: Edward Arnold, 1977), 195–230.

precipitated a commensurate redistribution of political power, which found expression in the ultimate political commodity: the commercially funded daily newspaper, a font of information available without social prejudice to anyone willing to spend the money for it.[8] The Russian situation, which had the press but not the vote, opens up new avenues for exploring the political utility of newspaper journalism.

The emergence of an active public opinion cannot be dissociated from the commercialism of its origins; as Michael Schudson argued in his social history of the American press, the economic foundation of the newspapers reflected the egalitarianism of the marketplace, which carried over into a liberal ethos in politics.[9] Integrating Russia's newspapers into journalism history promises to throw new light on the historically argued-for connection between political liberalism and a commercial press. Every newspaper analyzed here supported equal rights for all over gentry privilege, civil rights, and increasing the public's role in political decision-making; each paper fostered the same sort of legal guarantees for all citizens found in the contracts publishers drew up with advertisers. In Russia, even those newspapers that revered the person of the tsar inherently subverted the continuation of absolutism. This study categorizes Russian newspapers according to "liberal" and "conservative" editorial policies based on what positions their editors took on such issues as the extent of public participation in reform and the degree of toleration they would allow for non-Orthodox Russians, especially Jews. Editorial positions on specific topics, dividing papers between "liberal" and "conservative" instruments, though, must not be confused with what the daily newspaper projected as an institution.

Despite similarities in basic editorial orientation, the more fundamental differences between representative and autocratic governments prevented Russia's newspapers from reflecting a clear political image of their Western counterparts. Investigating the growth of liberalism in Russia through its newspapers tells only one part of the story; this study also explores the relationship between liberalism and socialism in the evolution of opposition to the autocracy, which was also rooted in its commercial press.[10]

Studying the relationship of newspaper journalism to Russia's nascent liberalism and commercialism, we exhume many remnants of its lost middle classes, who are the main protagonists of this story.[11] Economic logic

[8] Michael Schudson advanced this argument in *Discovering the News: A Social History of the American Press* (New York: Basic Books, 1978), 60.

[9] Ibid., 57–60.

[10] See especially Andrzej Walicki, *Legal Philosophies of Russian Liberalism* (Oxford: Clarendon Press, 1987).

[11] In addition to Habermas, on the relationship between the bourgeoisie and the culture

dictates that a prosperous newspaper industry has its social roots in a middle class that is substantial enough to provide the combined prerequisites of a large readership and advertising capable of sustaining it. I use the term *middle class* here to refer to a conceptual social category that established itself loosely amidst the crumbling pillars of aristocracy and peasantry. Peter Gay has artfully demonstrated that although there is no precise definition of this group, even within national boundaries, they shared similar experiences and values.[12] The rapid growth of commerce expanded opportunities for employment, creating a bourgeoisie and opening a variety of new kinds of jobs in the business and service sectors. Entrance into this new world required basic literacy skills, which encouraged newspaper reading. Attitudes toward social status also required adjustments, as those falling down from the gentry and those climbing up from the peasantry congregated with the merchantry in a group increasingly identified by a distinctive culture developing from the forces of modernization.[13]

Russia's arcane social system categorized the empire's subjects into four *soslovie*, or legal social estates (nobility, clergy, peasantry, and townspeople), who joined with the *raznochinets*, or "person of various estates." The nature of the *sosloviia* and Russia's peculiar path to industrialization prevented those groups that constituted the core of the middle class from successfully coalescing into a corporate body capable of identifying mutual interests and moving for political action based on those interests. However, as Gregory Freeze has argued, "the social structure . . . remained exceedingly complex and variegated, comprised of many distinct and often hereditary social groups, each possessing its own special status and constituting a *soslovie*."[14] This patchwork system held political as well as social sway into 1917, but especially following the Great Reforms, society's changing circumstances disputed the ability of a system of estates to manage modernization.

The middle group was tiered from upper to lower, but the daily newspaper provided its members with a place for a modicum of cultural co-

---

of news, see James W. Carey, *Communications as Culture: Essays on Media and Society* (Boston: Unwin Hyman, 1981), especially chapter 1; and Lennard Davis, *Factual Fictions* (New York: Columbia University Press, 1983).

[12] Peter Gay, *The Bourgeois Experience, Victoria to Freud: Education of the Senses* (New York: Oxford University Press, 1984), 3–68.

[13] Peter Stearns argued that "attention to the middle class and relevant sections thereof is in fact a beginning toward giving some necessary social context to modernization, considered as a shift in personality traits and not just a change in political and economic structure." "The Middle Class: Toward a Precise Definition," *Comparative Studies in Society and History* 21 (July 1979): 395–96.

[14] Gregory Freeze, "The *Soslovie* (Estate) Paradigm and Russian Social History," *American Historical Review* 91, no. 1 (1986): 35.

hesion.[15] As Leopold Haimson has pointed out, by the early twentieth century a chasm was growing "between the evolution of experience of various social groups and the legal statuses still ascribed to them by the state . . . [which] increasingly failed to provide any adequate indices of patterns of shared experience and collective behavior."[16] Here the daily newspaper, with its power to "make experience a common possession,"[17] stepped in to bridge the chasm. Because nowhere was a middle class homogenous, a variety of newspapers materialized to satisfy the differing tastes and interests. Contrasts in editorial orientation illustrate how Russians who disagreed on interpretations of a number of events nonetheless shared the same information. The newspapers also reflected the diversity of the middle; the lower-priced and urban-oriented papers played a particular educative role for their audiences, and the serious national press pulled readers into national and international issues. Yet differing editorial inflections did not outweigh the characteristics common to mass-circulation newspapers: themes of nationalism; editors' and publishers' convictions that they were serving broadly public rather than closed political interests; emphasis on the specifics of time and detail; and the growing importance of facticity.

The ascent of fact-mindedness led to a comparative decline in the role of the editorial, and newspapers were less didactic than political journals. A print medium, the newspaper promoted the advantages of literacy, but publishers' demand for reader participation enlarged the scope of the press, taking it out of the hands of the intellectuals who had previously dominated communications. Despite other differences, the mass-circulation dailies from St. Petersburg to New York had to fight the same battles against intellectual prejudice. Not only *what* was written was at stake, but also *how* it was written and to *whom*. Newspapers challenged the politicized journals of intellectual aristocracies and established themselves as the dominant medium for political discourse. The contest for influence was especially significant in Russia, where, in the absence of political parties to mediate differences, the intelligentsia had established a realm of political opposition for themselves in their so-called "thick" journals. Reporters everywhere had to earn the right to be counted

[15] As Stuart Blumin argued in support of work by Anthony Giddens, "[his] theory creates the opportunity for reformulating the hypothesis of middle-class formation in terms of the 'structuration' of certain types of social and cultural experience, to which expressions of class consciousness and awareness are related as a matter of secondary importance." *The Emergence of the Middle Class: Social Experience in the American City, 1760–1900* (New York: Cambridge University Press, 1989), 10.

[16] Leopold Haimson, "Social Identities in Early Twentieth Century Russia," *Slavic Review* 47, no. 1 (1988): 2–3.

[17] I have borrowed this phrase from Daniel J. Czitrom, *Mass Media and the American Mind* (Chapel Hill: University of North Carolina Press, 1982), 108.

among journalists, hitherto society's foremost political commentators. "Journalese" developed as the universal vernacular of the newspaper, with its compact phrasing, avoidance of two-ruble words, and the occasional blind eye to the rules of grammar. This use of a new language would lead to new ways of perceiving the world.[18]

A key to understanding both the language and political functioning of newspapers lies in nineteenth-century notions of objectivity. I use interpretations of objectivity as one way to explain related changes in concepts of public and politics. The term *objective* has a host of meanings, all relevant to my study: nonaligned politically; standing outside as an observer; empirical and factual; free of inherent bias. Central to faith in objectivity was the notion that the world could be understood and therefore mastered scientifically.[19] The doctrine of positivism, important to the middle class's sense of its distinctive importance, gave newspapers their philosophical foundation.

Recapturing the essence of Russia's prerevolutionary newspapers was not easy. Their history lay first in the hands of liberal intellectuals who, in their contempt for both commercialism and popular culture, ignored them. The very absence of references to the mass-circulation press in textbook histories written by Russia's disappointed and émigré historians, for example, A. A. Kizevetter, V. A. Miakotin, and P. N. Miliukov, provides insight into the authors, who denied readers knowledge of intellectual changes that contested their own hegemony in the interpretation of their times and the reconstruction of their history. Coming from the "thick" journal tradition, these keepers of the past recorded the life of the nation through the resentful eyes of those who sought to justify their inability to take control at the moment of revolution. Miliukov exemplified this best; having failed himself as both politician and publisher of a newspaper intended for mass circulation, he refused to come to terms with his editorial rivals in his histories of Russia, which enjoyed considerable influence in the West after 1917.[20]

Soviet historians have likewise snubbed the commercial press in favor of politicized periodicals, in their case the radical underground publications. Surprisingly, their Marxist orientations have not led to substantive new interpretations of the popular press. B. I. Esin has been the

[18] As Carey argued in "The Problem of Journalism History," "the central and as yet unwritten history of journalism is the idea of a report . . . that reflexive process wherein modern consciousness has been created" (5).

[19] Robert Park, "News as a Form of Knowledge," *American Journal of Sociology* 45 (1940): 669–86.

[20] For these historians' similar biases in their recording of the 1905 Revolution, see O. V. Volobuev, "Revoliutsiia 1905–1907 gg. v publitsistike russkikh burzhuaznykh istorikov," *Istoricheskie zapiski* 102 (1978): 287–325.

most prolific student of the prerevolutionary newspaper, but his thin studies only skim the surface of journalism.[21] A. N. Bokhanov has explored the business offices of several commercially successful newspapers, providing empirical data for the argument that connects industrialization to mass communications, but he stopped short of the kind of content analysis that might explain influences on readers' attitudes or behavior.[22] E. A. Dinershtein's biography of I. D. Sytin, whose *Russkoe slovo (The Russian Word)* was the empire's largest newspaper, has added significantly to our understanding of prerevolutionary Russia's most influential publisher, but he failed to integrate the one paper into the flourishing culture of popular journalism.[23]

The newspaper readers proved equally elusive. In the absence of outside sources, for example, readers' surveys, I drew conclusions about who read which papers from their contents. Audiences were not rigidly predictable; after all, every publisher wanted the greatest possible number of readers, and it is quite likely that more than a few educated snobs relished gutter fare on the sly. But the competitive basis of newspapers produced an overlap in contents that continues to make them a reliable indicator of audience; although today's *New York Times* features many stories differently than does the rival *Daily News*, articles about international politics lie alongside those on the sexual escapades of movie stars and billionaires in both papers.

I have organized my research around the emergence of "new journalisms," by which I mean innovations in newspaper reporting and publishing that intersected with broader socioeconomic changes. Chapter 1 establishes the theoretical context and the comparative framework, presenting a brief overview of the growth of commercial journalism in both Russia and the West. Most of the chapters—Chapters 3 through 6, then 8 and 10—center around the appearances of specific newspapers. Analyses of their contents illustrate how these papers exemplified what made journalism fundamentally "new." This organization allows the newspapers to serve as microcosms of the transformations that made commercial journalism both possible and important.

The first six chapters trace the growth of the daily paper into a public sphere and set the stage for the "dress rehearsal" for 1917, the 1905 Revolution. Chapter 7 introduces the newspaper journalists in order to ex-

---

[21] See, for example, B. I. Esin, *Puteshestvie v proshloe* (Moscow: MGU, 1983), *Russkaia dorevoliutsionnaia gazeta, 1702–1917* (Moscow: MGU, 1971), and *"Russkaia gazeta" i gazetnoe delo Rossii* (Moscow: MGU, 1981).

[22] A. N. Bokhanov, *Burzhuaznaia pressa Rossii i krupnyi kapital, konets XIX v.—1914* (Moscow: Nauka, 1984). See also A. Golikov, *Rossiiskie monopolii v zerkale pressy. Gazety kak istochnik po istorii monopolizatsii promyshlennosti* (Moscow: MGU, 1990).

[23] E. A. Dinershtein, *I. D. Sytin* (Moscow: Kniga, 1983), 79–114.

plain the effects of individuals and the occupational structure of reporting. Chapters 8 and 9 look at how the press created an agenda that contradicted that of the tsarist government, first in the Russo-Japanese War and then in the ensuing revolution. In Chapter 10, the role of the press in the crucial interrevolutionary period examines from a new angle the issue of how society was coping with the contradictory situation created by socioeconomic progress and political reaction. The final chapter considers the political impact of the news coverage of both World War I and the events of 1917.

My research covers St. Petersburg's press and includes Moscow's two most popular and influential newspapers, with both urban and national circulations. Russia's provincial press lies beyond the purview of this study; its history differs in many important respects from that of the major newspapers in the two capitals and therefore merits a separate study. Although the absence of Russia's provincial newspaper culture qualifies somewhat the conclusions drawn in this work, it must be remembered that the large dailies circulated widely in the provinces.

Methodologically, I began by surveying a random sample of issues over the span of their publications. At times my research was limited by the unavailability of the various newspapers. Where certain stories, for example, stories about war and assassination, dominated, I compared coverages to isolate variations in focus that would help to explain the different papers and their audiences. Sketched according to their contributions, newspapers disappear and resurface in the narrative at appropriate points. Footnoting posed a fundamental problem because of the literally dozens of stories that evidenced any paper's editorial positions. Therefore, in my notes I refer only to editions from which I have drawn specific material. To avoid overwhelming readers with both the fluctuating circulation figures of newspapers and the statistics that chart the censorship's attempts to supervise them, I have added two appendixes for immediate reference and easier digestion. A third appendix provides the skeletal structures of statistical content analyses for the newspapers fleshed out in the narrative.

Transliteration in this manuscript follows the Library of Congress system, although the more familiar proper names, for example, Trotsky, are spelled in their customary English forms. Dates conform to the "Old Style" or Julian calendar used in Russia until February 1918; in the nineteenth century, this calendar lagged twelve days behind the Gregorian calendar used in the West, and in the twentieth, thirteen days.

Unless otherwise indicated, all translations are my own.

1

The Origins of the Mass-Circulation Press

SURVEYING the historical sweep of the daily newspaper, Walter Lippmann, one of the most influential figures in communications theory, believed himself to have identified the historical logic that determined the
evolution of the modern press.[1] He focused his argument on the relationship between the changes in dominant political structures and the appearance of new types of newspapers that took correspondingly different
political roles. He isolated a pattern: at first, under autocracies, governments controlled communications by publishing information that they
wanted circulated. As social estates began demanding rights of representation and displacing autocrats, organized political interest groups began
to dominate published communications; the British, French, and American Revolutions all witnessed great flowerings of political journalism.
Journalists began to refer to themselves as the "Fourth Estate" to denote
their place in the political process.[2] In the nineteenth century, electoral
rights filtered down to larger sections of the populace at the same time
that commercially subsidized mass-circulation newspapers began to pros-
per. According to Lippmann's reasoning, these papers linked the independent consumer-*cum*-voter to the political system constructed by liberal capitalism. Lippmann's line of thought connected economics to
politics through the medium of the newspaper, which communicated political information to the voting consumer.

Although one can be caught short looking for the particulars of
Lippmann's argument because his theoretical framework fits so unevenly
over history's variations of time and place, the eminent journalist provided historians with an origin from which to explore the parallel changes
of the daily newspaper and politics that define the manifest, but poorly
understood, relationship between information and power. Even a cursory
survey of the industrializing West shows a correlation between widespread newspaper reading and increased opportunities to participate in
the electoral process. Lippmann's paradigm intrinsically made liberal

[1] Walter Lippmann, "Two Revolutions of the American Press," *Yale Review* 20, no. 3
(1931): 433–41.

[2] George Boyce, "The Fourth Estate: Reappraisal of a Concept," in George Boyce, James
Curran, and Pauline Wingate, eds., *Newspaper History from the Seventeenth Century to
the Present* (Beverly Hills: Sage, 1978), 19–40.

capitalism the necessary basis for political progress, insinuating that popular commercial newspapers were mandatory for the development of genuine democracy. These two preconceptions, which had characterized most thinking about politics and journalism before World War I, fell on hard times when social theorists, watching the rise of communism and fascism, expressed reservations about the role of communications in the emergence of undemocratic mass societies.[3] The most articulate challenge to the assumption that liberalism, capitalism, and a commercial press were the necessary prerequisites to democracy came from the Marxist-oriented Frankfurt School; Jürgen Habermas, heir to that intellectual tradition, has been the most influential theorist of mass communications since Lippmann.

Observing the same structural correspondence between changes in politics and journalism, Habermas gave greater weight to the precommercial political press as the more potent democratizing medium. Originating as a political domain carved out for itself by the liberal bourgeoisie, where traditional rule blocked their admittance to government, the public sphere opened by the political journals allowed readers to observe and discuss the formation of official policy; the ultimate objective of this function was to transform the nature of power.[4] A phenomenon of the developing capitalist system, whose economies of exchange were refashioning social relationships, the public sphere provided a place where private individuals could collect against the state and claim authority for themselves, "a space where citizenship can be negotiated."[5]

According to Habermas, however, when newspaper journalism became fully commercialized in the mass-circulation dailies, the influx of private values consistently eroded this press's value as a public institution. He argued for the superiority of the political press, Lippmann's second stage, because it provided a medium through which readers could engage in critical debates. The mass-circulation newspapers, developing from the competition of private commercial interests, conflated "public" and "private," which robbed newspapers of their legitimacy as genuinely public institutions. The consumer of the fully commercialized newspaper was a passive being, a mirror rather than a critic of his or her society. Even when these newspapers engaged public officials in debates over policy issues, their editors were not challenging the status quo as the political journals had. On the contrary, these papers facilitated psycho-

---

[3] Talcott Parsons and Winston White, "The Mass Media and the Structure of American Society," *Journal of Social Issues* 16, no. 3 (1960): 67–77.

[4] Habermas, "Public Sphere," 53.

[5] Jane Kramer, "Letter from Europe (Soviet Union)," *The New Yorker*, 12 March 1990, 79.

logical acceptance of the liberal capitalist state, with its attendant ineq-
uities.[6]

This study of Russian journalism is equally informed by the ideas of
Lippmann and Habermas. For all the thrashing that Lippmann has suffered, he still surfaces as more than a straw man for revisionists; the difficulty of separating freedom of the press from freedom of the market has
proved to be one of the recurring problematics in effecting *glasnost'* and
perestroika. Moreover, for all of the strengths of Habermas's insights, he
exaggerated the capability of the popular press to privatize public values.
Reading the histories of the mass-circulation presses of France, England,
and the United States, the relationship between the positivistic view of
progress and the popular newspapers voicing that idea is unmistakable,
as are the problems with commercialism that blurred differences between private and public. Integrating the Russian newspapers into journalism's history, with their host of differences from and similarities to
their Western counterparts, will expand both theoretical arguments.

The Mass-Circulation Press Develops in the West

Capsule histories of the development of commercial journalism in the
three Western countries selected for comparison will establish the context within which to analyze the Russian press. The United States, England, and France all adhered roughly to Lippmann's paradigm charac-
terizing the relationship between politics and the economic foundations
of publishing newspapers, giving way to the forces of commercialization
throughout the nineteenth century. But their newspaper journalisms did
not evolve either in unison or in direct proportion to the level of industrialization that made the commercial press both feasible and desirable;
national politics and the nature of their respective market economies affected the course of each press's development.

The Western newspapers did, however, share important commonalities of organization and purpose. Technology, for example, helped to give
the newspapers definition, just as it would govern the uses of radio and
television communications in the twentieth century.[7] German printer

---

[6] As Habermas argued, "The mass press was based on the commercialization of the participation in the public sphere on the broad strata designed predominantly to give the
masses in general access to the public sphere. This expanded public sphere, however, lost
its political character to the extent that the means of 'psychological facilitation' could become an end in itself for a commercially fostered consumer attitude." *Structural Transformation*, 169.

[7] Michael Schudson, "Politics of Narrative Form: The Emergence of News Conventions
in Print and Television," *Daedalus* 111, no. 4 (1982): 97; and Calder M. Pickett, "Technol-

Frederick Koenig had already connected steam power to the printing press by 1810. His basic design was improved upon by American inventor Richard Hoe, whose presses could run off four thousand double-sided sheets per hour; thirteen years later his rotary press tripled that output. New Yorker Samuel F. B. Morse had tested his telegraph successfully in 1844, at last making it possible for newspapers to disconnect communications from transportation. Londoner James Dellagana's advancements in stereotyping further improved production so that by the Crimean War New York, London, and Paris were all served by high-speed presses.

The popularity of newspapers in turn stimulated further technological developments. The Linotype, perfected in 1886, increased the speed with which printers could compose and remake pages, allowing for larger runs of papers produced more swiftly. Front pages could now be redone quickly to feature the latest news. Although the halftone effect, which made it possible to reprint photographs from rotary presses, was not commercially viable until 1897, the experiments leading up to proficiency would register refinements along the way. By century's end the telephone and the typewriter had improved communications in newspaper offices.

As technology expedited the collection and dissemination of information, news became an increasingly precious commodity. The value of facts proved pivotal in the separation of the newspaper from its financial basis in politics, whether party or autocratic, because it lessened the importance of the editorials written to persuade. Turning information into merchandise, however, allowed market mechanisms to mediate communications and brought into question the fundamental role of the newspaper in society. Since readers depended upon information to understand politics and to make personal decisions, did newspapers, as business enterprises, operate primarily for public or private interests? The contradiction inherent in a private enterprise functioning as a public institution continues to plague understanding of commercial communications. For example, the notion that a newspaper or a journalist would be deemed "corrupt" for misrepresenting information to make the paper sell better implied that, as a consumer product, news had a unique political value; news belonged to the community at large.

The newly appreciated value of information surfaced first in the American press, which also fit Lippmann's paradigm most closely. A revolutionary nation founded on principles that theoretically denied hereditary social standing a determining role in politics, the United States produced the archetypal commercial mass-circulation press. The politicized forerunners of America's popular newspapers could be traced back to the talents of rebellious exiles from the mother country in the persons of Benjamin Harris, Thomas Paine, and the Franklin brothers, James and Benjamin. These first journalists borrowed ideas extensively from flourishing British publications, and they used the press to fight the political controls exercised by the Crown. Following the achievement of independence, the infant republic's first newspapers pitted Federalists against Republicans in the struggle for votes.[8]

In 1835, however, when James Gordon Bennett introduced his *New York Herald*, priced at a penny and subsidized by advertising, he restyled print communications. As Michael Schudson has cogently argued, America's penny papers became the prototypes of modern journalism because they acted as "spokesmen for egalitarian ideals in politics, economic life, and social life through their organization of sales, their solicitation of advertising, their emphasis on news, their catering to a large audience, their decreasing concern with the editorial."[9] When more serious, higher-priced dailies began to appear, such as the *New York Tribune*, their publishers copied much of what had made Bennett so successful.

On the Continent, though, political interest groups maintained greater influence over a longer period in the publication of newspapers. Great Britain, the seedbed of the Industrial Revolution, was comparatively slow to develop a commercial press.[10] The politically oriented London *Times*, founded by John Walter as a private business in 1771, reached educated readers through its national circulation. However, the Stamp Act of 1765, which had applied the so-called taxes on knowledge by adding duties to newspapers and advertisements that would help to underwrite costs, made even lower-priced newspapers cost-prohibitive for mass consumption. An unstamped press surfaced illegally in times of political stress; England had an impressive history of radical working-class journalism.[11] The repeal of the tax on advertising in 1853, which predated by two years the revocation of the Stamp Act, paved the economic way for a commer-

---

[8] Edwin Emery and Michael Emery, *The Press and America: An Interpretive History of the Mass Media* (Englewood Cliffs, N.J.: Prentice-Hall, 1978), chapters 2–4. This book has gone through six editions with few significant changes; the fourth (1978) and the sixth (1988) are referenced in this study.

[9] Schudson, *Discovering the News*, 60.

[10] On the British press, see Stephen Koss, *The Rise and Fall of the Political Press in Britain* (Chapel Hill: University of North Carolina Press, 1981); Alan J. Lee, *Origins of the Popular Press in England, 1855–1914* (London: Croom Helm, 1976); and Lucy Brown, *Victorian News and Newspapers* (Oxford: Clarendon Press, 1985).

[11] Patricia Hollis, *The Pauper Press: A Study in Working-Class Radicalism of the 1830s* (Oxford: Oxford University Press, 1970).

cial press. The *Daily Telegraph*, founded in 1855, became England's first fully commercialized daily.

The English press's coupling of commerce and liberal politics appeared by the end of the next decade in papers oriented toward the lower classes, which subverted the radical tradition of the unstamped press.[12] Passage of the Education Act of 1870, which ordained universal primary education, enlarged the pool of ordinary readers and had a favorable impact on the growth of the popular press. Alfred Harmsworth (later, Lord Northcliffe) founded his *Daily Mail* in 1896, followed by his more infamous *Daily Mirror*, which reproduced the successful formula of the American urban press. England could then boast a thriving newspaper industry, headquartered along the euphonious Fleet and Grub Streets, that represented its diverse reading public.

France, like England, had a rich tradition of political journalism and was also quicker to develop a commercial press.[13] Emile Girardin, described as "perhaps the most influential figure in the history of the modern French press," founded his *La Presse*, the first French mass-circulation daily, in 1836.[14] The appearance of *Le Petit Journal* in 1863 gave Paris its first mass-oriented press, which combined serial adventure novels with *faits divers* (human interest stories) and, selling for five centimes, greatly expanded the base of newspaper readership.[15] Jean Dupuy took over the small, political *Le Petit Parisien* in the 1880s, and, spicing it up with human interest and entertainment, he made it the largest newspaper in the world by 1900, the first to circulate above one million.[16]

Despite these popular sensational periodicals, however, politics colored French journalistic traditions more deeply than they did British or American ones in the sense that editorial commentary lasted longer as a selling point over news. France's political turbulence throughout the nineteenth century helps to explain the directions its press took. The century witnessed a succession of imperial and republican governments, and even a flicker of socialism with the Paris Commune of 1871. Although France did not have England's taxes on knowledge, both its imperial and republican governments maintained censorship until reforms in 1881 allowed for expression of political differences.[17] As *New York Evening Post*

[12] Curran, "Capitalism and Control," 219.

[13] For example, Jeremy D. Popkin, *Revolutionary News: The Press in France, 1789–1799* (Durham, N.C.: Duke University Press, 1990).

[14] Theodore Zeldin, *France, 1848–1945*, 2 vols. (Oxford: Clarendon Press, 1977), 2:494.

[15] Claude Bellanger, Jacques Godechot, Pierre Guiral, and Fernand Terrou, *Histoire générale de la presse française*, 4 vols. (Paris: Presses Universitaires de France, 1969–1972), 2:327–29.

[16] Ibid., 3:304–5.

[17] Ibid., 240–41.

editor E. L. Godkin observed, as late as the 1890s Parisian journalists bragged about "the sensation they have made and the increase in circulation they have achieved by some sort of editorial comment or critique" instead of about scooping each other on the hard news stories in which American reporters took such pride.[18]

It was not simply French political and literary traditions that upheld the importance of newspaper commentaries. The means by which news had become a commodity in France had undermined its value as an independent item. From the origins of their commercial newspapers, the French had considerable difficulty trying to separate the public from the private value of information. In England and the United States advertising agencies had sprouted in the business atmosphere engendered by commercial journalism; these agencies operated as brokers between businessmen and publishers, directing publicity about a product to its probable users.[19] From their inception, though, French agencies operated differently. Charles Duveyrier set up the first advertising office in 1845, the Société des Annonces. A fascinating entrepreneur, Duveyrier had entered the world of political economics as a "missionary" of socialism, preaching the gospel of Saint-Simon. He lost his socialist sympathies to capitalism, though, when he discovered he could turn a profit for himself by "renting" the back pages of major newspapers and then "subleasing" occupancy to advertisers. Instead of fighting Duveyrier's quasi monopoly, French publishers responded by selling news space to middlemen, who peddled publicity items as newsworthy stories.[20]

British and American publishers, too, complained about this dilemma, and not all remained unblemished by corruption. But others responded by creatively rearranging the terms and placement of ads, for example, by breaking up static columns and offering discounts to regular patrons.[21] Graft in the French press became legendary, and local businessmen rightly feared the blackmailers who sat in editorial offices threatening negative publicity. Russia's government was not the only one that maintained a slush fund for French publishers; France's own Ministry of Internal Affairs kept one, too.[22] The corruption had an adverse effect on

[18] Quoted in Michael Schudson, "Deadlines, Datelines, and History," in Robert Manoff and Michael Schudson, eds., *Reading the News: A Pantheon Guide to Popular Culture* (New York: Pantheon, 1986), 81.

[19] Terry Nevett, "Advertising and Editorial Integrity in the Nineteenth Century," in Michael Harris and Alan Lee, eds., *The Press in English Society from the Seventeenth to the Nineteenth Centuries* (London: Associated University Presses, 1986), 149–67.

[20] Natalie Isser, *The Second Empire and the Press* (The Hague: Martinus Nijhoff, 1974), 34–35.

[21] On the American press, see Gunther Barth, *City People* (New York: Oxford University Press, 1980), 77; on the British, see Curran, "Capitalism and Control," 221–22.

[22] Bellanger et al., *Histoire générale* 3:249.

French commerce as well as journalism, and in 1911 French newspapers contained proportionally only half as much ad space as American papers.[23]

Russian Precursors of Commercial Newspapers

The mass-circulation press appeared in Russia in the 1860s when publishers welcomed their first genuine opportunity to found newspapers fully supported by commerce. The death of the small-minded reactionary Tsar Nicholas I in 1855 breathed life into journalism and every other aspect of society. The government enjoyed a monopoly over the political system, the printing presses, and the national economy. But the staggering defeat in the Crimea had made it clear to the new tsar, Alexander II, that the political and economic systems required an overhaul, one that when implemented would affect all aspects of mass communications. The populace at large was swept up in the spirit of reform, which could be measured quantitatively in the press: between 1851 and 1855, thirty periodicals had begun publication, but between 1856 and 1860, five times that number appeared.[24]

Central to Alexander's reforms would be the emancipation of 22 million serfs in 1861. All the reforms bore at least indirectly on newspaper publishing: an aggressive minister of finance committed to industrialization facilitated economic expansion and improved national communications; reforms of the army and educational system increased both the ability and the desire to read; and a legal system built around trial by jury made citizenship a relevant concept, as did the *zemstva*, or local organs of self-government. Journalism acquired added importance because periodicals reported information about the reforms, and newspaper reading became a prerequisite for mastering life in the new society. The censorship laws were revised in 1865 not only to allow for greater freedom of expression but also to facilitate the mechanics of publishing.

Before the Great Reforms, the Russian newspaper was neither especially urgent nor widely read. Readers turned to it for lists of decrees, book reviews or scattered other literary features, or perhaps tidbits about natural disasters and a crime or two. The tsarist government dominated newspapers completely as the major publisher and a principal source of information. Peter the Great had founded Russia's first quasi newspaper in 1703 to publicize his Great Northern War against Charles XII of Swe-

---

[23] Ibid., 493–573.

[24] A. V. Zapadov, ed., *Istoriia russkoi zhurnalistiki XVIII-XIX vekov* (Moscow: MGU, 1973), 316.

den. The semiliterate tsar himself contributed bits of rough prose extolling his military victory at Poltava in 1709.[25] Published in both Moscow and the tsar's "Window on the West," his new capital currently under construction, the erratic publication and circulation of this sheet of information disqualified it from being a real newspaper.[26]

The founding of the Imperial Academy of Sciences in 1725 made printing presses available through an educational, albeit still governmental, institution. After Peter's death that same year, his paper gradually ceased publication, and was replaced in 1727 by the Academy's *Sankt-Peterburgskie vedomosti* (*The St. Petersburg News*, hereafter *SPB vedomosti*). Dominated by imported German scholars, the Academy published its biweekly paper first in a German edition, which was then translated into Russian; both continued until 1917. The newspaper's sponsorship by academics meant that faculty squabbles could suspend publication until differences were repaired. A useful if also somewhat drab record of official activities and information about the works-in-progress at the Academy, the paper had occasionally enough spice to induce the tsarevna Elizabeth (1741–1762), Peter's ineffectual daughter, to begin the ill-advised Romanov tradition of forbidding the publication of any story mentioning a member of the royal family without imperial permission.[27]

The second of Russia's founding newspapers likewise originated with an official institution of higher learning. When Moscow University was chartered in 1756, a newspaper came officially with the printing presses, *Moskovskie vedomosti* (*Moscow News*). Winged Glory trumpeted the coming of a new, stylized age of imitation of Western classicism from the paper's masthead during its first years. Published with greater attention to news and with a more concerted effort to build an audience than its counterpart in St. Petersburg, *Moskovskie vedomosti* carried official announcements and decrees, plus information distributed by the court about royal weddings and births. News of the Seven Years War, raging on the continent from 1756, was translated and republished from European newspapers.[28]

When the intellectually inclined Catherine the Great, (1763–1796) rose to the throne, Russian journalism began to sparkle. Newspapers, however, played only a supporting role in the development of Russian intellectual life. Enchanted with the Enlightenment, the new tsarevna

[25] S. M. Tominskii, *Pervaia pechatnaia gazeta Rossii (1700–1727)* (Perm: n.p., 1959).

[26] Gary Marker, *Publishing, Printing, and the Origins of Intellectual Life in Russia* (Princeton, N.J.: Princeton University Press, 1985), 27–29; and A. Mal'shinskii, "Nasha pechat' v ee istoriko-ekonomicheskom razvitii," *Iv* 28, no. 6 (1887): 271.

[27] Marker, *Publishing*, 49.

[28] V. Korsh, *Stoletie "Moskovskikh vedomostei"* (Moscow: Tip. Moskovskogo Universiteta, 1857).

presided over the flowering of the "thick" journals, monthly assortments of literature, satire, politics, and science. Published by and for the native intellectual elite, Russia's all-important *intelligentsia*, these journals served as the dominant medium for political discourse well into the nineteenth century. Catherine dipped her own pen—more pompously than creatively—into these journals with her *Vsiakiaia vsiachina* (*Of All Sorts*). Her intellectual nemesis Nikolai Novikov showed his tongue playfully in his cheek with the title of his own "thick" offering, *Truten* (*The Drone*). The fun would cease when a peasant rebellion led by Emilian Pugachev in 1774 made the Enlightened Despot chary of criticism.[29]

The tsarist government concerned itself little with newspapers, and its relative neglect of these periodicals, far less influential than the "thick" journals, permitted scattered opportunities for political expression. With the intention of defraying costs, the government began leasing to private individuals the rights to publish the two *Vedomosti*, and therefore these papers could appropriately be considered no more than semiofficial. Themselves the bastions of intellectual deliberation, liberal and conservative alike, the leasing educational institutions welcomed critical voices so long as they exercised restraint. Even such foes of the autocracy as Novikov could publish *Moskovskie vedomosti*, although after making it Russia's most popular newspaper of the eighteenth century he had to give it up when the empress tired of his sardonic wit.

Until 1863 only one independent newspaper, *Severnaia pchela* (*The Northern Bee*), had permission to print "political news," that is, information about the government's activities emanating from official sources. With sycophants I. Grech and F. V. Bulgarin at the editorial helm, the autocracy had little cause for anxiety. The merchantry and lower ranks of the bureaucracy found their interests satisfied by this light fare, which circulated among three thousand readers in the 1830s, reaching a plateau of ten thousand in the 1850s.[30] When the fair-haired Romantics of the age, led by Alexander Pushkin and Baron A. A. Del'vig, wanted their own newspaper, Tsar Nicholas I would not allow them to add politics to the literary offerings of their *Literaturnaia gazeta* (*The Literary Gazette*), and the periodical foundered in 1831 after less than one year.[31]

Several ministries published newspapers in order to make available official information. The Ministry of Internal Affairs began its *Severnaia pochta* (*The Northern Post*) in 1809, and the Napoleonic Wars prompted

---

[29] P. N. Berkov, *Istoriia russkoi zhurnalistiki XVIII veka* (Moscow: MGU, 1952).

[30] Nurit Schliefman, "A Russian Daily Newspaper and Its Readership: *Severnaia pchela* 1825–40," *Cahiers du monde russes et sovietiques* 28, no. 2 (1987): 127–44.

[31] N. Zamkov, "K istorii *Literaturnoi gazety* barona A. A. Del'viga," *Russkaia starina*, no. 5 (1916): 245–81; and P. N. Polevoi, "Listki iz arkhiva *Literaturnoi gazety*," *Iv* 26, no. 11 (1886): 369–82.

the Ministry of War to publish *Russkii invalid* (*The Russian War Veteran*), originally intended to raise funds for veterans and their families. The *Journal de St. Petersbourg*, a French-language periodical published by the Ministry of Foreign Affairs, provided much of the news about the world beyond Russia's borders. The Senate and police departments also distributed sheets of information about their various operations. In 1869 *Severnaia pochta* became *Pravitel'stvennyi vestnik* (*The Government Herald*), a far more ambitious official forum. All ministries, departments, and even provincial administrations would forward "completely trustworthy" information to this central organ, which would publish the most important news and present the government's interpretation of events; it would "offer no private opinions or express independent views," nor would it accept paid advertising for "undignified" products, for example, French waters promising to cure sexual impotence.[32] The official nature of these newspapers did not, however, preclude license for critique, and aspiring writers of all political sympathies found careers with this press.[33]

By the end of the eighteenth century publishers were adding literary supplements and "unoffical sections" of news not issuing from governmental sources. So long as these additions were not provocative, the state ignored them. Translations from European periodicals and long, discursive letters from Russian observers in the provinces or abroad comprised these sections. Before the reforms a rudimentary newspaper culture had begun to take shape around the fragments of economics, European news, and, especially in *Severnaia pchela*, the births of two-headed calves, that painted the world in broad strokes. Circulations of the few major papers fluctuated between four thousand and twelve thousand. But as long as the state provided the basis for its legitimacy, newspaper journalism remained a political forum of secondary importance.

Censorship and the Newspaper

When the tsarist government had been by economic and educative default the exclusive source of printing presses and politics, "freedom of the press" had little conceptual meaning. But by the end of the eighteenth century, many of Peter the Great's education-oriented reforms were enjoying measurable success, and they had resulted in the development of an articulate political opposition. Two factors converged during the reign of Catherine the Great to suggest to the autocracy that it should consider

---

[32] TsGIA f. 785, dd. 1, 95.

[33] See A. G. Dement'ev, A. V. Zapadov, and M. S. Cherepakhov, eds., *Russkaia periodicheskaia pechat'* (*spravochnik*) (Moscow: Gos. Izd. Pol. Lit., 1959); and Esin, *Russkaia dorevoliutsionnaia gazeta*, for a survey of early Russian newspaper journalism.

establishing censorship as a necessary political institution. First, the intellectual elite came into contact with Western philosophies and many readers found republican ideals more attractive than autocratic controls. Coupled with this, the importation of printing technology allowed the elite to circulate their ideas. These new circumstances made freedom of the press a legitimate concern, as private individuals now had the resources with which to own and operate presses. Catherine permitted a few private presses to operate, but the appearance of Alexander Radishchev's biting indictment of serfdom, *A Journey from St. Petersburg to Moscow*, published in 1790 on Radishchev's private press with the nonchalant approval of a disinterested police captain, prompted the tsarevna to act against the subversive capabilities of the printed word. Shortly before her death in 1796 she approved the first official censoring administration.[34]

Catherine's successors, her son Paul I (1796–1801) and two grandsons, Alexander I (1801–1825) and Nicholas I (1825–1855), hoped to protect the autocracy by fixing the type of information the various periodicals could publish. Paul's fear of foreign ideas penetrating Russian borders resulted in stringent controls, and little progress was possible under this mentally unbalanced ruler. Under his son Alexander, greater toleration in printing resumed, and a statute produced in 1804 regulated relations between publishers and censors through the newly founded Ministry of Education. The censorship served a primarily educational function, and its preoccupation with morals and family honor reflected the government's interest in raising society's cultural level as it protected itself. The requirement that censors be well versed themselves in Russian and foreign literature created a corpus of sophisticated and often supportive reviewers.[35]

Alexander I's censorship failed to screen out all revolutionary ideas, and his sudden and mysterious death ignited a coup attempt by young officers, the "Decembrists," who had come into contact with political theories that had kindled the French Revolution. Although the coup was aborted, it fed the new tsar's paranoia, and Nicholas believed more fervently than his father and brother that by controlling information he could prevent it from being used against him. His government produced in 1828 the statute that would operate until the Crimean War. The new statute expanded the previous concentration on morals, reflecting Nicholas I's vision of himself as *paterfamilias* of the nation. It provided for a

[34] Charles Ruud, *Fighting Words: Imperial Censorship and the Russian Press, 1804–1906* (Toronto: University of Toronto Press, 1982), 21.
[35] The 1804 law is in PSZ, series 1, vol. 28, art. 21388.

centralized Chief Administration of Censorship and asserted official control over printed words and the technology that produced them.[36]

Until the post-Crimean intellectual euphoria, censorship of newspapers seemed little more than an afterthought. A concession extended in 1828 decreed that censors would look at periodicals before monographs because of the importance of timing, but it did not recognize an inherent difference between a daily newspaper and a monthly journal.[37] The necessity of approving a paper's contents by 4:00 P.M. before the next morning's circulation meant that the prereform press lacked the immediacy essential to the modern newspaper. The forced omissions of specific stories also undermined the need for newspapers. For example, the government restricted reportage of the two biggest stories of Alexander II's first decade, the military embarrassment in the Crimea and the new tsar's plans for reform.

Curtailing this information had political implications. However fervidly many Russians had opposed serfdom, censors had obstructed the periodical press from sounding an alarm to end it. Only Alexander Herzen's revolutionary tocsin *Kolokol* (*The Bell*) could openly attack serfdom, as well as the autocracy, because he published it in European exile. Literary realist I. S. Turgenev's *A Sportsman's Sketches*, a collection of essays depicting the humanity of the exploited peasantry, had sensitized many to the noxious institution, but it could not mobilize public opinion against serfdom to the degree that Harriet Beecher Stowe's *Uncle Tom's Cabin* politicized American readers because open discussion of Turgenev's book was restricted to private literary salons. Russia knew no William Lloyd Garrisons or Frederick Douglasses, whose newspapers strengthened through publicity the United States' concurrent abolitionist movement. Ironically, the censors could spare Alexander II the vituperative abuse heaped upon Abraham Lincoln by his unfettered critics, but could not save him from the same fate at the hands of an assassin.

By 1858 Alexander had admitted that the extant censorship regulations regarding the press did not fulfill the needs of the reformed Russia he envisioned. Revising the censorship in 1865, he made possible the first step toward developing a mass-circulation press along the same lines as that in the West. According to the reformed statute, politics pushed education aside as the basis for interpreting the printed word, exemplified by the transfer of the Chief Administration of Press Affairs to the Ministry of Internal Affairs. Most significantly, publishers in major cities could petition to have their papers removed from prepublication censorship, pro-

[36] Ruud, in *Fighting Words*, chapters 3–6, discusses the censorship under Nicholas I.

[37] The 1828 statute is in PSZ, 2d ed., art. 1979; points 21 and 49 regulate when censors will read which materials.

vided they deposited five thousand rubles with the state to guarantee payment of fines they were anticipated to accrue; banked in government securities, the deposits drew interest for the publishers waiting to be fined.[38] To the publishers' great satisfaction, the statute designated the newly reformed legal system as the adjudicator in offenses committed by the press; the function of the Chief Administration was now simply to ascertain that publishers complied with the rules for registering their publications and followed the rules laid out in the statute. Although those who drafted it had intended for this statute to be only temporary, through a series of amendments the 1865 regulations remained in effect until the 1905 Revolution.[39]

Despite its organization into a formal bureaucracy, the censorship lacked a coherent policy. Censors did not know how to prevent breaches in the rules that officials decided to keep from recurring. The rules could change at whim, as I discuss later. From the outset, executing the provisions of the 1865 statute proved frustrating for editors and publishers because the government, increasingly suspicious of the reforms it had begotten, moved more and more press crimes from the courts back to the arbitrary administrators. The 1865 statute had given the minister of internal affairs the license to issue warnings to publishers when he found a periodical's contents objectionable. Because three warnings could result in a temporary suspension, and the minister determined the duration, which could last up to six months, this power grew in significance.[40] Censors paid closer attention to editorials than to news, which, although irksome to writers trying to stimulate polemics, underscored the importance of factual information. Despite complications with censors, however, editors and publishers established a voice independent of that of the government.

The Financial Basis of Newspaper Publishing

Finances also determined independence because newspapers had to be weaned from state coffers. Because it produced all but one newspaper before the reform era, the tsarist government regulated the economics of publishing. Official papers could publish in the red because the ministries' budgets absorbed the losses, but this situation was hardly optimal.

[38] The 1865 statute was entered into PSZ on 6 April 1865, arts. 41988 and 41990. The mention of deposits is in part 2, arts. 19–20.

[39] Most of the laws relating to censorship were included in the 1866 *Ulozhenie o nakazanii*; the formal statute, the *Ustav o tsenzure i pechati*, entered the law code in 1890, incorporating amendments and revisions from 1865.

[40] 1865 statute, no. 41990, sec. 2, arts. 29–30.

To free itself from underwriting so many periodicals the government needed a solid commercial foundation as badly as aspiring publishers wanted one. Although the issue of paid advertising was not incorporated into any of the successive censorship statutes, the government decided which publishers could accept it, reserving most income from ads for its official publications. This policy derived from the fact that before the country had industrialized sufficiently to have an adequate financial base, most money spent to bear publishing costs came from the state's paying to print official notices.[41] In 1838 the government passed legislation allowing private individuals to take out advertising where they wanted, but prohibited government notices from appearing in private publications.[42] Two years earlier the protagonist in Nikolai Gogol's "The Nose" had tried to place an announcement in an unnamed paper for his missing proboscis, a fictional indication that advertising was starting to become familiar in St. Petersburg.

Official policies on paid advertising were never clearly enunciated. Deciding who could benefit from receiving the notices gradually evolved into determining who could secure advertising in general. Rules regarding the leased press varied haphazardly; before 1863 the Moscow *Vedomosti* did not publish state ads, but the one in St. Petersburg did. After this date the government legislated only permission to receive official announcements, a practice it manipulated into subsidies for favorite publishers. Two of the best-known conservative dailies, *Moskovskie vedomosti* and *Novoe vremia* (*The New Times*), both benefited from the lucrative state ads. The independently operated *Severnaia pchela*, despite the law of 1838, had been forbidden from accepting paid advertising from private individuals until 1862, although it received direct backing from the government.[43] But by the time the government eased up on economic controls, *Severnaia pchela's* time had already played out; it closed in 1864 for lack of subscribers.

If the right to accept advertising laid the financial basis for an independent press, peddling a single issue instead of an annual subscription made evident the economic novelty inherent in the contents of the new style of daily.[44] Designed for each issue to become obsolete while simultaneously stimulating an appetite for more, the commercial daily re-

---

[41] Regulations governing state ads can be found in PSZ, 2d ed., vol. 13, no. 10978, 16 Feb. 1838.

[42] PSZ, series 2, vol. 13, no. 10978, art. 21, 16 Feb. 1838.

[43] *Severnaia pchela*, 19 May 1862, no. 133.

[44] On the relationship between street sales, the commodification of news, and the changing stylistics of communications, see Richard Terdiman, *Discourse/Counter-Discourse: Theory and Practice of Symbolic Resistance in Nineteenth-Century France* (Ithaca, N.Y.: Cornell University Press, 1985), 119–21.

quired a format that would pique well beyond the reader's interest in the national government, Europe, and book reviews. Serialized fiction and continuing coverage of engaging stories kept readers anticipating the next issue, while the addition of regular columnists, or "feuilletonists," who addressed readers as friends, encouraged personal identifications with specific newspapers. In the first decades after the reforms a number of hopeful publishers tried their hand at mixing news and entertainment, but the lifespan of most of the initial entries barely exceeded a few months. Those few who prospered could attribute their successes not solely to their abilities to find an untapped audience but, more important, to their skills at creating one.

Signifying much more than a commensurate increase in the number of readers, the growing number of thriving newspapers measured the formation of different audiences. The newspapers available at kiosks mirrored the growing pluralism of tastes and interests that would characterize urban Russia by the turn of the twentieth century, a separation into distinct groups that the press itself had nurtured. Street sales fostered the emergence of a unique style of daily, the urban or "boulevard" press. Smaller and cheaper than newspapers circulated nationally, those from the boulevard reached out to the merchants, shop assistants, doormen, and petty bureaucrats caught up more in city than in national affairs. Levels of literacy in St. Petersburg and Moscow a decade after the emancipation reached 60 and 46 percent, respectively, when the populations of both capitals approximated half a million, forming a not insignificant pool of readers.[45] Recasting political questions for the non-elites and formulating new ones, the urban press chipped away at the social barriers of class and education segregating Russians in the middle of the nineteenth century.

Street sales were especially important to the urban press, and the government, still uncertain what to do with the noisy news hawkers, turned them over to the Ministry of the Interior in 1868.[46] Instead of legislating new rules of conduct, the ministry decided to turn the business of selling on the street to its own advantage. A law passed later that year gave censors the authority to suspend this type of sales, an ironic expression of the government's acceptance of commercialism in publishing.[47] This soon became a popular punitive measure for disciplining errant publishers, and until 1904 suspension of street sales constituted roughly one third of all punishments meted out (see appendix B, tables 11–12). In 1875 the censorship added to its arsenal the power to suspend a publish-

[45] Gregory Guroff and S. Frederick Starr, "A Note on Urban Literacy in Russia, 1890–1914," *Jahrbücher für Geschichte Osteuropas* 19, no. 4 (1971): 525.

[46] PSZ, 2d ed., vol. 43, no. 45973, 14 June 1868.

[47] The law was passed 14 June 1868. Mentioned in *Pv*, 6 April 1871.

er's right to accept paid advertising, although this never figured prominently among penalties (appendix B, tables 11–12). By the end of the
1870s the street sales and advertisements had become businesses in
themselves, and the agencies that handled them remained independent
of publishers.[48] One publisher's estimation in 1876 that the most industrious street peddlers were taking in eighteen thousand rubles per annum seems inflated, but by 1880 approximately twenty-three thousand
single issues of various periodicals sold on the streets daily.[49] Because
street sellers contracted for the right to return unsold papers, publishers
learned to make their products attractive to one-time as well as regular
shoppers.

The prosperity of the commercially funded newspaper prompted the
establishment in 1878 of an advertising agency, L. and M. Mettsl' and
Company, founded in St. Petersburg and soon opening branch offices in
other major cities. Based on the American models, the Mettsl' agency's
stationery read "Advertising Is the Engine of Commerce." The success
of the street hawkers and advertising agencies showed that a commercial
infrastructure had been laid for newspaper journalism. The tsarist government's recognition that economics could be utilized to keep journalists in line showed that it understood one basic premise of commercial
journalism: that money mattered sufficiently to publishers that they
would watch what they said about the autocracy. This was enough for the
government. But without a sense of the long-term implications of an institution in which public opinion could maneuver with relative freedom,
a sphere that by its commercial nature depended upon the public to give
it definition, the autocracy stood by while the mass-circulation press developed a political culture all its own.

Content to have at hand a censorship that could discipline publishers
when they stepped out of line, the government did not concern itself
with the subtler, more far-reaching consequences of the new journalism.
In fact, much of what the independent newspapers could accomplish
served the best interests of the reform-minded autocracy. For example,
circulating information and contributing positively to the growth of a consumer economy spurred the Great Reforms along. The contradiction between autocracy and commercial journalism would arise from the limits
that the tsar set on his reforms, limits that he and his successors believed
they could force upon recalcitrant publishers by keeping out of print
open discussion of topics that undermined their authority.

The newspapers did not need to engage in specifically polemical dis-

[48] The first *artel'* of street sellers was organized in St. Petersburg in 1878. Esin, *Puteshestvie v proshloe*, 138–40.

[49] Ibid., 139. Esin estimated that street sellers earned as much as thirty thousand rubles
annually, which seems grossly exaggerated.

cussions, however, to influence readers' perspectives and values. The press did this by its very structure and function. As Maxwell E. Mc-Combs and Donald L. Shaw have argued, the power of the press lies in its ability to identify specific subjects and present them for public discussion, that is, to set the political agenda; the press does not so much tell readers what to think as give them important issues to think about.[50] If Russian publishers were forbidden from editorializing against the autocracy, they were still not restricted from offering readers a wide assortment of ideas about what it meant to be Russian and how the many changes they were witnessing might affect them. This would in turn stir discontent among readers coming to want to decide for themselves the terms of policies that governed their lives. The tsar surrendered official control over print communications because he assumed that he could still maintain authority through censorship. But power and knowledge, both produced by communications, are not discrete objects independent of each other. Public access to the media but not to the government could not help but influence both.

The West understood the relationship between political power and mass-circulation journalism, especially from the second half of the nineteenth century, when Russia's newspaper industry began to evolve. In part because of the variety in the Western beginnings, and in part because of Russia's political structure and the fact that it began to industrialize later than the other three countries, it is difficult to pinpoint the origins of outside influence on Russia's newspaper industry. Educated Russians had long subscribed to foreign periodicals, so publishers were aware of what constituted a modern newspaper. Russians also borrowed extensively from Western print technology.[51] Of the three Western presses used for comparison, French influence could be felt most clearly, for several reasons. Cultural ties were strong between France and Russia, and this would be reflected in the literary offerings of the latter's press. Moreover, France had censorship controls until 1881, which also accounted for similarities of style in that both presses had significant immediate interest in establishing an oppositional public sphere. In business practices, though, Russians followed the less corrupt lead offered by the United States and England. Because American papers were universally the most influential in establishing concepts of news and developing the occupation of reporting, Russians also learned from them. If the Brit-

[50] Maxwell E. McCombs and Donald L. Shaw, "The Agenda-Setting Function of the Mass Media," *Public Opinion Quarterly* 36, no. 2 (1972): 176–87.

[51] On the history of print technology in Russia see B. P. Orlov, *Poligraficheskaia prommyshlennost' Moskvy* (Moscow: Iskusstvo, 1953); and Mark David Steinberg, "Consciousness and Conflict in a Russian Industry: The Printers of St. Petersburg and Moscow, 1855–1905" (Ph.D. diss., University of California, Berkeley, 1987), chapter 1.

ish impact was less easy to discern, 1855 turned out to be a pivotal date in the development of both presses, and the two would move together through a series of analogous stages.

Because contents, like technology, had to be adapted to the distinctly Russian circumstances, Russia's newspaper industry cannot be considered merely imitative or derivative. Its fit with both Lippmann's and Habermas's paradigms would be rough, but Russian journalism would make corresponding contributions to both theories. It would illustrate how a consumer-oriented press figured into the evolution of democratic ideals, and at the same time it would underscore the role of newspapers in opening a sphere in which public opinion could take shape and seek to revolutionize the political structure.

2

The Transition to Commercial Independence, 1863–1876

COMMERCE began to replace partisanal politics as the basis for periodical publishing with the appearance of the independent newspaper *Golos* (*The Voice*) in 1863. At the onset of the Great Reforms, two forces exercised hegemony over print communications: the government and the intelligentsia. The government could afford to lease its presses and permit private businesses to share the costs of publishing because it had the Chief Administration of Press Affairs to maintain its presence. Initially, therefore, the advent of market forces to mediate communications posed a more competitive challenge to the intelligentsia, whose political effectiveness derived from its domination of the "thick" journals, access to which was restricted by price and vocabulary. Sustained more by polemics than profits, these journals reached out to exclusive rather than inclusive audiences. Commercialism, which intrinsically changed the role of readers in the process of communication, broadened the base of what constituted "the public" by inviting more and different Russians to coalesce into a body of opinion.

Despite the absence of electoral politics and formally established parties, Russia was not without rival political interest groups. Educated Russians clearly identified camps among themselves. In the center stood apologists for the autocracy, and the government faced critics on both its right and left. On the right, the Slavophiles harkened back to a visionary ideal of the glory that was Muscovy. They urged Russians to shun the West and pursue instead a future based on Slavic traditions of a spiritual community between tsar and people. The more numerous Westernizers, in contrast, pushed to accelerate reforms along Western models that promised greater individual freedoms and constitutional restraints on the autocrat. For all the political freedoms that they desired to have guaranteed by a constitution, the Westernizers reserved doubts about how a free-market economy might conceivably allow consumers to circumscribe the leadership role they saw themselves playing in the imagined new order. By the 1860s, socialism was also attracting a following among the frustrated and disenfranchised young intellectuals.[1]

[1] Nicholas Riasanovsky, *A Parting of the Ways: The Government and Educated Public in Russia, 1801–1855* (New York: Oxford University Press, 1976).

Fig. 1. A. A. Kraevskii, publisher of *Golos*

The gradual transition to commercial independence in periodical publishing can be seen in the biography of Andrei Alexandrovich Kraevskii (1810–1889), who worked his way through all the different types of media, from the government's newspapers to the intelligentsia's journals, until the opportunity to publish an independent newspaper presented itself in 1863. Aware from past journalistic experience of the limitations inherent in the available media, Kraevskii inaugurated a substantively new journalism, one that enlarged the variety of offerings and invited readers to take an active part in producing the paper, making it "theirs." Even the name he chose, *Golos*, emphasized that he intended to speak out for readers.[2] Kraevskii consciously wanted to disentangle it from association with any of the established camps and to present a different kind of forum. The early history of *Golos*, like the biography of its publisher, captured the many transformations set in motion by the reforms. Through *Golos* Kraevskii helped to fashion an ideology for coping with the changes; his readers not only thought about the modern world, but

[2] V. Zotov, "Nestor russkoi zhurnalistiki," *Iv* 38, no. 11 (1889): 364.

could come to an understanding of it in terms that were themselves new. Making commercial profits and political objectivity the bases for his medium, he sought to include all readers rather than exclude those who did not share his interpretations of political events. Nevertheless, the price and contents of the paper suggest that it was read primarily by the affluent and well-educated.

Born into the nobility, Kraevskii came into his social status through the back door. The bastard son of the illegitimate daughter of a grandee at the court of Catherine the Great, the boy took his surname from one of his mother's lovers.[3] Like another nobleman's sexual blunder, his French counterpart Emile Girardin, denied a name, Kraevskii "made himself a reputation."[4] Growing up in his grandfather's house, he lied about his age and enrolled in Moscow University's department of philosophy at fifteen. Three years later Kraevskii embarked on his journalistic career at the "thick" journal *Moskovskii vestnik* (*The Moscow Herald*). Edited by historian M. A. Pogodin, it voiced the ultraconservative official ideology of Nicholas I: "Orthodoxy, Autocracy, and Nationality."[5]

Heading the bibliography section of the journal and occasionally writing articles on literature and philosophy did not provide much income, and when his family fortune declined, Kraevskii had to find steadier employment. He moved to St. Petersburg to look for a position in state service and landed at the Ministry of Education. As editorial assistant at the ministry's official journal, Kraevskii drew immediate attention with a controversial article casting doubt on the guilt of boyar villain Boris Godunov in the sixteenth-century death of the tsarevich Dmitrii, firstborn of Ivan the Terrible. His revision of the Godunov legend aided Kraevskii's admission into St. Petersburg's most prestigious literary salons when it attracted the attention of the dazzling Pushkin, whose recent drama on the boyar-tsar had probably inspired Kraevskii to investigate the subject. Pushkin pulled the obscure journalist into his Western-oriented intellectual circle. Kraevskii's new companions included such luminous figures as poet V. A. Zhukovskii and Prince V. F. Odoevskii, cofounder of the first philosophical circle, the Lovers of Wisdom.

Always a better editor than writer, Kraevskii presented his new colleagues' works in his various publications. He helped Pushkin out with the latter's organizational problems at the "thick" journal *Sovremennik* (*The Contemporary*), in the meantime negotiating for a periodical of his own. Staying in journalism while changing ministries, he edited the lit-

[3] Vl. Orlov, *Puti i sud'by* (Leningrad: Sovetskii pisatel', 1971), 452.

[4] Zeldin, *France, 1848–1945,* 2:494–95.

[5] Biographical information on Kraevskii is from *Russkii biograficheskii slovar'* (St. Petersburg: Tipografiia upravleniia udelov, 1903), 9:400–404; and M. I. Semevskii, "Andrei Aleksandrovich Kraevskii," *Russkaia starina* 63, no. 9 (1889): 709–14.

erary supplement of the Ministry of War's *Russkii invalid*. In 1839 he also procured the requisite approval to take over the nearly defunct "thick" journal *Otechestvennye zapiski* (*Notes of the Fatherland*). His first major hire proved his best; when he made the radical and outspoken Vissarion Belinskii his resident literary-*cum*-social critic, his became the most powerful journal in the 1840s. As aggressively hostile toward the autocracy as the censorship allowed, Belinskii inspired generations of frustrated young intellectuals with his call to social action. In the beginning, Kraevskii's bringing Belinskii to print prompted gratitude and respect for the publisher among leftist intellectuals. In time, though, his financial relationship with the renowned critic soured many of their colleagues toward Kraevskii because of the important role he gave to money and profits in journalism. The key to understanding much of the hostility provoked by Kraevskii's "new" journalism lies in the mini-scandal of their association.

The same age as his publisher, the brilliant critic grew up in Penza Province, the son of a poor naval doctor and a member of a social estate without pedigree or even proper definition, a *raznochinets*. Although forced to leave Moscow University because of his inability to pay, Belinskii became well known to Moscow's literati when he joined Nikolai Stankevich's fashionable circle of Westernizers. Kraevskii brought the destitute Belinskii to St. Petersburg on an annual salary of 1,200 rubles. The publisher had gone heavily into debt to commence operations, but by 1845 *Otechestvennye zapiski* was turning a profit. Kraevskii increased Belinskii's salary to six thousand rubles, a raise considered inadequate by those who resented Kraevskii's greater earnings.[6]

His contemporaries thought Belinskii deserved complete credit for the journal's success. They saw the most important critic of their generation constantly ill and in need of better living accommodations; Kraevskii saw creditors at his own door and a well-paid journalist who owed his career to *him*.[7] When Belinskii moved to the competition, N. A. Nekrasov's *Sovremennik*, in 1847 at twice the salary, he took away subscribers as well as prestige. Journalism suffered from Belinskii's premature death that same year, which exacerbated ill will toward Kraevskii. Novelist I. S. Turgenev wrote to *SPB vedomosti* to remind readers of Kraevskii's "commercial soul."[8] Pre- as well as postrevolutionary biographies of Kraevskii concur that although "he was a tireless journalist, he was not a man of

[6] V. I. Kuleshov, *"Otechestvennye zapiski" i literatura 40-kh godov XIX veka* (Moscow: MGU, 1959), 210–12.

[7] H. von Samson-Himmelstierna, *Russia under Alexander III and in the Preceding Period*, ed. Felix Verkhovsky, trans. J. Morrison (New York: Macmillan, 1893), 252–76.

[8] L. N. Maikov, "Pis'ma k P. V. Annenkovu I. S. Turgeneva," *Russkoe obozrenie*, no. 3 (1894): 24–25.

ideas or principles."[9] Kraevskii wanted not only to earn a living, but to get ahead. He had no family name or fortune upon which he could rely.

Selling words and opinions for money was not in itself the issue, as Belinskii himself had spoken on the importance of finance to keeping writers and periodicals afloat.[10] But the intelligentsia distinguished between "commercialism" and "professionalism," with Kraevskii committing the mortal sin associated with the former and Belinskii respected for representing the latter. They did not accept that without the means (Kraevskii's publishing enterprises) there could be no ends (Belinskii's intellectual impact). Throughout his career Kraevskii remained on the fringes of the liberal intelligentsia, hoping to make peace with that element from which he came.

Pioneering the Daily Newspaper

Both Kraevskii and his detractors held fast in their ideas about newspapers as well. Kraevskii pioneered in defining the novelty of the daily in its roles as both a communications medium and a financial venture. Together with A. N. Ochkin, another journalist who shared his sentiments about news and commerce, Kraevskii leased *SPB vedomosti* in 1850. Officials denied his request to renew the lease in 1862, approving instead the petition from Baron V. F. Korsh, a Westernizing supporter of Alexander's policies. Kraevskii could not have been disappointed, though, because the government approved his bid to publish his own daily.

During the first years of Alexander II's honeymoon with the Russian public, the government played a parlor game of musical chairs with editors of official papers. This ended in 1863 when Kraevskii received his own paper, Korsh moved from the Moscow to the St. Petersburg *Vedomosti*, and the well-established conservative M. N. Katkov returned to edit the Moscow edition for the second time. From the same circles, these three men shared a common background at "thick" journals and semiofficial newspapers. A colleague from Stankevich's circle and another impoverished *raznochinets*, Katkov competed with Belinskii for the charms of an actor's daughter, wrote a bit for *Otechestvennye zapiski*, and depended on Kraevskii to bail him out of occasional poverty.[11] When Katkov started his own "thick" journal in 1856, *Russkii vestnik (The Russian*

---

[9] *Entsiklopedicheskii slovar'* (SPB: Tov. Br. i I. Granat), 25:342.

[10] Robert A. Maguire, *Red Virgin Soil* (Ithaca, N.Y.: Cornell University Press, 1987), 55–56.

[11] Martin Katz, *Mikhail Katkov: A Political Biography, 1818–1887* (The Hague: Mouton, 1966); and V. A. Tvardovskaia, *Ideologiia poreformennogo samoderzhaviia* (Moscow: Nauka, 1978).

Messenger), Korsh's brother Evgenii sat on the editorial board. Initially, their personal connections imparted a clublike atmosphere to newspaper journalism. Katkov's support for the increasingly conservative government after 1863 set him apart from the other two politically, but it would be Kraevskii's ideas about newspaper publishing that would make him the odd man out of this trio. He suggested an enlarged realm of competence for the daily newspaper, like the type of medium he had created in *Golos.* Korsh and Katkov, in contrast, remained content to regard the newspaper, like the "thick" journal, as chiefly a forum for airing their views. Korsh, weary of doing battle with the reactionary minister of education Dmitrii Tolstoi, surrendered his platform in 1874 with the realization that Tolstoi, who oversaw publication through his ministry, "would not approve the Virgin Mary herself on his editorial board."[12]

Of the three, Katkov would receive the lengthiest footnote in Russian history because of his use of *Moskovskie vedomosti* to influence national politics. He achieved exceptional prominence as an ideologue of the right because the conservatism that had already estranged him in the 1850s from many in the Westernizing circles would make him a welcome companion to Alexander and other top officials having second thoughts about the momentum of the reforms. Read for its editorials by a politically critical element of the population until its publisher's death in 1887, Katkov's paper never reached out to a broader base and could not have endured without massive financial transfusions from the government, which came in the form of the right to publish official notices.[13]

Kraevskii's extraordinarily high profile in political journalism guaranteed that his paper would raise eyebrows and spark interest. Presenting himself as fundamentally a liberal Westernizer, he used some of the Slavophiles' chauvinistic tenets to argue his case. In times of reaction, when vociferous opposition would result in forced silence, Kraevskii declared his willingness to compromise.[14] Fearing the further erosion of his credibility among the intelligentsia, he lied about accepting minor funding from the conservative minister of internal affairs P. A. Valuev to get *Golos* under way. Strange bedfellows, Kraevskii and Valuev joined forces momentarily against their common rival, Katkov.[15] The animosity between

[12] E. V. Korsh, "Materialy po istorii russkoi literatury i kul'tury," *Rm* 34, no. 11 (1913): 90–113.

[13] Karel Durman, *The Time of the Thunderer: Mikhail Katkov, Russian National Extremism, and the Failure of the Bismarckian System* (Boulder, Colo.: East European Monographs, 1988).

[14] Maguire, in *Red Virgin Soil,* wrote that in 1848 Kraevskii volunteered to become a "government informer" (61), but did not elucidate what that would have entailed.

[15] B. B. Glinskii, "Kramola, reaktsiia i terror," *Iv* 115, no. 1 (1909): 234; and Esin, *Russkaia gazeta,* 97.

Katkov and Kraevskii erupted in a journalistic farce during the Pushkin
Celebration of 1880. The selection of ultraconservative Katkov to speak
at the ceremonies dedicating a statue to the poet excited much anxious
gossip about what kind of statement he might make. Katkov's magnanimous praise of Pushkin prompted thunderous applause from the relieved
onlookers. *Golos*'s correspondent, however, reported that the audience
had "decisively rebuffed" Katkov. Not even censures of *Golos* in the
other papers could elicit a retraction; Kraevskii preferred to wear egg on
his face rather than acknowledge that Katkov had performed admirably
in a role he had wished for himself.[16]

"Objective" Authority in the Comparative Perspective

In his opening editorial, Kraevskii announced his intent to remain politically independent and to chart a dynamic route for the independent
press: "What a responsibility lies on the newspaper, charged with ac-
quainting the public with contemporary social questions, and working
with that public to solve them. The obligation of a newspaper is to speak
honestly, to serve truth and action, and not people, parties, or reigning
theories."[17] He initiated a "For and Against" column that gave readers a
space for debating. Pandering to any special group would be "criminal"
now that the newspaper was assigned to safeguard the commonweal. By
stressing information over opinion, Kraevskii hoped readers of differing
sentiments would read his paper. This intent contributed to the intelligentsia's impression of him as "unprincipled" because in his bid for circulation he was relinquishing his responsibility, as they saw it, to take a
stance against the government. As his man in Italy, reporting on Gari-
baldi's fight for unification, ruefully noted: "If my responsibility as a correspondent permitted me to venture into my personal predictions about
the future, I would be able to tell you something about the ministry here.
But only information about what is happening here is required of me."[18]

Kraevskii's inaugural editorial read remarkably like the one James Gordon Bennett penned in 1835 to launch his *New York Herald* and that
Girardin wrote one year later for the first issue of *La Presse*. Bennett
promised in what would be the most influential organ of American journalism for the next fifty years, "We shall support no party—be the organ
of no faction or coterie, and care nothing for any election, or any candi-

---

[16] Marcus Levitt, *Russian Literary Politics and the Pushkin Celebration of 1880* (Ithaca,
N.Y.: Cornell University Press, 1989), 87–88.

[17] *Golos*, 1 Jan. 1863, no. 1.

[18] Ibid.

date from President down to Constable."[19] Also shunning political affiliation, Girardin explained to readers, "This is not [intended to function as] an inexpensive journal; the mission of *La Presse* is of a completely different order; it marks a radical reform of daily journalism . . . *La Presse* will attract [readers] through the most attractive editorial staff, the highest quality printing, and the cheapest subscription rates."[20] Kraevskii endured intellectual abuse, but was not called upon as Girardin was to defend his honor with pistols. When Armand Carrel, editor of the Republican *Le National*, denounced Girardin for having "reduced the noble mission of the journalist to that of news merchant," the latter called him out and created a lasting image of the commercial press killing off its political rivals when Girardin shot Carrel dead.

Of the three periodicals, *Golos* cost most at twelve rubles (silver), sixteen with delivery, but Girardin's price of forty-eight francs per year suggested that he could not fulfill his promise to bring "the greatest happiness to the greatest number."[21] Bennett's penny paper could better fulfill this promise, although in their first years each of these publishers had circulations of approximately twelve thousand. Vulgar by the standards of *Golos* and *La Presse*, the *Herald* reflected the rugged individualism that characterized Andrew Jackson's presidency. Kraevskii and Girardin did not bannerline murder to sell on the streets, nor did their editors tweak censors' noses with confrontational insults to public officials. Yet these publishers influenced the course of journalism in much the same manner. First, they reoriented their newspaper's political focus, making it over from the voice of one faction to the observer of all. Next, they distinguished the news report as a commodity they could make a business out of selling.

All three of these progressive publishers profited from the experiences of the Walter family of London, whose *Times* had made only a ripple when it appeared in 1771. John Walter had begun with the notion that commercial ads would make his paper independent, but he found himself in need of subsidies from the treasury and occasional employment by the government to cover publishing costs. Connections at the top did not guarantee security, and he spent 1790 in Newgate Prison for libeling a favored duke.[22] By the time of *Golos*'s appearance, the London daily had laid legitimate claim to being the world's most respected daily newspaper.[23]

[19] Quoted in Lippmann, "Two Revolutions," 435.
[20] Quoted in Eugene Hatin, *Bibliographie historique et critique de la presse periodique française* (Hildesheim: George Olms Verlags Buchhandlung, 1965), 400.
[21] Bellanger et al., *Histoire générale* 2:117–19.
[22] Arthur Aspinall, *Politics and Press, 1780–1855* (Brighton: Harvester Press, 1973), 75.
[23] Koss, *Rise and Fall*, 38–40.

Setting the Reformist Agenda

As permanent staff member V. O. Mikhnevich phrased it, "created by the reforms, [Golos] served the reforms."[24] If the Great Reforms made the new journalism possible, it was not yet evident in the reportage of the first of them, covering the emancipation. The coverage itself bespoke the government's insecurity about how the country would receive the emancipation. Nothing could be found on it in the press on the day Alexander officially signed the decree, 19 February 1861. Two days later *Moskovskie vedomosti* reported, "We have learned from a trustworthy source that the status of the peasant question, the affair that means so much to all of Russia, is coming to a close."[25] The careful tsar had waited until Lent began to make the news public, hoping that religious piety would diffuse hostile reaction. On Shrove Tuesday, 7 March, newspapers showed varying degrees of willingness to touch the story. Korsh noted simply that the manifest had been signed on 19 February, presenting the government's line that it had needed the extra two weeks to print copies, now available for one ruble. Kraevskii saved subscribers of *SPB vedomosti* that ruble by serializing the details of the decree on the front page for several days, but without comment. In the following days readers learned only about the displays of thanks by the grateful peasants; the reactions of the angry and disappointed did not find their way into print. But once the long-anticipated emancipation had become a reality, the mood to express oneself freely spread.

Many among the intelligentsia expected Kraevskii to challenge the ancien régime. Supportive of the Great Reforms in general, Kraevskii surprised them when he advised circumspection, urged readers to keep their expectations modest, and reminded them that it took seventy years after the appearance of *The Wealth of Nations* for Adam Smith's economic ideas to be realized.[26] The first cause célèbre in which *Golos* could partake that pitted liberals against the autocracy involved the latter's ruthless suppression of the Polish revolution of 1863. *Golos*'s coverage included such extras as biographies of key revolutionaries. Editorially, Kraevskii attempted the fragile balance between government and intelligentsia that he would maintain precariously for the next twenty years. Quoting the seventeenth-century Polish patriot Jan Kazimir's warning that Poland must put its house in order or be taken over by foreigners, he argued that "no one cannot find Poland responsible for its own fate."[27]

---

[24] V. O. Mikhnevich, *Piatnadtsatiletie gazety "Golosa"* (SPB: Tip. "Golosa," 1878), 2.
[25] *Mv*, 21 Feb. 1861, no. 42.
[26] *Golos*, 1 Jan. 1863, no. 1.
[27] *Golos*, 10 April 1863, no. 84.

Blaming the Catholic church and exploitative Polish landlords for fomenting the unrest, Kraevskii regretted that the Russian government had been forced to intervene. Katkov expressed considerably greater enthusiasm for the tsarist government's repressive measures, and Kraevskii resented the Moscow publisher's self-designation as the true representative of Russian public opinion on this issue.[28]

Kraevskii's refusal to defend the insurgents kept him a heavy with the intelligentsia, forcing him to deny publicly rumors of complicity.[29] Fear of a governmental reprisal cannot account for Kraevskii's stance on the Polish question. Three years later he showed his true colors when he sent a correspondent to Galicia, in Austrian Poland, who reported the deep affection of Poles for Russians, and especially for their language.[30] Kraevskii's politics of moderation appealed not only to censors, but also to cautionary readers frightened away from unquestioning support for the reforms by an unexplained rash of fires that had swept St. Petersburg in 1862. The Poles had given Russia's progressives their first post-Nicholaevan political litmus test, and Kraevskii's position suggested that even many reformists were upset by the Polish audacity.

The paper's immediate stake in the censorship kept debates about it on editors' desks. Because the statute issued in 1865 was intended to be temporary, Kraevskii wanted a say in the final regulation. Where the government feared that criticism in newspapers could create a public opinion hostile to it, *Golos* insisted that this lay beyond the power of the press. Because newspapers can only reflect a society's aspirations, "a state, strong from the mutual confidence shared between government and people, must be prepared for freedom of the printed word."[31] The paper disparaged the prerogative of the minister of internal affairs to issue warnings because an arbitrary ministerial decision would upset this mutual confidence. French publishers became models of editorial responsibility when Napoleon III discontinued France's comparable system of warnings in 1867.[32]

Golos Reporting the News

The news itself had potentially negative effects on the image that the autocracy hoped to convey. Like the relations between the government

[28] *Golos*, 4 and 20 Sept. 1863, nos. 231, 247.

[29] *Golos*, 30 Jan. 1863, no. 26.

[30] *Golos*, 14 April 1866, no. 102.

[31] *Golos*, 23 Jan. 1866, no. 23.

[32] *Golos* published the reformed French statute: 15 Feb. 1866, no. 46, and 22 Jan. 1867, no. 22.

and the populace, those between censors and journalists eroded in the aftermath of Dmitrii Karakazov's misfired shot at Alexander II in April 1866. The first event of national consequence on which journalists could report from the scene, the story demonstrated the newspaper's unprecedented ability to bring readers into the action. *Golos* re-created the drama of how an observant peasant, Osip Komisarov, had saved the tsar: "When the tsar stepped out of the garden, [Karakazov] pushed Komisarov so hard that he was forced to step aside. But this fellow was so unruly that Komisarov began following after him. When the tsar began to put on his greatcoat, Komisarov saw the fellow pull something out of his coat and aim it at the tsar . . . the cop standing by could only cry out, but Komisarov hit the culprit's arm the exact moment the bullet left the gun."[33]

Liberal outrage at the attempted assassination did not prevent the "white terror," a crackdown on potential sources of dissent that caught the press in its net. The white terror failed to paralyze the revolutionary movement, and suspicions centered on the printed word and its power to mobilize for antigovernment activities. In November 1869, mentally unhinged revolutionist Sergei Nechaev persuaded his followers to murder one of their own, a student whom Nechaev had accused of being a police informer. Although the psychopathic ringleader escaped abroad and lived in émigré communities until he was returned to Moscow in 1873, his coconspirators went on trial in the summer of 1871. *Golos* reprinted the stenographic account of the trial, which the government insisted be made available through its official *Pravitel'stvennyi vestnik*.

Alexander II had believed that informing the educated stratum about his reforms would encourage support for them, and the concept of *glasnost'*, or publicity, had been instrumental to his ideas about how to reform the censorship.[34] He now hoped that publicizing Karakazov's trial would engender public sympathy. Kraevskii agreed with the principle that glasnost would improve relations between government and readers: "Only by means of these court recordings can justice be guaranteed, can the cases be tried openly, can the public absent from the court be genuine witnesses to the open workings of jurisprudence. There is also a place in the newspaper for personal impressions and opinions of those present at trials, but in the interests of equality, the reading public has to be able to make judgments itself, based on the facts at hand."[35] Moreover, Kraevskii argued that glasnost would prove a sure deterrent against the revolutionary movement. He held that random individuals such as Karakazov

[33] *Golos*, 6 April 1866, no. 94.

[34] W. Bruce Lincoln, *In the Vanguard of Reform: Russia's Enlightened Bureaucrats, 1825–1861* (DeKalb: Northern Illinois University Press, 1982), 184.

[35] *Golos*, 5 Nov. 1876, no. 306.

and Nechaev, not society as a whole or even youth in general, must be held responsible, editorializing that "this trial should have a calming rather than upsetting influence on the public."[36]

The trial of Nechaev's murderous followers had begun not long after a special commission had been established to reconsider matters of censorship, one that *Golos* hoped would eliminate the arbitrary official warnings. The official committee reached the opposite conclusion, having decided that information about revolutionaries stimulated others to imitate them. When Nechaev himself went on trial, the increasingly insecure autocrat resolved to fortify his censorship by allowing the minister of internal affairs to remove specified subjects from the realm of published discourse. Thus began the much-hated issuance of circulars from censors to editorial offices, designating certain topics forbidden. Editors would be permitted to republish information from official sources, but could add no commentary.[37]

The policy of issuing circulars to try to prevent news itself from being reported reflected official policy in general throughout the 1870s, as the government retreated from reform in efforts to combat the growing revolutionary movement. However, it must be remembered that Karakazov and Nechaev had perpetrated political crimes. Although their trials were among the most important during the reign of Alexander II, coverage of them constituted a separate issue from that of other criminals standing trial by the new judiciary. In addition to crimes against the state, readers were also interested in crimes against society. Those brought up on charges would now be tried by their peers, and newspaper coverage of the reformed courts allowed readers to participate vicariously as members of a jury. This would kindle civic consciousness, as jurors and readers alike attempted to establish criteria for determining right and wrong.

In his study of crime reporting in the British press, Steve Chibnall argues that in no other section of the newspaper "is it made quite so clear what it is that newspapers value as healthy and praiseworthy and deplore as evil and degenerate in society . . . crime and the processing of offenders offers an opportunity for the celebration of conformity and respectability by redefining the moral boundaries of communities."[38] The first newspapers, especially *Golos*, helped to define the boundaries of the new community; this entailed redefining certain perimeters of the old. Stories on the exercise of justice in and of themselves acquainted readers with the new legal norms. Court reporting made available to readers the latest

[36] *Golos*, 9 July 1871, no. 188.

[37] M. K. Lemke discussed the circulars at length, listing 562 of them in his "V mire usmotreniia," *Vestnik prava* 35, no. 7 (1905): 97–156.

[38] Steve Chibnall, *Law-and-Order News* (London: Tavistock, 1977), xi. See also Frank Harris, *Presentation of Crime in Newspapers* (New York: Putnam, 1932), 7.

advances in social science, a discipline created by nineteenth-century reformers who believed that human behavior could be understood and de-
viancy therefore controlled. Coverage of Karakazov's trial was a case in
point. Trying to explain how a native Russian could shoot at his tsar, *Golos* showed Karakazov to suffer from melancholia, hypochondria, and possible addiction to opium.[39] Substantiating its diagnosis with medical findings that accounted for the would-be killer's actions, *Golos* applied
science to human behavior. Without exonerating the malefactor, *Golos*
still did not reduce the situation to absolute terms of right and wrong.
Perhaps this explained why no similar psychiatric profile accompanied
the details of the psychotic Nechaev's trial, held after the government
had begun to reconsider its position on glasnost.

Other criminals, however, saw society stand trial for their misdeeds.
Golos repeatedly brought attention to the novelty of cases with sociolog-
ical twists, as though to emphasize for readers their own newfound capacity for scientific understanding. When the jury found a *meshchanin*
(roughly, petty bourgeoisie) innocent on the grounds that he was out of
his mind with alcohol when he bludgeoned his wife, *Golos* concurred:
"This is not a felon, just an unhappy person upon whom has fallen the
accusation for the crimes committed by the masses of the social estate to
which he belongs. Must one man be asked to pay for the crimes of a
generation?"[40] Suicide was a crime, but when a peasant woman accused
her husband of driving her to a noose in the hayloft, he stood trial for
attempted murder. *Golos* introduced this unsavory type to readers: "He
has a small build, his face is red, ugly, he has droopy eyes, and his whole
demeanor suggests that he is obtuse; he doesn't speak clearly, but as
though his tongue is swollen. . . ."[41] Readers could read guilt in his face
even before the jury had returned its verdict.

The attempt to weigh the mental state of the accused contributed an
even more ambiguous scientific element to questions of criminal liability.
The insanity plea, which had been accepted first by Britain's courts in
the 1840s, came to Russia by the 1860s, and the newspaper's pages suggest that St. Petersburg psychiatrists were kept busy giving expert testimony. The study of psychiatry had only been added to the curriculum of
the Ministry of War's Surgical Academy in 1857, so the doctors were as
fresh to some of these ideas as the press. The insanity plea offered the
optimism that the criminal could be cured and returned to society. *Golos*'s editors did not flag in their support for the principle of innocence on
the grounds of mental incompetence, happy to see this defense applied

[39] *Golos*, 14 April 1866, no. 102.
[40] *Golos*, 20 Nov. 1866, no. 231.
[41] *Golos*, 6 April 1867, no. 98.

in a variety of suits, including slander and the rewriting of wills, but they worried about its misuse: a Jew who pleaded insanity (unsuccessfully) for committing a sacrilege in a Christian church also tried *Golos*'s toler-ance.[42] Pointing the finger of guilt so often at circumstances, Kraevskii subtly implied that society could and should intervene to correct the faults that led to crime.

Golos and the Worker Question

An important corollary to a reform platform that held society at fault for certain crimes committed by its members challenged the notion that the urban poor were to be blamed for their poverty. Nicholas I had pre-vented the terrible clustering of a landless proletariat in Russia's cities by opposing industrialization, but this was no longer possible under Alex-ander II. Yet a press of its own for Russian labor comparable to William Cobbett's radical *Political Register* (1817) or Philadelphia's *Mechanic's Free Press* (1827) was out of the question. Russian workers instead had to rely upon the sympathies of capitalist publishers to protect their inter-ests.

The position expressed in *Golos* and the other Russian newspapers on the worker question receives more attention in this study than its com-paratively small news space indicates that it should because it is impor-tant to trace the development of attitudes toward the lower classes. Newspapers provide an especially valuable source for exploring public opinion about social integration. Russia's mass-circulation newspapers, like their Western counterparts, supported equal civil and economic rights for all citizens, a reflection of the commercial press's underlying dependence on freedom of opportunity to operate in a market economy.

An editorial series in *Golos* cheering the abolition of debtor's prisons in 1873 echoed the progressivism expressed in society at large on a wide variety of topics. Followed by a multipart discussion of proposals for workers' legislation, *Golos* expressed "complete sympathy" for any proj-ect that would codify a fair relationship between employer and employee. An investigative piece on the cruel exploitation of women and children in Muscovite factories pronounced British conditions and legislation far superior, a backhanded jibe at *Golos*'s nationalistically self-conscious au-dience.[43]

Golos's relatively open discussion of the worker question is especially interesting in light of the government's decision to limit it as a topic open

[42] *Golos*, 11 Nov. 1873, no. 312.
[43] *Golos*, in 1873, nos. 67, 73, 88, 102, 107, 130.

to the press after the labor movement picked up momentum in the 1890s.[44] A reportorial tour of living quarters at a factory in 1873 was mindful of Friedrich Engels: "The ubiquitous filth is unimaginable. The workers number forty to a room. As a result, the oppressive heat is unbearable, and the workers eat and sleep in this room. . . . it is impossible to talk about cleanliness or fresh air, and this is where they wash their children and their laundry."[45] Incubators of syphilis and cholera, the factories were an abomination.

The government's response of restricting this sort of exposé exacerbated the problem, ultimately proving counterproductive. The capitalist-based reformist press in other industrialized countries helped to find nonrevolutionary solutions to the labor strife in ways that accommodated workers within the system. As David Paul Nord argued in his study of how nineteenth-century Chicago's newspaper editors responded to labor problems in the Windy City, "Newspapers seem to have been early proponents of progressive-era views on business and labor, notably, a commitment to public interest consumerism, an obsession with commercial order and social harmony, and a growing faith in organizational modes of conflict resolution."[46] Articles in Russia's newspapers, coupled with the patriarchal attitudes adopted by the major publishers toward their own workers,[47] suggest that most prerevolutionary editors tried to play the same socializing roles as did those in Chicago. Moreover, newspapers designed to foster a working-class consciousness lost out in popularity in France, England, and the United States to the solidly capitalist newspapers that attacked big business editorially in the name of the little man. Russia's different political and socioeconomic structures, however, would ultimately prevent a like editorial assimilation of workers.

News and Nationalism

One of the most significant aspects of the mass-circulation press as it developed everywhere, and one connected directly to the growth of a middle class, was its role in the formation of a national consciousness.[48] Dis-

[44] The first circular Lemke found prohibiting information on the worker question was from 1893. "V mire usmotreniia," 134, cir. 326.

[45] *Golos*, 12 May 1873, no. 130.

[46] David Paul Nord, "The Business Values of American Newspapers: The 19th Century Watershed in Chicago," *Journalism Quarterly* 61 (Summer 1984): 265.

[47] Steinberg, "Consciousness and Conflict," especially chapter 3.

[48] Benedict Anderson, *Imagined Communities: Reflections on the Origin and Spread of Nationalism* (London: Verso, 1986), 38–40.

seminating new ideas and symbols, Russia's newspapers furthered the development of an ideology that called into question previous symbols employed by the ruling elite to justify their power.[49] Nationalism also contributed to pluralism: how would races and religions be integrated into one geographical unit defined by political and economic concepts instead of segregated according to the happenstance of birth? Moreover, how would newspapers influence the use of one unifying national language?

Coverage of Russia's shifting national boundaries in the immediate postreform era, as the nation expanded in Central Asia while contracting in North America, illustrated how the newspaper marketed a positive image of Russia to the rest of the world. In the process, it generated a peculiar problem for the autocrat. Transferring the image of authority from the person of the tsar to the concept of the Russian nation separated the two in readers' minds, a division the newspaper did much to reinforce.[50]

Golos dissociated the tsar from the land in the concept of nationhood it presented to readers. Portraying Russia as the bearer of Enlightenment to Asia, the paper undermined the idea of autocracy by emphasizing the image of Russia as lawgiver to the chaotic hordes. When Tashkent fell in 1866, the jubilant editorial in *Golos* read, "Asians are not accustomed to a lenient victor; they expect violent retribution from us. But we are bringing them *laws*."[51] L. Kostenko, a correspondent who flavored his reports with the history and legends of Central Asia, justified Russia's activities: "Now that you have a sense of the various cultures here, you can understand the mutual antagonisms that led all of the tribes to want some sort of political change."[52] He implied that the changes the new subjects wanted would not simply substitute dynastic for tribal loyalties.

Fulfilling the imperatives of civilization, Russia joined Europe on a separate-but-equal basis: "Western Europe, taking pride in the great deeds it has done for humanity, has always looked on Russia with a sort of malicious prejudice, only reluctantly allowing it a place in the family of civilized nations. . . . even those who are friendly to us view us as half-Asian. . . . but now our fate is clear: Russia has been deemed the En-

[49] Harold D. Lasswell, "Nations and Classes: The Symbols of Identification," in Morris Janowitz and Paul M. Hirsch, eds., *Reader in Public Opinion and Mass Communications*, 3d ed. (New York: Free Press, 1981), 17–28.

[50] Jeffrey Brooks, "Russian Nationalism and Russian Literature: The Canonization of the Classics," in Ivo Banac, John G. Ackerman, and Roman Szporluk, eds., *Nation and Ideology* (Boulder, Colo.: East European Monographs, 1981), 315–34.

[51] *Golos*, 4 Feb. 1866, no. 35.

[52] *Golos*, 25 and 29 March 1869, nos. 84, 88.

lightener of Asia and the representative of Slavdom in Europe."[53] Thus
Golos bridged the divide between Slavophiles and Westernizers by bor-
rowing from both. Slavs were distinct from other Europeans, but the ra-
tional thought that freed the individual from ignorance and arbitrary rule
was now considered a part of their intellectual heritage.

Russia's culture, not its bullets, was trumpeted as the mainstay of a
polyglot empire composed of a variety of peoples. The Russian language,
which unlocked the doors of education, furnished the key to moving from
a multiethnic empire to a stable nation tolerant of diversity—the proverbial melting pot. Central Asia did not have scientists "in the European
sense of the word,"[54] but now Russia could correct this. The Russian ventures into the Caucasus marked a retaking of land that had belonged to
Slavs in an earlier time, before the warrior tribes had chased them to the
northeastern forest. Pacification of the Caucasus meant restoring that
prior, superior civilization.[55]

Where did the Russian Orthodox church, the Slavophile's citadel of
Russian culture, fit into *Golos*'s concept of nationalism? Kostenko had
argued that Islam in Central Asia had disintegrated from being a "con-
solidating link" uniting tribes into a divisive force. He did not, however,
argue specifically that Orthodoxy should replace Islam. Russia's mission
was to educate, not necessarily to baptize. The tsar's dwindling utility as
a unifying image became apparent when he was mentioned as a figure-
head of the Church and not the nation's political leader.[56] Because the
newspaper also defended freedom of religion, promoting the tsar as the
spiritual head of Orthodoxy meant that he was no longer even the religious leader of all Russians.

Golos and the government tangled on one territorial issue, the selling
of Alaska in 1867. When rumors about the purported sale surfaced, the
newspaper made light of them, joking, "What should we sell next, the
Crimea?"[57] As galling as the sale itself, a week later the *New York Herald*
sneered at the action as "Seward's Folly," referring to the American secretary of state who had consummated the deal. Swallowing the bitter
medicine of the dual loss of land and prestige, *Golos*'s editors lamely
hoped that the transaction would mean a stronger tie between Russia and
the United States against France and England.[58]

[53] *Golos*, 21 June 1866, no. 69.
[54] *Golos*, 29 March 1869, no. 88.
[55] *Golos*, 9 Aug. 1866, no. 218.
[56] *Golos*, 13 Nov. 1866, no. 253.
[57] *Golos*, 23 March 1867, no. 84.
[58] *Golos*, 14 April 1867, no. 103.

Technology: The Telegraph and the Newspaper

The technology that enhanced the capability of newspapers to collect and present the information that made them so valuable came later to Russia than to the West. Kraevskii's ambitions for Russia greatly outdistanced his ability to communicate them. He knew what he needed, but the obstacles of censors, money, and technology stood in his way. For example, although he could afford the telegraph only to report immediate events, for example, the fall of a fortress in the charting of Russian expansionism, Kraevskii wanted more of the "lightning lines." Trailing behind Western entrepreneurs, he made exceptional headway in the development of the Russian telegraph. He saw how Morse's contraption broke time down from a continuum to a second, a concept critical to the daily newspaper's role in restructuring notions of time itself. In 1876, for example, St. Petersburg was awaiting the verdict in a trial of suspected embezzlers at a Moscow bank. Throughout the trial, *Golos* had been publishing daily telegrams of latest developments, carrying also the stenographic records, delayed by post. *Golos* reported the precise minute that the jury had brought in the "guilty" verdict, followed by the exact time that the newspaper had received the telegraphed word of it.[59]

The telegraph was expensive, though, and it was desirable to form a separate organization capable of collecting and disseminating information among publishers who could share costs. Russia's first news agency had been founded in 1866 by *Birzhevye vedomosti*'s publisher K. V. Trubnikov to facilitate the flow of economic information to his various periodicals. Beset by management problems, this agency foundered, despite the escalation in the number of transmitting stations from 160 to 714 in the 1860s.[60] When the telegraph finally connected St. Petersburg to the Pacific outpost of Vladivostok in 1871, Kraevskii petitioned for official approval to establish a news service to rival Trubnikov's. Granted a twelve-year lease, he set up the International Telegraph Agency (ITA), augmenting the national network of correspondents he had set up for *Golos*.[61]

In the international news market, Kraevskii could not accumulate the resources necessary to declare his independence from the recently organized Western cartel of news agencies. To avoid cutthroat competition,

[59] *Golos*, 2 Nov. 1876, no. 303.

[60] *Bol'shaia sovetskaia entsiklopedia*, 3d ed. (Moscow: Sovetskaia entsiklopediia, 1976), 25:389.

[61] B. I. Esin, "K istorii telegrafnykh agenstv v Rossii XIX veka," *Vestnik MGU*, philology and journalism series no. 1 (1960): 61–62; and Tehri Rantanen, "A Historical Study of News Agencies—The Beginning of News Agency Activity in Russia," *Nordicom-Information*, no. 1 (1985): 7–12.

the "Big Three"—France's Havas, Britain's Reuters, and Germany's Wolff Bureau—combined energies in 1870 and carved the world up into "colonial" news territories.[62] Russia, falling into the German dominion, struggled with the unwelcome censoring capabilities of the Wolff Bureau, which supervised the stream of news about Russia as well as information into and out of the tsarist empire. The ITA would not be renewed in 1883; a new lease went instead to a small consortium of independent publishers. But none of the commercial agencies could establish independence from the Wolff Bureau. Major publishers such as Kraevskii tried to counteract the problem with their own international bureaus, but for years their private correspondents had to utilize the slow, less costly mails.

Ironically, the Russian press needed its government here. The Big European Three all received substantial subsidies from their respective governments, which in return enjoyed privileged access to the information gathered. The situation in the United States differed significantly; from the beginning, the government left telegraph news to its commercial distributors, refusing to acquiesce to the public's demand that it intervene and regulate.[63] Russia would have benefited from following the European rather than the American system because its poorly developed system needed the weight of its government to organize and fund it. By the time that tsarist officials discovered the possible benefits to them of a telegraph service, custom had already accepted news as public property guarded by the independent newspapers.[64]

Foreign news reported and reprinted in *Golos* had a distinctive Russian slant, but these stories brought attention to the inadequacies of the national communications system. The forced reliance on international news sources posed a serious problem, and Kraevskii struggled to free Russian news from the media imperialists in the West. As he pointed out, Russia could not get reliable news about the American Civil War. Caught between the French press, which favored a Northern victory, and the British media, which gave the sympathetic edge to the South, reports of the same battle would often name different victors.[65] *Golos* did, though, have a correspondent at Abraham Lincoln's second inauguration, and its readers learned of Vice-President Andrew Johnson's scandalously drunken behavior.[66]

The difficulty of getting a positive image of Russia in the Western press

[62] Graham Storey, *Reuters' Century* (New York: Crown, 1951), 53.

[63] Czitrom, *Mass Media*, chapter 1.

[64] I deal with this more fully in "Autocratic Journalism: The Case of the St. Petersburg Telegraph Agency," *Slavic Review* 49, no. 1 (1990): 48–57.

[65] *Golos*, 9 Jan. 1863, no. 8.

[66] *Golos*, 27 March 1865, no. 86.

would never be resolved satisfactorily. European fascination with Russia's revolutionary movement constantly irritated Kraevskii. Editorials in *Golos* time and again accused the West of "exaggerating the actions of three dozen youths in a population of eighty million."[67] The fact that so many of the revolutionaries' philosophies originated in Western countries whose media distinctly underplayed their own analogous problems added to editorial vexation. For *Golos*, the disinformation in the contentious European press projected a false image of Russia. As Kraevskii tried to defend himself, "everyone knows that there is no press in this world that stands farther from the actions of its government than the Russian, but we are in agreement about the revolutionary movement."[68]

New Functions of the New Journalism

For its considerable impact on communications in general, Kraevskii's brand of new journalism had less impact on other writing conventions. Potboilers that whetted appetites daily for the cheap urban press by the 1880s constituted a clearly identifiable literature created by newspapers. The short story and the genre of realism would also be heavily influenced when entertainment was added as a function of the daily paper. *Golos* published precursors of regularly published fictional entertainment, albeit irregularly. Characteristic of the scattered fiction in *Golos* was A. V. Eval'd's "Passing By," which combined the familiar travelogue with social commentary. Published in the fall of 1863, this episodic journey of an officer through the countryside gathering data about local reception of the emancipation contained no sustained action.

Entertainment was never more than an incidental section in *Golos*. Once Kraevskii even serialized a play, a genre particularly ill-suited to the newspaper. The best he could offer was translations of several French authors, including Emile Zola, Victor Hugo, and Henri Rochefort. Zola, one of the most influential literary stylists of the nineteenth century, had developed his naturalistic prose, which evoked the realism found in news reports, from an early career in journalism. Soon the rage in Russia, Zola wrote monthly "Letters from Paris" for the "thick" journal *Vestnik evropy* (*The Herald of Europe*). Peter Boborykin, Zola's second-rate Russian impersonator nicknamed "Pierre Bobo" in Parisian salons, ascribed Zola's popularity in Russia to his assault on literary traditions that Russians could appreciate, but were not yet capable of making themselves.[69] From

[67] *Golos*, 10 Dec. 1876, no. 341.
[68] *Golos*, 22 Aug. 1878, no. 231.
[69] V. Chuiko, "Emil' Zola v kharakteristike P. D. Bobrykina," *Bv*, 10 April 1878, no. 98.

a more journalistically sophisticated society, Frenchmen had to make do for Russian readers until their own writers found a literary style compatible with newspaper journalism.

Kraevskii expanded other conventions of the daily paper. Drawing on human vanity, he published the names of those who moved up the ranks of state service. The newspaper was an attractive medium for identifying the socially prominent, and the comings and goings of notable folk were chronicled in a back-page diary. Kraevskii also tied the reader's social conscience to the newspaper's social responsibility. Soliciting readers to donate to particular charity cases, Kraevskii would publish names and amounts of donations. This practice gave a blush of social consciousness to the press, buttressing in general the daily newspaper's claim to be an institution serving the public interest.

Kraevskii also stressed the immediacy of his product. When subscribers complained about late deliveries, Kraevskii published their names and grievances weekly, alongside a timetable of when he had delivered *Golos* to the post office. Blame fell on postal authorities, whom he chided and urged to recognize the gravity of timeliness in communications. This ruptured the original bond between post and press, dating back to the time when newspapers appeared only on days that the post office delivered.[70] Still dependent on the post to distribute *Golos*, Kraevskii made an important move in disengaging communications from dependence on transportation by reversing their relative importance. In a more consequential action, he pioneered the publication of the Monday edition. Beginning as sheets of supplementary news bulletins about the worsening crisis in Poland, by May 1863 Kraevskii had developed them into full-size editions. He thus broke the religious taboo of treating Sunday as a day of rest for journalists and printers. News did not defer to the Sabbath; readers could not go uninformed.

Free to accept advertising wherever he could find it, Kraevskii revamped the process of soliciting ads. He offered incentives through discounts to those who would buy space regularly and allowed advertisers to place their ads through the many locations at which one could sign up for a subscription to *Golos*. The length and style of ads determined the price, and woodcut illustrations could be purchased for an additional few kopecks. In the 1870s he added colored supplements, which proved too costly to continue.

Golos's initial circulation of four thousand had more than doubled by decade's end. How, though, had this audience changed after a decade of newspaper publishing? Kraevskii repeatedly attempted to combat the ap-

---

[70] Government legislation on home delivery can be found in PSZ, 2d ed., vol. 30, no. 29137, 16 March 1855, and vol. 37, no. 38121, 2 April 1862.

athy notorious among the gentry: "We want to be powerful people, leaders, lords, but under no circumstances will we get down to it and work
for the public's [as opposed to individual] welfare. Such is the cancer of
our society."[71] Whether or not the people shared Kraevskii's enthusiasm,
by reading his newspaper they at least indicated a willingness to consider
his ideas. An editorial in 1865 on the chronic difficulties of finding good
help gave another clue to the aggregate profile of the *Golos* reader.[72]
Some of those incompetent servants, however, and others for whom the
issues addressed in *Golos* held little interest, had found their own medium. The appearance of a newspaper from the boulevard enlarged the
public space as it brought more and different social groups into the general newspaper audience.

[71] *Golos*, 23 May 1868, no. 141.
[72] *Golos*, 14 Jan. 1865, no. 14.

3

The Newspaper from the Boulevard, 1864–1876

ON 15 MARCH 1864, residents of St. Petersburg welcomed the first spec-
imen of a unique kind of newspaper targeted specifically to city-dwellers.
It was nicknamed for the "boulevard" along which papers and readers
circulated: *Peterburgskii listok* (*The Petersburg Sheet*). The paper's original masthead depicted the bustle of Nevskii Prospect, the city's main
thoroughfare. The lead editorial promised that "we will speak exclusively
about life in Petersburg . . . life that boils like a whirlpool."[1] For a mere
three rubles a year, four with delivery, subscribers could buy into the
mainstream of Peter's great city. The preponderance of local news made
the paper an attractive window on St. Petersburg, and nonresidents
could be a part of the life of the national capital by receiving the paper
through the post office or retail outlets in Moscow and Warsaw. To ease
possible financial strains, office workers could pay on an installment plan.
Editors solicited readers for their interests and also encouraged them to
submit articles.[2]

Thus *Peterburgskii listok* and its audience began to shape each other
from their first encounter. Smaller than *Golos*, this lighter fare traveled
southeast along Nevskii Prospect, down from the Winter Palace toward
the vast marketplace, Gostinnyi dvor. *Peterburgskii listok* had to speak in
a new language. Flamboyant, sensational, and entertaining, this first of
the boulevard papers spoke in shirtsleeve Russian to ordinary residents.
It identified a political base in the city and accelerated the process by
which readers adapted to the urban environment.

Founder A. S. Afanas'ev, a provincial nobleman whose journalistic career paralleled Kraevskii's on a less distinguished level, likewise read opportunity into the reforms.[3] *Peterburgskii listok* forged a direct link between the city and its commerce. From the beginning, Afanas'ev had
accepted the importance of local business to his readership, and subscribers received the added bonus of the chance to publish six short ads gratis
during the course of the year. He worried, though, that economic news
would dominate. Promising daily information on stocks, he nonetheless
assured those who had no interest in the bourse that they would find

[1] *Pl*, 15 March 1864, no. 1.
[2] *Pl*, 4 June 1864, no. 44.
[3] N. A. Skrobotov, *"Peterburgskii listok" za 35 let* (SPB: Tip. Aktsion. dela, 1914), 3–4.

plenty else in the paper.[4] The newspaper's immediate success attracted another backer, A. A. Zarudnyi, proprietor of several brokerage houses. Temperamentally unsuited for the provincial nobleman's monotonous life, he had tried running a small circus before finding an outlet in the petty press. Another Zarudnyi brother, Nikolai, dipped into the writing side of journalism from his position in the Ministry of War. Tension developed quickly between the forces of commerce and art. Afanas'ev, who held the literary section paramount, resigned in November rather than give in to Zarudnyi's pressure to publicize his businesses.[5]

The new publishers, the Zarudnyi brothers, faced competition for the urban reader. The reasons for their success can be gleaned from what they did differently. The most immediate rival was Trubnikov's tabloid *Birzhevye vedomosti*, billed as "a commercial newspaper and journal for stockbrokers." Founded in 1861 primarily as a sheet of information pertaining to the national and international stock markets, the publisher soon added a telegraph news service that began to carry political stories as well. Trubnikov intended to provide the voice for the small businessman and others involved in petty commerce, and on several occasions he ran afoul of the censors by criticizing the Ministry of Finance when he saw it working against the interests of his prospective readers.[6] The publisher also supported the organization of mutual-aid societies for shop assistants to protect them from exploitation by his business peers.[7] But the paper's narrow focus and lack of attention to civic affairs prevented *Birzhevye vedomosti* from attracting a citywide bourgeois audience.

The Boulevard Press and the Public Sphere

The old social order, defined by birth, had to defend itself first against the newly legislated equality of all estates, and then against the determining role of earned versus inherited income in demarcating social status. The urban press led the attack. Priced and directed toward those pulling themselves up the social ladder, *Peterburgskii listok* championed the virtues of sobriety and honest work. A letter to the editor defending the rights of artisans and coachmen to smoke on the streets revealed much about who read this newspaper.[8] The Russian gentry's infamous "superfluous man," lounging about aimlessly in a stained smoking jacket, would have shuddered to see himself in the pages of *Peterburgskii listok*;

---

[4] *Pl*, 21 March 1864, no. 4.
[5] Skrobotov, *"Peterburgskii listok,"* 6, 9–10.
[6] Esin, *Puteshestvie v proshloe*, 82–99.
[7] *Bv*, 13 Jan. 1862, no. 9.
[8] *Pl*, 26 Nov. 1864, no. 143.

aristocrats who sniffed at those who imbibed cheap vodka were reminded of the excessive intake of alcohol in St. Petersburg's finest restaurants.[9]

This righteous voice criticizing the dissolute rich sounded consistently throughout the paper's history. Twenty years later, when a debutante died of drug overdose at a fashionable ball, *Peterburgskii listok*'s editors expressed disgust for a gentry that harped on alcoholism among society's lower strata while turning a blind eye to its own vices.[10] Yet at the same time that they chronicled gentry excess, *Peterburgskii listok*'s editors imitated *Golos* with a daily calendar of the movements of the socially prominent. Following the elite around hinted at intimacy, and the paper's format suggested that one day readers might find themselves mentioned alongside references to the Trubetskois or the Golitsyns.

The paper's often novel contents affected several journalistic canons. The boulevard press, initially forbidden from publishing what the censorship deemed "political news," which meant information about the government's activities, had to reconceptualize much of what constituted "news." With discussions of the Great Reforms off-limits, *Peterburgskii listok*'s editors had to content themselves with publishing selected factual information about reform legislation from official sources, for example, reprinting notification that the judiciary had been reformed with the sole comment that "this will be of interest to readers."[11] Even after censors permitted sections of political news, they maintained a close watch on urban newspapers' contents because the boulevard audience was presumed to be more credulous than *Golos*'s. Prevented from discussing national issues, editors made local topics all the more important.

The correspondent for the boulevard newspaper differed sharply from the combination of bureaucrats and intellectuals who staffed the precommercial press. Where *Golos* would feature the distinguished physician N. I. Pirogov writing from Heidelberg to compare Russia's university education to Germany's, *Peterburgskii listok*'s writers would take to the streetcars. In a technique that the future "King of Feuilletonists" V. M. Doroshevich would develop to perfection, A. Nedolin reconstructed a conversation overheard on public transportation. The poor and unhappy Misha lamented his fate with Zina, the girl he truly loved, whom poverty had destined to life as a governess. Engaged to a woman of wealth and title, Misha had the chance to escape the situation into which he had been born. Days later, Nedolin informed readers that he had eavesdropped once again on Misha and Zina, this time at Gostinnyi dvor. Happily, Misha had decided to follow his heart instead of his billfold. The

[9] *Pl*, 22 March 1864, no. 5.
[10] *Pl*, 21 Jan. 1887, no. 19.
[11] *Pl*, 24 Nov. 1864, no. 142.

tale ended with a clumsy pitch for the paper when Zina requested a subscription to *Peterburgskii listok* as a wedding gift, after Misha had offered her "Belinskii, or any of the best journals."[12]

The writer as escort-around-town, a rhetorical stratagem born of the petty urban press as it appeared everywhere, helped the daily newspaper to become the reader's companion. Nedolin located his audience in an everyday environment and introduced them to personalities with whom they could empathize. As the disembodied ear, Nedolin accentuated the personal attributes of the newspaper. Merging his identity with the paper's, he could enhance the image of the newspaper as a witness who could report with the authority of having observed the event firsthand. Nedolin had labeled the article discussed above a "story" (*rasskaz*), which obscured the boundary between fact and fiction, reality and fantasy.[13] This deliberate blurring of genres was common to the early newspapers intended for ordinary rather than educated readers. The style had its origins in the broadsheets that often retold events with the purpose of making them more entertaining.[14]

The boulevard press could help ease the transition phase of urbanization by introducing readers to the Zinas and Mishas, making their environment less intimidating through familiarity. In addition, *Peterburgskii listok* shrank the physical expanse of the city by setting up with great fanfare correspondents in all the different neighborhoods of the national capital.[15] Residents of the "Petersburg Side" could commiserate with those of the Vyborg district about frustrations with local sanitary conditions. A decade later, an added feature, "Around Towns and Villages," brought in communications from the rest of Petersburg Province.

One of the most valuable attributes of the boulevard paper was its ability to integrate inhabitants of the city into what sociologist Louis Wirth called "urbanism as a way of life."[16] According to Wirth, the necessity of substituting "secondary for primary contacts" constituted a basic element of adaptation for the emigrant, uprooted from the kinship ties that were alternately secure and stifling.[17] In the second half of the nineteenth century Moscow and St. Petersburg would see their populations more than double, each recording in excess of one million inhabitants in the 1897

[12] *Pl*, 21 March 1864, no. 4.

[13] Shelley Fisher Fishkin, *From Fact to Fiction: Journalism and Imaginative Writing in America* (Baltimore: Johns Hopkins University Press, 1985).

[14] Helen MacGill Hughes, *News and the Human Interest Story* (Chicago: University of Chicago Press, 1940; New Brunswick, N.J.: Transaction, 1981), chapter 6.

[15] *Pl*, 31 March 1864, no. 10.

[16] Louis Wirth, "Urbanism as a Way of Life," *American Journal of Sociology* 44, no. 1 (July 1938): 1–24.

[17] David Paul Nord, "The Public Community: The Urbanization of Chicago Journalism," *Journal of Urban History* 11, no. 4 (1985): 411–41.

census.[18] Emigrants to Russia's cities came from the provinces rather than foreign shores. Stories about hayseeds fleeced by city slickers appeared in the pages of the paper often enough to indicate the editors' consciousness of their readers. The trusting Russian abroad also had to beware.[19] The staff advised readers how living in the modern city required new modes of behavior: chatting aloud in the public library or with shop clerks when others wanted help, for example, was brought to readers' attention as an irksome practice.[20] The editors also commended the growing practice among merchants of putting visible price tags on their merchandise, because "the young generation of merchants should end the old ways."[21]

The boulevard press also drew from its origins in gossip. *Peterburgskii listok*'s regular "Notes, Rumors, and News," which often featured tidbits from the lives of ordinary people, made the paper over into a proto–town gossip. If the sheer size of the city overwhelmed the nameless, faceless reader, he or she could find a community-like atmosphere by being privy to the social goings-on. One could be relieved to learn, for example, that the worker who accidentally sliced his arm on the job a few days ago had not been injured seriously.[22] The integrity of news was also vital. When *Golos* rejected as "fabrication" a small piece about a sidewalk encounter between a brash young nobleman and a street-cleaning doorman, *Peterburgskii listok* leapt to vindicate its source.[23]

Although this street sheet stayed out of bedrooms, it gave keyhole access to enough accidents, knife fights, and alcohol-related incidents to keep tongues clucking. The paper provided a double-edged security. It could make the city less threatening by integrating readers into the life of the otherwise anonymous city as it unraveled around them. At the same time, it kept its distance, unlike the busybodies many had left behind. Robert Park, one of the first to apply sociology to the study of newspapers, evaluated the significance of this type of story: "It ceases to be the record of the doings of individual men and women and becomes an impersonal account of manners and life."[24] Substituting "objective" for "impersonal" better describes the newspaper's position, because the editors intended these stories to be taken personally. In *The Fall of Public*

---

[18] Population figures are from *Istoriia Moskvy* (Moscow: Akademiia Nauk, 1955), 5:15; and *Ocherki istorii Leningrada* (Moscow and Leningrad: Akademiia Nauk, 1956), 3:105.

[19] *Pl*, 5 Nov. and 15 Dec. 1864, nos. 131, 154.

[20] *Pl*, 4 Oct. 1864, no. 113.

[21] *Pl*, 21 Nov. 1864, no. 140.

[22] *Pl*, 26 March 1864, no. 7. The original news had been published on 19 March.

[23] The defense was in *Pl*, 13 Dec. 1864, no. 153. The story had appeared a week earlier.

[24] Robert Park, "The Natural History of the Newspaper," *American Journal of Sociology* 29 (1923): 277.

Man, Richard Sennett argues that this conflation of personal and impersonal, because it replaced the traditional community with a vision of a
new communal harmony so idealized that it could only disappoint, was
one of the unfortunate legacies of the nineteenth century.[25]

Limited by locale and the type of stories it could report, *Peterburgskii
listok* took an active part in civic life. Where Kraevskii hoped to influence
national issues, the Zarudnyis were determined to claim their authority
among common city-dwellers. "Notes, Rumors, and News," for example,
made plain the dangers of life in the big city. A story on the high inci-
dence of murder along the Neva River warned readers to avoid the area
at night.[26] The first *Peterburgskii listok* correspondent to report regularly
under a byline (of sorts), Z-S-V, reported his exciting but improbable life:
caught in a crowded theater when someone yelled "Fire!," only a few
days later he found himself cornered by wild dogs on a city street. He
avoided disaster by keeping a cool head.[27]

The paper also pledged to guard readers as best it could by publicizing
right and wrong. Two police officers who had refused to pursue an escap-
ing thief late one night read all about their inactivity in *Peterburgskii
listok*.[28] After twenty years the paper still watched out for "coldblooded-
ness to the public" and published, when it could attain them, badge
numbers of policemen lethargic about their duties.[29] An article on corruption at the customs office ultimately sent the culprits off to jail, and
an exposé of the meat packers' monopolizing practices spurred the government to investigate.[30]

The daily newspaper created a public by pulling together the interests
that many private individuals shared in common. Residents of St. Petersburg had any number of difficulties as individuals that could be addressed
collectively through the newspaper, and a feature begun in 1870 addressed "City Problems." Home delivery of fresh water was one. One
editorial writer at *Peterburgskii listok* took umbrage at the monopolizing
tactics of a water-supply firm, denouncing their high costs and poor service. The writer alleged that the firm "doesn't think that the enterprise
exists for the public, but that the public exists for the enterprise."[31] Proprietors and waiters who overcharged, dirty dining rooms, and places
that attracted a wild clientele could read at length about their shortcom-

[25] Richard Sennett, *The Fall of Public Man* (New York: Knopf, 1977), chapter 10.
[26] *Pl*, 10 Nov. 1864, no. 134.
[27] *Pl*, 29 Oct. and 5 Nov. 1870, nos. 127, 131.
[28] *Pl*, 10 Dec. 1864, no. 151.
[29] *Pl*, 5 June 1884, no. 152.
[30] *Pl*, 4 July 1864, no. 104.
[31] *Pl*, 2 June 1864, no. 43.

ings, just as those who offered wholesome entertainment at reasonable prices would find their efforts applauded in *Peterburgskii listok*.[32]

In the late twentieth century, the difference between "snooping" and "exposing" awards some newspapers Pulitzer Prizes and relegates others to the checkout stands in grocery stores. Before that distinction could be drawn, however, the newspaper *as an institution* had to become regarded as a watchdog for the public's interests. In their initial search for readers, *Peterburgskii listok*'s editors found success by giving the potential audience a personal stake in the information supplied by the newspaper. When a female reporter went undercover to expose a crooked firm promising to place well-qualified young women in private homes as governesses, she presaged by two decades the trendsetting era of reformist journalism in the United States. "Lialia" disguised herself as a poor-but-educated girl in desperate need of work, and recounted in the paper how the director took her money in exchange for promises of employment that he made no effort to fulfill.[33] Lialia had created simultaneously a news story and a political situation.

This particular example highlights the innovative ability of the urban press to insert itself into local politics. In England in 1885, when editor William Stead of the *Pall Mall Gazette* posed as a lecherer ready to spend whatever it took to buy a virgin in "modern Babylon," he popularized a type of reporting that led newspaper reporters directly into the political process. Matthew Arnold christened Stead's as the "new journalism," a term he intended to be derisive because he loathed Stead's overt sensationalism and pandering to base instincts. In the United States, at the end of the nineteenth century reporters appeared in a myriad of disguises to perfect "stunt reporting" as one of the daily newspaper's contributions to the reform movement. Publishers' skills at promoting social reforms by sensationalizing the need for them strengthened the interrelationship between mass-oriented communications and political action. Comparing what only barely flowered in tsarist Russia with the full bloom of the American street press points to the limits of participation in public affairs under the autocracy rather than to journalistic shortsightedness. This style of reporting could not carry the same punch in Russia because most consumers of street sheets lacked an immediate voice in reforms.

Limited access to decision-making circles did not prevent Russian editors from laying claim to membership in them, and, like their Western counterparts, they often used shocking stories to stake that claim. In another landmark feature that drew greater response than that of the incognito governess, the editors experimented with journalistic styles to bol-

[32] *Pl*, 4 June 1864, no. 44.
[33] *Pl*, 21 Nov. 1864, no. 140.

ster their declarations of social responsibility. Publishing excerpts from what would later fill two volumes, V. V. Krestovskii's serialized "Petersburg's Slums,"[34] they drew from the "thick" journal convention of using the *ocherk*, or "sketch," which gave fictional license to factual reporting in social commentaries.[35]

Krestovskii's seedy descriptions of St. Petersburg's underclass stood out for both the topic and his prose, sharpened by his eye for detail and his ear for the unhappy mutterings of this neglected populace. Although Krestovskii was not truly a newspaper reporter, he nonetheless steered those just taking up this newest of literary crafts toward the path of distanced, "objective" observation. Equally important, he wrote "sensational" narratives, in that the subjects he described and the words he used evoked an immediate sensation of shock or titillation. He could argue that he was aspiring to motivate his audience to pay attention to a very real problem, but the way in which he went about reproducing reality had implications for the development of the language of the newspaper; his reportage was "sensational" at the same time that it was "reasonable."[36]

A peculiar candidate to influence objectivity in journalism because he later moved on to the official press, Krestovskii could trace his noble ancestors to the pre-Petrine era, but the family had fallen on hard times. Born in 1839, the boy had adequate funds and connections for a university education in St. Petersburg, but he had to work to support himself. His writing competence put him on the periphery of the intelligentsia in the salad days following the death of Nicholas I, and respectable "thick" journals occasionally carried his poetry and fiction. Invoking Belinskii's assertion that all writing must serve a social purpose, Krestovskii argued that for literature to serve society best it must lose its "tendentiousness." He was one of the first to suggest that objectivity must replace "sentimentality," as he phrased it, in writing. As he further explained, didacticism and moralizing about the lower classes were no longer appropriate literary styles for presenting harsh realities, and his style was admirably suited for the daily press. Paradoxically, Kraevskii purchased excerpts from this work for *Otechestvennye zapiski* but not for *Golos*. This marked

[34] The story came in four installments in *Pl* in October 1864, nos. 111, 115, 118, 126.

[35] The *ocherk*, is discussed in Joan Neuberger, "Images of Crime and Poverty in St. Petersburg: The Sketch and the Popular Press, 1845–1914" (unpublished manuscript). See also Gary Saul Morson, *The Boundaries of Genre: Dostoevskii's "Diary of a Writer" and the Traditions of Literary Utopia* (Austin: University of Texas Press, 1981), 15.

[36] As John Stevens has pointed out, characteristically "little attention is given to the vital distinction between material that is made sensational by its manner of display and material that is inherently sensational." No distinction need be drawn in Krestovskii's case. "Sensationalism in Perspective," *Journalism History* 12, nos. 3–4 (1985): 78.

the end of the author's affiliation with the liberal intelligentsia, with whom he would find a second career doing infamous battle, to the point of dueling.[37]

Krestovskii's stories sparked the sort of attention that *Peterburgskii listok*'s editors wanted. The denizens of his slums, the petty thieves, mentally unbalanced old women, and the great unwashed, knew only two ways out: "prison and the cemetery." Krestovskii's graphic tour of the Haymarket district drew fire from the more sober newspapers, as yet unaccustomed to overt sensationalism as a selling point for the press. The Ministry of War's *Russkii invalid* charged that hyperbole had overwhelmed the author; Nikolai Zarudnyi jumped to his writer's defense, and his editors complemented the serial with an editorial campaign to clean up the area.[38]

These detailed descriptions of seedy people and lurid situations influenced the subject matter as well as the language of the popular press. Not only did the new jury trials have readers thinking like judges, but crime itself retained all the old elements that had made public executions a kind of popular drama, and visiting the courts had become a mass entertainment. *Peterburgskii listok* dutifully published listings of trials as it did of theaters. *Golos* also reported crimes, and in both papers the commission of a violent crime was at the same time a thrill and a matter of social concern, but the respective editors inverted the scale of importance. *Golos*'s attention to the insanity plea staked out a new territory for social psychology, not a significant subject for *Peterburgskii listok*. The journalistic styles of presenting crime news were deliberately different. Where *Golos* used stenographic recordings, *Peterburgskii listok*'s editors vowed not to bore readers with these "dry accounts." Instead, they sent their "own correspondents to court so that readers will get the effects of a living story."[39]

Attention to events that, like Krestovskii's tour of the slums, engaged readers at a gut level became increasingly pronounced. Another story recounted how a pair of inebriated fallen women had lured a wealthy gentleman into their apartment, where they poisoned, robbed, and chopped up their victim and packed him off to Moscow in a suitcase.[40] The language used to describe was important as well. Instead of, for example, a tactful mention of "death by her own hand," readers learned

---

[37] The fighting would not always be with pens; Krestovskii would find himself in court for slander and plagiarism in a case involving "Petersburg's Slums," later facing off with dueling pistols. See Iu. L. Elets's introduction to *Sobranie sochinenii Vsevoloda Vladimirovicha Krestovskago*, 2 vols. (SPB: Obshchestvennaia pol'za, 1899), 1, iv–lv.

[38] *Pl*, 17 Dec. 1864, no. 115.

[39] *Pl*, 14 Dec. 1876, no. 245.

[40] *Pl*, 29 March 1870, no. 50.

how a young governess "aimed the bullet directly into her mouth so that death was instantaneous."[41] In its attention to the city's underside, *Peterburgskii listok* was comparable to the first successful urban daily, the *New York Herald*. Bennett's initial popularity in 1835 has traditionally been attributed to his coverage of the trial of Richard Robinson, a bank clerk accused of taking a hatchet to the young prostitute Helen Jewett. Bennett energetically involved his paper in Robinson's defense and could probably claim some credit for the clerk's acquittal.[42]

By 1870, the year that the municipal reforms allowed at least some of the residents of St. Petersburg an electoral say in managing the national capital, *Peterburgskii listok* had achieved the consistent format that was to carry it through the next four decades. Fulfilling Afanas'ev's initial promise to report all news "quivering with life," *Peterburgskii listok* had become a well-known resident of the city. The front page invited readers to drop by editorial offices to sell articles, but the recurrence of several bylines indicated the presence of a growing permanent staff.

The most visible difference six years later was in the entertainment features, which mirrored the flourishing partnership between publicity and leisure time. Local stage productions now merited a resident critic and gossip-monger, S. S. Okreits, who would enjoy a long career in Russian urban journalism.[43] The newspaper produced for sale lessons on "How to Become an Actor." "Notes from a Whistler's Album," amusing and satirical ditties, appeared several times weekly. Serialized fiction, which depended on habitual rather than casual readership, signified the existence of a steady clientele. These serials produced spin-off publications sold through the paper. Krestovskii's slums had given way to "The World of Ballet," billed as "lively scenes characteristic of our contemporary morals," and the macabre "From the World of the Dead and Buried."

France, not the grave, provided the most endurable backdrop for these serial tales. The Zarudnyis, like Kraevskii, had to go to Paris initially to find fiction writers who had already developed a literary touch for popular periodicals. Serialized fiction was commonplace in periodicals from the eighteenth century, when Daniel Defoe sold fiction to the British press, and became ingrained in the commercial press when Girardin published Honoré de Balzac's "La Vieille Fille" in the inaugural year of his *La Presse*, 1836. Emile Gaboriau, whose "Detective Lecoq" roamed

[41] *Pl*, 15 Jan. 1886, no. 13.

[42] Dan Schiller has argued that readers may well have been more interested in a concurrent trial of tailors accused of forming a conspiracy to strike than in the Robinson-Jewett case. *Objectivity and the News* (Philadelphia: University of Pennsylvania Press, 1981), 57–61.

[43] S. S. Okreits, "Literaturnye vstrechi i znakomstva," *Iv* 144, no. 6 (1913): 613–42.

the Parisian underworld in *Le Petit Journal* from 1866, found his works
translated in greatly abridged form in *Peterburgskii listok*, and the paper
also sold Lecoq's adventures separately. Russians learned to imitate the
Frenchman's style, adopting as well his heritage in their pen names and
the settings for their dramas. Perhaps readers would never believe that
Russia could be so interesting.

The necessary ingredients of *Peterburgskii listok*'s serials suggested
that escapism competed favorably with reality: action was invariably set
abroad, usually on the Continent, and the attractive hero and heroine
had to suffer through days of unrelated misadventures, involving such
stereotypes as lascivious older men, concealed parentage, and mysterious
papers that held the clues to the final solution, before they could find
happiness. In a typical denouement, the scarlet woman drowned herself
and the evil count, while the young lovers sailed off to begin life afresh
in glamorous Baltimore.[44] The Holy Synod could not have been pleased
by "The Love of a Monk and a Female Corpse," subtitled "Crazy Love—
The Love of a Crazy Person," but no fictional man of the cloth broke his
vows by committing necrophilia.

The intellectual vacuity of such tales might distress critics of popular
culture, but in the images they gave of Europe, these stories fed directly
into the fancies of a population whose curiosities about the outside world
at last had a means of being satisfied. The foreign landscapes yielded an
exotica that was not explained away by balanced companion articles on
the contemporary European scene. International news received more attention by the new decade, but survey reports on Europe came from
someone sitting in an office on Nevskii Prospect, not the Champs-Ely-
sées. Moreover, *Peterburgskii listok* painted a lopsided view of Europe.
A typical report on the international situation began: "We now turn to
Spain. This unhappy country did not know one year of peace in the
thirty-year reign of Isabel II."[45] Life beyond insular national borders tantalized with suspicions of danger, but it was ultimately better to read
about these problem-ridden societies from the safety of a courtyard in
Petersburg.

Peterburgskii listok defended its readers against Western condescension. Observing European mores in 1876, feature writer "Uncle Parfutyi"
wrote sarcastically, "We, because of the primitive ways and general
crudeness in all circumstances, are just naive children in comparison with
cunning Europe."[46] He proceeded to discuss insurance frauds and exaggerated the sickening practice of sending infants' corpses through the

[44] *Pl*, 24 Dec. 1870, no. 203.
[45] *Pl*, 12 Dec. 1870, no. 196.
[46] *Pl*, 10 Jan. 1876, no. 14.

mail to churches for proper burial as evidence of European depravity. *Peterburgskii listok*'s readers found reasons for national pride and self-confidence in their paper.

The Russia that *Peterburgskii listok*'s editors believed in also had its native-born critics, especially among the youthful participants in the revolutionary movement. The nihilists and populists who dominate Soviet and Western histories of Russia's 1860s and 1870s made rare and brief appearances in the pages of the boulevard newspapers. In part, this was because the censors kept a close watch on the inexpensive papers. But *Golos* and the government's own *Pravitel'stevennyi vestnik* made available information about the revolutionaries' activities that trickled down to the urban populace. *Peterburgskii listok* portrayed the revolutionary movement as primarily the shenanigans of university students. Consciously intending their paper to be a source of intelligence about modern life, editors attacked "muzhikofil'stvo," the guilt-ridden sentimentalities of gentry intellectuals who had romanticized the Russian peasant into a noble savage.[47] After the "to-the-people" movement of students committed to educating the rural peasantry about the benefits of revolution had charged haplessly into unwelcoming arms in 1874, news in the "In Towns and Villages" section reminded readers that the brutal and ignorant countryside was Russia's past, not its future. The Nechaev Affair, which had put the murderous followers of a psychopathic revolutionary on trial, was cursed for "serving as food for foreign newspapers, overflowing daily with obviously exaggerated rumors."[48]

On the eve of Alexander II's assassination the paper was running Alexander Sokolov's "The Scandal-Makers, or Who Are These Socialists?," billed as "A Humorous Novel from the Days We Didn't Understand Each Other." This parody spoofed Turgenev, featuring an incompetent rural gentry and a well-intentioned, if disruptive, young provincial intelligentsia. The regicide halted the serial quickly because such character types were no longer playful or amusing.

Another Voice on the Boulevard: *Peterburgskaia gazeta*

In St. Petersburg in the 1860s, the choice between discussions of the American Civil War and Detective Lecoq did not whet all readers' appetites; audiences still lolled past kiosks, purchasing nothing, waiting to be discovered. As *Peterburgskii listok* began making its turn toward the provocative, one editor left in 1867 to take part in the organization of a

---

[47] *Pl*, 8 Feb. 1876, no. 28.
[48] *Pl*, 6 Jan. 1870, no. 4.

rival urban daily, *Peterburgskaia gazeta* (*The Petersburg Gazette*). I. A. Arsen'ev hailed from the company of politically minded journalists whose literary talents fell short of those who staffed the "thick" journals. These writers were in agreement that the government could slow down the pace of reform, perhaps even renege on a few of its promises, if such were necessary to prevent revolution.

When S. N. Khudekov, a St. Petersburg businessman and future member of the City Duma, took over *Peterburgskaia gazeta* in the 1870s, he continued the original editorial philosophy until 1917. The young Anton Chekhov appeared first in *Peterburgskaia gazeta*. Nikolai Leikin's lighthearted burlesques of the merchantry became a staple feature, and Nikolai Leskov, one of the best known of the ex-radicals of the 1860s turned antinihilist, sometimes contributed editorial essays. Like its precursor on the boulevard, it announced its respectability: a feuilletonist recounted a dream in which Kraevskii and Katkov offered him jobs, implicitly promising readers that their newspaper equaled the most prestigious.[49]

One of the sharpest distinctions between *Peterburgskii listok* and *Peterburgskaia gazeta* was the latter paper's greater devotion to international news. *Peterburgskaia gazeta* drew in the line that connects the bourgeoisie to nationalism through its commercially funded newspapers.[50] As the government expanded its empire into Central Asia in the 1860s and 1870s, coverage of the army's activities warranted an exclusive correspondent. D. Borzna's communiqués suffered the two-month postal time lag, but they underscored the newspaper's value as a tool of conquest, facilitating the incorporation of different peoples into one nation—with those in control of communications deciding the terms of nationhood.

Borzna's tone differed markedly from that set by *Golos*'s correspondents. One particular report summarized Borzna's presumptions: "Although the Kirghizy are officially members of the Muslim religion, they do not practice the rituals of Mohammed. I am convinced that if one of our missionary societies were to send some zealous missionaries it would be easy to convert the natives to Orthodoxy." Still, the Kirghizy required more than Christian baptisms to join the ranks of the civilized: "Their slovenliness is unbelievable. . . . they never wash, and they sleep on the bare ground, burying themselves in litter and ashes."[51] More than a decade later, when *Golos* suggested that money spent on the further conquest of Central Asia might be better spent on internal improvements,

---

[49] *Pg*, 12 March 1868, no. 34.
[50] Anderson, *Imagined Communities*, especially chapter 3.
[51] *Pg*, 12 March 1868, no. 34.

Peterburgskaia gazeta reminded readers that war had complemented Peter the Great's reforms splendidly, and to curtail its "civilizing mission" at this point would reduce Russia to a "second-rate" power.[52] Editors accepted accusations of "chauvinism," saying that they had always opposed territorial expansion for its own sake, but Russia must continue to "pursue the goals of liberation and tighten the knots of friendship between peoples."[53]

Europe's Great Powers received no greater welcome here than in any other Russian newspaper. Without a telegraph news service or foreign correspondents, information came from writers rehashing from other publications. France's Second Empire suffered the heaviest verbal assaults: "Although the government of France screams constantly about *freedom*, it still subjects its people to the official oppression of bureaucratic despotism. . . . France is not thriving but rotting, just as Austria and Turkey are rotting."[54] These were curious reproaches for Russians to level, but the humiliation suffered in the Crimean War would not be readily forgotten. In a symbolic gesture against the West, *Peterburgskaia gazeta* did not follow other Russian newspapers' practice of putting the European date, twelve days in advance of Russia's because of the different calendars used, in parentheses beside the Russian date on the front page.

Local news was also of exceptional importance, but promoting public welfare did not involve quite as much uncovering of local misdeeds as in *Peterburgskii listok*. The key to the new paper's popularity may well have rested in its somewhat more conversational style. Items in the "Rumors and News" section began with "We heard," or "We've been told," accenting the newspaper as a confidant. "We've heard," for example, "that the director of one of our railroads, conspicuous these days for its *substantial* inaccuracies, is going to ask the company to double his budget."[55] The paper kept one eye over the reader's shoulder, but it took the role of a tattletale instead of that of a hound of justice collecting the badge numbers of negligent policemen.

The investigative pieces run in *Peterburgskaia gazeta* also faded next to those in its more flamboyant competitor. In a four-part series on St. Petersburg's prison system, the correspondent pointed out that prisoners were often served garbage and beaten by guards, but he avoided the sensational particulars. Concluding that "the major shortcoming of our prisons is the lack of moral and physical labor," he echoed an editorial

[52] *Pg*, 13 Jan. 1881, no. 10.
[53] *Pg*, 20 Feb. 1881, no. 43.
[54] *Pg*, 7 March 1868, no. 31.
[55] *Pg*, 26 May 1868, no. 71.

preoccupation found throughout the paper.[56] Like proper Victorian reformers, the editorial board had faith in the healing powers of the work
ethic. A later story on a work colony for juvenile delinquents, for example, embraced rehabilitation through good, hard toil.[57] On the worker
question, *Peterburgskaia gazeta* shared *Golos*'s reasoning that factory
owners should take a patriarchal interest in protecting and educating the
families of those who put in a good day. However badly workers were
treated, though, recourse had to come through factory legislation rather
than workers' taking matters into their own hands: "Thank God the
worker question is being posed differently here than in the West. . . .
there cannot be two opinions about strikes."[58]

The sensationalism characteristic of *Peterburgskii listok* did not fill the
pages of *Peterburgskaia gazeta*, although incidents of crime found their
way into the latter's daily report on public occurrences. Instead of murder, suicide received the largest share of stories fashioned to appeal to
readers' emotions.[59] The manner in which *Peterburgskaia gazeta* presented suicide called for a rethinking of traditional religious beliefs about
individual responsibility versus divine will. Michael McDonald has argued that straightforward accounts of suicides, which conformed to the
strictures of other news reports, that is, with the formulaic listing of
name, date, place, and means, removed some of the diabolical taint to
suicide left over from medieval times.[60] Once variations of the insanity
plea were invoked and accepted for suicide, scientific reasoning excused
the person's actions. In the newspaper, melancholia, alcoholism, or an
impossibly hard life, not the devil, induced the deed. Reports of suicides
provide one more example of how newspapers could undermine the authority of the Orthodox church without challenging it directly.

The Feuilletonists

Through the use of feuilletonists, editors emphasized the mien of the
newspaper-as-companion. The mass-circulation press did not invent the
feuilleton; they came by way of the "thick" journals. M. E. Saltykov-
Shchedrin, whose "Letters to My Aunt" in *Otechestvennye zapiski* in the

    [56] *Pg*, 7 March 1868, no. 31.

    [57] *Pg*, 9 April 1876, no. 68.

    [58] *Pg*, 18 July 1886, no. 194.

    [59] I compared one week's worth of random issues of *Golos*, *Peterburgskii listok*, and *Pe-
terburgskaia gazeta* in 1870–1871. *Peterburgskaia gazeta*'s items on suicide outnumbered
the others' 2 to 1.

    [60] Michael McDonald, "Suicide and the Rise of the Popular Press in England," *Represen-
tations* 23 (Spring 1988): 36–54.

1870s remain classics of journalistic satire, best exemplified the role of the feuilletonist as leading social critic. Feuilletons began as satirical editorials, forums from which journalists of various political persuasions could engage each other in polemics. They compared to editorials much as *ocherki* corresponded to reportage. *Golos*, for example, had "Nil Admirari" writing regular columns on Sundays, and I. A. Shcherbak communicated frequently from Paris. Gradually, everything that appeared on the bottom half of a newspaper's front page, from the chapter in a serial novel à la the French "roman-feuilleton" to theater reviews, fell under the rubric "feuilleton."

The most common purpose of the feuilleton was to "repeat in light form what [the reader] has no time or inclination to read in serious form,"[61] but *Peterburgskaia gazeta* made it a friendly dialogue between writer and reader. N. Zaletnyi, "our correspondent" in Moscow, kept the second national capital on top of the doings in the first. Strolling through Aleksandrovskii Park on an afternoon in May, he waxed nostalgic as he guided readers around a former favorite retreat: "The cafes and restaurants from the years gone by were no longer around, but there was a bar of sorts, very dirty, and the proprietor charges double for everything." Chancing upon a wrestling match, he watched briefly and then disgustedly turned away.[62] Describing his activities and remembrances in thoughtful detail, he brought the afternoon to life for readers. Admirari, writing for *Golos* also on the subject of fistfights among the urban peasantry, told a similar story differently. He informed readers that the season for this "coarse entertainment" had begun, disturbed because it was a "dangerous inheritance" that the newly arrived Muscovites brought in from the countryside.[63] Admirari's readers got a social commentary, Zaletnyi's a view of the brawl in the street.

The Sunday paper brought "Excerpts from Captain Kopeikin's Diary." What could be more congenial than sharing a personal journal with readers? Apologizing once for "not having spoken with you, dear readers, for three weeks," he made it up to them by recounting his recent dilemma trying to find a governess. He and his wife finally found "Mlle. Annette." When his nephew dropped by to visit, the governess "walked into the room, saw my nephew and screamed 'mon Dieu!', and ran up the stairs. . . . Kolia shook with laughter. 'That's your wonderful Mlle. Annette? Last year in Paris she danced such a cancan!'[64] The writer brought read-

---

[61] This was how A. S. Suvorin, who played such an important role in the development of feuilletons in prerevolutionary Russia, characterized them. Quoted in Effie Ambler, *Russian Journalism and Politics* (Detroit: Wayne State University Press, 1972), 59.

[62] *Pg*, 23 May 1868, no. 69.

[63] *Golos*, 9 Nov. 1869, no. 310.

[64] *Pg*, 26 May 1868, no. 71.

ers into his household, introduced them to his family, and invited them
to laugh with him at a ridiculous situation into which he had stumbled.

Zaletnyi and the pseudonymous "Captain Kopeikin," like Nedolin and
Krestovskii, walked boulevard journalism's thin line between the literal
and the invented. Although they recorded everything down to the finest
details—the street sellers' wares, what Kolia said—every feuilleton could
have been recounted from the workings of a fertile imagination. In fact,
it is unlikely that the toast of Paris's cancan circuit would be seeking employment as a governess in St. Petersburg, a point probably not lost on
too many readers, who might also have wanted exotic French governesses, but had to settle for the services of some of the refugee females
from the Continent with no other employable skills who advertised in
Peterburgskaia gazeta. No matter. Zaletnyi and Kopeikin, whether real
people or figments of a journalistic imagination, wrote as if addressing
their next-door neighbors.

The career of *Peterburgskaia gazeta*'s most prominent feuilletonist, Nikolai Leikin, illustrated how the dimensions of the medium dictated the
daily newspaper's unique affinity between reader and journalist. The disposable newspaper, unlike the "thick" journal, lasted not much longer
than a witty conversation. Leikin could not distance himself from readers
as a sage. Writing weekly, sometimes daily, he had to cover a number of
subjects and spent less time choosing his words. He developed a broad
range of expertise and a brisk prose that made him the archetypal newspaper feuilletonist. His popularity motivated other papers to keep recognizable columnists in residence, and his vignettes of identifiable characters told in easily digestible prose affected the evolution of journalese.

Leikin's success cannot be separated from *Peterburgskaia gazeta*'s. Rumors in 1879 that he had been fired compelled an editorial rebuttal, complete with a pledge that he would write more often and exclusively for
Peterburgskaia gazeta.[65] Born in 1841 into a family that had registered in
the St. Petersburg merchantry under Catherine the Great, he was well
known in his readers' circles. His education could have entered him into
state service and raised him to gentry status, but he chose the family
business. Working in his father's shop at Gostinnyi dvor in the 1860s, he
realized that for the people around him "news" meant information about
fires, robberies, or gossip about other shops, not the British Parliament.
Although he placed short pieces in "thick" journals, he professed to be
intimidated by Kraevskii's galaxy of stars. He tried his hand first at *Peterburgskii listok*, but the tone set at *Peterburgskaia gazeta* suited his talents better, and he lasted as chief feuilletonist until his death in 1906.[66]

[65] *Pg*, 30 Oct. 1879, no. 213.

[66] *Kniga Nikolaia Alexandrovicha Leikina v ego vospominaniakh i perepiske* (St. Peters-

The nature of Leikin's satires suggests that he was writing about his readers, not for another group that might condescend to his characters. He put up a mirror to his audience, but it was not a fun-house reflection that perverted their images. He allowed them to admire, primp, or, if they so desired, make faces at themselves. As with the pseudo-European adventure writers, many of his feuilletons came as serial episodes in the lives of various Petersburgers. Leikin's heroes and heroines, however, did not find themselves facing a drunken foreigner with a pistol at the end of each installment. The sensitivity and wit of the writer from Gostinnyi dvor were especially evident in two of his best-known works, "The Stockjobbers" and "Where the Oranges Ripen."[67]

"The Stockjobbers" began amusingly enough with a Sunday morning encounter between two dandies on Vasilevskii Island, site of Petersburg's bourse. Both out for a summer stroll, decked out in the "uniform" of their job at the stock exchange, raspberry vests, shiny boots, and hats cocked at a swaggering angle, they paused to admire one another and discuss their wardrobe. A few days later, the first one encountered took on more human dimensions when readers learned that he had a wife in the provinces, a girl his father had forced him to marry because he wanted household help. The main character, loose in the national capital, had become quite the ladies' man.[68]

"Where the Oranges Ripen," described as a "humorous description of the travels of Nikolai Ivanovich and Glavira Semonovna Ivanov in Italy and along the Riviera," told the plight of a merchant couple from St. Petersburg, spending many homesick hours trying to absorb the highbrow culture of the Continent and the romantic thrill of the Cote d'Azure. Getting by in broken French proved a constant chore, but however comical Leikin's fictional characters, he did not create them with either spite or ridicule. More from the pages of Mark Twain's *Innocents Abroad* than Alexander Griboedov's *Woe from Wit*, Leikin's tourists commanded empathy as well as laughter from a nascent bourgeoisie that could laugh at itself in good fun.

Compared flatteringly to Brett Hart and fellow countryman Alexander Ostrovskii, Leikin did not create characters in the baseness of spirit that marked Ostrovskii's contemptibly corrupt stereotype of the merchantry,

burg: Golike i A. Vil'bor, 1907). Leikin was in the process of writing this autobiography when he died, so a few of his colleagues finished it for him.

[67] Although published shortly before he joined *Peterburgskaia gazeta*'s permanent staff, these assorted tales of misadventures of ordinary people were later partially serialized in the newspaper.

[68] The vignettes were published in collected form, *Apraksintsy: Birzhevye artel'shchiki. (Stseny i ocherki)* (SPB: Tip. R. Golike). The collection went through at least three editions; the third, which I referenced, appeared in 1886.

"Kit Kitych." He kept pace with social change by expanding his reper-
toire to include characters from the factory and the middle intellectual
stratum.[69] His parodies served the same purpose as Balzac's more famous
journalistic satires of the French bourgeoisie coming of age in the previous decades. Leikin's portrayals supplied "the felt need of a new class
looking for an image of itself."[70] Like other feuilletonists, Leikin had to
"personify social norms and values, [and] also set patterns for imitation
which are very much wanted in times when society is being unmade and
assembled in strange new ways."[71]

Situated somewhere between *Golos* and *Peterburgskii listok*, *Peterburgskaia gazeta* emphasized the notion that a newspaper should integrate the private into the public life. Its detractors could legitimately ac-
cuse it of being less newsworthy than the others, but the paper
compensated for this shortcoming by offering readers greater intimacy
and somewhat more personalized communications. By 1876, one thing
readers wanted seemed to be temporary diversion from what they had;
Ksav'e de Montepena, of dubious European heritage, had joined *Peterburgskaia gazeta*'s permanent staff to churn out escapist pulp. This suggested that the editors had taken a necessary measure to compete with
Peterburgskii listok, and also that they now had a stable readership.

The feuilletonists and entertainment features did not, however, overwhelm the seriousness with which Khudekov approached politics. Much
in the newspaper reflected Khudekov's aspirations for those like himself
and his readers to supplant the intelligentsia as political leaders in postreform Russia. The publisher vigorously involved his newspaper in Russia's first elections to a City Duma in 1870 by publishing biographies of
the candidates. Later this turned into "Busts and Statuettes," a feature
profiling local leaders. Khudekov did not use his newspaper to promote
himself, just his platform, in city politics. The publisher's real battle was
not with those who stood against him for election to the Duma. A number
of stories and editorials in *Peterburgskaia gazeta* illustrated how deeply
frustrated its primary audience was becoming with the revolutionaries,
who threatened to incite a governmental reaction that would forestall the
reforms. Angry that some "have found it necessary to call Peter the Great
a hopeless drunk and a loathsome degenerate," bitter at the cynics who
disdained their own past but eschewed working to improve the future,
an editorial writer criticized those who "write hymns of praise to honor

[69] "N. A. Leikin. Nekrolog," *Pg*, 7 Jan. 1906, no. 6.

[70] Joan Rockwell, *Fact in Fiction: The Use of Literature in the Systemic Study of Society*
(London: Routledge, 1974), 65.

[71] Ibid.

convicts," referring to political exiles. He closed with an admonishment to the press to work actively for the good of society.[72]

After the Nechaev Affair and the populists' trip "to the people" early in the 1870s, Khudekov ground the ax against the intelligentsia with new fervor. Annoyed by the term *intelligentsia* itself, so laden with connotations of a certain educationally privileged prototype, the publisher wanted to see it broadened to include all progressive types, including knowledgeable bureaucrats, educated peasants, priests, and scientists.[73] Students constituted a special target for *Peterburgskaia gazeta*; a story on the university's annual ball followed one on demonstrations, and the avuncular tone suggested that most students' energies had been exhausted in excusably bad behavior, and daylight had found them too hung over to participate in political mayhem.[74]

One feuilletonist narrated a visit to a childhood friend who had married a "liberal." As barefoot and pregnant as any peasant woman, his friend was forbidden by her husband to attend church and had been forced to read Darwin. The couple, adulterers both, lived in moral and material squalor, so much so that the writer returned quickly in disgust to Petersburg.[75] This writer, though, was speaking to the already converted. Many of his readers were undoubtedly already steeped in images of a morality as lax as the standards of cleanliness maintained by the young revolutionaries, having already read Krestovskii's *Panurg's Herd*, one of the racier and least forgiving of the antinihilist novels of the 1860s.[76] Not always innocent products of a malicious imagination, the youths who inspired the fictitious characters excited enough gossip on their own, strolling down Nevskii Prospect dressed sometimes in peasant garb, sporting peculiar hairstyles and blue glasses, not unlike the hippies of the next century.

The conspicuous differences among *Golos*, *Peterburgskii listok*, and *Peterburgskaia gazeta* said much about how Russians were adapting to the Great Reforms. After a decade of modifications, these newspapers had established patterns of communication that reflected distinct, entrenched, and literate communities of interest. Competitors sprang up, but their brief, debt-ridden lives attested to the successful publishers' sway with their respective audiences. True, these three papers' combined circulation of approximately forty thousand represented a tiny fraction of Russia's 100 million citizens, even after multiplying each subscrip-

[72] *Pg*, 24 Oct. 1868, no. 151.
[73] *Pg*, 26 March 1881, no. 72.
[74] *Pg*, 10 Feb. 1881, no. 34.
[75] *Pg*, 9 March 1876, no. 47.
[76] See Charles Moser, *Antinihilism in the Russian Novel of the 1860s* (The Hague: Mouton, 1964), 67, 72–73.

tion by the five to ten readers estimated to have access to each paper. Moreover, Katkov's *Moskovskie vedomosti* had considerably more influence with those in power than the two urban papers combined. The boulevard readers, though, constituted a crucial element of the population, encompassing not simply some who held positions of authority, but also many who aspired to better themselves. The daily paper demanded time and money of a world that was beginning to see a relationship between the two, and it helped those who could see this coming to refashion their lives accordingly; newspapers accrued power by stimulating needs that only they could satisfy.

In 1876 Russia's newspaper industry was still in its formative stage. Two subsequent national crises challenged the daily press's capabilities, accelerating journalism in the directions in which it had already begun to make headway. The brutal retaliation of Ottoman Turks against insurgent Slavs in the Balkan province of Bosnia would inflame public opinion in Russia, voiced loudly for the first time in newspapers, and push the tsarist government to war against Turkey in 1877. The murder of Alexander II four years later by terrorists resulted in a critical revision of the government's relationship to public opinion. Growing increasingly accustomed to newspapers as a feature of daily life, readers were coming to value the press as an institution that defended interests they shared as a public. As a result, they would also want to see their relationship to the autocracy changed, although not exactly in the way that the tsar had in mind.

4

The News Shapes the Medium

WAR AND ASSASSINATION, 1876–1881

BEFORE 1876 newspapers had not yet been put to a test that could effectively measure the strength of their ability to mediate between populace and government. Rising circulations and larger editions showed growing popularity, but how could newspapers involve their readers in the national political discourse? What effect would competition among publishers have on the evolution of the daily newspaper into one public institution where various readerships contested their different opinions? How would the autocracy respond to pressure from this public sphere, and how would the censorship be affected by public outcry to set a political agenda? Atrocities committed by Ottoman Turks against Orthodox Slavs in the occupied provinces of Bosnia and Herzegovina furnished the crucible that caused the Russian mass-circulation press to come of age. The incidents themselves were not unprecedented, but the manner in which they were communicated would influence the responses to them.

This chapter will demonstrate how the "new" journalism that came out of the crises in the Balkans stirred up readers with sufficient intensity that the press coerced the government to take action. Technology played an instrumental role because the telegraph and high-speed presses greatly facilitated the flow of communications. More important, though, were the personalities who realized the newspaper's potential. The war correspondent emerged as the first specialized journalist to make evident the significance of eyewitness accounts for the distant audience. War correspondence contributed to the evolution of journalese and elevated the status of reporters as readers came to fully appreciate the extent to which they depended on someone else's relaying events to them; the importance of news gave authority to the individuals who supplied it. Russia's reporters learned their journalistic skills directly from their more experienced Western colleagues.

Significantly, the creators of this journalism came from the first generation to have reached maturity in reformed Russia. Like the new types of journalism exemplified by *Golos* and the boulevard press, this one depended upon social and intellectual changes to define its character. A growing contingent among educated Russians had concluded by 1876 that the radical attitudes of the prereform era no longer applied. They supported the tsar's ambitions, and, deciding that society itself was insufficiently mature to achieve Alexander's objectives quickly, many ex-radicals accepted a conservative gradualism as the route to reform. More conservative than Kraevskii, these journalists were just as eager to develop the newspaper into a medium capable of influencing national politics. Rejecting (or being rejected by) the elite intelligentsia, the new journalists crossed over the bridge Kraevskii had tried to maintain between commercial and intellectual interests.

A. S. Suvorin and Generational Conflict in Journalism

Aleksei Sergeevich Suvorin forged his *Novoe vremia*, which reigned for some twenty years as the nation's most powerful newspaper, from his coverage of the actions that would push Russia into a luckless war and a humiliating victory. When Tsar Nicholas II sent a wreath to Suvorin's funeral in 1912, he demonstrated the extent to which independent commercial journalism had made its presence felt in the Winter Palace.

Suvorin's biographers have fallen too easily under the sway of his disparaging liberal intellectual contemporaries.[1] For them, the fact that the obscurantist tsar would honor the deceased explained why they despised him, and not even the pleadings of Suvorin's editors could entice them to the funeral. This controversial publisher's pages in Russian history are indexed under his conservative politics. As a result, his major contributions to journalism have gone overlooked. The more probing question is why a tsar would bother to honor a former peasant from Voronezh Province.

Suvorin's biography made Horatio Alger into a member of the Russian intelligentsia. Born in 1834, Suvorin was technically the son of a nobleman because his father, a peasant conscript, had distinguished himself at the Battle of Borodino. The paper title, though, did not allow the family to live like the heroes of *War and Peace*. Suvorin later capitalized on his up-by-the-bootstraps life by trumpeting it as an example of the mobility made possible by the Great Reforms. His mother's background also figured significantly in his upbringing. The daughter of a priest, she belonged to that minuscule category of nongentry Russian women who, through their father's tutoring, received a primary education which they

[1] Biographical information on Suvorin is from Ambler, *Russian Journalism*, 37–59; U. Solov'eva and V. Shitova, "A. S. Suvorin. Portret na fone gazety," *Voprosy literatury*, no. 2 (1977): 162–99; and N. Snessarev, *Mirazh "Novago vremeni." Pochti Roman* (SPB: Tip. M. Pivovarskogo i A. Tipografa, 1914). Suvorin also left a diary, *Dnevnik A. S. Suvorina*, ed. M. Krichevskii (Moscow and Petrograd: L. D. Frenkel', 1923).

Fig. 2. A. S. Suvorin, publisher of *Novoe vremia*

passed on to their children. But having neither the desire for state service nor the money for the university education he wanted, Suvorin became a schoolteacher in his native Voronezh Province, where he performed for six years as a yeoman intellectual. Enjoying the flurry of
journalistic activity that followed the death of the Iron Tsar, the future
publisher penned amusements for comic journals, translated French poetry, and corresponded with official newspapers about life in the provinces. Invited to Moscow by the publisher of *Russkaia rech'* (*The Russian
Speech*), a short-lived liberal political offering, Suvorin embarked upon
his newspaper career in the propitious year of 1861. He brought as intellectual baggage the radical expectations of the most educated of his generation. When Korsh took over at *SPB vedomosti* in 1863, he brought
Suvorin aboard. Under the pen name "The Stranger," Suvorin's Sunday

feuilletons landed Korsh in occasional trouble with authorities, but also attracted readers who found *Golos* too unpolemical.

Between 1863 and 1876, the popular journalist frequented the best liberal circles. He even enjoyed respectable notoriety for a brief imprisonment for his quasi-nihilistic *All Sorts: Sketches from Contemporary Life*, although the patchwork of unpublished feuilletons would scarcely have stirred up a fuss if it had not appeared two days after Karakazov fired at Alexander II in 1866.[2] In addition to Korsh's newspaper, Suvorin began to write regularly for *Vestnik evropy*, the "thick" journal of record for Westernizers. He joined the posthumous chorus of Belinskii's defenders against the money-grubbing Kraevskii. In 1876 he partnered with jurist V. I. Likhachev to take over the bankrupt *Novoe vremia*; those whom Kraevskii had disappointed cheered. The budding publishers secured investment capital from V. O. Kovalevskii, a prominent liberal whose wife Sofia, a renowned mathematician, wrote a bit for Suvorin's paper at first.[3]

Suvorin wrote ebulliently in his first editorial, "For me journalism is everything. It is my whole life, all my hopes and joys."[4] But once he had a newspaper of his own, Suvorin seemed to become a political changeling. The personality with whom Nicholas II empathized appeared, so his colleagues told it, as if from nowhere. The disillusioned Kovalevskii abandoned the enterprise without recovering his money, much less benefiting from the enormous profits Suvorin would reap.[5] His critics, who wanted a newspaper that functioned as a "thick" journal, would have been well advised to substitute their preoccupation with the message for one with the medium. Certainly Suvorin did. Although earlier he had harbored doubts about writing for newspapers because the medium was so fleeting that ideas became as disposable as words, when he later claimed that he preferred accusations of triteness to those of formalism, he showed that he had learned to value the other advantages offered by the less fixed presence of the daily paper.[6]

The often-drawn parallels between the Russian radicals of the 1860s and the militant American students of a century later can clarify the issue of Suvorin's supposed about-face. In both situations, the respective populaces underwent a series of social revolutions, brought on when a war backfired, spearheaded by young intellectuals, and stoked by a spirit that sought an idealized liberation of the individual. Suvorin's infamous *All*

---

[2] Ambler, *Russian Journalism*, 60.

[3] Ann Hibner Koblitz, *A Convergence of Lives* (Boston: Birkhauser, 1983), 134–35.

[4] Quoted in Esin, *Russkaia dorevoliutsionnaia gazeta*, 41.

[5] Koblitz, *A Convergence of Lives*, 135.

[6] Esin, *Russkaia dorevoliutsionnaia gazeta*, 41; and Solov'eva and Shitova, "A. S. Suvorin," 162.

Sorts, for example, had analogs in Abbie Hoffman's *Steal This Book* or Eldridge Cleaver's *Soul on Ice.* When the Russian publisher retreated from the radical vanguard to the comfortable shelter of personal and financial security, he behaved much like Yippie-turned-financier Jerry Rubin. Suvorin's actions could be attributed to a blend of burned-out idealism and the readiness to compromise after systemic changes had indeed made the system more accommodating.

Several prominent writers he invited to *Novoe vremia* were also spent radicals.[7] Nikolai Leskov was one. Like Suvorin, he came from a mixed social background and grew up in provincial poverty, in Orel. In his case, the priest came from his father's side of the family and the gentry element from his mother's. Her nobility was impure, blended with the local merchantry. Leskov made his way to St. Petersburg in 1860, but he ruined his reputation among the intelligentsia in his attempt to join them. When suspicion fell on the university students for the Petersburg fires of 1862, he tried to ingratiate himself by protesting their innocence in the newspaper for which he corresponded, the sycophantic *Severnaia pchela.* The intelligentsia, including Suvorin, infuriated at having this toady periodical come to their uninvited defense, soundly rejected his advances. The embittered Leskov responded with *No Way Out,* a novelistic portrayal of the nihilists as self-indulgent and out of touch with Russian reality. Best known for his short stories, Leskov had a productive adjunct career writing for a variety of newspapers, including *Novoe vremia* and *Peterburgskaia gazeta.*[8]

Another major figure in newspaper journalism's formative years, Alexandra Sokolova, shared much in common with Suvorin and Leskov. From a wealthy noble family in Riazan Province, Sokolova was schooled at Petersburg's elite Smol'nii Institute for Young Women. When she married beneath herself, her family disinherited her. Education gave her the writing skills she needed to get by after her husband died and left her with three small children. She met Suvorin when the two worked together at *SPB vedomosti,* and he occasionally employed her later when the two had established themselves independently. A prototypical *shestidesiatnitsa,* or "woman of the sixties," Sokolova joined essentially the same semiradical youth groups as Suvorin and Leskov. Abandoning her children, she escaped to Europe to avoid the "white terror" that followed

---

[7] Along with this background at *Novoe vremia,* the powerful literary critic V. P. Burenin had begun his journalistic career corresponding for Herzen's London-based *Kolokol. Kratkaia literaturnaia entseklopedia* 1:775.

[8] Hugh McLean, *Nikolai Leskov* (Cambridge, Mass.: Harvard University Press, 1977); K. A. Lantz, *Nikolay Leskov* (Boston: Twayne, 1979); and L. G. Chudnova, *Leskov v Peterburge* (Leningrad: Lenizdat, 1975).

the attempted assassination in 1866. After several years abroad she returned, reclaiming her children.[9] Like Suvorin, she found a niche in the new journalism and enjoyed a second career writing sentimental fiction for a number of popular periodicals.

Two editorials in *Novoe vremia* in the 1880s articulated the social and political views of the group Suvorin and his staff represented two decades into the reform era. The first commemorated the centenary of Catherine the Great's Charter to the Nobility of 1785. Suvorin had little truck with empty prestige, and he used the occasion to criticize the outdated *soslovie* system of social estates: "We should not talk about the influence of the nobility as a class on the state. It is true that many nobles have performed great service to the state, but they did this as *individuals* and not the *soslovie* as a whole."[10]

The second formative aspect of their lives that needed redressing was their leftist politics. In their minds they had been naive idealists, simply out to assuage the guilt of privilege and to repay the debt to the peasantry who had so long supported the lords. The Great Reforms, though, changed the terms of both social station and public service. Now, according to Suvorin, Jews and radicals had corrupted the higher ideals he had professed in his youth, and were exploiting the *narod* in the name of serving them. What "debt to the people," Suvorin wondered, was the Jewish lawyer fulfilling when he used slick histrionics to free common criminals?[11] With a swift pen he preserved the purity of his own motive by striking out against those who had taken the other road.

Suvorin built prerevolutionary Russia's first publishing empire. Through the A. S. Suvorin Publishing House, he printed not only his newspaper but also books, which he then sold through the bookstores he established in major cities. He also innovated the "Inexpensive Library" of pocket-sized books affordable to ordinary readers, making Pushkin and other major writers available to the masses. In 1880 he added a "thick" journal, the nationalistic *Istoricheskii vestnik* (*The Historical Herald*).[12] He, his staff, and his subscribers represented that public which evaluated the Great Reforms ten years later as an ambitious idea gone awry, derailed by radicals who wanted too much, too soon.

[9] Boris Glinskii, "A. I. Sokolova. Nekrolog," *Iv* 135, no. 3 (1914): 954–59; and A. P. Karelin, "Vlas Doroshevich, literaturno-biograficheskii ocherk," in V. M. Doroshevich, *Rasskzy i ocherki* (Moscow: Sovremennik, 1986), 6–8.

[10] *Nv*, 22 Jan. 1885, no. 3198.

[11] *Nv*, 15 June 1886, no. 3696.

[12] E. A. Dinershtein, "Izdatel'skaia deiatel'nost' A. S. Suvorina," *Kniga issledovaniia i materialy* 48 (Moscow: Kniga, 1984): 82–118.

War Correspondence Shapes Newspaper Reportage

Fortune appeared to have smiled on Suvorin and given him a news story of tremendous national significance just as he began his enterprise. Orthodox Slavs revolted against the occupied Turkish forces in the Ottoman province of Herzegovina in 1875. Inflamed by newspaper coverage, especially that in *Novoe vremia*, two wars erupted in quick succession in the Balkans. Suvorin's actions presaged William Randolph Hearst's telegram to a bored graphic designer dispatched to Cuba in 1898 to record a war that had yet to begin. The artist wanted to return to New York, but Hearst ordered him to stay put with the legendary message, "You furnish the pictures. I'll furnish the war." Suvorin no more started the Russo-Turkish War than Hearst did the Spanish-American War; the telegram may well be apocryphal, although it is assured a spot in journalism's folklore because it reflected what so many believed Hearst capable of doing. The two publishers both took pistols and notepads to the front lines themselves, personifying the newspaper's growing presence as a slice of the action, not just the record of it.

War has, understandably, always provided a catalyst to journalistic developments. Interest runs high when thousands of lives are at stake. Moreover, the conduct of war requires the kinds of sophisticated communications that newspapers rely on, which in the nineteenth century meant railroads and the telegraph. Correspondence from the battlefield transformed the style of reporting. An axiom holds that "the first casualty when war comes is the truth" because veracity rises to a premium.[13] Reporters have always depended awkwardly on military high commands for information, and relationships between soldier and journalist are often intensely personal. Especially in Europe, where the nobility dominated the officer corps, the war correspondent needed acceptance as a social equal. Personal relationships between officers and reporters counted for a great deal, especially when correspondents were asked to acquit themselves in battle. Many received military honors in the course of duty, which led in return to the camaraderie that allowed for omissions from reportage that might somehow discredit courageous soldiers. Their importance to both their readers and their sources imbued these correspondents with a renown previously restricted to writers from the intelligentsia.

When the London *Times* sent William Russell to the Crimea in 1854,

[13] Phillip Knightley, *The First Casualty: From the Crimea to Vietnam, the War Correspondent as Hero, Propagandist, and Myth Maker* (New York: Harcourt Brace Jovanovich, 1975).

it involved him in politics in a new way. Russell's reports on the British Army's poor accounting of itself were circulated from the War Office to Downing Street and resulted in changes in policy. Russell found himself a celebrity, and his reports of the horrendous medical conditions in the Crimea prompted civic action, too, when Florence Nightingale took her nurses to care for the wounded.[14] Significantly, Nicholas I forbade Russian correspondents from reporting on the war in the Crimea, tolerating only approved information from military dispatches to be reprinted in official newspapers.[15]

American reporters during the Civil War elaborated upon Russell's innovations. Woodcuts, used before primarily for advertising purposes, were now recognized for their newsworthy qualities and illustrated battles on front pages. The halftone effect would not be developed, which would make it possible to use photographs in newspapers, for another decade, but Mathew Brady's recordings of the "irrepressible conflict" anticipated photojournalism. The unprecedented demand for specific information and competition for the telegraph resulted in stylistic modifications to reporting; correspondents had to limit their words, abbreviating messages in "cablese," the language of the wires, and leading with concise summaries, lest the message not get through in its entirety. Union General Joseph Hooker, whose name entered the dictionary of popular culture for other reasons, demanded the use of bylines in hopes of forcing correspondents to report more responsibly. Receiving acknowledgment for an important story gave writers dignity and then celebrity, which began to make newspaper reporting an attractive occupation.[16]

After the Civil War, the Franco-Prussian War of 1870–1871 also had repercussions in the development of the European press. All major European newspapers sent correspondents to cover Bismarck's wars for German unification, and they drew heavily from the Americans' experiences. The *New York Tribune*'s George Smalley moved from Antietam to Sedan and taught to European reporters the tricks of his trade, including precision, conciseness, and the technique of pooling information.[17] Coverage of the Crimean and Franco-Prussian wars proved instrumental to the concept that the public had a *right* to information that newspapers therefore had an *obligation* to provide. As E. L. Godkin, the gifted Irishman who wrote human interest stories from the Crimea for London's *Daily News*, reflected, "The real beginning of newspaper correspondence

[14] Knightley, *First Casualty*, 4–17.

[15] Ruud, *Fighting Words*, 93–94.

[16] Emery and Emery, *The Press and America*, 4th ed., 165–79.

[17] Bellanger et al., *Histoire générale* 2:364–69; and Robert W. Desmond, *The Information Process: World News Reporting to the Twentieth Century* (Iowa City: University of Iowa Press, 1978), 234–46.

was the arrival of 'Billy Russell' to the Crimea. . . . It brought home . . .
the fact that the public had something to say about the conduct of wars
and that they are not the concern exclusively of sovereigns and states-
men."[18]

Russia's Daily Newspaper Goes to War

Russian publishers were not the first to use journalism to ignite the Balkan Peninsula between 1875 and 1878. An ousted British prime minister,
William Gladstone, and an American foreign correspondent, Januarius
Aloysius MacGahan, who had close friendships among the Russian officer
corps from his coverage of the fall of Khiva in 1873, lit the fuse. It all
began in 1875 when the peasants in Bosnia and Herzegovina rose up
against their Turkish overlords. By the following spring the insurrection
had spread to parts of Bulgaria, where troops of Muslim irregulars ruth-
lessly made an example of them for other Slavs. An estimated fifteen-
thousand men, women, and children were raped, butchered, and burned
out of their villages. The slaughter itself was not new, but now readers
well removed from the scene could feed on the violent and personalized
details.[19] MacGahan wrote from Bulgaria: "The procedure seems to have
been as follows: They would seize a woman, strip her carefully to her
chemise. . . . Then as many of them as cared would violate her, and the
last man would kill her or not as the humour took him. . . . There were
curly little heads there in that festering mass, crushed down by heavy
stones; little feet not as long as your finger on which the flesh was dried
hard."[20]

Gladstone, a Liberal leader with the righteous tone of an evangelical
minister, produced his notorious and widely circulated pamphlet on the
"Bulgarian Horrors" largely from MacGahan's stories in London's Lib-
eral-backed *Daily News*. When the popular press took up his call, Gladstone successfully pressured the Foreign Office to take action.[21] The British politician is far more closely associated with the atrocities than the
American who recorded them because Gladstone's successes were quan-
tifiable in the polls. The reporter, however, deserves proper recognition
for his impact on correspondence. MacGahan remained in the Balkans,
dying at age thirty-four of typhus en route to the Congress of Berlin. He
was in Bulgaria when Russia's first, inexperienced war correspondents

[18] Knightley, *First Casualty*, 17.

[19] R. T. Shannon, *Gladstone and the Bulgarian Agitation 1876* (London: Thomas Nelson
and Sons, 1963), 22.

[20] Quoted in Knightley, *First Casualty*, 51.

[21] Shannon, *Gladstone*, especially chapter 3.

came to cover the hostilities, and they flocked around him. Married to a Russian noblewoman, he spoke the language and became a great favorite among many of Russian journalism's raw recruits. *Golos* numbered among the newspapers to which he sold his correspondence. A street in the Bulgarian capital of Sofia stills bears his name.[22]

The Russian public had been waiting for what transpired in the Balkans that summer since the crippling Peace of Paris had ended the Crimean War in 1856. Inspired by their colonial advances into the Caucasus and Central Asia, Russians wanted to flex their Great Power muscles. Minister of Finance M. Kh. Reutern, chair of Alexander II's brain trust on industrialization, insisted that the nation could not afford a war. The tsarist government had agreed in December 1875 to a plan put forth by Austrian foreign minister Julius Andrassy that called for internal reforms from the Turks that would ameliorate the situation. But the combatant Slavs in the Ottoman provinces wanted unification with their Serbian brethren, not more obliging alien rulers. At this point the "Lion of Tashkent," General Mikhail Cherniaev, bane of the reforming minister of war Dmitrii Miliutin, stepped into the picture to lead the Russian public to where their government would not.

The son of a general from whom he had inherited a penchant for letting errata slip into his reports, Cherniaev earned his military reputation during the conquest of Tashkent, where he also earned Miliutin's wrath for his maverick behavior. Relieved of his post in Tashkent, Cherniaev had returned to St. Petersburg, where he mixed in the Pan-Slavic political circles. With its roots in Slavophilism, the broader-based Pan-Slavic movement saw Russia as the natural leader of Slavdom and took up the cause of freeing its ethnic brethren in Ottoman captivity. Following the Bulgarian horrors, Cherniaev resigned his commission in the Russian Army and, against Miliutin's orders, surfaced mysteriously in Belgrade to take command of the Serbian Army against the superior Ottoman forces. He would show the South Slavs that not all Russians had their government's yellow streak.[23]

Russian readers would have had abundant interest in Cherniaev's antics even had Suvorin not appeared to contest Kraevskii's quasi monopoly as the most important nongovernmental national newspaper. Readers made authority the spoils of their war, fought in public for the public. The shrewd young publisher provided the hard news that gave his cause validity, and he framed competition around who had the best informa-

[22] Biographical information from Dale L. Walker, *Januarius MacGahan, the Life and Campaigns of an American War Correspondent* (Athens: Ohio University Press, 1988).

[23] Biographical information on Cherniaev is from David MacKenzie, *The Lion of Tashkent: The Career of General M. G. Cherniaev* (Athens: University of Georgia Press, 1974), chapter 1.

tion. He made this orientation visible by restructuring the traditional front page, leading off with columns of telegrams instead of presenting the editorials first. Poised to declare a circulation war on Kraevskii just before the outbreak of hostilities in 1877, he had imported the most sophisticated high-speed presses into Russia. When Cherniaev led his ill-equipped and poorly trained Serbian forces against the Turks in June, Suvorin traveled to Serbia himself to report the war. He returned in August with adulation for Cherniaev but disdain for the shiftless Serbs and fury at the treacherous British in Constantinople. Battle lines for readers were drawn. Kraevskii added superbly detailed maps of the Balkans as supplements, with accompanying explanatory texts in *Golos*. (The enmity between the two publishers ended, however, at the business table; Suvorin advertised *Novoe vremia* prominently and expensively on the front page of *Golos*.) *Novoe vremia* set the terms of the match, forcing Kraevskii to rebut them. Both publishers turned their spotlights on the most attractive target, Cherniaev.

Suvorin and Kraevskii did not introduce the "Cherniaev Question" into print; the general did that himself. In 1873 he had purchased controlling interest in *Russkii mir* (*The Russian World*), an anti-Miliutin paper edited by Colonel V. V. Komarov that served as the voice of Pan-Slavism. Cherniaev hungered for military action and cared little about the business side of newspapers, but he took "Jupiter" Komarov with him to Serbia as his chief of staff and appointed another journalist, P. A. Monteverde, as Komarov's assistant. A Spanish adventurer, Monteverde had been in the Balkans peddling pro-Russian stories to *Russkii mir* and anti-Russian ones to the French press. These two "thugs," as Turgenev called Komarov and Monteverde, set up a "correspondence bureau" at Cherniaev's camp and circulated rather specious news bulletins among the foreign correspondents. Protests poured forth onto the Serbian government after this makeshift news agency distributed accounts of stunning victories, although correspondents in residence could see the bedraggled Serbian troops in retreat.[24]

The utter rout of Cherniaev's Serbian Army realized Miliutin's worst fears. In the first outpouring of Pan-Slavic ardor that followed the general's assuming command in Belgrade, several thousand Russian volunteers had responded to calls in *Novoe vremia* and other newspapers and had poured across the border to join Cherniaev's ranks. Therefore, the Turks had also spilt Russian blood. Alexander II forced an armistice on Turkey in October, but the Russian newspapers had already declared war on each other. Although St. Petersburg's publishers did not imitate Odessa's *Novorossiiskii telegraf* (*The New Russian Telegraph*) and publish a special

[24] MacKenzie, *Lion of Tashkent*, 110–23, 127–37, 185.

supplement of telegrams from Serbia on blood-red paper, their rhetoric was inflammatory enough without the pyrotechnical newsprint.[25]

All regretted the loss of Russian lives and agreed that the Serbs did not measure up to the sacrifice. The erroneous telegram from Cherniaev's camp that "The Serbs all fled, the Russians all perished!" during the final battle in October resounded throughout the Russian press.[26] Whereas *Golos* interpreted this as vindication for its antiwar stance, *Novoe vremia* used what happened in Serbia to illustrate the necessity of Russia's going to war against Turkey. *Golos* accepted that the majority of volunteers, earnest at the point of departure, had nonetheless been akin to Thomas Paine's "summer soldiers and sunshine patriots."[27] *Novoe vremia* saw in them the advance patrols for the coming war. When a few straggled home and began to tell their stories to the press, Cherniaev's dramatic actions were called into sharper question than when he had snuck off to Serbia.

Many publishers back on the home front preferred Cherniaev's Pan-Slavic version of the events. Kraevskii therefore concentrated on discrediting the general. Interviews in *Golos* with returned volunteers told of hungry, barefoot soldiers who watched while Cherniaev and his coterie dined sumptuously on white linen tablecloths. In *Golos*, Cherniaev's participation in the war had been inspired by his maniacal ego: "History punishes those who place their personal interests above their people, utilize others' blood."[28] Many volunteers had found Serbia depressingly different from the descriptions that had motivated them to sign up. As one veteran wrote, "volunteers died cursing the names of several publicists."[29]

Suvorin found allies in *Peterburgskii listok* and *Peterburgskaia gazeta*, which reprinted largely from *Russkii mir* and *Novoe vremia*. In *Peterburgskii listok*, Alexander Sokolov replaced the usual pseudo-French escapades with his "The Sister of Mercy," a serial novel of a nurse tending the Russian wounded in the Crimea. The primerlike language used to tell the history of Bulgaria revealed the limited sophistication of *Peterburgskii listok*'s audience: "At the end of the last century, a war between Russia and Turkey awakened in Bulgarians thoughts of a liberation from the Turkish yoke."[30] Sokolov assailed Kraevskii, demanding, "Isn't it time that the sanitation commission ordered this publisher dumped out at

[25] *Golos* estimated that the red supplement sold twenty thousand copies, well above the daily average. *Golos*, 20 Nov. 1877, no. 231.

[26] MacKenzie, *Lion of Tashkent*, 165.

[27] *Golos*, 20 Oct. 1876, no. 290.

[28] Quoted in MacKenzie, *Lion of Tashkent*, 186.

[29] *Bv*, 23 Dec. 1876, no. 354.

[30] *Pl*, 15 Dec. 1876, no. 246.

night [with the rest of the garbage]?"[31] Ten months earlier he had re-printed with congratulatory approval *Golos*'s unmasking of vice in the Russian Army's commissariat.[32]

More conciliatory toward Kraevskii, *Peterburgskaia gazeta* conceded that "he is not really a Turcophile," but *Golos*'s publisher simply did not understand the difference between Pan-Slavism and patriotism. Great Russian chauvinism won the day in *Peterburgskaia gazeta*. Arguing that "now is the time for Russian journalism to stand above personal consid-erations," Khudekov wanted all to understand that Russia must fight Tur-key for itself, not for Serbia. He also pointed out, "M. Kraevskii seems to forget that the Moscow merchantry sent their banner not to Serbia, but to the Russian volunteers there."[33] How Cherniaev treated the vol-unteers was beside the point; Russians had died and their graves had been violated. The fallen Russians had to be avenged: "There are no great rivers in Turkey, only wide bloody streams, created from Christian blood."[34]

It is impossible to isolate the point at which Alexander II decided to respond to public opinion and act against the advice of his most trusted advisors.[35] Miliutin, while warning of Russia's unpreparedness, ruefully accepted that Russia could not afford a complete disintegration of its prestige in the Balkans, but Reutern resigned in protest.[36] The dull-wit-ted tsarevich was a noted Pan-Slav, and it is by no means improbable that his father had tired of the bevy of Western-oriented reformers who con-tinually nipped at his autocratic prerogatives. The archipelago of Slavic Benevolent Committees collected considerable funds, but not all mem-bers wanted war; Kraevskii and one of his top writers, G. K. Gradovskii, for example, both belonged to the St. Petersburg chapter. Yet the par-venu Suvorin seemed to exert greater influence over the tsar than Kraev-skii, although Alexander admittedly agreed with the latter.[37] Ironically, it was *Golos*, not *Novoe vremia*, that the fickle tsar suspended for the first forty days of the war. Kraevskii had had the misfortune to publish a feuilleton dismissing as "rumors" the talk of war on the same day that Alexander decided to declare it.[38]

Although it cannot be argued that without *Novoe vremia* there would

[31] *Pl*, 11 Nov. 1876, no. 222.

[32] *Pl*, 8 Feb. 1876, no. 28.

[33] *Pg*, 23 Dec. 1876, no. 252.

[34] *Pg*, 11 Feb. 1877, no. 29.

[35] On the official deliberations, see Dennis M. O'Flahery, "Tsarism and the Politics of Publicity" (Ph.D. diss., Oxford University, 1974).

[36] A. L. Narochnitskii, ed., *Rossiia i natsional'no-osvoboditel'naia bor'ba v Balkanakh, 1875–1878 (Sbornik dokumentov)* (Moscow: Nauka, 1978), 226–28.

[37] Ibid., 14.

[38] *Golos*, 14 April 1877, no. 102.

have been no Russo-Turkish War, no previous tsar had been placed in a position comparable to that of Alexander II. Official policies had been conspicuously defied, and readers saw the guilty party lionized in *Novoe vremia*. If previously Russians had heard rumors about outrages against Slavs, they now had the gory details. A stream of eyewitnesses told their stories for mass consumption. Formerly, debates about the emancipation and subsequent reforms had been closely contained within the Winter Palace. But the press would not allow this issue to remain confined to the highest decision-making circles. Suvorin, like Hearst later, threw it raucously into the public arena. In his response, Kraevskii kept it there. The nature of Alexander's dilemma is of far greater consequence than the controversy about why he took the position he did, which he later had cause to regret when noncombatant Europe forced another humiliating peace on the Russians at the Congress of Berlin.

American history provides an instructive parallel. Another vain and insubordinate general led his men into ill-conceived battle that same June, George Armstrong Custer. Two peas from the same military pod, Custer and Cherniaev shared a braggadocio that earned them medals, and also the same carelessness that sent many a soldier unnecessarily to his doom. Both generals shouldered a sense of the white man's burden that gave them a right to snatch land from the non-Caucasian tribes, but their personal restlessness would not permit them to stay around to bring law and order to the territories once captured, the original purpose of their violent missions. Coincidence alone cannot explain the similarities in their careers, however remarkable the timing of the battle in Montana at the Little Bighorn River. The generals owed their reputations in considerable part to the newspapers that publicized their exploits, literally making them legends in their own time by re-creating images of their lives on the front page.

These two generals made for such colorful copy that reporters quite naturally gravitated to them, but the true significance of their relations with the press lay in the newfound potential for publicity. Cherniaev could not enter into Russia's historical lore in the same way that Custer could enter that of the United States for a variety of reasons, not the least of which was that the Russian general survived and therefore could not be accorded a martyr's rites.[39] Cherniaev, Custer, and the daily newspaper met at a crossroad when national identities were being formed. The histrionic generals embodied the contradictions and moral ambiguities of nineteenth-century expansionism. When the newspapers made the lives

[39] Richard Slotkin, *The Fatal Environment* (New York: Atheneum, 1985), chapters 15 and 18; and Evan S. Connell, *Son of the Morning Star* (San Francisco: North Point Press, 1984), include newspaper coverage.

and actions of these individuals public property, they offered up the contradictions for discussion, which helped to mobilize public opinion into pressing for political action.

The main ingredients of the agitation for war, Cherniaev, Serbia, and Pan-Slavism, turned out to be incidental to the campaign waged between Turkey and Russia in 1877. Editorial rivalry surrendered to cooperation, often quite amicable, among the correspondents in the war zone. The paucity of qualified journalists could not keep pace with the demands of so many publications needing reporters; even Kraevskii and Suvorin shared the services of at least one prominent reporter, N. S. Kairov. The Russo-Turkish War had the dubious benefit of making it possible for Russian journalism to catch up with Western journalism. Russia's first star reporter, V. I. Nemirovich-Danchenko, shone from the battlefield decades before his younger brother arose at the Moscow Arts Theater.

Russia's War Correspondents

Nemirovich-Danchenko, who enjoyed a slight reputation for his travelogues, found himself plagued by notoriety in 1876. Several years earlier, destitute, he had stolen books from the library of a publisher who had held back payment for an article. Admittedly guilty, the writer found himself exiled briefly to Astrakhan. Having paid his debt to society, he arrived in the national capital to remake a career in journalism. His welcome was painful; *Peterburgskaia gazeta*, for example, blacklisted him.[40] The editors of Nedelia (*The Week*), a weekly with pretensions to being a "thick" journal, dismissed his travelogues as too superficial for the serious press and, referring to his reputation as a dandy, insinuated that he should not be allowed in offices where women would have to work alongside him.[41] When the Russo-Turkish War erupted, the editors of a newly founded Petersburg daily, *Nash vek* (*Our Century*), hired him to cover it. The flimsy paper folded after 102 issues. This was just Nemirovich-Danchenko's luck, because Suvorin, always in need of men in the field, began to buy his correspondence.[42]

Born in 1844 in Tblisi, the first son in a family with a heritage of professional soldiers, Nemirovich-Danchenko's father had taken the boy along on several campaigns during the conquest of the Caucasus. His

[40] *Pl*, 21 Jan. 1876, no. 15.

[41] *Nedelia*, 11 Jan. 1876, no. 2.

[42] The publisher and war correspondent, although they hit their strides together, never enjoyed another professional collaboration. Suvorin recorded in his diary that he sat next to Nemirovich-Danchenko at a banquet in 1898 and found him "a completely boring conversationalist." *Dnevnik Suvorina*, 135.

Fig. 3. War correspondent V. I. Nemirovich-Danchenko

mother came from the Armenian aristocracy and instilled in him an abiding love for the ethnic peripheries of the Russian empire. Sent to Moscow to study at the Alexandrovskii Kadet Corps, he developed a passion
for writing. Significantly, this was his worst subject in the academic part
of his training because he could never master syntax. Instead of hinder-
ing his career in journalism, this shortcoming would ripen into a style of
reporting exceedingly well suited to newspapers. What caused the intelligentsia to shudder made Nemirovich-Danchenko one of the most popular and prolific authors in tsarist Russia. When the aspiring writer decided to forgo an army career, his father disowned the sixteen-year-old.
Vasilii Ivanovich did not lose his love of rugged camp life, but he preferred writing to fighting. He knew the military, made friends easily with
officers, and found his niche as a war correspondent.[43]

---

[43] The prolific journalist left a six-page autobiography in a pamphlet written in emigration
in Czechoslovakian exile in 1930. *Venok. Nezabvennomu starshin, dorogomu Vasiliu Iva-
novichu Nemirovichu-Danchenko soiuza russkikh pisatelei i zhurnalistov v Chekhoslovakii*,
12–17. Peter Bykov wrote a short biography of him to introduce the 1916 edition of his
collected works, *Novoe sobranie sochinenii* (Petrograd: P. P. Soikina, 1916), iii–xlvi.

Gradovskii, *Golos*'s correspondent with the army in the field who began reporting when the forty-day suspension was lifted, recognized the novel importance of his new assignment. The commander to whom he had been assigned had balked when the light-traveling reporter asked for provisions. "I held that the war correspondents have an importance equal to that of the officers and soldiers because they were working in the interests of society," he wrote. Startled at his vulnerability, he noted, "you could have a pocket full of gold, yet die of hunger if the military authorities do not want to help you." The hesitant commandant billeted the reporter, who sympathized with the officer's reluctance because "relations with war correspondents were entirely new for them, too. . . . They didn't know if we were there to write about their courage, or if we were some sort of spies or critics."[44]

In addition to Gradovskii and Nemirovich-Danchenko, Iulii Shreier and V. A. Giliarovskii, soon to rise to the top of the occupation, covered the war. V. V. Vereshchagin, a painter of growing stature, played the Mathew Brady of the canvas. Krestovskii, whose disdain for the intelligentsia had inspired him to assert his manhood and patriotism by joining the army, reported the war for the official *Pravitel'stvennyi vestnik*. But the writer had lost his flair from his days in the slums and among the slovenly nihilists. Collected in book form and made available for sale through the state printing office, his war stories gathered dust because readers greatly preferred others' narratives.[45] Having surrendered his talents and interest in petty journalism, Krestovskii ended his career fittingly as Cherniaev's chief of staff when the reaction following Alexander's assassination rehabilitated the commander.

Nemirovich-Danchenko made two fast friendships in Bulgaria, Mac-Gahan and General M. D. Skobelev.[46] The American reporter and Russian officer had become close more than a decade earlier, during the battle for Khiva. MacGahan had won admiration for having crossed Turkestan with only a guide in search of the Russian forces, and he lionized Skobelev in the *Daily News*: "He is a tall, handsome man, with a lithe, slender, active figure, a clear, blue eye, and . . . the kind of nose it is said Napoleon used to look for among the officers when he wished to find a general, and face young enough for a second lieutenant although

[44] G. K. Gradovskii, *Voina v Maloi Asii v 1877 g.* (SPB: A. Transhal', 1878), 34–35.

[45] TsGIA f. 785, op. 1, d. 17, ll. 1, 87, 137.

[46] Solov'eva and Shitova, in "A. S. Suvorin" (197) connected Custer to Skobelev rather than Cherniaev, noting the importance of the newspaper in making a superstar of Skobelev. Other similarities included Custer's insistence on wearing a bright red neck scarf so that his men could always identify him on the field, just as Skobelov wore white and rode a white horse for the same reason.

he is a general—the youngest in the army."[47] Small wonder that the general was taken with the reporter, or that MacGahan received such excellent information. They welcomed in Nemirovich-Danchenko a comrade-in-arms, but the privileges permitted by this chumminess did not go uncontested by other reporters.

The jealousy over access to Skobelev became more pronounced after the hostilities had ceased and the journalists began publishing their diaries of the war. Some charged the intrepid general with being a glory boy, arguing that his heroics were no more than a product of MacGahan's and Nemirovich-Danchenko's imaginations.[48] Not only did other reporters resent Skobelev's friends, but so did officers who felt overlooked in promotions and decorations because Nemirovich-Danchenko had not been on hand to glorify their activities.[49] The dispute about Skobelev's relations with favorite reporters was rekindled after the general's premature death in 1882. Just before dying of a heart attack, rumored to have been brought on by an orgy, Skobelev had made a provocative speech in Paris about Russia's need to rewrite the Treaty of Berlin. Skobelev had taken his case to the press, granting interviews. Nemirovich-Danchenko at once produced an adulatory biography of his patron, which became an immediate best-seller and, like his book on the Russo-Turkish War, was translated into French and English. In vintage lean prose, Nemirovich-Danchenko filled his pages with the adventures of a hero-in-uniform, interviewing many who knew or had fought under the general. Gradovskii set out to tell the other side of the story, to demonstrate that Skobelev had been a poor military strategist and that he had cost many a foot soldier his life unnecessarily because he wanted to see his feats in print.[50]

Gradovskii's observances reek of the sour grapes that make for less interesting reading, and as later analysts showed, the journalist was not a better military strategist than the general. Gradovskii did, however, make an astute observation about Skobelev's relationship with reporters. Arguing that "times of change begat character changes," he placed Skobelev as simultaneously "a product and reflection of the times." Gradovskii's sniffing that "we can only speculate about what his feelings toward the press might have been if he had not been the darling of journalism"

[47] Quoted in Frederic Bullard, *Famous War Correspondents* (Boston: Little, Brown, 1914; New York: Beekman, 1974), 135.

[48] A. E. Kaufman, "Za kulisami pechati. V. I. Nemirovich-Danchenko o Skobeleve," *Golos minuvshogo*, no. 9 (1914): 201–7.

[49] *Personal Reminiscences of General Skobeleff*, trans. E. A. Brayley Hodgetts (London: W. H. Allen, 1884).

[50] G. K. Gradovskii, *M. D. Skobelev: Etiud po kharakteristike nashego vremeni i ego geroev* (SPB: I. C. Lev', 1884), 81–82.

overlooked the fact that neither fate nor accident had made Skobelev a "darling." As Gradovskii himself pointed out, Skobelev identified journalism as one of the Great Powers.[51]

The element of personal competition between Nemirovich-Danchenko and Gradovskii figured into the different versions of Skobelev, but it was not a war fought between their publishers, Kraevskii and Suvorin. *Golos* had MacGahan, and Gradovskii enjoyed the patronage of Miliutin himself, so he too had privileged access.[52] What set Nemirovich-Danchenko apart was his reportorial style. Nemirovich-Danchenko, like Russell, earned his reputation unmasking corruption, and the instances he uncovered touched upon questions of intense public concern about why the brave fighting men were not receiving acceptable care. It was not just what he wrote, but how he wrote it. Unhindered by the rules of grammar, he wrote in short, choppy sentences, packing more action into fewer words. His background in travelogues enabled him to capture the sights and smells of Bucharest. He provided local color, describing the priests drinking beer with their parishioners, and the air thick with gun smoke at the Shipka Pass.

Another correspondent of sufficient reputation in the Balkans, A. N. Maslov, published correspondence alongside Nemirovich-Danchenko's in *Novoe vremia*. A comparison of their styles shows what singled Nemirovich-Danchenko out from the competition.[53] The person of Maslov is always present in his accounts: "I entered the Dar'ialskoe ravine on a dark November evening."[54] But MacGahan's pupil brought Bulgaria alive for readers: "It was a muggy autumn. The lush spring and marvelous Bulgarian summer had now left the village of Elena drowning in mud."[55] Maslov, when reporting conversations with uneducated peasants and others for whom Russian was not the native tongue, translated their slang and corrected their grammatical errors. Nemirovich-Danchenko showed the greater effectiveness of recording comments in the vernacular of his interviewees.

One important reason that Skobelev became a hero under Nemirovich-Danchenko's quill, a reason lost on Gradovskii, was that the more popular writer kept himself out of his texts personally, instead allowing the characters he interviewed to speak for themselves. The pronoun *I* made comparatively rare appearances in Nemirovich-Danchenko's three-volume history of the war. Gradovskii's works were intentionally chronicles

---

[51] Ibid., 104, 107.

[52] A. E. Kaufman, "Pisatel' s temperamentom," *Nasha starina*, no. 4 (1916): 307.

[53] Maslov's and Nemirovich-Danchenko's correspondences were published together in the three-volume *God voiny v Maloi Asii* (SPB: P. P. Soikin, 1878).

[54] Ibid., 3.

[55] Ibid., 142.

of his opinions. Nemirovich-Danchenko, in contrast, took pride that his were not. Believing it his duty to inform, not persuade, he was among the first to link descriptive with political objectivity.

The Assassination of Alexander II

With the Russo-Turkish War preoccupying people and kindling patriotism, the government continued to press its case against the young revolutionaries. In 1876, conflicting accounts about a rally to be held at the Kazan Cathedral in the heart of St. Petersburg had led to a clash between supporters of the Serbian War and political protesters. A year later, tsarist officials began to prosecute the notorious case of the 193 who had been caught in the roundup of those who "went to the people" three years earlier. A sad lot of political prisoners, these youths who had trekked determinedly into the countryside that summer were more guilty of naiveté than of treason. Their presence at the dock provided a greater source of piquant interest than fear among the curiosity-seekers who strained to see whether or not the accused really were copulating on the benches as rumor had reported.[56] The record of the trial, carried in *Pravitel'stvennyi vestnik* and reprinted in *Golos* and *Novoe vremia*, carried to readers images of overzealous, sometimes gullible and sometimes exploited participants who had irritated the status quo but had not substantially threatened it; eighty-eight were found innocent of any wrongdoing, and most of the rest got off lightly. The minister of justice began the trial confident that public opinion supported the government against these "revolutionaries," but the relatively light verdicts indicated otherwise.[57]

Women had a more significant place in the Russian revolutionary movement than in other European crusades, and their presence made for good copy in the press. The extraordinary trial of Vera Zasulich, who wandered ingenuously onto the stage of Russian history in the turbulent 1870s, is a case in point. The third of four daughters born to a despotic, alcoholic noble officer, she had followed her older sisters into the rebellious life of failed socialist dreams that characterized much of the youth movement in the 1860s. She witlessly became involved with the deranged and murderous Nechaev, and although she was not implicated in the murder perpetrated by some of his other followers, her association with the ringleader landed her in provincial exile. Back in St. Petersburg

[56] Vera Broido, *Apostles into Terrorists: Women and the Revolutionary Movement in the Russia of Alexander II* (London: Maurice Temple Smith, 1977), chapter 9.

[57] Richard Wortman, *The Development of a Russian Legal Consciousness* (Chicago: University of Chicago Press, 1976), 282–83.

in 1877, Zasulich's distress and alienation drove her to deliver a physical blow to the autocracy. In July, the governor-general of the national capital, the hard-nosed General Fedor Trepov, ordered a young prisoner from the Kazan Cathedral demonstration flogged for not doffing his hat in the general's presence. Outraged, Zasulich maneuvered her way into Trepov's office and shot him, though not fatally.[58]

The appearance of a young, troubled, wide-eyed female at the bar for a crime of moral indignation softened even conservative hearts. In his brilliant summation, presiding judge A. F. Koni told jurors that they must consider themselves "the conscience of society," a role they were only too happy to assume.[59] *Golos* carried much more information than simply the reprints from *Pravitel'stvennyi vestnik*; readers learned of Zasulich's tragic background and even about the jurors who would judge her crime. True to form, Kraevskii published the minute the jury brought in the "not guilty" verdict.[60]

Mea culpas emerged everywhere. *Novoe vremia* hailed the decision as "a verdict of social conscience not against state and law, but in defense of lawfulness and consequently for state and law."[61] Dostoevskii, whose politics fell to the right of Suvorin's, wrote that "to punish this young woman would be inappropriate and superfluous."[62] Gradovskii's ink flowed freely to endorse Koni's line of defense; he argued that a Russian society willing to accept the guilt of sin would atone for it.[63] His exhilaration earned *Golos* a warning from the Ministry of Internal Affairs. Only Katkov opposed the verdict, suggesting that it was an April Fool's joke because of the date of its delivery.[64]

The tsarist government, however, reneged on its promise to allow public opinion to participate in the judicial process and discounted the verdict. In radical response, a band of terrorists calling themselves the "People's Will" set upon the autocracy with a vengeance. Assassins felled several important figures, including one chief of the tsarist secret police. The terror literally entered the halls of the Winter Palace when a bomb exploded in the dining room. The frightened tsar at last agreed to consider returning to the reformist platform. In March 1880 he appointed General M. T. Loris-Melikov to reside over a "dictatorship of the heart."

[58] Barbara Alpern Engel, *Mothers and Daughters: Women of the Intelligentsia in Nineteenth-Century Russia* (London: Cambridge University Press, 1983), 93, 94–100.

[59] Quoted in Broido, *Apostles into Terrorists*, 150.

[60] *Golos*, 1 April 1878, no. 91.

[61] Quoted in Ambler, *Russian Journalism*, 163.

[62] Broido, *Apostles into Terrorists*, 150.

[63] *Golos*, 2 April 1878, no. 92.

[64] Tvardovskaia, *Ideologiia poreformennogo*, 175.

Loris-Melikov eased censorship restrictions and called in newspaper publishers to explain his positions and solicit their support. New Year's editorials of 1 January 1881 once again hailed the birth of a new Russia.

Interaction between Loris-Melikov and journalists, however, signified only what might have been. A few months later, when Alexander was on his way home, reputedly from signing a quasi constitution, the People's Will hit its mark. A bomb exploded close to the royal carriage. Instead of driving on, the tsar stepped out to investigate. Another assassin tossed a second bomb at the now stationary target. The last tsar's dying words, "I'm cold, I'm cold," reverberated on front pages across the country.

Reporting his murder, the press made the Tsar of all the Russias manifestly and profoundly human. *Golos* featured a starkly graphic description of the tsar's body: "Both legs between the knees and the feet had been reduced to a mass of scraps of muscles, with shreds of bone clinging in a few places. Traces of burns could be seen on some of the soft spots of his skin. There were also burns on his upper left eyelid. The glove on his right hand was bloody . . . the tsar summoned enough strength to ask that he be taken to the palace."[65] In one paragraph, journalists demystified the man who had ruled by divine right by accentuating his mortality in vivid depictions of shreds of bloody flesh and bones.

The assassination did not push the daily installment of "Love and Money" from *Peterburgskaia gazeta*'s front page, but its editors went to the hospital where the bystanders wounded in the double explosion were being treated. Other disfigured bodies had lain beside the tsar's: "One unknown person lay in an open coffin, what had been a bench. . . . He looked about thirty, a little taller than average, short hair, a dark red complexion, with a small mustache and thin beard."[66] Maintaining their intimacy with city-dwellers, the editors gave daily hospital reports on the other victims, assuring that the stories were "truthful accounts of people wounded at the site."[67]

Peterburgskii listok took another route. Its editors drew information largely from other papers, which led to confusion. One paper had reported the assassin captured, while another had him killed; *Peterburgskii listok* carried both versions without explanation. Editors interviewed witnesses and printed maps of the spot on the Catherine Canal that would allow readers to retrace the tsar's movements. The crudeness of these maps was counterbalanced by an extraordinarily intricate drawing of the

[65] *Golos*, 3 March 1881, no. 62.
[66] *Pg*, 3 March 1881, no. 92.
[67] *Pl*, 5 March 1881, no. 94.

internal construction of the "devilish device that was used to kill the the tsar, who rests now with God."[68]

Each newspaper brought the terrible crime into readers' homes with essentially the same stunning particulars. Editorially, all papers registered shock and indignation. In addition, they all solicited funds for the erection of a cathedral on the site; the Church of Our Saviour's Blood still stands in Leningrad, with a bright red mosaic on the floor where Alexander spilled his blood. The differences in reportage did not detract from the similarity of purpose in re-creating the particulars of the dramatic death of a man.

Symbolically, this event can be interpreted as the murder of the concept of tsar as the nation's only public person. As Richard Wortman has argued, "With the assassination, the sense of the tsar's inviolability died . . . much as it had in France with the execution of Louis XVI."[69] But by implementing the Great Reforms, Alexander II had already subverted the mythology of a "tsar father" domineering over his national family. What Alexander II accomplished institutionally, the People's Will did metaphorically.

The six assassins were quickly rounded up. Within less than a month they stood trial. Technology did not yet allow for the inclusion of photographs in newspapers, so *Peterburgskaia gazeta*'s editors found words to suffice: "Imagine that you are looking at photographic pictures. Rysakov: medium height, heavyset, *young*, of them all he has the most vulgar and antipathetic countenance . . . Gesia Gel'fman: an ordinary, ugly Jewish face. Overweight, a small nose . . . Sofiia Perovskaia: a flat, bloodless, smooth face with a small nose. She reminds one very much of Chinese women."[70] All received the death penalty, although it was commuted for the pregnant Gel'fman; all papers noted that she was a Jewess. On 4 April their executions were replayed in the press. Facts differed, but not significantly. In *Golos* the peasant terrorist Andrei Zheliabov relented and kissed the cross the priest held out to him, but in *Peterburgskii listok* he scorned it to the end. The account in *Golos* was the most complete: "At 9:20 A.M. the executioner Frolov completed the preparations, went up to Kibal'chich and led him to the high black dock, helping him up the two stairs. The executioner overturned the dock, and the criminal swung in the breeze."[71] The deaths of the other four followed with similar precision.

---

[68] *Pl*, 7 March 1881, no. 46.

[69] Richard Wortman, "Moscow and Petersburg: The Problem of Political Center in Tsarist Russia, 1881–1914," in Sean Wilentz, ed., *Rites of Power: Symbolism, Ritual, and Politics Since the Middle Ages* (Philadelphia: University of Pennsylvania Press, 1985), 248.

[70] *Pg*, 28 March 1881, no. 74.

[71] *Golos*, 4 April 1881, no. 94.

Epilogue on Russia's First "New" Journalism

The new tsar, named for his father, made short shrift of the "dictatorship of the heart." Editorial writers calling for the son to be faithful to the intentions of his parent did not realize that the intense familial animosity between the two carried over into ideas about ruling the empire. Deeply committed to the principles of autocracy in a society largely outgrowing such a system of government, the third and last Alexander reinvested where he could reactionary powers that limited freedom of expression. The successive harsh decrees distributed from the Ministry of Internal Affairs again forced editors to maneuver creatively to circumvent, or at least undermine, the censorship.

There was one more victim of 1 March 1881, although this one would not expire officially until February of 1883: *Golos*. Ironically, just prior to Alexander's death, a poem by liberal editor Nikolai Nekrasov that had long been forbidden by censors had at last appeared in his *Otechestvennye zapiski*. Two days before the assassination, stanzas had been reprinted in *Golos* with a sardonic retort that the censors who had prevented its publication did not themselves understand why it might be considered dangerous.[72] It was the last snide remark *Golos* could make about the bureaucrats in the Ministry of Internal Affairs who scouted out sedition. Warnings and temporary suspensions followed in rapid succession.

Alexander III brought Dmitrii Tolstoi back from the shadows of repression and appointed him minister of internal affairs, giving him the authority to force newspapers to submit to preliminary censorship after three warnings. Moreover, a Supreme Commission of Press Affairs established in 1882 was empowered to move even without the warnings. Tolstoi vented his ire against his former nemesis from the 1860s. Attacks on *Golos* continued with such arbitrariness that even *Novoe vremia* jumped to Kraevskii's defense, pointing out that he suffered even when supporting official policies.[73] *Golos* received the necessary three warnings within a year. Thus did Russia's first generation of newspaper journalists end much as it had begun.

[72] *Golos*, 28 Feb. 1881, no. 59.
[73] Zotov, "Nestor russkoi zhurnalistiki," 368.

5

The Newspaper in Battle with the "Thick" Journal

COMMERCIALIZATION AND OBJECTIVITY IN THE 1880s

BY THE 1880s technological advances had improved the quality of many goods and increased their availability. The daily newspaper, which could now be produced faster and more cheaply, figured among the items benefiting from the changes. The result was a "new" journalism that emphasized more than ever the importance of the reader as a consumer, a person with interests to be satisfied and the ability to make choices. People also had more reason to read newspapers. A number of political changes by the second half of the nineteenth century had made it all the more important for governments to assimilate social groups into a stable consensus. Socialism had threatened where workers remained disenfranchised, which had induced Western governments to include greater numbers of them in the electoral process. British reform legislation had extended suffrage to three quarters of the male population by 1884, and France began its third republican experiment in 1875. In the United States the majority of white males had enjoyed voting rights free of property qualifications since the first quarter of the century, but now the continuing waves of immigrants had to be taught how to exercise them. Although electoral rights did not constitute an issue in autocratic Russia, two decades into the Great Reforms growing numbers of Russians wanted more opportunities to participate in government.

The heightened relevance of politics to the newly enfranchised did not, however, result in a popular press with greater space devoted to political issues. Instead, sensationalism characterized this new consumer-oriented journalism, which alarmed those who watched as their partisanal periodicals lost ground to what they considered trivia. This conflict between the new journalists and their critics represented a very serious struggle for control of the public sphere. The elites wanted to keep the new groups out, primarily because they distrusted the commercialism that could allow private issues to dictate public ones. There was a class-based component to this struggle, since those being excluded came primarily from the lower rungs of the middle class. In the West, this group would include a number of enfranchised workers hoping to be integrated into the liberal capitalist system.

Charting the growth of consumerism is especially important to tsarist Russia because it helps to fill a lacuna in the history of how the middle strata came into existence. The first part of this chapter describes the evolution of commercial consumerism in Russia with an analysis of the newspaper that fueled it most conspicuously, newcomer Nikolai Ivanovich Pastukhov's *Moskovskii listok* (*The Moscow Sheet*). What Pastukhov (1822–1911) and his paper epitomized, however, would not become established without a struggle, and the second half of this chapter chronicles the competition between the traditional and the new forms of communications. In Russia, not only the nature of the battle but its very existence is especially significant for the way in which it has been written out of the history of the pivotal decade of the 1880s, when the new tsar, Alexander III, threatened to turn back the clock of reform that his murdered father had wound up.

Consumerism and Counterreform

Alexander II and his assassins had disappeared from the headlines, the mourning bands no longer decked newspapers' front pages after the requisite six months, and *Golos* was languishing under a temporary suspension when Sarah Bernhardt arrived to help Russians put the traumatic year behind them as they began the Christmas season of 1881. Playing to packed houses, "La Grande Sarah" dominated the urban press, whose reporters found no minutiae about her personal or professional life too trivial. Although she disappointed some admirers by leaving her coffin at home, sleeping instead in a more prosaic bed at Moscow's Slavic Bazaar, she awed them by paying a lordly thirty rubles per diem for the comfort.[1] Leikin, *Peterburgskaia gazeta*'s most distinguished writer, met her train and related her triumphal entry into the national capital.[2]

Newspapers' advertising pages, too, heralded her arrival by peddling everything from theater seats to gingerbread frosted with her portrait. Among others, she performed her most popular role, Marguerite Gautier, the consumptive heroine of Alexandre Dumas's (*fils*) tragic "La Dame aux Camelias." Leikin thrilled readers with a personal visit to her dressing room, from where he could report that she received admirers in Marguerite's theatrical style, reclining on a chaise lounge.[3] The French

[1] *Pg*, 29 Nov. 1881, no. 282.
[2] *Pg*, 5 Dec. 1881, no. 287.
[3] *Pg*, 12 Dec. 1881, no. 293.

actress, after mixed receptions for her highly stylized interpretations in Odessa and Moscow,[4] acquitted herself admirably in aristocratic St. Petersburg: "At last even the skeptical critics are beginning to recognize that there is art in Sarah Bernhardt."[5]

When Bernhardt added her name to the list of theater stars who became international celebrities in the nineteenth century, she bore witness to the evolving view that consumers could select and crown their own royalty. Such veneration of entertainers had begun forty years earlier when adoring fans cheered in the streets as well as the theaters for Viennese dancer Fanny Elssler and "Swedish Nightingale" Jenny Lind. Crowned heads of the new age of consumption, the stars of the stage found everything from clothing to confectionary named for them. Dependent upon publicity for fame so widespread that it won them the privileged status of the new age, they developed a symbiotic relationship with the media that introduced them to customers of art, candy, and images. Horace Greeley's puritanical refusal to solicit ads from New York theaters for his *Tribune* as late as 1841 because "we consider the stage . . . rather an injury than a benefit to the community"[6] sounded the last gasp of the moral separation of mass communications from mass culture, a separation ill affordable to proprietors of both.

By the time of Bernhardt's tour, Russians had long held Italian soprano Adelina Patti dear; prattle about her wealthy private life appeared everywhere, and *Golos* advertised the French champagne named for her. Over and above this, though, loomed the symbolic date of Bernhardt's arrival. As Russia's intelligentsia was bracing itself for the counterreformation threatened by the new tsar, its mass-circulation newspaper industry was preparing for the next successful wave of "new" journalism, one explicitly reflected in the interests and values Bernhardt represented and spoken in the voices of her fans.

Historians have remembered the liberals' dejection with considerably greater clarity than they have the confident tones set by the newspapers. Those who recorded the events of the 1880s by and large distorted the past by omitting the growth of the mass-circulation daily because they themselves, the learned elite, fought and lost a battle for influence among a critically important segment of Russian readers. Writing in exile after 1917, for example, prerevolutionary historian V. A. Miakotin entitled his section on postassassination journalism "The Impotence of the Press." Claiming incorrectly that the number of periodicals had declined in this era, this alumnus of the "thick" journal *Russkoe bogatstvo* (*Rus-*

---

[4] Laurence Senelick, "Chekhov's Response to Bernhardt," in Eric Salmon, ed., *Bernhardt and the Theatre of Her Time* (Westport, Conn.: Greenwood Press, 1984), 165–82.

[5] *Pg*, 12 Dec. 1881, no. 293.

[6] Quoted in Hughes, *Human Interest*, 6.

sian Wealth) fortified his argument that "the matter offered by the survivors was being visibly impoverished under the double influence of governmental rigors and the general discouragement that had taken hold of the public."[7]

The historian pitied the disconsolate intelligentsia, not the vast majority of newspaper readers. Many intellectuals had resigned their fates to the new tsar's Supreme Commission on Censorship. In their despondency they held up *Grazhdanin* (*The Citizen*), the ultraconservative paper published by the "troubadour of reaction" Prince V. P. Meshcherskii from funds supplied by the Winter Palace, as the newspaper that best depicted Alexander III's reign. Dubbed "Prince Period" for editorializing in favor of "putting a period to all the reforms in Russia," Meshcherskii made a convenient target for the bitter recriminations of those whose hopes had been shattered by Alexander III.[8]

His contemporaries exaggerated, however, Meshcherskii's leverage. A persona non grata in royal social circles for unacceptable behavior that included more than a suspicion of homosexuality,[9] only his boyhood friendship with the deceased tsarevich Nikolai Aleksandrovich kept money flowing into *Grazhdanin*. The extravagant publisher had no special access to inner politics and no license with the censors, who punished him only slightly less often than they had Kraevskii for different indiscretions.[10]

Miakotin might have learned from picking up the "thin" journal *Zritel'* (*The Spectator*), where clever young satirist "Antosha Chekhonte" scribbled at great length about how the local audience greeted the century's greatest actress as the era of the consumer dawned in Russia: "Two days ago Moscow knew only four elements; now it won't stop talking about a fifth. It knew seven wonders; now a fraction of a second doesn't go by without it discussing an eighth. Those who had the luck to get even the worst ticket are dying with impatience for nightfall."[11] Soon to join the ranks of newspaper journalists himself, Anton Chekhov, together with his older brother Alexander, would be important as representative figures in the contest for intellectual influence that Miakotin neglected in his chronicle of the 1880s.

[7] Paul Miliukov, ed., *A History of Russia*, trans. Charles Markham (New York: Funk and Wagnalls, 1960), 146.

[8] A. V. Zapadov, ed., *Istoriia russkoi zhurnalistiki XVII–XIX vekov* (Moscow: MGU, 1973), 492; and W. E. Mosse, "Imperial Favorite: V. P. Meshchersky and the *Grazhdanin*," *Slavonic and East European Review* 59, no. 4 (1981): 529–47.

[9] *Dnevnik Suvorina*, 315–16.

[10] Daniel Balmuth, *Censorship in Russia, 1865–1905* (Washington, D.C.: University Press of America, 1979), 98.

[11] Quoted in Senelick, "Chekhov's Response to Bernhardt," 169.

Fig. 4. N. I. Pastukhov, publisher of *Moskovskii listok*

N. I. Pastukhov and *Moskovskii listok*

Pastukhov began publishing a newspaper in Moscow only three months before Bernhardt's arrival, one intended for those most likely to purchase candies wrapped in her portrait. Like Suvorin and Leskov, Pastukhov followed his ambitions from provincial poverty to city lights. From a small town in Smolensk Province, Pastukhov had been forced to substitute personal drive for education; even as one of Moscow's foremost publishers and a popular writer, his articles needed a second reading at the rewrite desk. Born into the *meshchane*, or petty bourgeoisie, Pastukhov developed a talent for trade. Nearing the age of sixty when he started his newspaper, he overcame the hardships of his youth and died a wealthy man, legendary for his generosity, in 1912. During Russia's first post-emancipation experiments with newspaper journalism, Pastukhov could be found drawing beer in his pub in Moscow's central Arbat district. With a canny intuition for popular tastes, he founded *Moskovskii listok* on the advice of the reporters who frequented his tavern picking up bits of news and hearsay. The rumors in which Pastukhov's patrons bartered were as marketable as his alcohol, and Pastukhov took up the trade himself and improved upon it. A local businessman, he appreciated the correlation between publicity and sales. When reporting, he developed a system of collecting special receipts in lieu of cash from the papers to which he sold stories, and he used these receipts in area shops to emphasize his close connections with the press.[12]

The first capital was long overdue for an urban daily on the order of Petersburg's established two, and Pastukhov had entered journalism as an occasional contributor to St. Petersburg's urban papers.[13] In 1881, Moscow could boast the nation's two most important specifically politicized papers, Katkov's *Moskovskie vedomosti* and its self-styled loyal opposition, *Russkie vedomosti* (*The Russian News*), both of which had received contributions of local news from Pastukhov. The latter daily, whose sobriquet "the professors' newspaper" indicated its staff and the audience to which it was addressed, remained the flagship of the liberal intelligentsia until 1917.[14]

The inaugural issue of *Moskovskii listok* appeared on 1 August 1881. Promising that "life itself will be our senior reporter," Pastukhov borrowed from the imagery of the ineffectual gentry and assured that his paper would not be "a superfluous man in the already large family of the Russian press."[15] Because in the wake of the assassination the censorship had been adjusted with special harsher provisions for periodicals costing less than seven-and-a-half rubles a year, Pastukhov charged this minimum for his paper, nine with delivery. The advertisers who subsidized him also enticed the ordinary consumer; the restaurants, circuses, bicycles, and cures for venereal diseases found advertised in the pages of *Moskovskii listok* reflected a sizeable population with leisure time and money to spend filling it.

In no time he assembled a staff, including the talented young V. A. Giliarovskii.[16] Under several pen names, including "Granddad from the

---

[12] Jeffrey Brooks, *When Russia Learned to Read: Literacy and Popular Literature, 1861–1917* (Princeton, N.J.: Princeton University Press, 1985), 118–23; and Pastukhov's obituary by "Osa" (I. A. Batalin) in *Pg*, 3 Aug. 1912, no. 210.

[13] Skrobotov, "*Peterburgskii listok*," 8; and Esin, *Puteshestvie v proshloe*, 96.

[14] "50 let *Russkikh vedomostei*," *Golos minuvshogo*, no. 1 (1913): 10.

[15] *Ml*, 1 Aug. 1881, no. 1.

[16] Giliarovskii left behind the most informative account of the early years at *Moskovskii listok*. See his "Moskovskie gazety v 80-kh gg.," *Byloe*, no. 6 (1925): 119–30, in addition to his three-volume collected works, *Sobranie v trekh tomakh* (Moscow: Moskovskii rabochii, 1960). Volume two, *Moskva gazetnaia*, covers his life as a reporter in Moscow.

Fig. 5. *Moskovskii listok* correspondents. *Top row (left to right)*: E. V. Barsov, editor
A. V. Smirenskii, I. I. Miasnitskii. *Bottom row (left to right)*: A. M. Pazukhin, A. P.
Landsberg, E. N. Opochinin, A. A. Sokolov.

Arbat" and his most famous personality, "Old Acquaintance," the publisher himself wrote popular feuilletons and serial novels. He also hired
ex-radical Sokolova and her son, future star Doroshevich. Mother and
son did not, however, get along well; he never forgave her for removing
him from the happiness of the adoptive home where he had lived during
the years she lived in Europe in the 1860s.[17] The rift between Doroshevich and Sokolova had broader implications than a retelling of the oe-
dipal myth, though, because it personified the generational differences
between the old journalism and the new. Sokolova had returned to Russia after deciding that she would put her revolutionary past behind her,
and her work for Pastukhov was typical of her neoconservativism.[18] For
the teenager, on the other hand, what mattered was the novelty of Pastukhov's newspaper and its cornucopia of opportunities. Studying his

[17] S. V. Bukchin, *Sud'ba fel'etonista* (Minsk: Nauka i tekhnika, 1975), 14.
[18] A. I. Sokolova, "Vstrechi i znakomstva," *Iv* 135, nos. 1–3 (1914): 135–44, 498–511, 849–
65.

trade at the most popular of the boulevard dailies, the bright young writer learned considerably more than he had from the various educational institutions that sheer boredom had forced him to abandon. Although with Giliarovskii he outgrew *Moskovskii listok* and they moved on in the next decade, working for Pastukhov Doroshevich developed a writing style with broad appeal and an almost arrogant sense of nationalism that turned him into the most popular star in Russia's mass-circulation press by the turn of the twentieth century.

Pastukhov employed the services of writers with a background in the "thin" satirical journals, including Doroshevich and Giliarovskii, whose audiences overlapped considerably with that of the popular press. Like his publisher, feuilletonist I. I. Miasnitskii (Baryshev) combined business sense with "thin" journalism. Educated in a commercial training school, the "Moscow Leikin" aspired to a more creative career in literature. Churning out feuilletons and melodramatic serials for Pastukhov, Miasnitskii carried on a second career managing the finances of millionaire book publisher K. T. Soldatenkov and his heirs, who owed their fortunes at least in part to Miasnitskii's pulp literature. Miasnitskii's considerable output, better measured for quantity than quality, never rose above the middlebrow standards maintained by urban journalism.[19]

Pastukhov's News

"La Grande Sarah" gave Pastukhov his first big feature story, although his critic was one of those with reservations about Bernhardt's somewhat technical interpretations. A clever ditty by another contributor corroborated this, capturing local ardor for the visiting actress in its rhymed assembly of new words entering the Russian vocabulary punning her name: "We no longer play games [srazhat'sia]," for example, "but we bernhardt around [zabernarivat']."[20] This echoed the tenor of the paper in general. Stories from around town pushed aside world events, and the publisher could claim assorted provincial correspondents, but not a national news network.

Pastukhov captured the city's attention immediately, primarily because of his willingness to overreach the boundaries of propriety maintained by the Petersburg papers. The renegade Muscovite publisher capitalized on the craving for insight into personal lives in a variety of daily features that could fall under the rubric of "Moscow Confidential." Bernhardt and Patti had relinquished their private lives to the ticket-purchas-

[19] Obituary for I. I. Baryshev-Miasnitskii, *Ml*, 3 June 1911, no. 126.
[20] *Ml*, 27 Nov. 1881, no. 104.

ing public, and Pastukhov decided that his prospective audience should be equally susceptible to snooping. The Muscovite publisher dug for dirt in ways that Khudekov never tolerated in *Peterburgskaia gazeta*'s poking into the activities of his merchant readers. The gossipy asides in the Petersburg paper directed attention to slightly shady business dealings, but Khudekov tacitly kept hearth and home off-limits. Pastukhov, however, offered an "Advice and Answers" column with tantalizing candor: "To the merchant Mi-v at the Serpukhovskie Gate. Tell your stepson Misha, who recently married a pretty woman from a good family, that he should cast his glances less often at the wife of the innkeeper A-vich. The neighbors are already laughing."[21] This section often contained cryptic messages in apparent response to readers writing in for advice. Such exposés could also be read in the more notorious "Along Streets and Alleys," which made every merchant family vulnerable to Pastukhov's scandalmongers. Occasionally a subtext of social responsibility could be detected when the prying divulged misconduct among public servants, but such was not Pastukhov's primary purpose. For all its titillation, *Moskovskii listok* also published such religious material as naming the patron saints of each day, as if to say that God and gossip were not incompatible.

If inhabitants of the Winter Palace and Holy Synod did not have to look over their shoulders to see which of Pastukhov's reporters was following behind, the bureaucracy stood a fair and fitting target. Pastukhov brought the same cheekiness to political commentary that he did to gossip. In his first issue, he made light of *Golos*'s Moscow business office next door to his own: "We are reminded of the problems of getting carried away and playing with only the high notes; one can lose unexpectedly not only one's voice, but also the right to one's voice."[22] Attacking the City Duma with the flair with which he did the wayward merchants, Pastukhov moved against local politicians. Establishing clean water, fresh air, and streetlights as basic inalienable rights of the citizenry, he reproached those who expended their reformist energies on the young revolutionaries, claiming that in hiding behind national issues they dodged their responsibilities to solve the city's most pressing problems.[23] A factory owner who had allowed his architect to cut corners so that now falling bricks from his crumbling building endangered passers-by was humiliated by a woodcut illustration of his negligence.[24]

Pastukhov's defense of the public interest was tenacious. His counsel to reporters to address "my janitors and shopkeepers" recalled the standard American dictum about reporters writing for the "Iowa milkman";

[21] *Ml*, 8 Sept. 1881, no. 31.
[22] *Ml*, 1 Aug. 1881, no. 1.
[23] *Ml*, 18 and 19 Sept. 1881, nos. 41–42.
[24] *Ml*, 22 Aug. 1881, no. 17.

both cases refer to a lowest common denominator that allows for a broad range of readers. In addition to snickering about their neighbors' sins, Pastukhov's audience of merchants, bureaucrats, and artisans read about their weddings and similar events that gave them social respectability. Through the paper readers could also call on the socially prominent, as when it transported them to the most elegant mansions during the height of the holiday season, allowing them to mingle with the likes of Governor-General V. A. Dolgorukov: "Prince Vladimir Andreevich was, as is his custom, charming to everyone and constantly surrounded by his guests, all of whom had fabulous impressions of this, honestly, simply marvelous ball."[25]

Just as he overstepped the unstated restrictions on prying, Pastukhov's sensationalism could churn the strongest stomach. Corpses found on Vladimirskii Road, victims of highwaymen, were depicted in gratuitous detail: "A horrifying sight rose before the eyes of passers-by: from under a sheepskin coat, which appeared to be tossed over people asleep, eight human legs were sticking out in various positions, and in the place above the legs, where one would expect to find heads, four streams of blood flowed from under this cover, still warm. . . . When they took the cover off these people, you could see that all four heads had been beaten in, and that their brains and blood were all dribbling together."[26] Grislier than accounts of the regicide, this passage is equally noteworthy for its ability to transport readers to the scene of the crime. If shockingly sensory detail is a hallmark of the tastes of the common reader, this passage points to a key segment of Pastukhov's audience.

The Government and the New Journalism

The Moscow censorship committee, bothered by the license Pastukhov took with civic decorum, forced him to terminate "Advice and Answers." Although this did not keep all gossip out of *Moskovskii listok*, the censors' reprimand of the publisher for his refusal to differentiate between public and private here revealed an appreciation of the kind of threat Pastukhov could pose. Divulging the pecadillos of a few Muscovite merchants did not menace the political order, but becoming an independent source of information did. Further investigation into the government's attitude toward the developing popular culture, however, points instead to official shortsightedness; censors assessed the issue as one of public conventions rather than public authority. The reasons for limiting Pastukhov's ability

[25] *Ml*, 3 Jan. 1887, no. 3.
[26] *Ml*, 1 Aug. 1881, no. 1.

to scandalize took the censorship backward in time, returning it to its prereform preoccupation with morals instead of moving it forward to address the importance of a popular and independent medium.

The government's toning down of Pastukhov complemented a broader official program that intended to use newspapers to bring the emancipated peasantry into the government's fold. The government decided to launch, under the aegis of its national *Pravitel'stvennyi vestnik*, a far more ambitious project, this one aimed at the rural peasantry. *Sel'skii vestnik (The Village Herald)*, a glossy weekly tabloid made available at local township headquarters or through subscription at the nominal annual cost of one ruble, offered information on subjects the government wanted its peasant populace to know more about, especially the legal system, the beneficent royal family, and the Orthodox church. *Sel'skii vestnik's* own "Advice and Answers" section dealt primarily with readers' queries about laws, agrarian issues, and advancements in farming techniques. Editors initiated several press campaigns, including one on alcoholism, that drew readers into public discourse on national questions. Yet the official newspaper could not create a public in the same way that Pastukhov's could because it preached to rather than communicated with readers.[27] Its readers were too few, and it rarely addressed topics of real concern to the peasantry. Holding fast to the myopic view arrived at during the Nechaev Affair that if the public did not read about an event it had not occurred, the government continued to publish *Sel'skii vestnik* as a rickety defense against revolutionary propaganda in the countryside. When offered a choice between *Sel'skii vestnik* and *Moskovskii listok*, peasants preferred the latter hands down.[28]

The relationship between Pastukhov and the government is particularly instructive because the publisher's revolutionary ideas about newspaper publishing did not stem from a political desire to dethrone the tsar. His personal and editorial politics reflected the end-of-the-century interpretations of the symbols of authority of Nicholas I: "Orthodoxy, Autocracy, and Nationality." The counterreformation forged by Alexander III was directed primarily against the peasantry and the intelligentsia, and it imposed no real hardship on those who constituted the bulk of Pastukhov's readers. The most provocative of the counterreforms—Dmitrii Tolstoi's University Statute of 1884 and the implementation of noble land

---

[27] James Krukones, *To the People: The Russian Government and the Newspaper "Sel'skii vestnik" (The Village Herald), 1881–1917* (New York: Garland Press, 1987).

[28] Two readership surveys taken in Moscow Province produced these results: "Gazeta v derevne," *Moskovskii statisticheskii ezhegodnik za 1905*, 170–78; and I. Stepnoi, "Chto chitaet derevenskoe naselenie," *Dlia narodnogo uchitelia*, no. 17 (1916): 26–28. Some peasants, however, preferred *Selskii vestnik* to *Ml* because the former contained valuable agricultural information. T.R.B., "Pervaia russkaia narodnaia gazeta," *Iv* 36, no. 6 (1889): 679.

Fig. 6. The *Moskovskii listok* building

captains five years later—stultified critical inquiry in all academic disci-
plines and returned the gentry to administrative control of the countryside. But gloomy students and peasants beyond Moscow Province were
unlikely to have had extensive contact with *Moskovskii listok*. Of greater
immediate relevance to Pastukhov's readers was the revision of the statute on town government in 1892 that increased property qualifications
for the electorate. This did not stimulate editorial agitation on either side
of the issue, but because of the general apathy of the Moscow voters, the
newspaper's readers might not have had much interest in the polemics
surrounding this particular issue.[29]

[29] Joseph Bradley, "Moscow: From Big Village to Metropolis," in Michael Hamm, ed.,
The City in Late Imperial Russia (Bloomington: Indiana University Press, 1986), 25.
Thomas C. Owen discusses the apathy with which much of electoral Moscow met the re-

Moskovskii listok and the Market Mentality

Given that the increasing popularity of newspapers in the 1880s evidenced the growth of consumerism, editorial positions on economic growth offer insights into the development of a market mentality. Recurrent tirades in Russia's mass-circulation press spoke to chronic shortages and problems of supply of critical goods and services, which posed persistent obstacles to the development of a free-market ideology among even the bourgeoisie. Private enterprise might well have its place, but only so long as consumers were protected from potentially harmful monopolies. Basic foodstuffs, meat and bread, for example, were better distributed by a responsible Duma or zemstvo than left to the greedy producers charging whatever they could get.[30] Successful publishers, themselves enterprising beneficiaries of the market, did not argue that market forces could be relied on to arbitrate equitably between buyers and sellers of essential products.

The statist nature of Russian capitalism looms especially large in publishers' reservations about laissez-faire economics. It affected how Russians perceived the West, which they both feared and envied for various reasons relating to its free-market capitalism. A paradox seems to arise here, because the commercial papers were driven by market demands. However, the Russian consumer had many reasons to beware of Western capitalism; the parallels between M. S. Gorbachev's *perestroika* and Alexander II's Great Reforms include the problematic of how a consumer market might operate in an economic system supported by a kind of state capitalism. Although editorial hostility did not commence with Pastukhov, *Moskovskii listok* gave significant attention to the conflict of interest between Russian nationalism and Western investment in the tsarist empire. A protest against foreign investors in Russian railroad companies sounded an early alarm that Pastukhov would repeat throughout his career.[31]

The debates about capitalism resurrected the unresolved issue of Russia's uncertain relationship to the West. Russia's merchantry, the nucleus of its potential entrepreneurial class, still had to function too much in the caste-like *soslovie* system. Legally prohibited from forming politicized mutual-interest societies, merchants had to depend upon the paternalism of the autocracy to sustain them. Traditionally xenophobic, they feared that "reliance on foreign skills and capital could turn Russia into a depen-

---

form in *Capitalism and Politics in Russia: A Social History of the Moscow Merchants, 1855–1905* (New York and Cambridge: Cambridge University Press, 1981), 158–59.

[30] *Ml*, 19 Jan. 1895, no. 19.

[31] *Ml*, 4 Aug. 1881, no. 3.

dency of the West without a shot being fired."[32] In journalism, they responded more readily to Slavophile influences than to the Westernizers because they sought voices that would preserve their culture as well as protect their livelihoods.[33]

Yet at the same time many recognized the dynamic capabilities of an economic system that offered them greater say in national development, and they sought to lessen the threats of capitalism by ascertaining that its promises answered uniquely Russian needs. Pastukhov represented the interests of those who wanted a modern industrial Russia, but kept a skeptical eye out for what might be imported from the West to achieve that goal. The protective tariff instituted in 1891, the highest in Europe, reflected the dual desires to allow Russia's industry to develop and also to keep the West at bay. The belief that Russia could profit from the mistakes that other countries had made in the process of industrializing and could therefore contain the most jarring repercussions was attractive. Newspaper journalists emerged in the 1880s to speak for this ideal.

Doroshevich grew into the most popular of these representatives from the press. He made *capitalism* synonymous with the degenerate West, just as he used *bourgeois (burzhui)* as an adjective of contempt. Doroshevich played easily with vocabulary, giving Western words a Russian conceptual definition. When Pastukhov started a special newspaper to cover the annual trade fair in Nizhnii Novgorod, Doroshevich edited it while also corresponding for the parent paper. Exalting in the Russianness of it all, he wrote of visitors who "listen to Russian choirs, eat Russian food with Russian merchants in Russian restaurants and leave overstuffed but utterly charmed." The "yoke of capitalism," about which he often protested, menaced that charm. He had special venom for the grain monopolies, which sent Russian food westward to underwrite the costs of industrialization. Despairing that "not a single grain will reach a mouth, but rather it will all fall into the hands of the all-powerful firms," he waxed eloquent about the "thousands of acres of Russia's golden fields of grain." The Nobels and the Rothschilds brought with their "armies of millions" the "storm clouds of capitalism" to wreak devastation. When workers struck at the Hughes factories in 1892, he leapt to their defense: "Exploitation exists everywhere, wherever there are people who work and people who utilize the labor of others. But never in Russia, not at a single factory, has it taken on such grandiose proportions of 'misunder-

---

[32] Alfred Rieber, *Merchants and Entrepreneurs in Imperial Russia* (Chapel Hill: University of North Carolina Press, 1982), 178.

[33] Thomas C. Owen, "The Moscow Merchants and the Public Press," *Jahrbucher für Geschichte Osteuropas* 23, no. 1 (1975): 26–38; and Rieber, *Merchants and Entrepreneurs*, especially chapter 5.

standing.' . . . mortality among the Hughes workers significantly exceeds that among prisoners in the Siberian mines."[34]

Doroshevich's Soviet biographer, S. V. Bukchin, cited this and other of the journalist's invectives against the evils of capitalism to demonstrate the former's sensitivity to the class struggle. Sympathy for the toiling masses did not make Doroshevich a Marxist any more than his defense of Russian culture made him an agent of official nationality. His voice assured that Russia could be modern, strong, and just, without sacrificing its integrity to a West that had by no means resolved all the problems of industrialization.

The worker question remained one of the most problematic repercussions of the Industrial Revolution that the West had not resolved to satisfaction. The former bartender's concerns about arbitrating the relationships between business and labor echoed those of the other mass-circulation publishers who held social serenity paramount while assuming the authority to speak for workers. *Moskovskii listok* supported the rights of employees for health insurance and freedom from economic exploitation.[35] Pastukhov blamed the working class's first restive stirrings in the strike movement of 1885 on outside agitators, and justified the factory administration's bearing down to protect the rights of those who wanted to stay on the job.[36] This was not to say that factory managers were beyond reproach in all disorders; at the trial of workers accused of striking at the Nikolskii factory in 1886, Pastukhov hesitated to condone the strike, but acknowledged that "the factory was hell on earth for [the workers], and the management treated them worse than the plantation owners did their Negroes in Beecher Stowe's novel."[37]

Popular Fiction, Popular Culture

One of the Moscow entrepreneur's most enduring contributions to the growth of an urban-based culture came from the serial novels that he and his steadiest writer, former rural schoolteacher A. M. Pazukhin, authored. Instead of featuring pseudo-Europeans gallivanting through Parisian streets with suspiciously Russian-sounding names, *Moskovskii listok*'s serial adventures took place almost invariably in Russia. A European setting or character portended iniquity. Paris, for example, gave bitter refuge only in the end to an adulteress from the Moscow merchantry who forsook love and respectability to dally with Russia's "golden youth," pre-

[34] Bukchin, *Sud'ba fel'etonista*, 37–39.
[35] *Ml*, 8 Sept. 1881, no. 31.
[36] *Ml*, 8 Jan. 1885, no. 8.
[37] *Ml*, 30 May 1886, no. 148.

tentiously imitating the prodigal lifestyles of the wastrels in European salons.[38]

Historical novels also reinforced the paper's nationalistic tones. M. Staritskii, who turned out better-than-average historical pulp, contributed irregularly to *Moskovskii listok*. The two tsarevnas who preceded Catherine the Great, herself suspicious for being both German-born and Westernizing, appeared occasionally as background figures in these novels. The wicked Anna (1730–1740), who had brought her German lover, the infamous Count Biron, to tyrannize Russians at their own court, made an apt fictional foil for Catherine's aunt-in-law Elizabeth. The latter, a daughter of Peter the Great, was inevitably cast as the savior of Russia from alien domination.[39] Even the most villainous of tsars, Ivan the Terrible (1533–1584), got a fair hearing in A. Golubev's "The Brother of Ivan the Terrible." Vowing that he had drawn his story from "true materials," Golubev introduced readers to the illegitimate Iurii, firstborn and therefore rightful heir to the throne upon which the young Ivan sat. Iurii, a common foot soldier, saved his younger brother from Polish invaders, but refused the tsar's invitation to join him as coruler and faded back into history.[40] Coarse but imaginative illustrations often accompanied the texts, a first in the Russian press.

"Old Acquaintance" himself dramatized the most exciting and notorious newspaper protagonist of the era, the bandit Churkin. Based loosely on the exploits of a real-life desperado, a hard-drinking ex–factory worker who with his brother terrorized Moscow Province in the first decades after the emancipation, Churkin captured the imaginations of everyone from children to the tsar's council when he sprang from the pages of *Moskovskii listok* in 1882. A novel literary experiment, Churkin afforded Pastukhov the opportunity to introduce factual rebellion through newspaper fiction. This serial complemented the not infrequent news reports of enduring lawlessness beyond the urban perimeters.

Deliberately obscuring the border between fact and fiction, news and entertainment, the fictional Churkin drew even more blood than his factual counterpart. The outlaw had died around 1880, rumored poisoned by his wife or murdered by vengeful peasant victims. The reprehensible bandit gave Pastukhov problems with the censors, who found cause for apprehension in the lionizing of a thief and killer who reveled in the rural lawlessness that the government was in fact as well as fiction helpless to

[38] A. Pazukhin's "Zhenskaia dolia," serialized in the spring of 1887.

[39] N. Chirev's "Boiarin Petr Basmanov" began serialization in January 1887.

[40] This story began in January 1895. Perhaps Golubev found the answer to the historiographical question that continues to plague: Did or did not Ivan correspond with the renegade Prince Andrei Kurbskii? In this account brother Iurii wrote the letters, signing Ivan's name.

subdue.[41] The concern about the mass media's ability to spread pernicious ideas that had prompted higher prices for periodicals also forced
Pastukhov, after going several rounds with the local censorship committee, to kill off his legendary protagonist in 1885. As further punishment,
Pastukhov lost for several years the right to illustrate his stories, which
probably cost him marginally literate readers whose gaze would be
caught first by the pictures, and whose interest would then help them
piece together words in the text. Although curtailing the use of the prints
narrowed the horizons of Russian popular journalism, Pastukhov admitted that in the 1880s the technology of reproduction had itself limited his
operations.[42] Barely a year after the fictional Churkin's fateful demise,
another real-life criminal stepped into the imaginations of those who devoured the boulevard papers. Sofia Bliuvshtein, notorious as "The
Golden Arm," a convicted pickpocket and suspected murderess, made
news with her daring escape and recapture by authorities. Still alluring
at age forty, Bliuvshtein found tinges of admiration in the accounts of her
seduction of her jailor.[43] Despite the government's wishes, law and order
could not suppress fascination with so spirited a personality, and she too
found her escapades fictionalized.

Facticity, Mediation, and Cultural Politics

Pastukhov's extraordinary success forced Russia's intelligentsia to recognize that a substantively new print culture had begun to set the terms for
social discourse. A prophet had raised the cry in 1879 that "the newspaper has killed the journal!"[44] but the passing was not mourned until the
next decade. *Moskovskii listok* made the threat to the intellectuals' hegemony over the printed word manifest as never before. Although the
intellectual elite had demoted Kraevskii and Suvorin to pariahs, they
nonetheless acknowledged the publishers as part of their crowd. But
when an uneducated bartender came out with the flashiest assortment
yet of gossip, murder, and audacity, and his newspaper jumped to prominence in a city noted for its political press, they realized that they had
not been paying sufficient attention to the phenomenon at hand.

The rise of *Moskovskii listok* coincided with the demise of *Golos*, but
the censorship delivered a more debilitating blow in 1884 when it si-
lenced *Otechestvennye zapiski*, the liberal intelligentsia's most popular

[41] On Churkin, see Brooks, *When Russia Learned to Read*, 123–25, 177–87.

[42] Supplement to *Ml*, 1 Aug. 1906, no. 29.

[43] *Pl*, 14 July 1886, no. 188.

[44] "Gazeta ubila zhurnal!" *Russkaia pravda*, 20 Aug. 1879, no. 109; and V. P. Baluev,
Politicheskaia reaktsiia 80-kh godov XIX veka i zhurnalistika (Moscow: MGU, 1971), 103.

medium. Such a turn of events gave the intellectuals pause to take stock of their situation and face up to their isolation among readers. In addition to newspapers, other periodicals had changed, influenced by the insights of German immigrant A. F. Marx. In 1870 he founded *Niva (The Cornfield)*, a periodical that combined aspects of the informative, instructive, and entertaining elements of other media into a magazine format oriented toward a middle-class family audience. Like its American complement *The Ladies' Home Journal*, *Niva* became the first periodical with a national audience that exceeded one hundred thousand.[45] Although Russia's intelligentsia had not anticipated mass circulations for their "thick" journals, the popularity of periodicals beyond their editorial control forced them to recognize how the competition for influence in postreform society had stiffened. Their impotence in the face of Pastukhov, Marx, and others testified to an intellectual crisis deeply rooted in the changes in print communications.

The dilemma of the intellectual staring at a kiosk filled with an assortment of inexpensive and entertaining newspapers was by no means restricted to tsarist Russia. On the contrary, because this chapter was written out of the history of prerevolutionary journalism by those such as Miakotin, Russia's newspaper industry of the 1880s has appeared quite different from those in the West.[46] When in 1885 Matthew Arnold labeled as the "new journalism" William Stead's salacious romp through "modern Babylon" to expose the buying and selling of child virgins, he did so while dismissing it as "featherbrained."[47] At first blush the primary issue seems to be sexy detail, which would make Arnold's disdain intellectual snobbery. The debate, however, stretched well beyond the question of what type of reader preferred scandalous reading matter. The language of sensationalism continued to influence how news was received as a text.[48]

There was nothing "featherbrained" about this; when Arnold emphasized the vulgarity of Stead's approach, he was camouflaging "class" behind judgments of "refined" or "course" tastes. In the United States, publishers Joseph Pulitzer and Hearst are most closely identified with what their competition colored "yellow." As Warren Francke has argued, however, "yellow" journalism must be viewed within the larger context

[45] E. A. Dinershtein, *"Fabrikant" chitatelei: A. F. Marks* (Moscow: Kniga, 1986), 38.

[46] For a comparative analysis of this phase in Britain, France, and the United States, see Lee, *Origins of the Popular Press*, 224–33. *Histoire générale* begins the section on "L'apogee de la presse française" in 1880, (vol. 3, chap. 3). See also Amy Kaplan, *The Social Construction of American Realism* (Chicago: University of Chicago Press, 1988), chapter 1.

[47] Matthew Arnold, "Up to Easter," *Nineteenth Century* 21, no. 123 (1887): 638–39.

[48] Edmund Carpenter, "The New Languages," in Alan Casty, ed., *Mass Media and Mass Man* (New York: Holt, Rinehart and Winston, 1968), 35–46.

of the changing newspaper and must be regarded as a continuation of other changes. In the 1880s the changing techniques of reporting, coupled with the growing importance of reporters, greatly enhanced possibilities for sensational license.[49] Pulitzer was then credited with beginning the next new journalism, one which held the accuracy of detail paramount, and the origins of this second "new" journalism in the techniques of the first become readily discernible. Those who separate Pulitzer's influence into two discrete waves, first "yellow" and then "accurate," have underestimated the extent to which they were functions of the same process. Sensationalism threw a splash of yellow on a supremely political issue, hiding from view the agitation brewing among the new readers which was to enter the public sphere of newspaper journalism.

Pulitzer's first newspaper, the *St. Louis Post-Dispatch*, read not unlike *Moskovskii listok*. Major stories included the assassination of President James Garfield and the subsequent execution of his killer, and the tales of how Jesse and Frank James robbed their way through southern Missouri and into American folklore. Headlines read "An Adulterous Pair" and "Does the Rev. Mr. Tudor Tipple?"—showing Pulitzer no less keen than Pastukhov to enter private lives.[50] The Hungarian Pulitzer, a Jewish refugee from the Habsburgs, inspired the slur "yellow journalism" when he moved to New York in 1883 and took his *World* to war with Hearst's *Journal* in the 1890s.[51] His aside that "like everybody else, Matthew [Arnold] buys and reads the newspapers that are racy"[52] reflected an opinion shared by many others that even snobs surrender greedily to piquant prose. This sort of self-defense sidestepped the real issue as nimbly as had Arnold's contemptuous dismissal.

Both the critics of "yellow" journalism and its producers missed the point that the relationship between sensationalism and the class basis of its audience was connected to the growing importance of objective description in the news report. In his biography of circus impresario P. T. Barnum, whose gaudy enterprises raised similar questions of popular tastes and political change, Neil Harris concluded that the showman's life reflected a broadening of the American Revolution under Andrew Jackson to "relocate . . . all authority—social, moral, aesthetic, even reli-

---

[49] Warren Francke, "Sensationalism and the Development of 19th-Century Reporting: The Broom Sweeps Sensory Details," *Journalism History* 12, nos. 3–4 (1985): 80–85.

[50] Quoted from Emery and Emery, *The Press and America*, 4th ed., 221.

[51] The adjective *yellow* applied to journalism as a pejorative for cheap sensationalism derived from the first color comic-strip character, the "Yellow Kid." Begotten by Richard Outcault for Pulitzer's *World* in 1896, the cartoonist and his renowned creation became caught in the war between Pulitzer and Hearst for the most popular newspaper personnel, and the "Yellow Kid" followed the competitive salaries offered to his creator, appearing in both publishers' newspapers for a time.

[52] Quoted in Schudson, *Discovering the News*, 117.

gious—in the hearts and minds of the ordinary citizen."[53] Barnum relied on the popular press to advertise and publicize his numerous extravaganzas, beginning with his arrangement of Jenny Lind's first American tour. More important, though, he depended upon newspapers to alter his audiences' worldviews and expectations. When he showcased midget Tom Thumb or the fraudulent Feejee Mermaid, or paraded Jumbo the Elephant across the Brooklyn Bridge, Barnum made fact indeed stranger than fiction in ways that complemented the works of Bennett and his successors, Pulitzer, Stead, and Pastukhov. Nor was Barnum's clever intuition about the public appetite for the curious limited to post-Jacksonian America. He had no shortage of imitators, and makeshift museums along Nevskii Prospect advertised an enticing variety of freaks in Russian newspapers, just as Pastukhov himself became embroiled in a highly publicized feud with a local circus owner and one of his popular clowns.[54] The feud started when the owner refused to give Pastukhov a good seat. Pastukhov proceeded to write a negative review of the circus, and the clowns then parodied him and *Moskovskii listok*.

The sensational and the absurd astounded, but they also constituted a democratized form of intelligence. Barnum and the boulevard press took knowledge out of the exclusive province of the elites and made it available to all who could move beyond their imaginations to contemplate the escapades of a Churkin or touching an elephant. In so doing, they transferred to ordinary readers the sense of power that comes from access to information about the world, however minimal the comprehensions of the newly exposed. As Roger Chartier has argued, "representations of the social world" must be viewed as "constituents of social reality,"[55] and news is one of the most important means by which society is represented. Moreover, James Carey's observation that "when we grasp the history of journalism, we grasp one form of human imagination . . . in which reality has entered consciousness in an aesthetically satisfying way" captures this affinity between sensational reportage and the audience it beguiled.[56] Arnold and the other critics correctly recognized its importance in attracting readers who might otherwise have ignored the issues altogether through lack of exposure, had they not found themselves drawn to the new journalism.

By 1880, technology had facilitated the spread of information and in-

[53] Neil Harris, *Humbug: The Art of P. T. Barnum* (Chicago: University of Chicago Press, 1973), 3.

[54] Brooks, *When Russia Learned to Read*, 121.

[55] Thomas Childers, "The Social Language of Politics in Germany: The Sociology of Political Discourse in the Weimar Republic," *American Historical Review* 95, no. 2 (1990): 358.

[56] Carey, "Problem of Journalism History," 5.

creased its attractiveness with illustrations; the higher the circulations, the greater the reach of influence. Newspapers could physically relocate a considerable degree of the authority derived from information by taking it away from "thick" journals, and the transfer of authority to which Harris referred had political implications for Russians. In the course of the decade, the drive toward hard news would be more sensational as it also brought in more readers. This would follow the intelligentsia's outburst, and signal their failure.

Fact-mindedness formed the literary foundation of the struggle between the intellectual elite established at "thick" journals and the upstart newspaper reporters. Battle lines were drawn around the nature of news and the relevance of views. Anyone could read and decipher the fact-based report without the need of a third party to decode the message. Newspaper readers denied intellectuals their long-held and supremely politicized function of interpreting events. The daily paper directly confronted the didactic tradition, which had conferred upon the intelligentsia the authority obtained from explaining texts.

The doyen of Russia's intelligentsia, Alexander Herzen, went straight to the heart of the matter when he slighted reporters as "grasshoppers, devouring events before they have time to ripen."[57] He chastised these writers for not allowing for reflective pause, for describing instead of analyzing. The writer who had proclaimed the death of the journal had pointed out that "the journal is an *opinion*, the newspaper a *fact*," with obvious preference for the former. A nostalgic remembrance of the golden age when Belinskii reigned, when "thick" journal writers were "priests of social progress," focused on the changed function of the press and how newspapers demeaned those who communicated through them.[58] Belinskii, after all, "would not have been able to find it in his soul" to write for newspapers.[59] Luminary satirist from *Otechestvennye zapiski* Saltykov-Shchedrin remarked condescendingly that *Russkie vedomosti* was the only newspaper he was not ashamed to read.[60] He regretted that it was a newspaper, not a journal,[61] and those who turned to his "thick" journal for wisdom were his "reader-friends," whereas the consumer of newspapers was discarded as a "reader-simpleton."[62]

N. P. Shelgunov, a "thick" journal publicist who also contributed oc-

[57] Gal-in, "Sredi khronikerov," *Rm*, no. 5 (1913): 19.

[58] *Gazeta i publika* (SPB: n.p., 1902), 13.

[59] Nikolai Engel'gardt, *Ocherk istorii Russkoi tsenzury v sviazi s razvitiem pechati* (SPB: Suvorin, 1904), 369.

[60] "50 let *Russkikh vedomostei*," 10.

[61] P. A. Zaionchkovskii, *The Russian Autocracy under Alexander III*, ed. and trans. David R. Jones (Gulf Breeze, Fla.: Academic International Press, 1976), 161.

[62] N. Valentinov, "Obyvatel' i gazeta," *Kievskaia mysl'*, 10 July 1911, no. 188.

casionally to *Russkie vedomosti*, surveyed the situation in 1895 and announced the battle lost. Accusing the intelligentsia of giving into the apathy and pessimism generated by the counterreforms of Alexander III, Shelgunov chided them for letting the opportunity to take control of editorial offices slip past them. Echoing Herzen's derision of reporters for not digesting facts for readers, Shelgunov argued that the primary weakness of the commercial press was that it provided factual information in place of theoretical interpretations.[63] Publishers who trafficked in the bare facts obviously had no personal philosophies; Shelgunov rebuked Suvorin and others for giving into public opinion instead of directing it: "The reader does not need facts, but a crystal ball to explain them. . . . the reader needs ideas."[64] However correct his accusations of anomie among the intellectuals, he strayed off the mark when he argued that the growing appeal of objectivity could have been contained. Moreover, with Herzen he presaged the Marxist attack on the journalistic notion that "objective" can be equated with "politically neutral."[65]

Like Miakotin, Shelgunov could have learned from reading the works of Suvorin's latest hire at *Novoe vremia*, Anton Chekhov. Trained as a medical doctor, Chekhov was comfortable with the obligation to describe and did not feel the need to explain. Preferring the facticity associated with newspapers to the didactic tradition inherited from Belinskii, he responded to his critics: "You criticize me for objectivity, calling it indifference to good and evil, lack of ideals, etc. You desire me, in depicting horse thieves to say: horse-stealing is an evil. But this has been known for a long time without me. Let juries judge horse thieves. My job is only to show what kind of people they are."[66] Acclaimed for his realistic portrayals of Russia's fluctuating social hierarchy at century's end, he composed these caricatures in the language of the times.

The line between fact and fiction, directly related to that between didacticism and objectivity, began to be obscured as the 1880s drew to a close.[67] Where Nedolin had professed his feuilleton a "story" in 1864,

[63] Moran, in *Century of Words*, found German intellectuals equally bothered by "perfidious neutrality" (275).

[64] N. V. Shelgunov, "Gazetnyi opportunizm i ideinost'," *Ocherki russkoi zhizni* (SPB: n.p., 1895), 883–903.

[65] Walter Benjamin, "Karl Krauss," in Peter Demetz, ed., *Reflections*, trans. Edmund Jephott, (New York: Harcourt Brace Jovanovich, 1986), 249; Stuart Hall, "The Determination of News Photographs," *Working Papers in Cultural Studies*, no. 3 (1972): 84; and Terdiman, *Discourse/Counter-Discourse*, 131.

[66] Quoted in Richard Pipes, *Russia under the Old Regime* (New York: Macmillan, 1974), 280.

[67] Emery and Emery, in *The Press and America*, 6th ed. (217), analyzed the rise of "objective" reports, showing that between 1864 and 1874 one third of news reporting met "objective" criteria, a percentage that had climbed to two thirds by 1905–1915.

twenty years later Pazukhin identified an analogous story as "fact." Recounting the sad tale of a husband who had killed his servant, whom he mistook to be molesting his wife, Pazukhin felt no more need than Chekhov to add a sermonizing postscript.[68] His obligation to readers had already been fulfilled. Facticity had replaced didacticism; the report had replaced the interpretation.

Facticity and objectivity also had moral authority. Like sensationalism, the moral component of the competition over control of communications obscured the class bias. Pioneer Bennett had paid first for introducing a socially provocative medium that upended traditional print communications. The publishers of the Wall Street papers targeted his *Herald* for a "Moral War" in 1840 in an attack that previewed Arnold's. Intimidating Bennett's advertisers and rebuking his editorial philosophies, the organized publishers declared Bennett's "dirty sheet . . . off-limits to self-respecting men and women." Successful enough to lose Bennett more than two thousand of seventeen thousand subscribers for several years, the battle was staged over rightful control of communications. As Schudson has cogently argued, this war was "not so much business competition as deadly serious social conflict, a class conflict in which [the Wall Street publishers] were on the defensive against a new way of being in the world which we awkwardly summarize as 'middle class.' "[69] Stead's expedition in search of a virgin likewise lost him financial support from shocked advertisers who declared an analogous moral war.[70] Russia's literary elite found inadvertent common cause with censors in their class-based misgivings about the new newspapers, and left it to the latter to shut down Pastukhov's indulgences.

Moral authority was at stake because it was closely connected to the politics of interpretation, although this was not how the aggressors justified their attacks. The sensational contents of the petty press, with its roots planted deeply in the cautionary tales of the premodern era, reflected the new morality of fact-mindedness. Recent studies of England's and France's newsbooks and news ballads, forerunners of the popular yellow press, have demonstrated that the writers' listing of bloody details was of secondary importance to the morals they intended for readers to draw.[71] As Mitchell Stephens has argued, "Sometimes the presentation of a news story was simply interrupted for some undisguised preach-

---

[68] A. Pazukhin, "Rokovaia oshibka," *Ml*, 2 Jan. 1887, no. 2.

[69] Schudson, *Discovering the News*, 55–57.

[70] Brown, *Victorian News and Newspapers*, 23.

[71] Mitchell Stephens, "Sensationalism and Moralizing in 16th and 17th-Century Newsbooks and News Ballads," *Journalism History* 12, nos. 2–3 (1985): 92–95; and Robert Darnton, *The Literary Underground of the Old Regime* (Cambridge, Mass.: Harvard University Press, 1982).

ing."[72] Although a message could still be read into such stories as the case of the clerk Robinson accused of murdering the prostitute Jewett and Stead's "Maiden Tribute," the incidents themselves were unlikely to be related as scenes from a morality play. *Moskovskii listok*, for example, provided a factual rendering of the highwayman's victims without further comment.

The disappearance of the sermon did not herald an end to morality in journalism. On the contrary, the rise of objective reporting required acceptance of facts on ethical, not just intellectual, grounds because reporters of this era "understood facts to provide moral direction."[73] Nemirovich-Danchenko had argued for objectivity in his war correspondence, and he explicitly intended it to have a moral complexion. His opinions about journalistic responsibility came from the same store as Belinskii's, albeit from a different shelf. Nemirovich-Danchenko believed writers had a sacred duty to society, but saw that their service should remain objective. Fifty years earlier Belinskii had charged that such detachment was immoral. Nemirovich-Danchenko, on the other hand, rejected efforts to categorize him within one of the "politically defined camps," but he felt a strong moral underpinning to his objective reporting.[74] Nemirovich-Danchenko considered it his duty to make facts available to readers; he connected objectivity to morality and spoke in favor of democratizing knowledge.

The Triumph of the New Journalism

By the 1900s Pulitzer had become a paragon among newspaper journalists because of his relentless pursuit of a good story, precise detail, and commitment to standards of truthful and objective reporting. He had taken off the gloves and stepped out of Hearst's ring, but his *World* was still printing much that would have been deemed "yellow" in an earlier time. After 1900 both Pulitzer and Pastukhov claimed that they had resorted to sensationalism at the start to attract attention, and then subtly improved the qualities of offerings once readers had swallowed the yellow hook, but the contents of their papers suggest that the publishers overstated their enlightened editorial practices.[75] To be fair, by the end of the century readers found more religion than gossip in *Moskovskii listok*, and Pulitzer's *World* was a calmer place in which to live, but jour-

[72] Stephens, "Sensationalism and Moralizing," 93.
[73] Schudson, *Discovering the News*, 87.
[74] Interview in *Bv*, 10 May 1903, no. 228.
[75] Emery and Emery, *The Press and America*, 6th ed., 209; supplement to *Ml*, 1 Aug. 1906, no. 29.

nalism still bore the effects of their initial experimentation. The dictum that hung in Pulitzer's newsroom—"Accuracy! Accuracy! Accuracy!"— had redeemed him in the minds of many who sat on high in judgment of mass-circulation journalism.

One fundamental reason for the changing stylistics of communications lay in the importance of commercial factors and the marketplace in determining who read what; let it not be forgotten that Pastukhov and Pulitzer amassed impressive personal fortunes. The Russian intelligentsia distrusted the intrusion of earned income into print communications, never having put to rest their antipathies toward Kraevskii. The writer who announced the newspaper's slaying of the journal saw it as a victory of commerce over literature; allowing that moral or serious readers would not read commercial newspapers, he worried about what their mass-circulations said about societies.[76]

The successful challenge to journalistic tradition launched by the Pulitzers, Steads, and Pastukhovs reflected the collective stamina of the consuming classes that formed the basis of the new readership. Accepting the new journalism required acquiescence to commerce as a determining factor in journalism. Writing on the French press, Theodore Zeldin pointed out that "by the twentieth century . . . the power of journalism had become too obvious for these moral doubts to matter too much, just as the *nouveau riche* financier was eventually welcomed into the aristocratic society that had once disdained him."[77] The same held true in Russia's newspaper industry. The two—reporter and financier—were part of the same social transformation read in the new journalism of the 1880s. The beliefs in both facticity and commercialism at the end of the nineteenth century were connected by the common faith that the new way of reading, like the new way of living, revealed progress, improvement over the past and into the future.

Like the Russian intelligentsia, Western political parties lost their domination over print to the forces of commerce. In his study of the growth of a popular press in England between the repeal of the Stamp Act in 1855 and the onset of World War I, Alan J. Lee focused on the growing capitalization of newspapers, the replacement of politics with commerce in the basis of publishing. Elaborating on the competition in England between the old journalism and the new, the political and the consumer-oriented, Lee gave considerable attention to the disillusionment among Liberals when the beneficiaries of their social legislation did

[76] Quoted in S. P. Melgunov, *O sovremennykh literaturnykh nravakh* (Petrograd: n.p., 1916), 4; and V. P. Berezina, N. P. Emel'ianov, N. I. Sokolov, and N. I. Totubalin, eds., *Ocherki po istorii russkoi zhurnalistiki i kritiki*, 2 vols. (Leningrad: LGU, 1965), 2:450.

[77] Zeldin, *France, 1848–1945* 2:506.

not turn to their political press for guidance.[78] Instead, the new audience preferred the trivia churned out by the likes of Harmsworth.

Just as Harmsworth's fare fed those left hungry by the political press, Pastukhov provided for Muscovites indifferent to Katkov's or "the professors' " soapboxes. He suffered excessive opprobrium for recognizing the new audience and catering to it, but the typical vituperation that "every drunk had to have his issue of *Moskovskii listok*" showed a tinge of wishful thinking about who actually read his news sheet.[79] There may well have been thirty thousand alcoholics in Moscow in the 1880s, but there were not many who were also literate and could afford the paper. Miakotin's failure to mention Pastukhov as an important figure in journalism in the 1880s suggests an adaptation of tsarist policy toward journalism: if it does not get mentioned in print, it did not happen. Returning the Muscovite publisher to his rightful place in Russian history restores as well a missing piece in the puzzle that pictures tsarist Russia's middle classes: consuming, curious, nationalistic, boasting the time and money for both useful information and escapist entertainment, and enjoying more opportunities to determine the course of their own lives. In the following chapter I describe how this new journalism spread its roots throughout society, affecting the conduct of politics, abetting the growth of commerce, suggesting new ways of looking at the world, and in general assuming a principal role in the process of bringing Russia's Old Regime into the modern world.

[78] Lee, *Origins of the Popular Press*, especially chapters 4 and 7.
[79] I. A. Volkov, *Dvadtsat' let po gazetnomu moriu* (Ivanovo Voznesensk: n.p., 1925), 69.

6

The Grounding of a Public Institution in the 1890s

IN THE LAST two decades of the nineteenth century, the cumulative effects of the Industrial Revolution were clearly recognizable in a variety of changes in newspaper journalism. Circulations everywhere continued to climb, while publishers took advantage of technological opportunities that allowed them to adapt contents to the differing tastes of their increasingly heterogeneous audiences, as well as to distribute their papers more quickly and more widely. As Russia underwent rapid industrialization in the 1890s, its mass-circulation press registered the social and political repercussions of the transformation. Enlarging the space within which public opinion could maneuver and diversifying the constituents of that public which took shape, the daily paper extended its role in the conduct of politics. My purpose in this chapter is to integrate the new journalism of developing industrialism with the new politics that emerged from the adjustments that political systems made to the continual expansion of this public space. Although it is premature to consider Russia as developed industrially, not to mention politically, the innovations in its mass-circulation press followed patterns similar to those established elsewhere by popular commercial newspapers.

What constituted this so-called new politics, and how did it tie in directly with newspaper journalism? In the West, the broadening base of the electorate corresponded to the rising numbers of newspaper readers, and in both cases "mass" cut across demographic categories.[1] This translated politically into greater competition in the preparation of the political agenda. Western political parties sensed the developing relationship between the new politics and the new journalism, wrestling with what appeared to many contemporaneous observers to be a discouraging anomaly: increasing the electorate had been followed by a decrease in circulations of partisanal periodicals, which suggested that the new reader/voter had less than the anticipated interest in politics. England's Liberals were scarcely the only disappointed group who had to learn how to reach the masses through the media of the latter's choosing; in the United States, the mass-circulation newspapers were accused of "taking

[1] David Paul Nord, *Newspapers and New Politics* (Ann Arbor, Mich.: UMI Research Press, 1981); Lee, *Origins of the Popular Press*, especially chapter 5; and Bellanger et al., *Histoire générale*, vol. 3, chapter 3.

the politics out of politics."[2] What these papers did, however, was edit political discourse as they transformed how it was communicated. As Alan J. Lee has argued, "Until the 1880s the universe of political discourse was tolerably well-known and understood, its vocabulary and conceptual store were common change. The widening of the electorate and of newspaper readership meant that this helpful symmetry no longer obtained."[3]

David Paul Nord, exploring how communications affects both the content and formation of political debates, has laid important groundwork for the analysis presented in this chapter. Looking at the role of the new journalism in the development of progressivism, Nord found in it the "origin of modern political communication."[4] He rests his central argument on the theory that readers accepted newspapers for one of the same important reasons that they did political parties: both mediated between them and the public forces that affected their private lives. Shifting the focus away from organized parties and onto communications, the Russian example can inform subsequent debates about the relationship between information and agenda-setting. The point stretches, for example, but does not break, that Russian censors had counterparts in smoke-filled backrooms filled with party bosses deciding who would run and on what platform.

Viewed optimistically, this was a time in which readers demonstrated a growing sense of individualism by exercising their freedom of choice, of which selecting which newspaper to read was a small but representative example. It was also a time to celebrate modernization, and the daily newspaper was one of the best-kept promises of industrialization. Such antics as the contest to beat Jules Verne's fictional circling of the world in fewer than eighty days, a self-promoting gimmick used by both French and American newspapers, applauded the limitless possibilities of the new age.[5] The reporters racing around the globe personified the newspaper's conquest of time and space in the name of their audiences.

The calm before the storm unleashed in July 1914 permitted the flowering of a progressive and sanguine mass-circulation press. On the Continent, this was "La Belle Epoque," and the French press reached its apogee, with circulations stretching laterally as well as vertically: Jean Dupuy's tabloid *Le Petit Parisien* became in 1902 the world's first news-

[2] Nord, *Newspapers and New Politics*, 5.

[3] Lee, *Origins of the Popular Press*, 212.

[4] Nord, *Newspapers and New Politics*, 3.

[5] Gaston Stiegler of Paris's *Le Matin* beat the rest with his time of sixty-three days and thirteen hours in 1901. Nellie Bly was the fastest American, circling the globe for Pultizer's *World* in seventy-two days in 1889. Emery and Emery, *The Press and America*, 4th ed., 225; Bellanger et al., *Histoire générale* 3:300.

paper to reach the benchmark of one million subscribers, circulating more in the provinces than in Paris.[6] The United States recorded this as its "Gilded Age," and heralded newspapers as "the people's champions" because they assumed political postures that made them instruments of progressivism.[7] The end of Britain's Victorian epoch witnessed the "Northcliffe Revolution," named for the publisher who "exploited the thirst for knowledge and entertainment among women, the newly literate, and those acquiring leisure,"[8] that is, the previously marginal groups now entering journalism's mainstream.

In Russia, this era included the counterreformation of Alexander III and the first decade of the rule of his weak-willed son, Nicholas II. Traditionally, this era was identified by the generation of "doers of small deeds," referring to the social reformers who, discouraged by the persistence of reactionary tsars, decided that change could be achieved only gradually, through the accumulation of piecemeal personal efforts. Paradoxically, it was also a time of protracted economic and industrial growth that could not be confined by gradualism. The newspaper journalism of the age enlivens this latter image, depicting the development of an assortment of channels for taking action, based in part on public opinion and complementing those official policies that called for progressive change.

Industrialization boosted Russian confidence and made urban society resemble increasingly its Western counterparts. The journalism of the urban industrial boom mirrored the development of a pluralism of interest groups. Firmly established, pluralism works as a kind of social cement that develops from tolerance of differences, and its effectiveness at keeping disparate social and interest groups functioning both autonomously and for the shared general culture serves as an indicator of modernization; like the newspapers, pluralism both signifies and measures this process. Such visible socioeconomic similarities as a wide variety of commercial newspapers made the political differences between autocratic Russia and the democratic West loom even larger.

To explore the interaction of journalism and politics and what it meant to the development of pluralism in late imperial Russia, I have arranged this chapter into three separate sections, each of which presents one aspect of how developments in newspaper journalism figured into other changes sweeping through Russian society. The first relates how *Birzhevye vedomosti*, the best-selling newspaper in the empire by 1900 with its circulation of one hundred thousand, represented the relationship be-

[6] Bellanger et al., *Histoire générale* 3:239–405; *Petit parisien*, 304–8.

[7] Emery and Emery, *The Press and America*, 6th ed., chapter 10.

[8] Colin Seymour-Ure, *The Press, Politics and the Public* (London: Methuen, 1968), 22.

tween the new journalism and the new politics in the Russian setting. The second part introduces two important newspapers published only during this era. In the concluding section, I discuss the kinds of organizational changes that the newspapers underwent as competition among them heated up; and I contrast the different newspapers' coverage of the same stories in order to illustrate specifically how the newspapers reflected the growing pluralism.

Birzhevye vedomosti: The New Press and the New Politics

Even before the archreactionary minister of internal affairs Tolstoi had harassed Kraevskii out of business in 1883, a potential publishing rival had appeared quietly in St. Petersburg, S. M. Propper. The Jewish emigrant, who purchased *Birzhevye vedomosti* from financier and publisher Trubnikov in 1880, gradually assumed Kraevskii's place in offering a nationally circulated newspaper with a liberal editorial slant. The timing of *Golos's* closing, however, explained only one aspect of how Propper replaced Kraevskii. Differences between *Golos* and *Birzhevye vedomosti* balanced likenesses; Propper compared best with Kraevskii as a publisher with the shrewdness to foresee the future of communications and to adapt his newspaper in such a way that it would take part in the changes as it recorded them. Propper's purchase predated by three years that of journalism's other renowned Jewish expatriate from the Hapsburgs: Pulitzer bought his *World* from railroad tycoon Jay Gould, who, like Trubnikov, appreciated the power of the press but lacked the skill to utilize it effectively.

Another figure appeared in St. Petersburg in the 1880s, one who would find his career closely intertwined with Propper's during what were for both their formative years: S. Iu. Witte. The association between the two introduced a new relationship between the government and the mass-circulation press, one indebted to both men's ambitions for industrialization. Tsarist Russia's most imposing minister of finance, architect of the economic system that made possible rapid industrialization, and builder of the metaphoric national artery, the Trans-Siberian Railroad, Witte valued even the most subtle capabilities of mass communications. His career on the railroad began in a ticketing office in Odessa, and he moonlighted as a correspondent for one of the local papers. "The press," he was arguing when others in government were regarding it as at best a nuisance, "is a powerful force with which the whole world must reckon!" Under the pen name "The Green Parrot," he entertained as a feuilletonist in the port city, developing a rapport with reporters that served him well all his life. His congenial relations with journalists landed several of them desired posts in government, and he also had a reputation for coming to the aid of friends on poor terms with censors. Equally important, the practice of writing for newspapers taught Witte how to express complex economic ideas in language nonspecialists could understand, and this helped him to enlist public support for his ambitious projects.[9]

Journalists' memoirs refer to the common knowledge that Propper and Witte maintained professional ties, but the two left skimpy details in their own writings about their association.[10] In concrete terms, Witte would intervene with censors on Propper's behalf, although the calculating publisher kept up a second front, for example, by hiring chief censor M. P. Solov'ev's son as a music critic and remembering the censor's wife on holidays.[11] Witte preferred a strictly business relationship. The minister procured permission in 1893 for Propper to produce a second, provincial edition of *Birzhevye vedomosti*, which gave him the necessary reach to become a major publisher. Witte did not write for *Birzhevye vedomosti*, but he sometimes gave Propper copies of his speeches delivered *in camera* to the State Council, which frustrated censors as well as competitive publishers.[12] Propper's ringing endorsement of Witte explained in part the ministerial patronage. Witte's appointment to head the Ministry of Communications in February 1892 in order to oversee construction of the Trans-Siberian inspired an editorial only in *Birzhevye vedomosti*. The delighted Propper bubbled that "there has never been an official appointment that has created such a sensation or been accompanied by such high hopes . . . hopes based on the personality of the new minister."[13]

The Trans-Siberian, which would require considerable outlays from a nation with precious few rubles for investment and critical deficiencies in its social services, had its opponents. Propper, however, conceded no legitimate point of contention. Even a superficial comparison of *Birzhevye vedomosti* with St. Petersburg's other newspapers shows Propper's paper to be the best source of information, overwhelmingly positive, on the capabilities of the Trans-Siberian. Protesting that money should not be an issue, Propper called it "a great cultural undertaking for

[9] A. E. Kaufman, "Cherti iz zhizni S. Iu. Witte," *Iv* 140 (1915): 220–31; Theodore H. Von Laue, *Sergei Witte and the Industrialization of Russia* (New York: Atheneum, 1973), 36–70, 117; and B. A. Anan'ich and R. S. Ganelin, "I. A. Vyshnegradskii i S. Iu. Witte—korrespondenty *Moskovskie vedomosti*," in N. G. Sladkevich, ed., *Problemy obshchestvennoi mysly i ekonomicheskaia politika XIX–XX vekov* (Leningrad: Izdatel'stvo LGU, 1972), 12–34.

[10] A. E. Kaufman, "Iz zhurnal'nykh vospominanii," *Iv* 130, no. 12 (1912): 1067–78.

[11] I. I. Iasinskii, "Moi tsenzora," *Iv* 126, no. 2 (1911): 533–57.

[12] Kaufman, "Iz zhurnal'nykh vospominanii," no. 12, 1071.

[13] *Bv*, 18 Feb. 1892, no. 48.

all Russia": "We do not ask what income we earn from our courts, from our administration, from our schools . . . we do not ask if the sums spent on these would be better spent on the military . . . because we know that they are contributing to the benefit and prosperity of Russia."[14] The new minister made even the human interest section of Propper's paper when a group of his former subordinates gave him a commemorative photo album.[15] Six months after being named to transportation Witte was promoted, and Propper spoke glowingly of the energy now radiating from the Ministry of Finance.[16]

In addition to their consensus on the railroad, the protective tariff, and industrialization in general, Witte enlisted Propper in his bid to create a governmental monopoly on the sale of alcohol. Criticism surrounded this policy because it would add to official coffers at the moral expense of the drunken poor. In 1895, Witte set up experimental monopolistic operations in selected provinces. Five years later, Propper furnished the minister's cause with a survey conducted among the populace of several of the target sites, all of which registered enthusiastic response to Witte's scheme. Published in part in *Birzhevye vedomosti* and as a separate monograph, Propper's poll lacked the scientific basis of random sampling or calculations of margins of error, but he had the more useful documentation provided by quotes, for example, as in one respondent's proposal to erect a statue of Witte in thanks for his contribution to the war on alcoholism.[17] Propper's social conscience did not, however, prevent him from accepting advertisements for liquor.

Publishing and politics have long made natural bedfellows, and the coming together of Propper and Witte signified that politics in Russia was being conducted at a different level than previously under Tolstoi's heavy hand. Where publicists ruled at periodicals, such as Katkov at *Moskovskie vedomosti* or even Meshcherskii at *Grazhdanin*, there was no occupational distinction. But nor did the politician-*cum*-publisher have to mediate between public and government in the same way that editors of independent papers had to both maintain credibility with a sizeable readership and keep censors at bay. The ethos of public service and potential for influence intrinsic to both journalism and politics has customarily carried publishers outside their newsrooms, and the Russians duplicated in their fashion Western publishers who ran for elective office.[18] Like Khu-

[14] *Bv*, 25 Jan. 1891, no. 25.

[15] *Bv*, 17 July 1892, no. 195.

[16] *Bv*, 4 Sept. 1892, no. 243.

[17] *Kazennaia prodazha pitei i obshchestvennoe mnenie. Issledovanie S. M. Proppera.* (SPB: Izdanie *Birzhevikh vedomostei*, 1900).

[18] Emile de Girardin served in Parliament under various governments, although the desired ministerial portfolio always eluded him. Harmsworth lost his election to the House of

dekov, for example, Kraevskii remained active in city politics, serving on the committee to improve public education until the end of his life, and many of their colleagues followed in their footsteps. (Suvorin recorded in his diary that Kraevskii, a notorious ladies' man, was rumored to have used his position on the school board to secure teaching jobs for young women whom he later "defiled.")[19]

The currying of favors between Witte and Propper, in a context in which neither could be elected to office but together they could serve their own and national interests, gave essence to Russia's variant of the new politics because it symbolized the correlation between the spread of information and the broadening base of politics. Although it is premature to discuss a mass readership in Russia comparable to the audience for the most popular Western newspapers, Witte turned to Propper because he believed that policies should not be implemented in isolation. Nor was Propper the sole publisher with newly cordial relationships at the top; Suvorin left behind scattered pages from a diary whose entries reveal that his readership gave him Witte's ear, if not necessarily the minister's backing, because the latter's economic schemes were not always welcomed in *Novoe vremia*. Suvorin depended upon other patrons, such as future prime minister Ivan Goremykin, to serve as exclusive sources of news and to protect his interests when he ruffled censors' feathers.[20]

Witte also turned to other media besides Russian publishers. For example, he was instrumental in arguing for the tsarist government to establish a telegraph news agency that would free Russia from the imperialistic Wolff Bureau, and he opened a slush fund for corrupt French editors when he was trying to attract investment capital.[21] Ironically, his ideas about mass communications undermined the authority upon which his own power ultimately rested. Working through the alternative political channels, circumventing the established ones, he undermined the autocracy by appealing to a public opinion that would, so encouraged, want its own say. Whatever his feelings for the ineffectual Nicholas II, Witte never seriously entertained the idea of replacing his autocratic prerogatives with electoral politics; what the minister wanted was unrestricted access to the tsar's ear, and he believed that a show of public

---

Commons in 1894, but entered Parliament as Lord Northcliffe in 1905. Also unsuccessful at the ballot box, Horace Greeley received the presidential nomination in 1872 from both Democrats and liberal Republicans disgusted by the corruption of President Ulysses S. Grant's administration, running on the Mugwump ticket. No American tried harder than William Randolph Hearst to use his or her newspaper as a catapult to the White House; unable to grasp the brass ring, Hearst nonetheless managed to serve two terms in Congress.

[19] *Dnevnik Suvorina*, 216.

[20] Ibid., 24, 39, 79, 88.

[21] McReynolds, "Autocratic Journalism," 48–49.

support for his plans would help his enterprise.[22] His attitude toward mass communications showed how keenly he understood the mechanisms of informing, just as his desire for control of those communications revealed his taste for power without institutional checks.

Witte fell at odds with Propper when the latter tried to change the nature of their relationship and hold Witte accountable to the public through the newspaper. The minister would not accept that this was the logical culmination of his policies. Just after the 1905 Revolution Propper insisted that Witte, newly appointed as Russia's first prime minister, respond to the demands of assembled publishers, and the minister dismissed the publisher as "impertinent."[23] The calling of the press conference itself had chalked a high water mark in the development of the new politics in Russia, although it also revealed to Witte the frustrating limits on his ability to manipulate. However clearly the minister saw into the future, he still could not extricate himself completely from traditional political discourse. Like the contemptible Nicholas, Witte opted to ignore a public opinion whose declared independence of him intrinsically set it in competition with him. As prime minister during the first few months of 1906 he repudiated the principle of working with a successful independent publisher and produced *Russkoe gosudarstvo* (*The Russian State*), a daily intended to get his message to "one reader alone—his Majesty."[24]

The alliance forged between Propper and Witte marked a transformation of relations between journalists and officials based on commonalities of interest and purpose. If the officials still had the upper hand with regard to making decisions, the journalists had gained significant leverage by virtue of their access to the views of the reading public. But the affiliation between press and government explains only in part the far-reaching consequences of both the new journalism and the new politics. Interactions among the newspapers themselves, increasing in variety and circulation, established the daily newspaper as an institution explicitly "public" because it spoke on the general welfare in so many voices.

New Newspapers, New Audiences

The kind of competition that integrated the many papers into the one convention of the daily newspaper began with Suvorin and the way in which he struggled with Kraevskii. Editorial rivalry predated the mass-

[22] Daniel Turnball, "The Defeat of Popular Representation, December 1904: Prince Mirskii, Witte, and the Imperial Family," *Slavic Review* 48, no. 1 (1989): 54–70.

[23] S. Iu. Witte, *Vospominaniia*, 3 vols. (Moscow: Izd. sotsialno-ekonomicheskoi literatury, 1960), 3:60–64.

[24] Ruud, *Fighting Words*, 224.

circulation press, but the addition of commercialism to newspaper publishing had altered the stakes. Katkov and Korsh, with Kraevskii still playing by some of the old rules while writing some of the new, waged their contest by speaking for the most influential circles at court and in society. Certainly *Novoe vremia* cut a distinct political profile, but it also provided superior news coverage on national and international issues. The more populous the audience, the greater the potential to influence worldviews by informing. To a considerable degree, the publicist-publishers were speaking to the already converted. Suvorin, following Kraevskii's initiative, had seen the possibilities for doing the converting himself. Other publishers followed suit.

In addition to *Birzhevye vedomosti*, two other major newspapers appeared in St. Petersburg and enjoyed sizeable circulations during the industrial boom. The papers were more polemical than Propper's, neither was as popular, and censors quickly ended their publication. Of the numerous dailies that sprouted and died for whatever reason in the national capital during this time, the histories of *Novosti* (*News*) and *Rossiia* (*Russia*) warrant special attention because of the relative importance of their publishers and readerships.

The first, O. K. Notovich's *Novosti dnia i birzhevaia gazeta* (*News of the Day and the Stock-Market Gazette*), known simply by the shorthand *Novosti*, never achieved the prominence of a *Novoe vremia*, but many of the most important journalists passed through its doors at some point. Despite his ultimate failure, the publisher's struggles paint a vivid picture of the world of journalism. The son of a rabbi from Kerch, Notovich's early pursuits read like so many others. Beginning at *Novoe vremia* early in the 1870s when it was still one of Trubnikov's financial papers, he soon united with L. M. L'vov to assume editorial management of *Novosti dnia*, a St. Petersburg daily founded in 1871 by newly crowned "King of Reporters" Iu. O. Shreier.

The paper's liberal editorial orientation made it competitive with *Birzhevye vedomosti*, and familiar contributors included Leskov, Afanas'ev of *Peterburgskii listok*, and A. M. Skabichevskii, whose name often appeared in the popular press. Editorially the paper slanted westward: Bobrykin provided middlebrow entertainment, liberal publicist K. D. Kavelin wrote numerous lead articles, V. V. Stasov of *Vestnik evropy* served as arts critic, and Gradovskii joined the staff after *Golos* closed. The young D. N. Mamin-Sibiriak got his start in writing at *Novosti*, and recaptured some of Shreier's weight in journalistic circles in his quasi-autobiographical *Scenes from Pepko's Life*.[25]

[25] I. A. Dergachev, *Knigi iz sud'bi. Stranitsy literaturnoi zhizni Urala* (Sverdlovsk: Sredne-uralskoe knizhnoe izdatel'stvo, 1973), 56–74.

In 1880, Notovich took over as sole publisher and merged the paper with yet another of Trubnikov's failing ventures, *Birzhevaia gazeta*, with which he formed a publishing joint-stock company.[26] The competition paid enough attention to the paper to mock it. A sarcastic joke in *Peterburgskaia gazeta* profiled Notovich's paper well: "They say that people of great *weight* write for *Novosti*, which explains why the articles are so *heavy!*"[27] The anti-Semitic Suvorin referred to *Novosti* repeatedly as a "synagogue," and in its pages Suvorin was a "Pharisee." When the conflict between these two publishers intensified, however, Notovich once lost his sense of humor and fined a reporter for mentioning *Novoe vremia* in print.[28] Suvorin also tried to use his influence to get censors to crack down on the "*zhid.*"[29] A pundit referred to Suvorin and Notovich as the Montagues and Capulets, but no children would unite the feuding families through love.[30]

Novosti's circulation of twenty-thousand readers fell far short of *Novoe vremia*'s and *Birzhevye vedomosti*'s, which tripled and quintupled, respectively, that figure. Notovich could not maintain a consistent editorial policy. He used serialized sensational novels to complement his serious news and progressive editorials, aiming for the readers between *Birzhevye vedomosti* and *Peterburgskaia gazeta*. Future populist V. G. Korolenko, who copyedited *Novosti* for a short while in the 1870s, drew a less flattering picture than Mamin-Sibiriak's portrait of influence. Fortunately for Notovich, Korolenko never finished his piece, so it remains unpublished, but the writer left other testimonies of his annoyance at the publisher's excessive frugality and pandering to street traffic (the paper went so far as to reprint ads from other newspapers to make the languishing *Novosti* appear prosperous).[31] Others suggested that collisions with censors early in his career made Notovich editorially gun-shy, so he avoided controversies on which his prospective audience wanted him to take a stand. Notovich has more generously been credited as the first in Russia to make wide use of the interview, a journalistic technique only then coming into vogue in the West.[32] During the 1905 Revolution he printed the infamous "financial manifesto" of the St. Petersburg Soviet in *Novosti*, which resulted in the closing of his paper and a warrant for his arrest. Notovich died of stomach cancer in Parisian exile in 1914, remem-

[26] Zapadov, *Istoriia russkoi zhurnalistiki*, 490.

[27] *Pg*, 25 Jan. 1887, no. 24.

[28] Kaufman, "Iz zhurnal'nykh vospominanii," no. 10, 142.

[29] *Dnevnik Suvorina*, 119.

[30] Temtovich, "Literaturnye zametki," *Nizhegorodskii listok*, 1 Feb. 1903, no. 31.

[31] V. G. Korolenko, *Istoriia moego sovremennika*, 4 vols. (Moscow: Pravda, 1985), 2:547–51. The unfinished satire, "Istoriia odnoi gazety," lies in the ROBL, f. 135, no. 8.458.

[32] Zapadov, *Istoriia russkoi zhurnalistiki*, 490.

bered by his colleagues better for his flashes of liberalism than for any major journalistic contributions.[33]

The second newspaper, *Rossiia*, had a much briefer but also more distinguished record than *Novosti*. The rise and fall of this short-lived daily, published from 1899 until January of 1902, delineated Russia's singular blend of ambitious newspaper personalities and autocratic politics. Technically, the censors closed *Rossiia*, but only after one of the coeditors, A. V. Amfiteatrov, had provoked them.

Amfiteatrov, a priest's son who had originally pursued a law degree, had the schizophrenic career of a Russian *intelligent* unable to decide where he belonged when so much fell into flux at the end of the Old Regime. Doroshevich knew Amfiteatrov from their days together in Odessa, where the latter had, like many an oppositional journalist, gone to cool his heels, evading the censors in the national capital. Amfiteatrov had begun in newspaper journalism as a student correspondent in Italy for *Russkie vedomosti*, but had made his mark as "Old Gentleman" (*sic*) at *Novoe vremia*; Suvorin's paper offered too much exposure, and presumably too much pay, for its publisher's politics to be dismissed lightly. Moreover, for all his political liberalism, Amfiteatrov had a decided streak of anti-Semitism.[34] But in 1905, Amfiteatrov ended up with Notovich in exile in Paris, publishing the radical antiautocratic *Krasnoe znamia* (*The Red Banner*). Returning to Russia several years later, he continued to straddle journalism's political fence.[35]

He was joined on *Rossiia*'s editorial board by Doroshevich, now well established as a popular and important writer, and former populist G. P. Sazonov. Their combined efforts were hoped to succeed where Notovich had not. Businessman M. O. Al'bert invested a quarter of a million rubles in their enterprise, paying generously for the reputations of his editors because he wanted the status of a Propper or Suvorin.[36] "Old Gentleman" reappeared in the national capital, Doroshevich wrote on the courts and the social ills that lent themselves best to his style, and Sazonov's presence assured notice from the intelligentsia. Shady nobility in faraway places did not find their escapades serialized beneath *Rossiia*'s fold; rather, H. G. Wells appeared in translation in the glossy weekly supplement. Nemirovich-Danchenko published travelogues, and the paper quickly sprouted a network of national and international correspondents

[33] Notovich's obituaries in *Rm*, no. 3 (1914): 51; *Iv* 136, no. 2 (1914): 216–21; and Zapadov, *Istoriia russkoi zhurnalistiki*, 490.

[34] See, for example, his descriptions of Russia's "cowardly" and "greedy" Jews in *Strana razbora. Balkanskie vpechatleniia*, 2d ed. (SPB: Obshchestvennaia pol'za, 1907), 49.

[35] *Kratkaia literaturnaia entsiklopediia* (Moscow: Sovetskaia entsiklopedia, 1967), 1:189–90.

[36] Bokhanov, *Burzhuaznaia pressa*, 71–74.

that included such outstanding occasional contributors as chemist D. I. Mendeleev and artists I. E. Repin and V. V. Vereshchagin. Within two years *Rossiia*'s circulation had reached forty thousand, with more than one fourth going to the provinces. Even Suvorin admitted, if only to himself, that "there's something free and honest about *Rossiia* . . . next to it, *Novoe vremia* seems gray."[37]

The editorial trio put themselves immediately at the forefront of liberal reform. An editorial commemorating the fortieth anniversary of radical critic N. A. Dobroliubov's death inspired a nostalgia for the 1860s with the reminder that "his courageous and energetic call to social work is still, and always will be, imperative to us."[38] Sazonov's influence surfaced in support for the maintenance of the *obshchina*, the rural peasant communal organization, and his argument that the peasantry should own their land collectively complemented certain fears of Doroshevich's about Russians' rejecting their own heritage in favor of slavish imitation of the West.[39] Intensely nationalistic without the stigma of being so officially, *Rossiia* was en route to becoming a mass-circulation daily of great relevance.[40]

"Old Gentleman" ended its ascent in midflight. On 14 January 1902, Amfiteatrov published the feuilleton "The Obmanov Family," a play on the name of Romanov that translates as "swindlers." Lest any reader miss the object of his satire, he named the father "Alek" and the son "Nick." Thinly disguising common gossip about the court, Nick Obmanov had a dual personality, was terrified of his father, and was having an affair with a ballerina. The public was stunned that the feuilleton had been published. Suvorin's diary for that week recorded the gossip that told more than the censors' archives. Rumors abounded: Suvorin had promised Amfiteatrov fifty thousand rubles for an article that would close down *Rossiia*; Amfiteatrov had spent two weeks at an orgy and was drunk and beside himself; Amfiteatrov had shot himself in a fit of self-destruction after having written the provocative lampoon. The most plausible explanation came from V. P. Burenin, who had confided that Amfiteatrov had a "psychopathic envy" of the more popular Doroshevich, and that he wrote the article "in a white heat."[41]

The episodic histories of these papers revealed opportunities unfulfilled by the relative immaturity of Russia's newspaper industry. They

[37] *Dnevnik Suvorina*, 207.

[38] *Rossiia*, 16 Nov. 1901, no. 920. This edition of the newspaper featured a special supplement devoted to Dobroliubov.

[39] *Rossiia*, 18 Nov. 1900, no. 564.

[40] Anton noted to Alexander Chekhov, for example, that *Rossia*'s influence was rising at the expense of *Novoe vremia*'s. Bukchin, *Sud'ba fel'etonista*, 126.

[41] *Dnevnik Suvorina*, 276.

also showed the continuing presence of the government in ways that undermined the development of the new politics associated with Witte, Propper, and *Birzhevye vedomosti*. If these papers demonstrated by their demises the limits of the freedom to maneuver within the public space, in their successes and even some of their other failures they also expanded that area in which opinions were formed.

Institutionalizing Pluralism

The variety in the Russian press at the turn of the century evidenced society's growing ability to accommodate diversity. The extent to which Russia was developing a pluralism capable of providing the social support for industrialization raises a fundamental question about its ability to withstand revolution. Although the appearance of mass-circulation newspapers signaled the breaking down of the old order, the press could not lay claim to entrenching the new. In its first stages, pluralism corrodes the cement of tradition, and this has destabilizing side effects. As diversity emerges, the potential for conflict is great. The pluralism represented by the independent press was distinctive, but the society of diverse reading groups still fragile. Ideas, values, and symbols needed to be generated that would create a common culture strong enough to buffer internal confrontations over claims to that culture.

The continuing differentiation of the newspaper-reading public into separate interest groups could be seen first in structural reorganizations in a number of areas. The newspapers made adjustments continually to keep pace with their changing readerships. The street-corner kiosks in St. Petersburg during its Belle Epoque could satisfy any number of appetites, and additions to or modifications of the contents of the various papers illustrated how the readerships themselves had been reconfigured since the 1870s. Patterns of circulation also told of significant shifts and extended reaches. Not only *who* read the newspaper, but *when* and *where* it was read increasingly affected journalism.

Trubnikov had begun the first afternoon edition in 1865 with *Vechernaia gazeta* (*The Evening Gazette*), a smaller, cheaper version of *Birzhevye vedomosti* with business news updated by the telegraph. Suvorin improved upon this in 1881 by publishing morning and evening editions of *Novoe vremia*, and Notovich then brought out two editions of *Novosti*. Although all newspapers circulated in the provinces via the mails, the expanding railroads facilitated timely distribution. The relative paucity of commercial newspapers in the provinces made those published in the two capitals all the more valuable.[42] Suvorin, so quick to realize the business possibilities of mass communications, had paid ten thousand rubles in 1883 for the charter to manage kiosks at railroad stations and was servicing six hundred of them by 1913.[43] Also by that date special distributing agencies supplied 409 cities with papers from the two capitals in time for daily delivery and street sales.[44] Propper, however, had engineered in 1893 the first newspaper especially designed for provincial delivery: a tabloid-sized version of *Birzhevye vedomosti*, combining national and international news with feuilletons that spotlighted provincial issues, and subsidized primarily by advertisers selling national brands or through mail order.

Increased diversity in contents gave more people reason to buy a newspaper. The boulevard papers had added games and riddles, the answers to which were promised in a future edition. Suvorin used similar ploys for his more educated crowd, teasing their intellects with chess and card puzzles. In 1900 *Birzhevye vedomosti* held a literary competiton, offering publication in the paper as first prize. By the 1890s commentaries on the latest Paris fashions were a must in all papers. Suvorin was publishing Natalia Lukhmanova's melodramatic short stories for the woman of the bourgeois household; she would soon be writing feuilletons and articles about women's and other social issues for *Birzhevye vedomosti* and *Peterburgskaia gazeta*. Khudekov extended his paper to the female component with regular advice on planning meals. *Peterburgskii listok* by the 1890s occasionally featured excerpts form sermons delivered at the magnificent Kazan Cathedral.

Faced with a new form of competition from the growing popularity of family-oriented magazines, publishers began adding slick Sunday supplements of fiction and photographs too expensive for reproduction on newsprint; a little religion and a lot of entertainment became standard by the end of the century. Propper began to include a weekly "thin" journal in the 1890s, and after several years his *Ogonek* (*Little Flame*) turned into a successful separate publication. By 1900 all the major dailies offered illustrated weekly supplements, and the Sunday paper gradually became a unique publication specifically associated with the day of rest.

All papers added one striking feature that in and of itself told much about social change: coverage of horse racing. No longer simply the sport of kings, racing captivated readers from all newspapers because of the gambling that had become integral to it. The invention of the mechanical

[42] A. V. Peshekhonov, "Russkaia politicheskaia gazeta," *Rb*, no. 3 (1901): 1–21.

[43] Esin, *Russkaia dorevoliutsionnaia gazeta*, 34; and E. G. Golomb and E. M. Fingerit, *Rasprostranenie pechati v dorevoliutsionnoi Rossii i v Sovetskom soiuze* (Moscow: Sviaz, 1967), 29.

[44] Golomb and Fingerit, *Rasprostranenie*, 29.

totalizator, a pari-mutuel device that made it possible to compute odds quickly as thousands of rubles poured in, fashioned horse racing into the first genuinely mass-based spectator sport. Its popularity confirmed the existence of a sizeable crowd with time and money to burn and suggested the presence of the urban criminal element associated with easy money. Russia's editors faced the same moral qualms as those in the West who also felt pressured to report on the races: should they contribute to the erosion of social ethics by subtly sanctioning gambling with their coverage of the tracks?[45] Their audiences won the battle over their consciences, and the urban newspapers often went so far as to offer tips on horses, although the Ministry of Internal Affairs put a stop to publicizing the favorites between 1898 and 1905.[46]

The variety in Russia's periodical offerings pictured the accomplishments of industrialization, still moderate but ably measured according to the evolution of different social strata and the clusterings within them of subgroups based on gender, age, and political leanings. What follows here is a comparative study of how various newspapers covered three major stories: the lethal mugging of a tourist during the height of the summer season just outside St. Petersburg; the national commemoration of the fiftieth anniversary of Pushkin's mortal wounding in a duel; and the trial of a young Jewess who pleaded insanity in the hotel-room shooting of her estranged lover. This comparative look at news clarifies how newspapers affected the political implications of events in nonparty Russia.

The murder of an innocent tourist went beyond sensationalism because of what the man represented about socioeconomic change. By the summer of 1886 the boulevard papers offered special sections on "dacha life," a feature that revealed much about the growth of the city and the newspapers' readers. The upper classes were no longer the only ones able to afford second residences, and the proliferation of small summer houses served by urban railroad lines bespoke the connection between social and technological mobility. Therefore, when two badly beaten corpses were discovered in the woods next to the railway station that connected the capital with its suburb of Ligovo on 19 June, shock waves reverberated throughout the city. Identifying the bodies increased tensions, because although one turned out to be a thug whose friends had battered him to death when all three were in an alcoholic stupor, the second was a well-liked young student who had apparently been grabbed at the station by the drunken three. Apprehending the two on the loose came quickly after one tried to pawn the student's stolen coat.

<hr />

[45] See, for example, Tony Mason, "Sporting News, 1860–1914," in Harris and Lee, *The Press in English Society*, 168–86.

[46] Lemke, "V mire usmotreniia" (156), lists a circular from 1898 prohibiting the publishing of "favorites," but advice to bettors returned to the popular press after 1905.

The heinous crime at Ligovo contained ingredients of interest for all of Petersburg's different newspapers, but it received the largest play, naturally, in the boulevard press. Both *Peterburgskaia gazeta* and *Peterburgskii listok* provided crude maps of the wooded area and graphic details of the corpses, following the story closely through the trial. *Peterburgskaia gazeta* interviewed the student's bereaved family,[47] but minutiae about the bruised bodies could satisfy readers of *Peterburgskii listok*.[48] *Novoe vremia* sent a reporter to investigate the scene of the crime and to talk with the police; readers were reassured when the city's commendable detective force had the culprits behind bars.[49]

Commentaries on the killers emphasized the differences in the coverage. *Novoe vremia* and *Peterburgskaia gazeta* viewed the murders as symptoms of social illness: the killers were educated, had options for employment, and had murdered for the sense of exhilaration, not the money. Moreover, neither felt remorse for his actions. These papers played up the story to illustrate how social morals were in sad and dangerous decline.[50] *Birzhevye vedomosti*, in contrast, treated the entire affair with a lighter hand. The correspondent sent to cover the trial focused on the atmosphere at court, the crowd of thrill-seeking women who "treated the affair as an adventure story by popular French novelist Ponson du Terrail." Unfortunately for the bloodthirsty, nothing lurid happened at court.[51] *Peterburgskii listok*'s lengthy excerpts from the trial read not unlike its serial novels. Before the trial had ended, the paper's attention had shifted to an explosion of artillery shells in a residential area that had claimed fifteen lives, three of them children.

The differing approaches revealed the variety of opinions in the larger frame of the public sphere. For some readers, the murders stood as one of a series of shocking events that no one, neither themselves nor the state, seemed able to contain. For other readers, the event was a sign of loss of control, a red flag waving to alert them that control would need to be reclaimed. *Peterburgskaia gazeta* concluded that the swift trial and guilty verdict underscored the value of the jury system, suggesting to its readers that it might well be up to them to take command to halt society's decline.[52] After putting the killers on display as dangerous omens, *Novoe vremia* and *Peterburgskaia gazeta* turned considerable attention to the exploded artillery and repeated their insinuations about official incompetence to protect the public. Following up particularly vivid descrip-

[47] *Pg*, 20 June 1886, no. 166.
[48] *Pl*, 20 June 1886, no. 164.
[49] *Nv*, 20 June 1886, no. 3701.
[50] *Nv*, 22 June 1886, no. 3307; *Pg*, 24 June 1886, no. 170.
[51] *Bv*, 16 July 1886, no. 190.
[52] *Pg*, 14 July 1886, no. 190.

tions of body parts in the courtyard, the papers demanded to know why the government had so negligently sold live shells as scrap metal.[53] On the same story, the yellowest *Peterburgskii listok* told readers to "look for the Jew," as the French always direct, "cherchez la fêmme," when determining responsibility for the explosion.[54] Besides, it was time for this paper's readers to move on; "The Golden Arm" had just escaped by seducing her jailor and had surfaced on the Warsaw railroad, flirting and robbing her way from car to car.[55]

Less than a year later, the fiftieth anniversary of Pushkin's death appeared on the calendar. Seven years earlier, the dedication of a statue to the poet had turned into one of the first opportunities the mass-circulation newspapers had enjoyed to participate in an issue of national cultural significance. More to the point, the newspapers were instrumental in rescuing the poet from the intelligentsia and turning him over to his fans among ordinary readers. The writer whose appeal cut across all strata and whose literature made profound cultural and political statements appeared made-to-order as a national symbol.

As nationalism and secularization exposed the clay feet of Russian culture's traditional agents, tsar and patriarch, substitutes had to be found. Significantly, the popular press originally had not been invited to participate in the preparations for the 1880 celebration because its organizers viewed it from a narrow elitist perspective. Therefore, when the mass-circulation newspapers had jumped with great enthusiasm to cover the celebration, they were also staking a claim to Pushkin for their readers. The chocolate bars, cigarette packages, and other inexpensive souvenir items stamped in the poet's image on sale in 1880 provided further evidence that Pushkin belonged to ordinary Russians, that he could not be held prisoner by the elites. The flagrant consumerism played more prominently in 1887, horrifying the intelligentsia with the crassness that threatened to rob the poet of his political utility. The candy bars, exemplifying consumerism as a way of life, had political resonance all their own.[56]

Pushkin had become a commodity on several accounts. As the essence of Russian culture, all groups could rightfully lay a claim to him. Suvorin and Notovich saw in the upcoming anniversary an opportunity to manipulate the symbolic Pushkin in order to establish credentials as the truer authority on the subject. *Novosti's* staff tried to organize a commission similar to that of 1880. Suvorin exploded. The self-appointed commission was not representative, he argued, and the whole notion that the poet's

[53] *Nv*, 4 July 1886, no. 3715; *Pg*, 4 July 1886, no. 180.
[54] *Pl*, 8 July 1886, no. 182.
[55] *Pl*, 14 July 1886, no. 188.
[56] Levitt, *Russian Literary Politics*, chapter 3.

death would be observed by festivities rather than mourning was blasphemous. Nor did Suvorin look favorably on the proposed public readings of Pushkin's works in foreign translations of Russia's national languages, especially Yiddish.[57] Suvorin and members of the proposed commission had another point of contention; each was poised to release an inexpensive collection of Pushkin's works on the anniversay, the day the copyright expired.[58]

Birzhevye vedomosti suggested a truce because Pushkin, after all, "belonged to all of Russia."[59] In Propper's paper Pushkin was a conciliator, equally of the people and of the nobility into which he was born, a patriot who loved both his tsar and humanitarian progress.[60] On 29 January, the date of Pushkin's death, *Novosti* did not border its front page in black as the other major papers did. Instead, *Novosti* offered the poet as a living spirit for all Russians, and several students who had followed after him at his lycée were interviewed to give the human connection between past and present.[61] *Novoe vremia* took readers to the graveside, recalled the poet's dying words, "It is difficult to breathe," and emphasized how Pushkin had saved Russia from the pernicious influences of European languages and literature then dominating Russian culture.[62]

In 1887 Pushkin had found a home on the boulevard. For several weeks, Khudekov's paper had made Pushkin a daily feature. Reporter Dmitrii Lobanov had been dispatched to find the exact spot where the poet had fallen in the duel. *Peterburgskaia gazeta* consciously sought to humanize Pushkin, literally: "All of Russia bows before the talent of our great poet, but what do we know about A. S. Pushkin *as a man*? In any other country even the boots of such a great national poet would receive much attention, but we do not even know the topography of the spot where he died."[63] Leikin headed off to Chernaia Rechka, the area where the shooting had occurred, and interviewed elderly residents to try to track down a possible eyewitness.[64]

Still astride the ambiguous border between factual and fictional sensationalism, on 27 January, the day on which the duel took place, *Peterburgskii listok* took readers out to the clearing in Chernaia Rechka and reported the incident as a contemporary news event. Two days later, the poet lay dying in his bed: "Someone else came in and told him there was

[57] *Nv*, 13 Jan. 1887, no. 3906.
[58] Levitt, *Russian Literary Politics*, 155–56.
[59] *Bv*, 18 Jan. 1887, no. 17.
[60] *Bv*, 29 Jan. 1887, no. 28.
[61] *Novosti*, 29 Jan. 1887, no. 28.
[62] *Nv*, 29 Jan. 1887, no. 3922.
[63] *Pg*, 6 Jan. 1887, no. 5.
[64] *Pg*, 7 Jan. 1887, no. 6.

almost no hope. Pushkin heard his sentence bravely and asked them not to tell his wife." An accompanying editorial explained Pushkin's grave importance to Russia: "Pushkin made his contemporaries respect their Motherland, respect their nationality."[65]

Pastukhov claimed the poet for Moscow, the place of his birth and the site of the 1880 celebration. *Moskovskii listok* recounted the details of every day, it seemed, that Pushkin had spent in the first capital.[66] Appropriated by six different readerships in as many different ways, the historical Pushkin demonstrated the possibilities for a pluralistic culture. His flexibility as a symbol which the different groups could share allowed for a variety of interpretations. The newspapers spoke to different interests, but there was enough of Pushkin to go around for all.

The curiosity-seekers disappointed by the lack of thrills at the trial of the Ligovo murderers would be satiated in 1895 when Olga Palem, a mentally unstable Jewess, went before the bar for killing the man who had jilted her. Her nationality and state of mind figured directly into news coverage and the trial itself. If the boulevard papers gave the story proportionally more space than did the national papers, the latter nonetheless devoted unusual attention to such a scandalous affair. For all the debauchery that captivated prurient interests, this was also a story about religious tolerance, scientific medicine, sexual politics, and the legal system.

The story came in bits and pieces, with the defendant interrupting witnesses, falling into hysterics, and collapsing regularly on the bench. Born into a poor family in Simferopol, Palem had moved to Odessa in her teenage years and had taken up with a wealthy older man. She passed herself off at various times as a Tatar princess or a wealthy Crimean Muslim. Twenty-five at the time of the trial, five years earlier she had fallen madly in love with a young student, following him to St. Petersburg when he was accepted for study in the Institute of Communications attached to the ministry. Her love went unrequited. There was no shortage of testimonials about her erratic behavior; once her lover had been hospitalized with typhus, and she had thrown so many scenes that the hospital's administration forbade her presence. She had gone to the Ministry of Communications with lies about his having swindled her out of a fortune. By May 1894, the time of the shooting, he had long since refused to see her. One afternoon she persuaded him that, dying of consumption, she was off to Italy and simply wanted to say good-bye. He let her in and she pulled her gun.

Entering a plea of insanity, Palem faced one jury in the courtroom and

---

[65] *Pl*, 29 Jan. 1887, no. 27.
[66] *Ml*, 29 Jan. 1887, no. 29.

several others composed of newspaper readers. *Novosti, Novoe vremia,*
and *Peterburgskaia gazeta* had the most revealing reactions; *Peterburgskii listok* gave the trial great play, piling up the scandalous particulars
from the courtroom, maintaining its sensational slant. But *Novosti* mar-
shaled the testimony of witnesses who swore to her mental incompetence, saying that "everyone who has seen her during the cross-examina-
tion has testified unanimously that she was completely despondent, and
had a dead, depressed countenance."[67] When one court psychiatrist cer-
tified her mentally competent at the time of the crime, *Novosti* excerpted
the parts of his statement where he contradicted himself.[68] Although a
matter of record, her ethnicity was not mentioned in Notovich's paper,
where the issue of insanity as a legitimate defense constituted the heart
of the case. In *Novoe vremia,* to the expected contrary, she was cast as a
typical depraved, lying Jewess.

Peterburgskaia gazeta agreed in part with both of them. Like *Novosti,*
this paper had no qualms about the insanity plea in principle, but like
Novoe vremia, it questioned whether or not Palem was truly deranged or
"another Sarah Bernhardt" with her courtroom histrionics.[69] Her religion
was not a problem; A. R. Kugel', who wrote on the trial for *Peterburgskaia gazeta,* was Jewish. But she was a woman, and as such she suffered
"the disease of reality. . . . Neuropathologists still have not identified it
or found a cure for it, but it wreaks havoc among many women."[70] Rather
than mocking women, Kugel' was addressing the sophisticated concerns
of his readers, as neurological disorders had become quite fashionable
among middle-class women at the end of the nineteenth century. Three
years earlier, when American Lizzie Borden was accused of having taken
an ax to her parents, many similar concerns arose about distinctively female neuroses. Although the sentiments expressed here seemed to suggest that Palem was giving an excellent performance, the editors left it to
the jury to decide.[71]

Peterburgskii listok, in contrast, played up the number of society ladies
at the trial, but did not care why Palem fell into frenzies, only that she
did.[72] Like the Ligovo murders, this one was removed from the broader
context and reported as melodramatically as the serial adventures. David
Ray Papke has argued that framing the coverage thus "ignored the more

[67] *Novosti,* 30 Jan. 1895, no. 30.
[68] *Novosti,* 19 Feb. 1895, no. 49.
[69] *Pg,* 18 Feb. 1895, no. 47.
[70] *Pg,* 17 Feb. 1895, no. 46.
[71] *Pg,* 23 Feb. 1895, no. 52.
[72] *Pl,* 14 Feb. 1895, no. 43.

profound social and political aspects of crime."[73] The escapism it offered daily undoubtedly explains much of *Peterburgskii listok*'s popularity, and although the paper would later pay closer attention to the origins and implications of some crimes, the presence of readers who preferred emotional stimulation to political discourse identified some of the changing contours of late imperial society.

When the "innocent" verdict was returned in the Palem case, the defendant swooned, *Novosti* exalted, *Peterburgskaia gazeta* polled its readers, *Peterburgskii listok* moved on to the next murder/suicide attempt, but Suvorin telephoned a contact of his at the Ministry of Justice. The freed defendant spent a restless night in a hotel room, only to find out that the Senate had protested the verdict and was reviewing the matter. She stood trial again one year later and found herself sentenced to ten years when the psychiatrists' testimony was overturned.[74]

Twenty years earlier, the government had overturned the decision of a jury to free Vera Zasulich after her attempt to assassinate Governor-General Trepov. The Zasulich case had considerably more bearing on society and politics than this rather pathetic affair. But several aspects of the Palem case merit deliberation. In 1877 the independent press, including *Novoe vremia*, had applauded the acquittal. In reversing the court's decision, the tsarist government had acted against public opinion. In this trial, Suvorin had reversed his prior stance and called into question the jury system.[75] He moved against Palem because of his rabid anti-Semitism, but other aspects of the case bothered readers who need not have shared his phobia. More important, when a publisher could make a call that would reverse a court's decision, even when the case involved two insignificant characters and a vulgar homicide, he flexed the muscles of the daily newspaper.

Opening an arena for discussion of questions that the tsarist government did not declare off-limits, the Russian mass-circulation press by the end of the century provided a valuable forum for its disenfranchised audience. The disparate focuses in the coverages of the murders in Ligovo, the Pushkin anniversary, and Olga Palem's trial elucidated how the press edited discourse on topics with political implications. As Western political parties were losing ground to newspapers in deciding which issues would reach the public agenda, so too were Russian newspapers estab-

---

[73] David Ray Papke, *Framing the Criminal: Crime, Cultural Work and the Loss of Critical Perspective, 1830–1900* (New York: Archon Books, 1987), 70.

[74] Articles in *Novosti*, 21 Feb. 1895, no. 51; *Pg*, 20 Feb. 1895, no. 49; and *Nv*, 25 Aug. 1896, no. 7361. See also N. P. Karabchevskii, *Rechi. 1882–1914* (Petrograd and Moscow: M. O. Vol'f), sec. v.

[75] *Nv*, 20 Feb. 1895, no. 6817.

lishing a space in which readers could determine and debate issues of relevance to all. The Russian press exercised its ability to generate a forceful body of opinion when war broke out with Japan in 1904, and it accelerated the events of 1905 when the new politics confronted the old in the streets. But before moving to the war, the next chapter presents an in-depth analysis of the journalists who assembled this medium, largely in the image of their collective ambitions.

7

The Newspaper Reporter

THE GREAT DOROSHEVICH, soon to be cruising the streets in the same make of sleek, black automobile that transported Nicholas II around St. Petersburg, relished his position as a star of the first magnitude. Married to two actresses, the first of whom was apparently bisexual and the second of whom replaced him in his declining years with a younger man, Doroshevich shared with Nemirovich-Danchenko an eye for more than just a good story.[1] The flash and dash of his personal style, like that of his reportorial prose and the front pages he produced, announced the successful scaling by the newspaper reporter of heights of esteem in readers' minds. These were not entirely the same peaks as those conquered by the preceding generation of intellectuals, but they reached into the same realm, where the authority to speak for the public was being contested. Driving the same car that the tsar did, Doroshevich adroitly used a symbol of the modern age to connect competing images of royalty and power in the popular imagination. His larger-than-life posturing implied to other reporters that they had "arrived."

The growing importance of the daily newspaper thrust those who wrote for it into positions of influence. The triumph of the new journalism in the 1890s caused the decade to be recorded in the West as the "age of the reporter" because, as even so scholarly a journalist as Godkin could write, reporting had become "a new and important calling."[2] In France at this time the "job of the journalist" was no longer dismissed as "suitable only for vagabonds and men without any means of support," and differences dimmed between *ecrivains* and *journalistes*.[3] Russian reporters faced an especially challenging situation because journalism still provided the most meaningful forum from which they could launch opposition to the autocracy.

A major part of the reporter's contribution, the relationship of the new descriptive techniques to sociopolitical change, has already been intro-

---

[1] Doroshevich's personal archive, maintained in TsGALI f. 1063, contains a rather steamy letter, op. 2, l. 4, written by his wife to another woman discussing what they would be doing as soon as she got her husband on the train.

[2] Quoted in Schudson, *Discovering the News*, 70. Robert Park believed that "one of the most important events in American civilization has been the rise of the reporter." "News as a Form of Knowledge," 686.

[3] Zeldin, *France, 1848–1945* 2:506; Bellanger et al., *Histoire générale* 2:277–78.

Fig. 7. V. M. Doroshevich, the "King of Feuilleton-ists"

duced. The growing importance of facticity at the expense of commentary had evolved more from changing informational needs than from the conscious design of reporters, although the impersonal forces had required individuals to give them force and direction. This chapter shifts the focus to the men and women themselves to show how their personal backgrounds and attitudes toward their work affected the development of newspaper journalism. To the extent that who they were influenced how they selected their occupation, which had reciprocal effects on what and how they reported, the biographies of several of the most important journalists will provide some of the specifics on how individuals took advantage of opportunities extended by newspapers. The newspaper became a public institution in part because that was the expressed intention of those who wrote for it.

But the mass-circulation daily was fundamentally a commercial institution, and serving its readers entailed giving them what they wanted, not just what the writers believed they needed. A significant portion of the reporters' story consists of how they tried to harmonize the potentially contradictory notions of commercialism and public service. Russians, like their Western counterparts, hoped to circumvent possible conflict by organizing their occupation on a professional basis. In neither Russia nor the West did journalists succeed in their efforts to organize their occupation into a profession, but their ultimate failure does not detract from the importance of how the original arguments were framed. Those who argued for professionalization believed that news provided vital empirical data from which readers could construct society; they saw themselves as social scientists and reiterated the importance of accurate and objective reporting.[4] Opponents considered news a commodity like any other and, pointing to the excesses of yellow journalism, questioned the ability to serve at the same time both public and commercial interests. The reasoning that the reading public has the right to all information that a journalist can accumulate has never set as squarely as other arguments for professional service, such as those of the rights of the ill to medical treatment. In asserting that readers had a *right* to news, however, reporters were claiming the authority to get that information into the public domain.

The movement for professionalization in the newsroom had several political implications. Following the trends of other occupational groups who defined themselves according to their training and commitment to an ideal of public service, reporters at the end of the nineteenth century sought to provide one component of the professional middle class that, as some argue, in Western societies formed the nucleus of the liberal democratic political system.[5] Their activities in this direction are therefore worth exploring because of how they fit into the larger process that was under way of other educated Russians' forming professions to manage industrialization.[6]

Russia's reporters drew from the legacy of the importance of the writer to society that they had inherited from the intelligentsia. If on the one hand newspaper journalists wanted the respect and occupational controls associated with professionalization, on the other they wanted the prestige enjoyed by the generations of intellectuals whom many reporters revered

[4] In this, reporters sought status along the same lines as historians. See Peter Novick's distinguished study *That Noble Dream: The "Objectivity Question" and the American Historical Profession* (Cambridge: Cambridge University Press, 1988).

[5] Burton J. Bledstein, *The Culture of Professionalism: The Middle Class and the Development of Higher Education in America* (New York: W. W. Norton, 1976).

[6] See Harley A. Balzar, ed., *The Professions in Russia* (Ithaca, N.Y.: Cornell University Press, 1991).

as role models. The "age of the reporter" in Russia witnessed the emergence of a new intelligentsia, exemplified best by Doroshevich. The new intelligentsia did not completely supplant the old any more than the newspaper truly killed the "thick" journal, but it forced adjustments in the intellectuals' perspectives on communications.

Social Profile of the Newspaper Journalist

The first successful commercial publishers were guided by complex motivations stemming from the combined desires of making money and wielding influence; they wanted to ascend to places denied them by birth. It seems not entirely coincidental that Kraevskii and Suvorin, like their French counterpart Girardin, came from the fringes of the social elite and needed to support themselves financially while many of their peers did not. By the same token, Pastukhov had social complements in Bennett, Dupuy, and Harmsworth, all of whom came from insignificant commercial families and had to create new avenues for attaining prestige and power because their lowly rung on the social ladder prevented them from climbing higher. The uniqueness of the newspaper, its untried potential, and the contempt in which it was held by those whose money and education would have offered them the first chances to edit and publish, made the daily paper an excellent prospect to become an avenue leading upward.

The first publishers counted on the efforts of men and women who shared their appreciation of the newspaper as a means of social mobility. If Kraevskii was at times ambivalent about his loss of stature, at the low end of the social scale status could only be gained. All self-made men, these publishers found and publicized a route that led out of financial want and toward positions of influence in the community. Those leaving the gentry did not meet directly with those entering from the other *sosloviia* to constitute one homogenous group, but collectively they illustrated how the mass-circulation press opened up a space in the middle by pulling in members of various social estates.

The addition of biographies of leading reporters to those of the publishers further expands this middle space. Some such reporters have already been discussed. Sokolova and Leskov, for example, went to newspapers after being ostracized by family and colleagues. Leikin and Miasnitskii, members of their merchant audiences, could communicate easily with them. Doroshevich and Nemirovich-Danchenko, born more literally into their trade than into an estate, not surprisingly became reporting's first celebrities.

Few trades offered comparable opportunities for those who had to substitute ambition for traditional qualifications, and the conventional barriers of gender, ethnicity, and *soslovie* dissolved in the face of tremendous demand. Despite the critical need for printable stories, publishers could seldom afford to keep more than a select few writers working under restrictive contracts like the one Leikin enjoyed. The inability to maintain a permanent staff, coupled with the heavy requirements for sufficient materials to fill a daily newspaper, kept publishers from being choosy about whom they employed. Pressure for news sometimes brought it from questionable sources, and many a "foreign correspondent" sat in a bar in Moscow, clipping stories from international periodicals. As one quipster noted, "they wrote from a Chinese junk anchored in the Petersburg Canal."[7]

Newspapers offered geographical mobility, too. Urban papers beckoned to those in the intellectually undernourished provinces. The military and the land-poor nobility furnished a seemingly limitless supply of talent. Ace reporter Shreier led the archetypal life. He graduated from the Moscow Cadet Corps, and, serving in Poland on military assignment, found himself appointed to the local censorship committee. There he discovered an excitement about the press that overwhelmed his other interests, and the ex-censor made a second career frustrating his former official colleagues in St. Petersburg.[8] Reporters' obituaries dating from the 1880s identify a common pattern: born in the provinces into an obscure noble family, many a future correspondent found an opening to the outside world through the army or the university, from whence writing ambitions led to the local newspaper offices. State service, which often began with a posting in a backwater town, stimulated a number of men to connect with life in the two capitals through the press by contributing as stringers. University students often subsidized their educations by selling stories. By virtue of their birth into an increasingly anachronistic social station, most of Russia's first generation of reporters came from the nobility.

M. O. Menshikov, who later became a dominant figure at *Novoe vremia*, wrote in 1892 in praise of his chosen calling, pointing out how its requirements caricatured social mobility: reporters could come from any *soslovie*, spend a night in a flophouse, and then arise the next morning to interview a prominent government official.[9] Clichés abound on the window of opportunity opened by newspaper journalism. Alexander Kuprin, a reporter who became one of the leading figures in realism during the Silver Age of Russian literature, waxed nostalgic in claiming that a

[7] A. E. Kaufman, "Za kulisami pechati," *Iv* 133, no. 7 (1913): 118.

[8] Shreier's obituary in *Pv*, 5 Feb. 1887, no. 28.

[9] M. O. Menshikov, "Prizvanie zhurnalistiki," *Knizhki nedeli*, no. 4 (1892): 137. The article appeared in four parts: no. 4, 137–54; no. 5, 121–38; no. 6, 166–85; no. 7, 137–62.

successful reporter needed only "mad courage, audacity, breadth of vision, and an amazing memory."[10] His life echoed this refrain. A young army officer who had been denied entrance to the prestigious Academy of the General Staff for political reasons, Kuprin resigned his commission and took off for Kiev in 1894 with but a few kopecks in his pocket. He supported himself easily by writing for the local newspapers, serving one as its bogus Paris correspondent. Recapturing his past with affection, he made the hero of his scandalous frolic through St. Petersburg's red-light district, *The Pit*, a newspaper reporter with the soul of a frustrated reformer. Kuprin caught the attention of another reporter destined for a remarkable career after leaving newspapers, Maxim Gorky at *Samarskaia gazeta* (*The Samara Gazette*).[11]

It took frustration with the status quo for Varvara Menshikova, who wrote under her married name "Ol'nem," to pack up and leave her father's estate in Poltava Province in 1889 and move to Kiev to pursue a life in journalism. The daughter of a noble landlord, Ol'nem did not enjoy particular wealth or social standing. Her mother, the child of a village priest, suffered the scorn of her snobbish in-laws. Lineage through the clergy, however, had the advantage of education, and Ol'nem found sanctuary with her mother in the meager provincial arts and libraries. Three years after her mother's death and deeply frustrated by the patriarchal attitudes prevailing in her household, Ol'nem boarded the train for the nearest big city. Personal connections to the provincial intelligentsia landed her an interview with the editor of *Kievskoe slovo* (*The Kievan Word*). No sooner had she walked in the door than she was dispatched to get the verdict in an important trial. She had what her editor needed most: legs and literacy. She enjoyed a long and satisfying career at *Kievskoe slovo* on a variety of beats and as one of the best-paid members of the staff. Her memoirs imply that brushes with sexism were few and far-between.[12]

An atypical Russian woman, even among the educated and noble, because she took such forthright action, Ol'nem nonetheless represented a stock figure in newspaper offices.[13] If only a fraction of educated Russian women worked in newspaper journalism, their numbers represented a challenge to traditional roles for the Russian female. Suvorin was noted for hiring women, and some called *Novosti* a "feminist club" because Notovich kept a number of them on the payroll to present the "woman's

---

[10] Nicholas Luker, *Alexander Kuprin* (Boston: Twayne, 1978), 30.

[11] P. N. Berkov, *Alexandr Ivanovich Kuprin* (Moscow and Leningrad: Akademiia Nauk, 1956), 16–25.

[12] V. N. Ol'nem's two-part memoirs appeared in *Golos minuvshago* in 1913: "Iz reporterskikh vospominanii," no. 7, 123–59, and "Iz zapisok reportera," no. 8, 119–51.

[13] F. Shipulinskii referred to "the old maid [*baryshnia*] on salary" as a "familiar member of the newspaper family." *Zhurnalist*, no. 3 (1914): 12–13.

question."[14] Trubnikov's wife, like Sokolova an educated and liberal "woman of the sixties," had participated in every aspect of the publication of *Birzhevye vedomosti* before their divorce in 1867.[15] Significantly, however, unlike female reporters in the West, the Russian women did not develop a specific "women's journalism" that stemmed from a gender-based consciousness. Signs of it, however, had begun to appear in the popular press before the outbreak of World War I.[16]

Just as newspapers could save the unlucky from genteel poverty and provincial boredom, so could they spare the lower social strata from poverty, intellectual as well as financial. Two of tsarist Russia's most gifted reporters, Giliarovskii and A. I. Svirskii, used the newspaper to escape the unkind fate of their fathers. Able to write about social decay from personal experience with it, they enriched Russian journalism as two of the most articulate visitors to Gorky's "lower depths." Crusading journalists, they picked up where Krestovskii had left off in using the newspaper as an agent for social reform. Both remained in Russia after 1917 and enjoyed greater reputations under the new regime. Their humble beginnings and devotion to the plight of the lower classes accounted for much of their esteem among postrevolutionary readers, but their insights into what a newspaper could accomplish also formed a part of the unsteady bridge that connected Russia's two journalisms on either side of 1917.

The more dynamic Giliarovskii epitomized better Kuprin's axiom, and his vision was broad enough to enable him to see all openings made possible by the daily newspaper, including those for the advertising agency he began to operate in the 1890s. His personal stationery bore a sketch of him dressed in his signature Cossack attire, a pictorial reminder of how far he had traveled from his birth in 1853 Vologda Province where his father held a minor bureaucratic post. Like so many of his generation, he fell under the romantic spell cast by N. G. Chernyshevskii with his 1863 cult classic *What Is to Be Done?* Infatuated by the idealized rugged-but-enlightened laborer Rakhmetov, the young Giliarovskii took up his hero's wandering ways, including a stint as a bargeman on the Volga. Newspaper reporting began for Giliarovskii as one of a series of odd jobs that, like the others he took up, allowed him to travel freely.[17]

Svirskii had authentic working-class credentials. Born in Petersburg in 1865, his father worked in a tobacco factory. When his parents separated, he moved with his mother to Zhitomir. Only eight when she died, he found himself in the care of destitute relatives. At age fifteen he began to

---

[14] Kaufman, "Iz zhurnal'nykh vospominanii," no. 11, 613.

[15] Esin, *Puteshestvie v proshloe*, 90.

[16] I deal with this issue more fully in "Female Journalists in Prerevolutionary Russia," *Journalism History* 14, no. 4 (1987): 104–10.

[17] E. Kiseleva wrote a short biography of Giliarovskii as an introduction to the third volume of his *Sobranie sochinenii*, 6–12.

Fig. 8. Reporting star V. A. Giliarovskii

tramp, much like Giliarovskii, also spending time on the Volga. Writing
vignettes about the slums, which he began selling in Rostov-na-donu in
the 1890s, constituted one of many odd jobs. Notovich recognized his
flair for depicting life among the lowly and bought his work for *Novosti*.
Svirskii's interests were considerably more circumscribed than Giliarovskii's and therefore so was his career in journalism. His focus remained
on one subject, the urban poor, and he contributed to comparatively few
newspapers, although he became widely read as a social critic of the slums
in the interrevolutionary period. The censors terminated his brief career
as a publisher after only forty issues of *Novaia gazeta* (*The New Gazette*)
in 1906.[18]

Svirskii had another unique attribute that also influenced Notovich to
purchase his works: he was Jewish. The open-door policies that made the
obstacles of birth and sex surmountable worked the same for racial dis-

---

[18] A. I. Svirskii, *Istoriia moei zhizni* (Moscow: Gos. izd. khnd. lit., 1947); I. Kubikov,
"Bibliograficheskii ocherk," in A. I. Svirskii, *Polnoe sobranie sochinenii*, 2 vols. (Moscow
and Leningrad: Zemlia i fabrika, 1930), 1:7–18; and Joan Neuberger, "Crime and Culture:
Hooliganism in St. Petersburg, 1900–1914" (Ph.D. diss., Stanford University, 1985), 118–
23.

crimination, and the Jewish intellectual was also a standard figure in the newsroom. Not only was the rampant anti-Semitism psychologically restrictive, but Jews without official permission to live elsewhere were confined geographically to the Pale of Settlement. Newspapers offered a means to combat anti-Semitism for some, and a way out of the Pale for others. Some journalists resorted to registering in St. Petersburg as "pharmacists' assistants," typical Jewish employment, while others lived in fear that their illegal presence would be discovered by authorities.[19] The sense of being surrounded by belligerent forces, however, nurtured an ethnic solidarity and infrastructure of mutual support that gave Russian Jews a position in journalism disproportionate to their place in the population. Their role at newspapers had significant ramifications with respect to the contents and the political posturing of the Russian press.

Although raw numbers are not available for calculating what percentage of journalists were Jewish, the presence of this minority in positions of power indicated that they held substantial leverage. Propper and Notovich have already been mentioned. After the censors closed *Novosti* and Notovich emigrated to Paris, a Jewish financier funded *Rech'* (*The Speech*), organ of the Constitutional Democrats' (Kadets) political party, because he wanted to ensure continued editorial opposition to Suvorin.[20] M. B. Gorodetskii, who began the first "kopeck" paper in 1908, was a Jew who had worked for Notovich and had brought Svirskii to the publisher's attention. Gorodetskii's leading feuilletonist at *Gazeta kopeika*, O. Ia. Blotermants, was also Jewish.[21] Prominent newsman and editor A. R. Kugel', A. E. Kaufman, an editor at both *Novosti* and *Birzhevye vedomosti*, and L. M. L'vov (Kliachko), also of *Novosti* and other periodicals, were all Jewish. The "King of Reporters" himself, Iulii Shreier, was a Jew, although he played this fact down. These journalists did more than counter the rank anti-Semitism of the Suvorins and the Pastukhovs; their efforts guaranteed that channels of opposition to all forms of conservatism and oppression would remain open.

Professionalization and Commercialization

Reporters had to come to terms with the apparent contradiction between the commercial underpinning of what they did and the nobler tradition of journalism that combined literature with politics and carried it beyond the banality of putting opinions on sale. Writers had always needed

[19] L. M. L'vov (Kliachko), *Za kulisami starogo rezhima*, 2 vols. (Leningrad: n.p., 1925), 1:4–5; I. V. Gessen, *V dvukh vekakh* (Berlin: Speer of Schmidt, 1937), 273; and Svirskii, *Istoriia moei zhizni*, 522.

[20] Gessen, *V dvukh vekakh*, 221.

[21] O. Ia. Blotermants, "Chernaia ten'," *Leningrad*, nos. 17–18 (1940): 25–26.

money to maintain themselves, but for the intelligentsia it was hardly their *raison d'écrire*. Reporters, who sold information instead of interpretation, had the thornier problem of trying to justify their occupation on the same grounds as the intellectuals who gave thoughtful guidance. The notion of public service gave reporters an important connecting link to the intelligentsia. Still, the commercial structure of the mass-circulation press raised serious doubts that were themselves often signs of misunderstanding. The unscrupulous reporter collecting free drinks on the sly was the most notorious illustration, but also the least significant example in the long run, of the problematic relationship between capitalism and newspapers.

Commerce did much more than wave temptation in front of journalists, and the notoriety of the French press has created too convenient a peg upon which to hang the ready threat of capitalism gone awry. Attention to the eradication of venality has caused important aspects of the multiple roles played by commerce in the development of newspaper journalism to be misconstrued. The business side of publishing had a crucial impact on the organization of the editorial office, which carried over into reporting. As they scrutinized their balance sheets ever more closely, actively engaged in the pursuit of profit, publishers in the West were not so specifically concerned with distancing themselves from party coffers as they were with restructuring their businesses to increase the revenues earned from advertising and subscriptions. The same held true for Russia, where Propper's *Birzhevye vedomosti* was distanced from the polemics associated with Kraevskii's *Golos*. The loudly proclaimed independence of the first commercial publishers owed as much to business as it did to political practices.[22]

The farther removed the daily paper grew from partisanship, the more valuable the news report became as an autonomous commodity. Reporters hunted and gathered, collecting bits of information and selling it wherever they could. One observer compared them to clerks in a department store, simply handing over the counter whatever the customer wanted.[23] As dailies grew in circulation, more reporters found permanent employment at specific papers. The additional staff members played increasingly specialized roles with the development of the "beat," which sent individuals daily to specific assigned locales. Bennett's somewhat laughable advertisement in 1835 for a "Police Reporter of genius and education" anticipated this future.[24] The transformation of newspaper pub-

[22] Alfred M. Lee, *The Daily Newspaper in America* (New York: Macmillan, 1937), 206.

[23] Quoted in Ted Curtis Smythe, "The Reporter, 1880–1900: Working Conditions and Their Influence on the News," *Journalism History* 7, no. 1 (1980): 1.

[24] Quoted from Charlene J. Brown, Trevor R. Brown, and Wilbur L. Rivers, *The Media and the People* (New York: Holt, Rinehart and Winston, 1978), 55. The first advertisement

lishing into a commercial enterprise caught it up in the sweep of func-
tional rationalization, making it comparable to any other big business.
When its practitioners sought to improve their positions by establishing
professional criteria in order to regulate their ranks, they were behaving
as their peers in other occupations behaved.

The argument that newspapers must be regarded essentially as business enterprises sets forth critical analytical boundaries. News became
merchandise, which reporters found, bought, or sold without regard for
the editorial positions that identified periodicals according to political
camp. Many of the same stories ran in all papers, a situation that permitted publishers from across the political gamut to purchase from the same
source. In the West this had the perceptible effect of reducing the party
orientation of newspapers. Publishers' political lines formed loosely, not
with rigid predictability. Giliarovskii, for example, sold to the most conservative as well as to the liberal press. As long as the information itself
remained unblemished by interpretation, the reporter could not be held
accountable for editorial positions.

It does not, however, follow from this that correspondents were politically indifferent, despite the intelligentsia's accusations otherwise.
Rather, the point is that reporters, because of how they conceived of
their jobs, understood politics to be something other than negotiations
among partisan groups. Seeing themselves as objective mediators directing the flow of information without personal bias, they helped to transfer
the formation of the political agenda out of the elites' jurisdiction and put
it into the public domain. When Shreier, for example, lied to a bailiff in
order to gain entrance to a closed trial, or when another reporter disguised his voice to coax secret information out of a bureaucrat, their actions made for more than good storytelling. Reporters' quest for news
showed an implicit belief that the public had a *right* to information that
authorities chose to withhold, and therefore that they had a *duty* to supply it. Other Russian reporters acknowledged that they had learned this
"resourcefulness" from their American colleagues and, like the latter,
they argued that they used cunning as a tool to open doors that should
not remain closed to the reading public.[25]

The method of payment of newspaper reporters also influenced the
formation of the occupation because it took the business side of publishing directly into newspapers' contents. Before permanent staffs offered
the security of salaries, most reporters sold by the line, peddling various
versions of each story wherever possible. Reporting was treated not un-

I found in a Russian newspaper for a beat reporter was for one who could cover sports. *Rs*,
23 July 1899, no. 201.

[25] Kaufman, "Za kulisami pechati," 116–118.

like piecework in a factory, which undermined the contention that journalism was a profession. The highly competitive structure of finding and
peddling news laid the grounds for possible cutthroat rivalry. Instead,
being intellectual outcasts and sharing the same sense of purpose, reporters developed professional friendships that would affect their occupation as a whole. Tempers, of course, could flare into fisticuffs, and some
of Russia's most prominent reporters, including Gradovskii of *Golos* and
Burenin of *Novoe vremia*, challenged each other to duels that never came
to pass.[26] But the general atmosphere was not tense. The brilliant Baltimore wordsmith H. L. Mencken, whose *Newspaper Days* recaptured the
age of the reporter in America, told of congregating with his colleagues
in informal clubs, sharing notes and standardizing spellings of names and
other bits of information because they held accuracy in collective responsibility.[27] (Mocking with the same tone of Doroshevich's "burzhui,"
Mencken minted the term *the booboisie*.) More recently, Robert Darnton, recalling his own newspaper days, corroborated Mencken's remembrances that "nothing could be less competitive than a group of reporters
on the same story."[28]

Although selling by the piece rather than working on salary tended to
keep pay artificially low, it also boosted the entrepreneurial spirit. Prices
ranged between three and ten kopecks per line for average reporters; at
the opposite ends of the scale, Shreier could command up to twenty kopecks, while those with reputations for overselling the same story received less. The typical reporter averaged two hundred rubles per
month, while the best earned between five hundred and seven hundred
rubles. One reporter designated a monthly income of one hundred rubles
as the poverty line because reporters had so many out-of-pocket expenditures, especially payments to informants for news tips.[29] Moreover, reporters did not have the subsidized housing or meals that accompanied
most other positions, such as those in state service. Doroshevich's phenomenal annual income of forty thousand rubles early in the twentieth
century constituted a remarkable exception to all general rules, as did so
much about him.[30]

Despite fluctuations in income and lack of job security, the intrepid

[26] Kaufman, "Iz zhurnal'nykh vospominanii," 140, and "Za kulisami pechati," 120.

[27] Discussed in Smythe, "The Reporter," 6–7.

[28] Robert Darnton, *The Kiss of Lamourette* (New York: W. W. Norton, 1990), 75–77.

[29] The several reporters who left comments on salaries were in general agreement. See
Gal-in, "Sredi khronikerov," 69; Alexander Chekhov, "Zapiski reportera," *Iv* 109, no. 7
(1907): 81; L'vov (Kliachko), *Za kulisami* 1:84; and Ol'nem, "Iz zapisok," 126.

[30] Doroshevich's contract with I. D. Sytin gave him an annual salary of between thirty
thousand and forty thousand rubles per annum, plus a percentage of the profits of *Russkoe
slovo*, the paper he was hired to edit. Bokhanov, "Russkie gazety," 119; and Volkov, *Dvadtsat' let*, 70–71.

reporter could live comfortably in tsarist Russia. The financial advantages probably made reporting all the more attractive to those such as Ol'nem, who could have drawn a yearly pay of only approximately two hundred— no more than nine hundred—rubles in the likelier career open to educated women, teaching elementary school.[31] As even a skilled laborer Svirskii could have hoped for little more than three hundred rubles annually.[32] The upper ranks of the civil service paid six thousand rubles, plus subsidies and pensions, but the average bureaucrat scraped by on much less.[33] In the medical profession pay was uneven, but seldom abundant. Estimates for doctors' salaries range from nine hundred to three thousand rubles per annum, with female physicians averaging sometimes one-third less than the males.[34] The less skilled feldshers earned slightly more than schoolteachers.[35] The scale for professors' salaries ranged from fifteen hundred to fifty-five hundred.[36] Moonlighting was common, not just because of the relative instability of employment, but also because of the pleasure of seeing one's work in print. Kievan lawyer L. A. Kupernik both enjoyed writing feuilletons and appreciated the favorable publicity he generated for his practice in *Kievskoe slovo*.[37]

Looking at what was essentially the same financial structure in the American newsroom of the late nineteenth century, Ted Curtis Smythe arrived at a considerably different interpretation of the effects of the market economy on journalists. His alternative assessment merits discussion because it summarized the most pointed case against regarding journalism as a profession. Smythe had a wholly pessimistic view of the same picture: payment by line led to padding stories with contrived sensationalism, insecurity about the next paycheck kept graft rampant, and reporters lazily pooling their resources made an easy virtue of accuracy. Reporters in need of a scoop might tamper with legal evidence, and fabricating stories was commonplace. The root of the problem lay in the profit-oriented demands of publishing. It was clear that an industry geared toward earnings could not provide disinterested service to the public at large.[38]

Commercialism made an easy target for Russians ambivalent about the

[31] V. P. Leikina-Svirskaia, *Russkaia intelligentsiia v 1900–1917 gg.* (Moscow: Mysl', 1981), 62, 65.

[32] Iu. I. Kir'ianov, *Zhiznennyi uroven' rabochikh Rossii* (Moscow: Nauka, 1979), 103.

[33] Don Karl Rowney, "Higher Civil Servants in the Russian Ministry of Internal Affairs: Some Demographic and Career Characteristics," *Slavic Review* 31, no. 1 (1972): 109.

[34] Nancy Frieden, *Russian Physicians in an Era of Reform and Revolution, 1865–1905* (Princeton, N.J.: Princeton University Press, 1981), 214.

[35] Leikina-Svirskaia, *Russkaia intelligentsiia*, 59.

[36] Frieden, *Russian Physicians*, 215.

[37] Kaufman, "Za kulisami pechati," 104–5.

[38] Smythe, "The Reporter," 1–10.

market economy. The crooked and cynical reporters begat an erroneous stereotype of what the commercial element had supposedly knocked askew in the traditional relationship between journalist and reader, that of teacher and pupil. Russia's heirs to the intelligentsia were particularly sensitive to this issue. *Birzhevye vedomosti* editor A. E. Kaufman complained as late as 1912 that Russia as yet had published no history of its newspaper industry and that reporters were still met too often with contempt.[39] Other than Kuprin's Platon, Russia's few scattered fictional reporters surrendered happily to temptation. In the 1916 serial *The Journalist-Detective*, for example, the main protagonist forswore the mirrored ceilings in hotel rooms that he had enjoyed as a reporter to recover as a soldier at the front the virtue he had lost in sleazy pursuit of the scandals.[40] World War I certainly awarded value to soldiering, but the hero theoretically could have earned his stripes as a war correspondent in the tradition of Nemirovich-Danchenko.

Anecdotes from working journalists' memoirs could appall and amuse. L'vov recalled, for example, an incident involving the practice of slipping money into reporters' napkins at important affairs whose sponsors wanted generous coverage. The amount of the bribe was relative to the importance of the newspaper, and in this instance Suvorin's audience gave his reporter the largest cut. When the correspondent from *Birzhevye vedomosti* received by accident the napkin intended for *Novoe vremia*'s representative, he threw a party for all reporters in attendance with his booty.[41]

Corruption makes for entertaining stories, but the larger issue of which it was merely one aspect must be addressed. Tellingly, Russian journalists found it fashionable to blame Western market influences for instances of corruption. In their minds, accusing the market permitted them to connect with the intelligentsia's legacy of public service and maintain moral superiority over the "burzhui." When Menshikov counseled that Russians should be watchful of the Europeanization of their press, he referred to the reporter in pursuit of a fast ruble.[42] The spirit of competition that allowed for vice was the unhealthy influence creeping in from Europe, and the ambivalence among Russians reflected their view of capitalism in general.

Market forces were very much in operation. However, just as sensationalism concealed the importance of objectivity, calling attention to corruption obscured the subtle influences of the market on the development of attitudes about information and the knowledge to which this in-

[39] Kaufman, "Iz zhurnal'nykh vospominanii," no. 10, 122–23.
[40] P. D. Kurbatov, *Zhurnalist-Syshchik* (Petrograd: n.p., 1916).
[41] L'vov (Kliachko), *Za kulisami* 1:84.
[42] Menshikov, "Prizvanie zhurnalistiki," parts 3 and 4.

formation opened access. Shreier and his colleagues, even those clipping from the international press and passing stories off as theirs, worked from the premise that information bowed before no authority other than the person willing to spend a few kopecks for it. Reporters embodied as well as disseminated a cultural paradigm that embraced the social mobility, individualism, and entrepreneurial spirit that their occupation epitomized.[43] When Shreier tinkered with the truth for a scoop that would also profit him financially, he was serving a public interest that complemented rather than contradicted his own private concerns. Newspaper journalism brought the market and the reading public together rather than separating them. Despite instances of corruption, when reporters entered the marketplace looking for news, there was nothing inherent in reporting that forced private considerations to overwhelm public ones. This became more readily apparent in their attempts to organize an institutional basis to advance their professional goals.

Training and Organizing the Reporters

After public service, a second aspect of professionalization calls for specialized education to prepare prospective members to execute the duties that those without advanced instruction cannot. The requirements for particularized training relate directly to the concept of servicing the public: someone acting without the required training, such as one who practices medicine without having studied it, would harm the public interest. Notions of specialization have continually plagued would-be professional journalists because, unlike in the field of medicine, fundamentals learned in elementary school can suffice for competent reporting. Furthermore, expertise could be gained perhaps more easily on the job than in the classroom. In Russia, for example, Pastukhov and Suvorin emulated the examples of Bennett and Greeley by instructing the first "schools" of reporters. Many journalists referred to *Birzhevye vedomosti* as their "alma mater" because they worked there at some point in their careers.[44]

A feeling prevailed among reporters from the 1880s that their work had progressed beyond something anyone chatting in a saloon could do. Because in their opinion facticity gave journalism a basis in social science, they wanted it taught in an academic environment. The United States, as usual, pioneered. After several schools experimented with courses in journalism history, the University of Missouri in 1908 became the first to

---

[43] Schudson, in *Discovering the News*, argued that "a culture of the market became a more pervasive feature of human consciousness" through this aspect of the development of the mass-circulation press (59).

[44] L'vov (Kliachko), *Za kulisami* 1:85.

establish a separate school of journalism with a unique curriculum. Four years later, Pulitzer endowed Columbia University to found a similar school, and other Western countries followed suit, but Russian reporters petitioned in vain to add journalism courses to university curricula.[45] Aspiring reporters could study at night schools or through correspondence courses.[46] In Moscow in 1905, for fifty rubles per semester Professor L. E. Vladimirskii would conduct special evening classes on journalism to "members of both sexes" without demanding "any documents or any official educational qualifications."[47]

In addition to maxims of public service and specialized education, a third facet of professionalization expects that members will regulate their group to maintain high standards of ethical behavior. This requires a formal institution. The autocracy obstructed the development of an institution that would permit Russian journalists to meet and debate professional considerations, so they had to depend upon voluntary associations to discuss matters of mutual concern. The overarching problems of censorship and restricted civil liberties could overwhelm at these discussions. Many of the most prominent journalists met informally at dinners to deliberate the quandaries besetting their occupation.[48] The struggle between the intelligentsia and reporters spilled over into these discussions. For example, intellectuals who banded together to pressure the newly coronated Nicholas II to relieve the burdens of censorship categorically excluded representatives from the boulevard press; Notovich was the only newspaper publisher invited to sign their petition.[49] Journalists could organize legally into mutual-aid and credit societies, such as the Literary Fund.[50] Dependent largely on private donations, however, they could only afford to assist a needy few.[51]

A protoprofessional assembly, the Society of Journalists, appeared in St. Petersburg in 1898, and its members prepared to take on the matter of ethics. Composing makeshift "courts of honor" to put the "dirty yellow

[45] Esin, *Puteshestvie v proshloe*, 156–59.

[46] P. and D. Kumanov produced *Rukovodstvo dlia nachinaiushchikh gazetnykh korrespondentov* (Moscow: Luch', 1916), a 126-page guide in ten parts on how to become a provincial correspondent for newspapers in the two capitals.

[47] The advertisement appeared on the front page of *Rs*, 3 Jan. 1905, no. 3.

[48] G. K. Gradovskii, "Iz istorii russkoi pechati," *Mir*, no. 4 (1908): 49–53.

[49] Ibid., 49–50.

[50] See the article on the "Literaturnyi fond" in *Entsiklopedicheskii slovar'* 17(a) (SPB: Brokgaus and Efron, 1896): 797–99.

[51] Kaufman established a mutual-aid society in the 1890s that went bankrupt in 1918. His personal archive, maintained in TsGALI f. 252, contains scattered communications about it. Suvorin and Pastukhov also organized societies for their employees. *Kak pechataetsia gazeta Novago vremeni* (SPB: Suvorin, 1911), 15; *Bv*, 19 Jan. 1895, no. 19; and "Iz obshchestvennoi khroniki," *Vestnik evropy*, no. 12 (1902): 882–90.

blackmailer" on trial, these determined few represented an ideal but could not levy an enforceable authority.[52] In 1905, when all occupations, from laborers to lawyers, coalesced under the umbrella of the Union of Unions, journalists convened and voted to remove items about professionalization from the agenda and to concentrate exclusively on the overthrow of the Old Regime. Significantly, those who considered themselves reporters rather than journalists objected to this definition of goals.[53] The 1905 movement led to the creation of the most productive of tsarist Russia's journalistic organizations, the Society of Periodical Press and Literature Workers, organized in 1907 to "defend the professional, ethical, and material interests" of its members.[54] But even with branches in major cities and a short-lived house organ, *Zhurnalist* (*The Journalist*), the group could boast only 553 members in 1915.[55] The absence of the famous and influential from its roster suggests that the organization had minimal influence on the conduct of newspaper reporters, although the pages of *Zhurnalist* expressed the continued concern over the broad goal of professionalization.

Reporters as a New Intelligentsia

The Russian intelligentsia constituted a singularly important pillar of tradition because of its historical role in articulating opposition to the autocracy. This elite claimed to speak for the public that could not share in the advantages they themselves enjoyed through birth or education, and they saw themselves as holding knowledge in trust for the masses. Enter the newspaper reporter to dispute the basis of the intelligentsia's claims to authority.[56] As Martin Malia pointed out, "Under the impact of [the social changes brought about by industrialization in the 1890s] the intelligentsia began to have self-doubts about their self-righteousness and apartness."[57] The intelligentsia purported to speak *for* readers, the re-

[52] Esin mentions these courts in *Russkaia dorevoliutsionnaia gazeta*, 60. See also V. Miakotin, "Nabroski sovremennosti. O pisatel'skom s"ezde," *Rb*, no. 8 (1908): 117. Suvorin discussed being called to one in his diary. *Dnevnik Suvorina*, 195–204.

[53] The proceedings from this congress are in TsGALI f. 1694, op. 1, d. 744, ll. 178–83. See also V. G. Khoros, "Pis'mo N. F. Annenskogo o pervom s"ezde zhurnalistov Rossii," *Vestnik MGU*, journalism series, no. 1 (1968): 84–85.

[54] *Ustav obshchestva periodicheskoi pechati i literatury* (Moscow: n.p., 1907), art. 1.

[55] Leikina-Svirskaia, *Russkaia intelligentsiia*, 143.

[56] As Amy Kaplan argued, "If the realists engaged in the construction of a new kind of public sphere, they were also formulating a new public role for the author in the mass market." *Social Construction*, 13.

[57] Martin Malia, "What Is the Intelligentsia?" in Richard Pipes, ed., *The Russian Intelligentsia* (New York: Columbia University Press, 1960), 17.

porters *to* them. The popularity of newspapers reflected clear-cut changes in the nature of audiences, changes that threatened to leave the intelligentsia out in the bitter Russian cold. Reporters had usurped power by eliminating a key function performed in the past by the intelligentsia: they made knowledge available instead of holding it in trust. The circumstances of industrialization had, quite simply, altered informational needs.

The intelligentsia balked at responding to the new demands because of their preference for interpretation over presentation. The same easy dismissal of commercial culture as beneath their dignities led intellectuals in the West as well as in Russia to ridicule newspaper journalists. Theodore Zeldin noted that as late as 1875 Larousse's *Encyclopedia* called the reporter " 'an inferior writer', whose legs were more important than his style, and who 'is in general rather poorly thought of by serious people who regret seeing news taking on exaggerated importance.' "[58] A professor of medicine took scientific aim in 1871 with his *Influence of Journalism on the Health of Body and Mind*, diagnosing journalists as "jealous, ambitious . . . living in a state of pathological excitement and hot fever."[59] A frustrated "thick" journalist bemoaned, "It has become contemptible to be called a correspondent!"[60] His more pensive contemporary tried to explain the differences by arguing pseudoscientifically that those who wrote for newspapers used a different part of their brain than those who wrote for journals; he offered more cause for reporters to take heart than the French doctor, though, pointing out that through rigorous exercise of their upper brain centers they, too, could acquire intelligence.[61]

Reporters had to replace the type of leverage they could wield with the extent of it as their personal measure of success. The divergent paths taken by the Chekhov brothers illustrated this. Both trained for medicine, but turned to the boulevard press in search of careers in journalism and ended up influential writers, each in his own way. Anton, while working for newspapers, never overcame his feelings of intellectual inferiority associated with this medium. Priding himself on having made his reputation the hard way, in newspaper journalism, he gladly took credit for improving the quality of newspaper literature sufficiently to attract literary critics.[62] But he confided to his brother that among reporters, "I am in the lowest company, and working with them, I am becoming a scoundrel."[63]

[58] Zeldin, *France, 1848–1945* 2:504.
[59] Ibid., 505.
[60] "Korrespondenty novago tipa," *Nedelia*, no. 19 (1887): 617.
[61] Sozertsatel', "Obo vsem," *Rb*, no. 2 (1887): 173–94.
[62] B. I. Esin, *Chekhov-Zhurnalist* (Moscow: MGU, 1977), 32, 75.
[63] Ibid., 30.

The older Chekhov, Alexander, who had studied math and physics at Moscow University, typified the new reporters. Alexander set great store by his vocation, recalling in his memoirs the thrill of being welcomed by the coterie of St. Petersburg's finest reporters.[64] He spent almost his entire career as a primary reporter and feuilletonist at *Novoe vremia*.[65] Although he did not describe himself as either a social scientist or a reformer, Alexander appreciated that reporting allowed him to operate as both in service to the public.[66] He covered science, including the growing discipline of social science, and one of his most famous series of articles was an investigation into the social consequences of alcoholism. Epitomizing what one of the daily newspaper's continued adversaries described with condescension as "an American type, energetic, inventive, and with all the necessary connections," sneering that legwork should not substitute for brain power, Alexander showed how legs had become important to technique.[67] With Doroshevich, he supplied a respectable, even enviable, role model.

It is not his brother Alexander, though, but Doroshevich who contrasts most imaginatively with Chekhov. A comparison of the styles the two writers used to cover the same story, but through different media and for different audiences, pulls together the importance of the end of didacticism and the sensationalism of the mass-circulation press. Emerging into the national spotlight after he left Pastukhov in the 1890s, Doroshevich made his mark translating a story Chekhov had written for the "thick" journal *Russkaia mysl'* (*The Russian Thought*) into the language and experience of newspaper readers. In 1890 Chekhov had traveled to the penal colony on Sakhalin Island, intending to collect data for a scholarly dissertation. His startling findings about the brutal life on the island attracted an audience wider than academic circles, and the stir produced by his series in the journal prompted Doroshevich to follow in his wake. By the mid-1890s Doroshevich had left Moscow for Odessa, where he worked for the liberal *Odesskii listok* (*The Odessa Sheet*). He quickly became a local celebrity here, and from his new forum branched out nationally when newspapers around the empire reprinted his stories from Sakhalin.[68]

The striking difference in approach the two writers took in recording their observations can be attributed to the contrasting requirements of the media for which they wrote. Chekhov wrote long, detailed descrip-

---

[64] Alexander Chekhov, "Zapiski reportera," 81.

[65] A third Chekhov brother, Mikhail, also worked for Suvorin, operating *Novoe vremia's* railroad concessions for a time.

[66] Alexander Chekhov, "Zapiski reportera," 71.

[67] M. Gal-in, "Sredi khronikerov," *Rm*, no. 5 (1913): 20.

[68] Kaufman, "Iz zhurnal'nykh vospominanii," no. 11 (629), remembered Doroshevich's popularity in Odessa.

tions, as if recording in a diary, because his audience would be able to read and reflect on his work at their leisure. Doroshevich, on the other hand, wrote short, vivid pieces in order to attract the immediate attention necessary to sell newspapers. He also wrote for emotional appeal. Setting the mood, Doroshevich reported melodramatically how, en route to Sakhalin via a prison ship, he would eavesdrop on prisoners' sorrowful conversations through the ship's ventilating system, and then retire to his stateroom to weep for them.[69]

Compare, for example, the two descriptions of the pathos of a convict's life among other criminals. Chekhov narrated: "The vices and perversions common to people who are for the most part dependent, enslaved, hungry and in constant fear can be observed everywhere. . . . In order to escape from hard labor or corporal punishment, and to procure for oneself a crust of bread, a pinch of tea, salt or tobacco, the prisoner resorts to guile, because experience has taught him that in the struggle for existence, deception is the most tried-and-true means."[70]

Doroshevich, in contrast, used interviews, as when he tracked down the infamous "Golden Arm" and returned her to her curious followers. This "Rocambole in Skirts" invited pity rather than censure, though, when Doroshevich allowed her to speak through her tears: " 'I have two daughters. I don't even know whether they are dead or alive. Maybe they're embarrassed to have such a mother, they've forgotten me . . . I know only that they became actresses in operettas, in cheap little places. Good God! Of course, if I'd been there, my daughters never would have become actresses.' "[71]

Doroshevich's interview with Bliuvshtein was as significant for the way in which he reported it as it was for the subject matter's recognized standing in the popular press. The writer demonstrated his mastery of what sociolinguists have termed "situated language," that is, "writing in which the author conventionally attempts to approximate the speech of everyday life."[72] Doroshevich's convention of replicating dialogues, an established aspect of journalese but perfected here by its most talented sociolinguist, accentuated the newspaper's ability to reconstruct reality. Turning readers into eavesdroppers enhanced his "claims to professional competence and verisimilitude."[73]

Doroshevich also pioneered the use of investigative reporting to free

[69] V. M. Doroshevich, Kak ia popal na Sakhalin (Moscow: Tovarishchestvo I. D. Sytina, 1903), 14.

[70] Anton Chekhov, Ostrov Sakhalina (Moscow: Sovetskaia Rossiia, 1984), 286–87.

[71] V. M. Doroshevich, Sakhalin, 2 vols. (Moscow: Tovarishchestvo I. D. Sytina, 1903), 2:10.

[72] Schiller, Objectivity and the News, 110.

[73] Ibid.

Fig. 9. Sofia Bliuvshtein, pickpocket-heroine "The Golden Arm," imprisoned on Sakhalin Island

two peasants in Poltava wrongly accused of murdering a state official. He lived in the area for two weeks, interviewed witnesses, and exerted the power of the press to intervene in, not simply to report on, the legal system.[74] If his professions of impartiality were naive, his trust in facts was sincere.[75] Like other civic reformers, reporters such as Doroshevich maintained "faith in the power of facts and information. This faith allowed them to make the bridge between science and morality, between efficiency and democracy."[76] Moreover, using the newspaper to correct a miscarriage of justice by providing factual information pertinent to the case, he greatly enhanced its image as an institution serving society.

Whether taking into consideration first the style or the substance of the new journalism, whether reading Chekhov's rejection of didacticism or Doroshevich's racy descriptions, the cumulative changes evident in journalism by 1900 confirm the appearance of a new type of writer. Their efforts to maintain objectivity, to stand outside as observers, impartially

[74] Discussed in *SPB vedomosti*, 13 Jan. 1904, no. 12.

[75] Schudson, *Discovering the News*, 176–93. See also Herbert J. Gans, *Deciding What's News* (New York: Pantheon, 1979), especially chapter 6.

[76] David Paul Nord, "The Paradox of Municipal Reform in the Late Nineteenth Century," *Wisconsin Magazine of History* 66, no. 2 (1982–1983): 141.

recording details and conversations rather than interpreting for readers, separated this new intelligentsia from the old. Both groups had an equally strong sense of social responsibility, but they did not share the same ideas of how to communicate it. Those from Belinskii's tradition held a particularly subjective view of Russian life, with distinct notions about their duties as national cultural leaders. The new group, significantly, did not consider that they were living an existence isolated from much of contemporary life. Gathering facts instead of interpreting them, reporters showed greater confidence in their readers' abilities to make decisions about what they read. By stimulating readers to think of themselves as actors in the world unfolding around them, reporters encouraged aspirations among readers to influence the course of events.

The rising prominence of the reporter and the influence of the language of newspaper journalism forced the intelligentsia to adapt themselves and their media. Korolenko's career shows how. Beginning by serving time on *Novosti*'s copydesk in 1876, he built a modest career as a "thick" journalist in the next decade. Siberian exile for refusing to swear an oath of allegiance to Alexander III had restricted his options, and he published where he could in the 1880s.[77] Freed from exile, he took his family to Nizhnii Novgorod, and rose to prominence on *Volzhkii vestnik* (*The Volga Herald*) in the 1890s, a decade known there as the "Korolenko epoch." This writer, who would become one of the major voices of populism in the twentieth century, disturbed the local intelligentsia with his realistic reporting. "His work comes from the brain," complained one reader, "but people respond only to what comes from the soul."[78]

Korolenko's principal forum became the "thick" journal *Russkoe bogatstvo*, where he dominated editorially after replacing legendary populist N. G. Mikhailovskii upon his death in 1904. He arrived with Anton Chekhov's literary technique of lengthy, fact-based narrative descriptions that differed more from Belinskii and Saltykov-Shchedrin than from Doroshevich. Some of Korolenko's most important stories, for example, came from covering sensational trials that had volatile political undercurrents, from the 1896 trial of a Siberian tribe accused of conducting human sacrifices, to the celebrated case in 1913 of Mendel Beilis, the Jewish factory watchman charged with the ritual murder of a Christian boy. Instead of stooping to Pastukhov's level, a new generation of writers would contribute to the creation of a press that would be culturally uplifting and politically aggressive and would appeal to a broad audience.

[77] For a short comparison of the early careers of Korolenko and Chekhov, see L. E. Obolenskii, "Obo vsem," *Rb*, no. 12 (1886): 166–85.

[78] *Autobiography of Maxim Gorkii*, trans. Isidor Schneider (New York: Citadel, 1949), includes Gorky's comments on his tenure in Nizhnii Novgorod during the "Korolenko epoch" (559–62).

M. K. Lemke, prerevolutionary Russia's most prolific historian of its journalism, his studies heavily accented by attention to censorship, made a concerted effort to bridge the divide between "journalists" and "reporters" in his *Thoughts of a Journalist* in 1903. Torn himself between the prestige of the "thick" journal and the obvious power of the daily newspaper, he decided hesitantly in favor of the latter. Considering all points of the familiar debate, he railed against the negative potential of commercialism and resurrected Saltykov's farcical publisher Ivan Remembersnothing. But then he concluded that Saltykov and Shelgunov, who had blamed the intelligentsia for not taking control of the mass-circulation press when it first appeared, had overreacted against newspapers because they were insecure about their own place as writers in society. Arguing against the theory of small-deeds gradualism, he echoed Menshikov and pointed to the importance of the role of the daily paper in the more important "large deed," by which he meant the functioning of modern society. When he told readers, "You must appreciate your own strength. Without your support the journalist is no more than a bureaucrat," he brought the argument about public service full circle. Not only did he insinuate reporters into public service, he entrusted readers with at least partial responsibility for the contents of their newspapers. Lemke drew the vital link between servant and public as the government tottered toward crisis in the Far East.[79]

The newspaper journalists took their place in the new gathering of socially committed and educated Russians. Dedicated to serving readers, they borrowed both from the Russian intellectual heritage of commitment to the people and from the late-nineteenth-century movement toward professionalization. Developing into a new type of intelligentsia, their reciprocal relations with the old-style intellectuals affected both groups. At the end of the nineteenth century, reporters gained in respect and authority by offering to readers a medium for understanding the world around them. Many became recognizable personalities, and some feuilletonists continued in the role of explaining change to the less sophisticated readers. The development of a new reportorial intelligentsia also produced the interpretive reporter, someone between the fact-gatherer and the feuilletonist who lent the weight of expert commentary to news; Alexander Chekhov's series on alcoholism and Doroshevich's Sakhalin stories exemplified this combination of journalistic investigation and the personal prestige of the writer. The higher profile enjoyed by newspaper journalists would become evident in their coverage of the new century's first major story, the Russo-Japanese War.

[79] M. K. Lemke, *Dumy zhurnalista* (SPB: n.p., 1903), 4, 7, 46, 64, 180.

8

The Journalism of Imperialism

THE RUSSO-JAPANESE WAR

As JAPANESE soldiers stormed the Russian stronghold at Port Arthur in December of 1904, driving toward the Christmastime surrender of tsarist forces that would betray Nicholas II's folly of fighting a "small victorious war" in the Far East, readers of *Russkoe slovo* learned that one of their correspondents was steaming home from Japan with intimate details of life in the Land of the Rising Sun. V. E. Kraevskii had traveled incognito as tourist "Percy Palmer" aboard an American cruise ship in September, braving the dangers of exposure that would have surely marked him a Russian spy. Landing safely in San Francisco en route home, he telegraphed news of his triumphal voyage to his editors in Moscow, who blazoned the stunt with a bannerline and a woodcut portrait of their intrepid reporter.[1] This feat rivaled the journalistic gambit of circling the world in fewer than eighty days.

Unfortunately for poor Percy, the subsequent events of 1905 trivialized his exploit. On 9 January, when Father Grigorii Gapon was leading a peaceful demonstration of workers to the Winter Palace, toward the bloody confrontation with troops that would give this particular Sunday its historical epithet, *Russkoe slovo*'s readers were treated to fatuous photos of Percy in a rickshaw. Using the mails instead of the telegraph for his longer stories meant a time delay, so his opinion that "personally, I feel that it will be difficult work for the Russians to subdue the Japanese, but they will do it" did not sound so insightful when published after the fall of Port Arthur.[2] But because this study focuses on journalism, looking at the war from the perspective of the role of the daily newspaper, it can therefore restore Percy's ingenuity to its rightful place.

This chapter is about the new journalism Percy's escapade epitomized. The main protagonists are his publisher, Ivan Dmitrevich Sytin, and his editor, Doroshevich. Through their efforts *Russkoe slovo* was on its way to becoming tsarist Russia's most widely circulated and influential newspaper. *Russkoe slovo* provided the most news, the best coverage, the most popular journalists; it was also the first paper to lure contributions

[1] *Rs*, 9 Dec. 1904, no. 342.
[2] From *Russkoe slovo*'s Sunday supplement, *Iskra*, 9 Jan. 1905, no. 9.

from the intelligentsia. Its publisher's insistence that his paper be both "accessible to everyone" and "truly Russian," when realized successfully, meant that its readership, in addition to being the largest, incorporated the widest variety of subgroups.[3] The Russian prototype of the great Western mass-circulation dailies, *Russkoe slovo* was correctly identified by Doroshevich as a genuinely *public* institution because its readers came from all classes, educational backgrounds, political leanings, and regions of the empire.[4]

This chapter is divided into three parts. The first introduces *Russkoe slovo*, the second presents the growth of Russia's journalism of imperialism, and the third connects the press, especially *Russkoe slovo*, to the Russo-Japanese War, the culmination of imperialist expansion. *Russkoe slovo* and the war both developed from the same forces of modernization that had allowed Russians to reassert their claims to Great Power status after the Congress of Berlin in 1878. As Dietrich Geyer has argued in his study of Russian imperialism, "The nationalist ideology which insisted that Russia must be a great power was a social product of frenetic modernization."[5] Industrialization had made possible the mass-circulation press and its audience, and had supplied both with the imperialist ambitions characteristic of the modern states at the turn of the twentieth century.

Insofar as this is a comparative study, reportage of the Spanish-American War of 1898 and the Boer War that erupted a year later provide the appropriate context. This was the journalism of Rudyard Kipling, whose writing career began on a colonial newspaper in the Punjab and culminated in the Nobel Prize in 1907 in large political measure for urging readers to "take up the white man's burden." The mass-circulation dailies established a beachhead in the imperialist wars by glorifying the prowess of their respective nations. The Industrial Revolution had made possible the new imperialism by giving those nations who underwent it a material strength, which in turn imparted a sense of self-righteousness and purposefulness. The Russo-Japanese War originated in the contest between the world's most recent industrial powers for the right to exact Korea from China's decomposing Manchu empire, until the Russian populace localized it into a fight for political authority at home.

The beneficiaries of the political changes associated with industrialization, the burgeoning middle class, constituted the most avid consumers

[3] Lead editorial in *Rs*, 1 Jan. 1898, no. 1, Sytin's first edition as publisher.

[4] The Sytin Publishing Company produced a lavish monograph commemorating Sytin's fifty years in publishing in 1916; Doroshevich contributed the chapter on *Russkoe slovo*. *Polveka dlia knigi* (Moscow: Sytin, 1916), 420.

[5] Dietrich Geyer, *Russian Imperialism: The Interaction of Domestic and Foreign Policy, 1860–1914*, trans. Bruce Little (New York: Berg, 1987), 317.

of this new journalism.[6] The socioeconomic changes that begat the popular press contributed much to the new imperialism; to quote Geyer, "Modern imperialism . . . cannot predate the development of modern bourgeois society."[7] The growth of manufactories and subsequent search for raw materials and markets for finished goods had given rise to expansionism. The profit motive, however, proved an inadequate moral justification for conquest, and imperialist powers also laid claim to performing a sacred mission by advancing modern civilization. *Golos* and *Peterburgskaia gazeta* had taken different tacks on the colonization of Central Asia from the 1860s, but both newspapers had promoted the image of a Russian nation that had duties to fulfill as a member of the civilized world. Later, the Russo-Turkish War allowed the Russian press to demonstrate its power to mobilize a nationalistic public opinion of sufficient force to influence official policies. Although it was the Japanese Navy, not the press, that forced an end to the hostilities, the revolutionary movement had begun to force concessions from the government before the disaster at the Tsushima Straits in 1905. Russia's journalism of imperialism challenged the autocracy's supreme authority to define national interests.

"Imperialism" meant "nationalism" to Russia in ways that it did not to Western powers because Russia's territorial expansion differed from that of the West on several important points. Physically, the Russians absorbed contiguous territories instead of sailing to new continents. The tsarist nation's relative economic poverty not only denied it the kinds of financial controls that other powers enjoyed, but, moreover, made it at times a victim of fiscal intervention that smacked of imperialism. But certain fundamentals held the same for all, especially the "interdependence of expansionist strategies and more rapid socio-economic change" brought on by rapid industrialization.[8]

By the same token, Russia's imperialistic journalism had surface parallels that changed course under closer examination. Russian imperialism took the country to war with Japan, just as the United States fought Spain and Great Britain went to battle in the Transvaal, but their respective mass-circulation newspapers did not carry public opinion in the same directions. America's and England's newspapers agitated for war, so much so that in the case of the United States the press is often credited with

---

[6] In her study of Britain's imperialistic journalism, Catherine Hughes argued, "It was, however, the newly affluent lower middle classes who were most vociferous and unquestioning in their reception of things imperial, and their new wealth coupled with their recent enfranchisement made them a social and political force of no little importance." "Imperialism, Illustration and the *Daily Mail*, 1896–1904," in Harris and Lee, *The Press in English Society*, 187.

[7] Geyer, *Russian Imperialism*, 17.

[8] Ibid., 11.

having ignited it. The jingoism that gave journalism one of its most jaundiced characteristics, richly illustrated by Hearst's offer of fifty thousand dollars for the "Conviction of the Criminals Who Sent 258 American Sailors to Their Death"[9] aboard the battleship Maine torpedoed in Havana Harbor on 15 February 1898, was not a part of Russian coverage of the war with Japan; the burst of patriotism following the surprise attack by the Japanese on 26 January 1904 had abated months before defeat was imminent. Even when Percy wrote that he thought the Russians would eventually prevail, he did so with a heavy heart.

The racist aspect of imperialism also played differently in Russia. A central feature of imperial philosophy, race figured prominently into definitions of civilization. The "white men" Kipling addressed specifically were citizens of the United States, and their "burden" lay in civilizing the Philippines, newly won from Spain. Cecil Rhodes, the most aggressive advocate of Britain's imperial policies, had always wanted something more than financial bounty from his enterprises in southern Africa, where he governed as prime minister of the Cape Colony in the 1890s. A regular villain in the Russian press, Rhodes at twenty-four had dedicated his life "for the furtherance of the British Empire, for the bringing of the whole civilized world under British rule, for the recovery of the United States, for making the Anglo-Saxon race into an empire."[10] Such bombast gave Slavs cause for alarm.

Russia did not shoulder the white man's burden in the same manner the British did, and the war that pitted white Russians against yellow Japanese touched upon an issue that the European powers did not face: How was Russia to integrate the Asian and European halves of its geographical character? Race, only one component of nationalism, could be regulated by abstractions of class or culture that alternately obscured or intensified racial distinctions. The challenge of cultural assimilation gave Russia's imperialistic journalism one of its most compelling editorial questions.

Russkoe slovo: Accessible and Truly Russian

The birth of neither publisher nor newspaper suggested so bright a future. Born in 1852 to a state peasant clerking in the bureaucracy of Kostroma Province, the young Sytin had only a few years of schooling. Like Pastukhov's and Suvorin's, Sytin's biography told of entrepreneurial ge-

---

[9] Headlines in the *New York Journal*, 17 Feb. 1898, no. 5572.

[10] Walter L. Arnstein, *Britain Yesterday and Today* (Lexington, Mass.: D. C. Heath, 1976), 170.

Fig. 10. I. D. Sytin, publisher of *Russkoe slovo*

nius. Apprenticed in his teens to a Muscovite fur trader who ran a small publishing firm on the side, Sytin capitalized as the other two innovative publishers had on the Nizhnii Novgorod Fair, the Russo-Turkish War, and literature affordable to the masses. Peddling at first *lubki*, colorful prints with religious and adventure motifs, Sytin took a major step when he produced a map of the Balkans for insertion in newspapers just as war was declared in 1877. But Sytin did not share the other two publishers' conservatism, and in the 1880s he joined with archrival of the autocracy, novelist, and religious philosopher Lev Tolstoi, in the Posrednik (Intermediary) Publishing House, which functioned under the principle of providing good books cheaply.[11]

Although Sytin was not bound to Tolstoi and his highly controversial followers, his association with them brought problems with censors, difficulties that in time served to the publisher's advantage. He had

[11] Sytin left an "autobiography" of questionable authorship, *Zhizn' dlia knigi* (Moscow: Kniga, 1978). See also Robert Otto, *Publishing for the People: The Firm Posrednik, 1885–1905* (New York: Garland, 1987), 60–90.

branched into periodicals in 1892 with an illustrated family weekly, *Vokrug sveta* (*Around the World*), not affiliated with Posrednik, and in the next year began applying for permission to publish a newspaper. At first, however, his relations with the Tolstoians made censors too suspicious to approve his publishing a periodical with a political section, and Sytin had to enter the newspaper industry as a clandestine backer of A. A. Aleksandrov's ultrareactionary and un-newsworthy *Russkoe slovo*, subsidized by the state, which appeared in 1895.[12] When Witte put an end to this financial drain in 1897, he forced Aleksandrov to sell the paper.[13]

The last six months of 1897 saw Sytin hustling to secure permission to publish, which came only when he agreed to keep Aleksandrov on as "responsible" editor, although he was kept on salary in a contrived position and earned his pay by working as Sytin's liaison with officials.[14] The accusation that Sytin had turned *Russkoe slovo* into "the pettiest street sheet" was an exaggeration, but his paper resembled the other boulevard fare.[15] Veteran of the boulevard N. N. Zhivotov, the "Crown Prince of Reporters," kept readers abreast of social life around town writing under the pen name "The Pink Domino." "The Iron Mask" entertained, serial novels mixed patriotic histories with mutilated corpses strewn along "The Path of Blood," and Miasnitskii contributed feuilletons while continuing at *Moskovskii listok*.

Sytin knew that his future prosperity did not depend on his attracting whomever he could from Moscow's boulevards. He wanted a newspaper that appealed to a broad national spectrum, affordable to the lower end of the readership scale without pandering to it or alienating the upper. Giliarovskii laughingly recalled the lean years, when *Russkoe slovo* was such a sorry institution that the doorman cleaned fish in the lobby, not bothering to wipe his hands before helping the mortified visitors off with their coats.[16] Like Hearst, who was spending these same years launching his *Journal* in New York, Sytin's other investments allowed him to absorb the first years' staggering financial losses, amounting to forty thousand rubles in 1899, a number that was double the circulation.[17] By 1900, the

---

[12] E. A. Dinershtein, "A Leviathan among Newspapers," *Soviet Studies in History* 25, no. 1 (Summer 1986): 36–48. Dinershtein's chapter on the "leviathan" is translated from his biography *I. D. Sytin* (Moscow: Kniga, 1983). Subsequent references will also be from the translation. Prince B. A. Shchetinin, "V literaturnom muraveike. Vstrechi i znakomstva," *Iv* 123, no. 3 (1911): 875–90.

[13] Witte rejected Aleksandrov's petition for the sum to continue in 1897. TsGIA f. 565, op. 14, d. 109, l. 61.

[14] Dinershtein, "A Leviathan," 49, 54.

[15] Shchetinin, "V literaturnom muraveike," 875.

[16] Giliarovskii, *Moskva gazetnaia*, 216.

[17] Dinershtein, "A Leviathin," 50. In another tale from the Hearst legend, the publisher's accountant was said to have warned Hearst that he had lost one million dollars on the paper

Fig. 11. The *Russkoe slovo* building

losses had been cut in half and circulation had risen by one third. But it would take the closing of *Rossiia*—more specifically, the unemployment of Doroshevich—to make available to Sytin the journalist capable of turning his enterprise around. Personifying Sytin's dual goals of making his paper "accessible" and "truly Russian," Doroshevich developed the language of Russia's imperialistic journalism, a writing convention of nationalism and braggadocio.

The publisher and writer already enjoyed a professional relationship, as Doroshevich had been selling feuilletons to *Russkoe slovo* since 1898.[18] The terms of Doroshevich's contract attest to Sytin's complete confidence in the journalist's abilities. Doroshevich had "general supervision" of the paper, the power to make final decisions that not even Sytin could veto, and no one could edit his copy. For this, and at least two feuilletons weekly, Doroshevich earned approximately forty thousand rubles per annum plus 20 percent of the paper's profits, an incentive Western publish-

in the past year. "Good," replied Hearst, "At this rate we can publish for another sixty years!" The story was retold in Orson Welles's classic film biography of Hearst, *Citizen Kane*.

[18] *Rs*, 19 Feb. 1917, no. 41; and I. R. Kugel', "Sytin," *Leningrad*, nos. 23–24 (1940): 17.

ers also used to attract top editors.[19] The only stipulation was that Do-roshevich stay within the confines of the censorship, a skill at which he was adept, having outridden both official disapproval of the Sakhalin pieces and the uproar at *Rossiia*.[20] Yet Sytin's son-in-law, F. I. Blagov, a medical doctor by training, held the post of "responsible" editor, with Doroshevich as "chief" (*glavnyi*). The latter spent much of the first few years traveling abroad, observing the Western press and reporting inter-national public opinion about Russia.[21]

Even before Doroshevich, who may well have been influenced by his tacit presence at the paper, Tolstoi stood as the figurative standard-bearer for *Russkoe slovo*. The chimerical Tolstoi commanded indisputable le-verage among all segments of the population by virtue of his stature as Russia's most famous contributor to world civilization. One feuilletonist's sentiments that "with Tolstoi we pay our debt to Europe" captured the newspaper's quintessential nationalism in the symbol of the figure who embodied Russian culture and was second to no one in the West.[22] Idol-ized for his preoccupation with ethical questions of justice, his unprag-matic doctrine of Christian Anarchy nonetheless troubled many on both right and left. *Russkoe slovo*'s serialization in 1899 of *Resurrection*, Tol-stoi's quasi-autobiographical account of a spiritually bankrupt nobleman redeemed through peasant piety, underlined the paper's identification with the moral titan.[23] In contrast, *Birzhevye vedomosti* rebuked Tolstoi, together with his American soulmate Henry David Thoreau, as "enemies of civilization and contemporary progress."[24]

Much of what the Russian philosopher stood for had little truck with the new journalism, which suggested a paradox in his relationship to this most modern of newspapers. *Russkoe slovo* resolved the contradiction between Tolstoi's convictions and contemporary communications by adapting the writer to the medium, creating a media-specific Tolstoi, a political character who functioned symbolically in the public sphere. Without editorializing in favor of his most questionable theories, *Russkoe slovo*'s editors could still use the fascination with his extraordinary life to sell both newspapers and themselves as sympathizers with the larger, imprecise concepts of equality and democracy for which he stood. An

[19] Bukchin, *Sud'ba fel'etonista*, 166; and Bokhanov, "Russkie gazety," 119.

[20] Bukchin, *Sud'ba fel'etonista*, 111–12.

[21] TsGALI f. 595, op. 1, d. 7, l. 1.

[22] *Rs*, 6 Sept. 1907, no. 205.

[23] A readership survey among workers in a local factory showed that "many" had begun to read *Russkoe slovo* because of *Resurrection*. P. Shestiakov, "Materialy dlia kharakteristiki fabrichnykh rabochikh," *Russkaia mysl'*, no. 1 (1900): 179.

[24] *Bv*, 24 June 1903, no. 307.

inflamed vein in Tolstoi's leg would make news,[25] and his views were sought on everything from constitutionalism to Mikhail Artsybashev's quasi-pornographic novel *Sanin*.[26] The writer himself could use *Russkoe slovo* to have personal appeals published.[27] In a time and place where newspaper readers had such limited opportunities to involve themselves in politics, the medium's ability to keep such symbols as Tolstoi at the forefront of public discussions in whatever form enhanced its merits as a serviceable alternative arena for political discourse.

The addition of maverick Orthodox priest G. S. Petrov, who corresponded as both a reporter and a feuilletonist, also contributed significantly to the paper's new tone.[28] Petrov's outspoken opinion that Orthodoxy did not respond to the legitimate needs of the masses would lead to his excommunication in 1907, only a few years after Tolstoi's expulsion from the Church for similar views. When modernist writer and philosopher Dmitrii Merezhkovskii began writing regularly for *Russkoe slovo* in 1903, he became the first member of the intelligentsia to join a newspaper's regular staff. The presence of these two writers accentuated *Russkoe slovo*'s commitment to addressing the historically important politics of Russian culture.

Doroshevich wrote in 1916 that he and Sytin had made the editorial decision to improve the paper gradually, hooking readers in and then moving them up "from class to class" as they brought in the better educated in the process.[29] Price hikes also came slowly, and never went as high as the national competition: in 1904, *Russkoe slovo* cost six rubles, but *Birzhevye vedomosti* cost ten and *Novoe vremia* fourteen. In editorial policy "truly Russian" did not equate with Great Russian: "*Russkoe slovo* will appeal equally to all the peoples inhabiting the Russian land, and it will consider these people as children of one family." Despite this disclaimer, there were intentionally few ethnicities represented on the staff.[30] Another of Sytin's objectives was to keep his paper "open to persons of different convictions," and he featured writers from both right and left.[31]

Above all, editor and publisher wanted this newspaper to provide the most accurate and complete news, and Doroshevich stressed facticity and

[25] *Rs*, 5 March 1909, no. 51.
[26] *Rs*, 17 July 1907, no. 163, and 7 March 1909, no. 54.
[27] Open letter from Tolstoi in *Rs*, 21 Sept. 1907, no. 208.
[28] Censors worried about what this dual hire of two popular critics of Orthodoxy and autocracy portended for *Russkoe slovo*'s editorial politics, but the appointments went unchallenged. TsGIA f. 776, op. 8, d. 847, l. 29.
[29] Doroshevich, *Polveka dlia knigi*, 418.
[30] Ibid., 400.
[31] Dinershtein, "A Leviathan," 59.

objectivity as the paper's guiding editorial principles.[32] The paper's national and international networks of correspondents, "representatives of the editorial board," compared with the best anywhere in the world. Moreover, Sytin insisted that his provincial correspondents work exclusively for him.[33] Students of a correspondence course on how to become a reporter were advised that *Russkoe slovo* would be the best paper to work for as a stringer.[34] Reputedly, Sytin engaged his own pony express, theatrically using a rider on a white horse as one means of getting information speedily to *Russkoe slovo*'s offices.[35] The Ministry of Post and Telegraph ultimately opened a branch at *Russkoe slovo*'s offices to handle the paper's "Niagra of telegrams."[36] Combining excellent coverage with an editorial policy that criticized official inadequacies in the language of the ordinary reader's favorite journalists, and priced to sell, *Russkoe slovo* acquired a national audience and an international reputation.

Russkoe slovo determined to speak out on the most pressing social issues. God lost out to the newspaper as the arbiter of social problems, and reporters encouraged the development of a civic consciousness with their critical coverage of local issues.[37] Joining in the debate about the nature of humanity, *Russkoe slovo* accepted insanity not only as a perfectly reasonable defense for murder, but possibly the only logical explanation for violent crime.[38] Syphilis was presented as a social rather than a personal disease, and the paper insisted that hiding it behind a curtain of shame instead of educating youth about its consequences would only end in more casualties.[39]

Russkoe slovo's editorial politics reinforced the progressive public opinion that wanted immediate and meaningful reforms of the political system, changes that would allow for more direct participation in matters of public concern. Like other paternalistically inclined publishers, Sytin vigorously supported settlement of the worker question with a reformative eye to the rights of labor: the working class deserved insurance, legislation protecting workers' rights on the job needed to be strengthened, and safety regulations had to be better enforced at the factory.[40] The sort

[32] Doroshevich, *Polveka dlia knigi*, 398, 402.

[33] TsGALI f. 595, op. 2, d. 4 contains letters to editor A. V. Rumanov from provincial correspondents about their contracts.

[34] *Kak korrespondirovat' v gazetu*, parts 12 (Odessa: n.p., 1912), part 10, 292–93.

[35] Ruud, *Fighting Words*, 218.

[36] Doroshevich's history of *Russkoe slovo*'s editorial policy in *Polveka dlia knigi*, 393–422.

[37] One reporter, for example, assured readers that they no longer needed to attend meetings of the local zemstvo because he would report the proceedings accurately. *Rs*, 28 Jan. 1898, no. 28.

[38] *Rs*, 2 and 3 April and 25 Aug. 1899, nos. 90–91, 234.

[39] *Rs*, 26 June 1902, no. 173.

[40] *Rs*, 18 July and 10 Nov. 1899, nos. 196, 311.

Fig. 12. *Russkoe slovo* rolling off the presses

of patronizing suggestion that the children of the poor be trained to fill the vacancies in domestic help disappeared after Sytin found a niche that included both employers and servants.[41] After the violent destruction of private property in 1905, some of the more conservative publishers would rethink their sympathetic defenses of exploited laborers, but not Sytin, even though he would lose his typography house when government troops attacked his workers holed up there in a revolutionary "hornets' nest."[42] On the critical peasant question, *Russkoe slovo* did not waver in its stance that peasants should be treated equitably as citizens of the empire and that the government must redress the centuries of inequality.[43]

The critic who disdained *Russkoe slovo* as having "the physiognomy of the man-on-the-street. . . . This newspaper always conforms to the mood of the crowd and invariably takes financial considerations into account"[44]

[41] *Rs*, 2 July 1902, no. 183.

[42] Sytin was unable to collect one ruble of the insurance money because the company charged that he had incited the government to burn down the typography house with his revolutionary politics. Sytin, "Pozhar moei fabriki," *Zhurnalist*, no. 12 (1925): 26–27. *Russkoe slovo*, published in a different building, was not affected by the fire.

[43] *Rs*, 21 and 24 June 1902, nos. 168, 171.

[44] Dinershtein, "A Leviathan," 59.

belonged in the era of the pre-*Golos* press. Financially successful it was; Sytin had made his newspaper for a time the most profitable subsidiary of his publishing empire, no mean feat for the man also producing one quarter of the books in Russia.[45] He did not achieve this by avoiding political encounters; rather, he softened their impact by keeping up a good front with his erstwhile foes. Responding to critics who rebuked him for compromising with authorities, he pointed out that his willingness to be flexible afforded him opportunities denied others.[46] Heavy expenditures for a lavish history of the Romanov dynasty to celebrate its tercentenary in 1913, the publication of a costly encyclopedia of the Russian military, or producing inexpensive, and largely unsold, religious books for the masses bought Sytin good will without compromising his own principles. Besides, his decidedly antiautocratic views were camouflaged by a genuine nationalism that pleased official Russia. Describing *Russkoe slovo* as the "loyal opposition,"[47] Sytin intended his paper to be a sort of quasi parliament, tendering "opposition that goes beyond incidental criticism of personalities and policies and claims its own constitutional standing."[48]

The Nationalism of Industrialization

Witte's industrial policies had made readers all the more sensitive to their place in the world, and correspondence from abroad both increased and acquired greater relevance. Doroshevich had ventured West first in 1895 as a foreign correspondent for *Odesskii listok*. Instead of relaying news of events in other countries, Doroshevich enjoyed the special editorial license of a feuilletonist. The evils of private capitalism remained one of his favorite themes, and he never tired of haranguing Western syndicates pocketing profits from their imperial enterprises, which included Russia by investment if not by direct colonial administration. Broadening his scope to the international setting allowed Doroshevich to intensify the predatory images of Europe, and he drew by contrast a magnanimous picture of Russia accepting its moral responsibility as a Great Power.

[45] According to the Sytin Company's annual report, *Otchet tovarishchestva Sytina*, in 1909–1910 *Russkoe slovo* brought in more earnings than the books or stores. Dinershtein, *Sytin* (192), also mentioned the great financial contribution the newspaper made to the firm. According to Bokhanov, Sytin's was the only publishing house that traded shares on the St. Petersburg stock exchange; when in 1912 the average dividend was 6.4 percent, Sytin's investors received 12 percent. "Russkie gazety," 120.

[46] *Rs*, 19 Feb. 1917, no. 41.

[47] Doroshevich, *Polveka dlia knigi*, 421.

[48] Moran, *Century of Words*, 272.

Among popular journalists, Doroshevich affirmed most eloquently the cultural virtues which Russians believed gave them the right to speak for those oppressed by other nations. Striking the same chords as in his attacks against the foreign businesses endangering Russia's economic integrity, Doroshevich oriented his readers toward a place where they could find self-esteem instead of belittlement in the outside world. He showed readers the United States, where "the dollar is everything," introducing them to the wealthy plantation owners who, exploiting the natives of the Hawaiian Islands, had made a mockery of political equality when they stamped out the nascent republic and forced instead a trusteeship status that would allow them to escape paying import duties. Sympathy for the Hawaiians carried over to the underpaid and overworked laborers in the foreign-controlled Baku oilfields, where decision-making was as evanescent for the Russians as for the aspiring Hawaiian republicans.[49]

The profit motive behind capitalism had made hypocrisy the quintessence of Western culture, and Doroshevich took it upon himself to expose this. His first trip abroad produced a series of feuilletons unique to the Russian press. Doroshevich specifically wanted to debunk notions of Western superiority that would make Russians think comparatively less of themselves. Anti-Semitism might be bad in Russia, but not compared to Vienna, where the Jewish fever to assimilate resembled an ethnic suicide. A Veronese marquis would be exalted for beneficence after throwing crusts to the poor, but a wealthy Odessan would pass unnoticed for a more generous contribution. And for all of Europe's lip service to labor equality, Russia's roving reporter witnessed bloody confrontations between workers and police in every country he visited.[50]

Disdain for the West carried over to those Russians who adopted European mannerisms. One of the first pieces Doroshevich had sold Sytin was "Gentlemen: The New Generation of Merchants," the saga of "Sila Silych," a fop whose lackey confided in the writer that he earned extra for calling the master "Lord."[51] The hapless Sila entered a tradition of Russian literary characters who slavishly mimic Western ways. Doroshevich supplied, in addition to the mirror that reflected ridiculous behavior, the outspoken opinion that one should not desire to emulate a morally inferior people. Although he did not find the issue quite so humorous, Menshikov, by 1904 one of *Novoe vremia*'s leading feuilletonists, shared Doroshevich's negative assessment of the same stereotypes, who "worked for the destruction of life, not its creation."[52]

Doroshevich took for granted Russia's status as a Great Power, and it

[49] Bukchin, *Sud'ba fel'etonista*, 142–43.
[50] Ibid., 66–67.
[51] *Rs*, 23 Dec. 1898, no. 356.
[52] *Nv*, 23 May 1904, no. 10137.

might have seemed to Westerners that he presumed too much for sec-ond-rate Russia. In order to claim such stature, a nation must be able to exert its authority beyond its own borders. If the Crimean War had hu-miliated Russians by exposing them as incompetent masters in their own house, the Congress of Berlin following the Russo-Turkish War had deep-ened the disgrace by showing up the inability of the Great Reforms to restore Russia's parity with the other Great Powers. Bulgaria, tradition-ally the most reliant ally, had further injured Russian pride when its dual provinces united in 1885 under Ferdinand of Saxe-Coburg, a move that increased Austrian influence at the expense of Russian. But industriali-zation had given Russians their second wind by the turn of the century, inspiring an eagerness to recover the international esteem that had crum-bled with the defenses around Sevastopol.

The Balkans for centuries had been the focus of Russian foreign policy directives because of the ethnic and religious ties to the Slavs under Ot-toman rule. But relationships had changed since the war fought twenty-five years earlier. In 1901 Amfiteatrov traveled to Macedonia, the slim strip of territory claimed by Greeks, Bulgarians, and Serbs alike because of the access it held to the Mediterranean. The series of articles from this trip combined travelogue with interpretive commentary and was striking for its absence of a declaration of a Russian historical mission based on race or religion. Amfiteatrov showed instead an irritation with Bulgarian demands that Russia support its claims to Macedonia. Pointing out that all the peasants in the Balkans enjoyed a higher standard of living than those in Russia, he shifted attention back to nationalist-oriented con-cerns. Amfiteatrov criticized Russian foreign policy directly, commenting that "unfortunately, when we speak in St. Petersburg about Russia spending so much for influence with a government, it almost always means that Russia spent too much for pensions, gifts, subsidies to some such prominent representative of this government or that people."[53]

Propper, too, criticized the Ministry of Foreign Affairs. In 1903 he served as foreign correspondent for *Birzhevye vedomosti*, traveling from Sofia to Constantinople. He toured the Balkans interviewing Ottoman officials, South Slavs, and Bulgarians about the claims all made to Mace-donia. His series, which included detailed maps of the territory in ques-tion and lists of the demands of the various groups wanting to control it, brought readers directly into the international mainstream. Like Amfi-teatrov, he did not argue for a Russian duty or destiny in the region. Having returned just when assassins ended the reign of King Alexander of Serbia, Propper gave great play to the bloody murder and outscooped

[53] Amfiteatrov, *Strana razbora*, 169–75.

the competition with his fresh personal insights into politics on the Balkan Peninsula.[54]

As Propper's and Amfiteatrov's reports implied, Russia's relationships with the Slavic territories of the Ottoman Empire fell into a state of flux when the increasingly better organized nationalist movements among the diverse ethnic groups began to rely less and less on Russian patronage. Therefore, when the decision to build the Trans-Siberian offered new directions in Russian foreign policy, many readers turned willingly away from contemptuous Westerners and ungrateful Slavs. Propper emphasized the "two-ocean" status of the empire and referred to Russia's "cultural obligations" in the Far East, a concept he did not apply to the Balkans during his extended visit.[55]

As the Trans-Siberian neared completion, interest in Asia mounted with every verst of track laid. At *Rossiia* Doroshevich joined with Amfiteatrov on a series of feuilletons published collectively as *The China Question*, setting straight for readers who was threatening whose interests.[56] They presented the ominous "yellow peril" as a British contrivance, arguing that the yellow man was rightfully more fearful of the white man than vice versa. Russian soldiers had recently fallen to Chinese bullets in a border skirmish at Taku, but the patriotism that had roused the earlier generation to take up arms against the Turks was not invoked here. Instead, the authors pointed to the Chinese corpses also littering the frontier, decrying the wasted lives on both sides. Blaming the British for standing behind the scenes egging Chinese and Russian governments to act against their own best interests, the journalists recalled the injustice meted out at the Congress of Berlin. It was bad enough that the Russians had been abused by the west. Why should they wish the same fate on their Chinese neighbors?[57]

The deterioration of Russo-Chinese relations to gunfire recalled how six hundred years earlier Russians had been asked, as they interpreted the situation, to protect the rest of Europe from the Mongol hordes. Traditionally, many Russians blamed their relative economic and political backwardness on the conquest by the Golden Horde. They asked special indulgence from Europe for having sacrificed so much in shielding the West, a forbearance Stalin would later demand when the USSR suffered the brunt of Hitler's campaign in World War II. Doroshevich and Amfiteatrov told readers to stop whimpering about what Europe owed them. Was Russia being called upon again to save the West from the East?

[54] For example, *Bv*, 1, 5, and 7 May 1903, nos. 213, 220, 223.

[55] *Bv*, 11 and 17 May 1903, nos. 230, 239.

[56] The feuilletons were collected and published in monograph form in 1901 as *Kitaiski vopros*.

[57] "The Chinese Threat," in ibid., 26.

"What an honor!" the reporters exclaimed sarcastically, putting the word *civilization* in quotation marks when applied to the West.[58] When Western powers justified their behavior on moral grounds, arguing that through imperial conquest they were raising the standards of civilization, the Russian writers responded with an approving commentary on China's distinguished millenium of culture: "Even if one wants to say that European civilization is 'good' and Chinese civilization 'evil'—although we know this not to be the case—so what if China wants to maintain its 'evil' ways instead of pursuing the 'good' of Jesuits and opium? . . . you say that it is the duty of cultured nations to civilize the wild ones? China is hardly a primitive country, it's just that its civilization differs from ours."[59] European civilization was portrayed as technologically advanced, but atavistically violent. China would be quite literally beaten into acceptance by a civilization distinguished by the death penalty and the dumdum bullet.[60] Although Doroshevich and Amfiteatrov did not outline how Russia's civilization differed from that of the rest of Europe, they implied strongly that Russians had accepted Western ideas too readily and should learn from China's predicament to rethink their own national experience.

Doroshevich and Amfiteatrov struck a highly nationalistic note that could also be found in the other mass-circulation newspapers. *Golos's* optimism that Russia had been accepted as "Enlightener of Asia and representative of Slavdom in Europe" had proved premature. Frustration with an unappreciative, hostile Europe began to find a popular voice in 1872 with Nikolai Danilevskii's intensely chauvinistic *Russia and Europe*. Pastukhov, watching the dissection of China, concluded that Russia should also be the "Enlightener of Europe": "Our fatherland, because of the upsurge in both its spiritual and material interests, would in fact provide the best defense of both peace and truth, in the West as well as the East."[61] Propper argued that Russia was a humanistic imperializer, giving education instead of taking profits.[62] Russia's beneficent imperialism also contrasted favorably to the violence that the United States used against its minorities both at home and in its rapidly expanding empire, not to mention the force employed by the French and the notorious Belgians in Africa.[63]

The boulevard papers provided another reading of the nationalism associated with imperialism. Many of the serialized adventures in *Peterburgskii listok* and *Peterburgskaia gazeta* now took place in Russia. He-

---

[58] Ibid., 27.
[59] Ibid., 32.
[60] "Miss Civilization," in ibid., 15–24.
[61] *Ml*, 26 Feb. 1895, no. 57.
[62] *Bv*, 26 Oct. and 30 Nov. 1901, nos. 292, 327.
[63] *Bv*, 18 Oct. 1901, no. 284; *Rs*, 22 Feb. 1905, no. 51.

roes no longer needed to go to France for excitement, but could find
ample love affairs and murder victims in their own country. Locating action in the "Petersburg Side," or district of the national capital heavily
populated by the working class, was in part a response to the curiosity
workers had generated about themselves with their strikes of the 1890s,
but the shift to Petersburg also suggested the loss of the need to look to
Europe. The Petersburg papers, however, only rarely published the historical novels so typical of their Muscovite counterparts; this sign from
popular culture suggests that Petersburg's urban audience might have
been more cosmopolitan than readers in Moscow.

Peterburgskii listok guarded Russia more tenaciously than did the protective tariff of 1891. Surrounded by malevolent forces, blameless Russia
had to worry about the "intrigues" plotted by foreign powers.[64] Nor did
one need to exit the empire to confront Western malice. The Finnish
citizens were "ungrateful" for the Russian umbrella, concealing behind
reputedly false statistics a standard of living that was seriously lower than
Russia's. Although *Peterburgskii listok*'s generalizations strain the imagination, when its editors argued that poverty, homelessness, infant mortality, illegitimate births, and alcoholism all measured higher in Finland,
they told their readers to ignore snubbing by such as those who pledged
allegiance to the West.[65]

Pastukhov burned most intensely the torch of chauvinism. But his was
a retrograde patriotism, a reactionary dread of modernity. Pastukhov's
unhappiness with the West reflected a contentment with the autocratic
status quo that would become perceptible in the fear that gripped the
pages of *Moskovskii listok* when the tsar stumbled in 1905. Valuable as a
yardstick of conservatism, *Moskovskii listok* held fast to its readership of
forty thousand. Pastukhov offered the false security of nostalgia, which
appeared repeatedly in his melancholic reflections on the loss of Alexander III as possibly the last hope of Christian Russia. The royal family,
which shielded itself from a public it perceived—not without reason—as
armed and dangerous, remained a subject of abiding interest to Russian
readers, but Pastukhov treated the Romanovs with exceptional reverence. The death of Nicholas's tuburcular younger brother Georgii in 1899
received most moving play in *Moskovskii listok*. Describing in pathetic
detail how a passing milkmaid had discovered the tsarevich, fallen from
his bicycle, "spitting up thick blood," Pastukhov made human this royal
personage whom illness had consigned to the shadows.[66]

When the long-awaited heir was born to Nicholas and Alexandra, the

[64] *Pl*, 15 Sept. 1892, no. 253.
[65] *Pl*, 21 Jan. 1892, no. 20.
[66] *Ml*, 29 June 1899, no. 179.

boy, like his uncle, suffered from an incurable disease that made it diffi-cult for his parents to allow him in the curious public's eye. The hemo-philiac Alexei, however, arrived in July 1904 amidst the war with Japan, when the rights of political succession to rule Russia had started to move out of the House of Romanov and into the public sphere.

Coverage of the Russo-Japanese War

The Japanese sneak attack on Port Arthur has often been compared to the "day of infamy," 7 December 1941, when they surprised the Ameri-can naval base at Pearl Harbor and brought the United States into World War II. The Russian autocracy, however, not only had been awaiting the war but welcomed it. Since 1896 Russia and Japan had shared a condo-minium over Korea, but the deeper the Russian penetration into Man-churia with the Trans-Siberian, the more the Japanese wanted an agree-ment that would allow them to dominate politically in Korea in exchange for the Russian presence in northern China, a balance of power to Witte's liking. But the tsar had lost confidence in his minister and had begun to fund speculator Alexander Bezobrazov, who was negotiating with the Ko-rean government for timber concessions along the Yalu River. Bezobra-zov's actions threatened the Japanese on the opposite bank, and Witte resigned in 1903 primarily over the tsar's rash policies there. (*Birzhevye vedomosti*, characteristically, had made public the disagreements be-tween the minister of finance and the shady Bezobrazov Company.)[67] In 1902 the Japanese entered into an alliance with England, which did not bode well for the Bezobrazov clique.

The press had followed closely the negotiations over spheres of influ-ence between the Japanese and Russian governments. Two weeks before the attack Doroshevich, in a feuilleton entitled "War," had suggested the inevitability of one, unless the worldwide phenomenon of imperialism ended of its own accord.[68] An editorial, "On the Eve," argued that the war would be fought because Western Europe had frustrated Japan's un-derstandable search for markets, adding that the Russian government should have begun weighing the consequences of its behind-the-scenes activities in Korea a decade ago.[69] When the unavoidable occurred, *Russ-koe slovo* invoked Tolstoi's name to remind readers how Russians hate war and must hope for a quick peace.[70]

First news of the battles came from the Russian military and European

[67] Kaufman, "Iz zhurnal'nykh vospominanii," no. 12, 1071.
[68] *Rs*, 13 Jan. 1904, no. 13.
[69] *Rs*, 27 Jan. 1904, no. 27.
[70] *Rs*, 30 Jan. 1904, no. 30.

news agencies based in the Far East, especially the British Reuters Agency. Technology also affected news; Guglielmo Marconi's wireless telegraphy had been operational for news services since 1898, and many correspondents from around the world had remained in Asia following the Boxer Rebellion in China in 1900. *Russkoe slovo* already had several correspondents in place, although none had immediate access to a telegraph, so the largely human interest stories were delayed publication by several weeks. Improved halftone technology allowed for better maps to be published in the newspapers, so Sytin did not need inserts. Moreover, the appearance of woodcut drawings of ships, maps, and military leaders the same day Moscow learned of the attack showed *Russkoe slovo*'s preparedness. By the end of February, letters from an officer's wife provided the engaging human interest particulars of housekeeping under siege.[71] The editors also solicited family photographs of anyone at the front for publication in *Iskra (The Spark)*, *Russkoe slovo*'s slick Sunday supplement. Although most newspapers' circulations jumped with the interest in the war, none equaled *Russkoe slovo*'s surge forward.[72]

Nemirovich-Danchenko set the pitch of *Russkoe slovo*'s attitude toward the war, and he opposed it from the outset. Signing him up with great fanfare, Sytin's editors announced his exclusive contract with a personal interview and a biography that accented his close friendships in the military.[73] Russian copyright law allowed the other newspapers to reprint Nemirovich-Danchenko's reports twenty-four hours after they appeared in *Russkoe slovo*, which the boulevard papers did occasionally, but he was Sytin's correspondent.[74] Sytin had not, however, hired Nemirovich-Danchenko just to report news as he had the hostilities in the Balkans in 1877. The publisher had purchased the writer's reputation and connections, and Nemirovich-Danchenko sent in stories in the form of a diary, this time using the first-person form that he had previously eschewed. Still an eyewitness, the writer could draw from his expertise to provide interpretive reporting. His fact-filled pieces complemented other news, but the additional insights he provided emphasized his importance as a newspaper personality. Throughout, like Doroshevich on Sakhalin, he kept the focus away from himself, but maintained his individualized voice.

Riding a troop train along the Trans-Siberian, Nemirovich-Danchenko

[71] *Rs*, 1 and 4 March 1904, nos. 61, 64.

[72] *Russkoe slovo* also sold the most on the streets. Garri, "Interview s gazetchikom na Tverskoi," *Zhizn'*, 15 Dec. 1908, no. 1.

[73] *Rs*, 29 Feb. 1904, no. 60.

[74] Entertainment and feuilletons could not be republished without permission, but news could. On the Russian copyright law as it applied to newspapers, see D.L., "O gazetnykh perepechatkakh," *Rb*, no. 2 (1902): 1–14.

described the "monotonous" expanses of Siberia, introducing readers to the various ethnicities whose incorporation was changing what it meant to be Russian. He passed along, for example, the observations of a stationmaster when the train stopped briefly: "The *buriaty* are good people, but the *tunguzy* are the best of all. They have well-built wooden huts, and tea is always boiling in their large copper kettles."[75] His primary theme, though, was the war toward which he headed, and he spent much of the long journey ruminating on the Russo-Turkish conflict. Remembering it later not exactly as he had reported it, Nemirovich-Danchenko recalled how enthusiasm had soured as the fatalities mounted, asking rhetorically, "What is more precious to us than youth?" Since 1878 "we have grown up, grown disappointed." Searching for a reason for this war, he blamed "the foreign sources of information upon which Russians must depend for information about the subjects nearest and dearest to them." Like Doroshevich, he argued that the "yellow peril" was a myth dangerous to peace and public opinion. Praising the Japanese on the integrity of their ancient civilization, he commended the skill and courage of the Japanese fighting men as sincerely as he did the Russian soldiers, "no less honorable or brave than those at Shipka or Plevna."[76]

Nemirovich-Danchenko enjoyed entry into the Mukden camp of General Aleksei Kuropatkin of the First Manchurian Army. No other correspondent could duplicate his conversations with the generals, whom he could mention casually as having "bumped into in the hall."[77] Taking readers behind the lines, he reported, "I watched Kuropatkin closely. He was exhausted. He didn't take his eyes off the fog in the distance, off the grey curtain that had been concealing the battle for days."[78] The last days of Port Arthur gave Nemirovich-Danchenko his final story, and he returned to Moscow to lead a press campaign to end the hostilities. Beginning his series on "The Blind War," he stressed his objectivity, denying that he was taking a stand: "My job is to tell readers clearly and exactly what I saw and, as well as I am able, to let the facts speak for themselves."[79] The facts he presented indicted the government for gross mismanagement, faulty plans, and unpreparedness. For example, he brought military training to task: "The Japanese soldiers are not braver than ours, they are just better practiced."[80] Many an officer wrote an approving letter to the editor for carrying these stories.[81]

[75] V. I. Nemirovich-Danchenko, *Na voinu* (Moscow: Sytin, 1904), 73.
[76] Ibid., 6, 9–11, 43, 95.
[77] Ibid., 158.
[78] *Rs*, 24 Dec. 1904, no. 357.
[79] *Rs*, 23 May 1905, no. 137.
[80] *Rs*, 12 June 1905, no. 156.
[81] *Rs*, 10 June 1905, no. 154.

Doroshevich complemented Nemirovich-Danchenko's diary with stories about the Asian perspectives on the war. Retaking a familiar journey by steamer through the Orient, he collected opinions on the war in the countries he visited. He began this trip as he had begun the one to Sakhalin, telling how he had to fight back tears of sadness for the young Russian sailors preparing to sail around the world to die in fruitless battle. Distinguishing immediately between Russians and their government, he separated pride in the former from contempt for the latter. Irritated but not surprised, he found a nearly unanimous chorus among other Asians in favor of a Japanese victory.[82]

Just as he had felt that European interests had pushed Russia into an unnecessary conflict with China, he saw Britain's imperial hand manipulating the Eastern puppets. By attacking the British, Doroshevich was not simply switching enemies in order to justify Russian claims to Manchuria; on the contrary, he had argued against Russian expansion into China. He found that fear of Russia was based on ignorance of Russia. Everywhere he went, he found Russia getting bad press, and English money behind the publications. Like Nemirovich-Danchenko, Doroshevich avoided conveying any anti-Japanese feelings, and he showed the same respect for them as a people.

Not all editors, or liberals, had such forbearance for the Japanese. Even "the professors' " Russkie vedomosti referred to a Russian "historical destiny" in the Far East that dictated the use of armed force against so treacherous an enemy.[83] Anger, though, receded, and depictions of the Japanese as no different from ordinary Russians replaced the villainy. Possibly, Sytin's prominent corps of correspondents had influenced others. If other publishers could not match Sytin's immediacy, they did not lag far behind. All of the major newspapers had special correspondents aboard the Trans-Siberian by May, and woodcut illustrations had become a front-page staple. They also published letters from officers and interviews with returning soldiers. Every paper collected money, clothing, and Christmas gifts for families of men at the front.

Unlike with the hostilities in the Balkans twenty-five years earlier, editorial opinion did not split over the nature of Russian involvement. Birzhevye vedomosti featured a professional analyst from the military academy and used its European correspondents to cull the usually better information from the foreign press. Birzhevye vedomosti supplemented news about the battles with information about and photographs of ordinary life in Japan, insights almost soothing in their implications that these

[82] Doroshevich's feuilletons were published collectively as Vostok i voina (Moscow: Sytin, 1905).

[83] Abraham Ascher, The Revolution of 1905: Russia in Disarray (Stanford, Calif.: Stanford University Press, 1988), especially 46–47.

Fig. 13. *Novoe vremia* caricatures of "John Bull" during the Russo-Japanese War. *Left*: "Soon you can carry this yourself. I'm tired of it." *Right*: "War is a profitable business. . . . Someone else's war. . . ."

cultured and interesting people could not truly be an enemy. A series on "How Do They Feel?" interviewed the returning wounded, a feature common to all the newspapers by November 1904. Asked "What impressions did the Japanese make on you?" an officer answered typically, "Excellent [*Molodtsy*]! They are remarkably well educated, strictly disciplined, and have a superior understanding of what they must do."[84]

Suvorin took a more conservative stand on the war. The only major publisher to still be pro-war by the end of 1904, Suvorin has been credited with convincing the government to send the Baltic Fleet on its ill-fated voyage to the disaster awaiting at Tsushima.[85] Although official sources do not comment on this, *Novoe vremia* stridently chastised the Turks, who had trapped the Black Sea Fleet behind the Straits. But Suvorin, too, focused primarily on the British, whom he accused of goading the Japanese into war.[86] *Novoe vremia* saw the sneak attack as evidence that "Asians always behave treacherously," citing the problems Russians

---

[84] *Bv*, 1 Nov. 1904, no. 561.
[85] Snessarev, *Mirazh*, 67.
[86] *Nv*, 20 Jan. 1904, no. 10014.

had faced in their conquest of Central Asia.[87] Nor did those who supplied the human interest stories about Japan have Percy Palmer's cultural respect; *Novoe vremia* showed the Japanese "weird" and their customs "ludicrous."[88]

Like Doroshevich, though, Suvorin's reporters were distressed to find that "Russia has more enemies than friends abroad."[89] Suvorin's writers, too, blamed the Western media for distorting images of Russia, which they found more repugnant than the Japanese providing the unhappy news.[90] But Suvorin the proud nationalist found no comfort in the fall of Port Arthur, and decried those papers that welcomed what the collapse foreshadowed for politics. To those who would compare this to the Crimean War in anticipation of a second chance at Great Reforms he queried, would it not be preferable this time to gain both political change and military victory?[91]

The boulevard press stretched out the sensationalism. *Moskovskii listok* accepted the war initially as fulfillment of Russia's "historical mission . . . [its] holy crusade to the East" and reminded readers that the sainted Alexander III had identified the Japanese threat after the attack on Tsarevich Nicholas's life during a state visit to Tokyo in 1891. Drawing the parallel of the Mongol conquest, it added the nationalistic caveat that "the Russian people have already repulsed with their breasts the Asian blows directed against Europe, but Europe did not value then as it does not value now our standing on guard."[92] The war coincided with the fiftieth anniversary of the siege of Sevastopol, and no publisher made more use of the analog than Pastukhov. The serial "Sevastopol and its Defenders" not only called to mind the current siege of Port Arthur, but also reminded readers that Europeans had in recent memory put Russia in this bleak position.

Among the urban papers, *Moskovskii listok* vacillated most on the issue of patriotism: did one serve Russia better by defeating the Japanese or by ending the war? At first Pastukhov's paper fanned the rumors of the Japanese committing atrocities, but a later interview with a Russian officer in the active army corrected this misinformation; the soldier extended only compliments to the Japanese in battle.[93] A letter from a Russian prisoner of war warning readers not to believe the Japanese press's favorable portrayal of prison conditions was followed a week later by a story

[87] Quoted in Ascher, *Revolution of 1905*, 46. Also, *Nv*, 28 Jan. 1904, no. 10022.
[88] *Nv*, 17 and 18 March 1904, nos. 10070–71.
[89] *Nv*, 1 Feb. 1904, no. 10016.
[90] *Nv*, 3 May 1904, no. 10117.
[91] *Nv*, 16 Feb. 1904, no. 10040.
[92] *Ml*, 29 Jan. 1904, no. 29. See also Ascher, *Revolution of 1905*, 47.
[93] *Ml*, 28 Feb., 1 July, and 3 Oct. 1904, nos. 59, 182, 276.

about a correspondent for *Moskovskii listok*, seized at Port Arthur, receiving only kind attention from his captors.[94] But this paper also resurrected the image of the Golden Horde when Port Arthur fell and prophesied a war between Japan and all of Europe within the next decade.[95]

Peterburgskii listok also carried descriptions of "maniacal" Japanese on the battlefield, determined to "convert the whole world to its taste, beginning with Russia."[96] Patriotism penetrated the entertainment features first in the serial "Partizan," a predictable story of love and courage during the Napoleonic Wars. But then the fiction moved to contemporary Japan with Count Amori's "Secrets of the Japanese Court" because "it is not only useful but necessary to learn all we can about this country . . . that is already dreaming about creating a colossal Asiatic state and a battle with Europe."[97] The intrigue began with the mysterious disappearance of a German baron, but the plot did not thicken politically any more than those set in France, and the geishas seduced just as temptingly as the café-chanteuses.

Peterburgskaia gazeta sent mixed signals, expressing both liberal optimism and genuine anxiety. Popular feuilletonist "Baron Igrek" wrote hysterically that "the 'yellow peril' is no longer an apparition but now a fact . . . that faces not only Russia but the whole civilized world."[98] In June a picture of a demolished train was captioned, "The Japanese, as is well known, shot at this train despite the fact that it was flying the flag of the Red Cross."[99] Yet another story in the same edition shifted the accent to the paper's recognizable style: interest in the human psyche had continued, and the newspaper interviewed Professor V. N. Sirotinym about the ill effects of war on soldiers' nerves. To stir up human interest, popular female writer N. A. Lukhmanova joined the Sisters of Mercy temporarily and proceeded to Mukden as a special correspondent to interview the wounded, to whom she administered aid. Her sentimental outpourings of affection for the Russian foot soldier echoed Doroshevich's remorse at the senseless waste of lives, but she voiced no criticism of the Japanese who had provided her with patients.[100]

Although outrage at the attack receded into an atmosphere of respect for the courage of the fighting men on both sides months before the capitulation of Port Arthur, when in May 1905 the Japanese virtually destroyed the Russian Navy in the Tsushima Straits, *Peterburgskaia gazeta*

[94] *Ml*, 21 and 29 Dec. 1904, nos. 355, 362.
[95] *Ml*, 1 Jan. 1905, no. 1.
[96] *Pl*, 26 July 1904, no. 204.
[97] *Pl*, 2 June 1904, no. 150.
[98] *Pg*, 27 May 1905, no. 136.
[99] *Pg*, 2 June 1904, no. 150.
[100] *Pg*, 30 Jan. 1905, no. 22.

evidenced gut-level patriotism, but also a keen awareness of the opportunities for reform made evident by the defeat. This newspaper's editors looked back to the Crimean War and argued in political rather than military terms that history was repeating itself: "They defeated not *us*, but that which was wounded at Sevastopol. . . . it is absolutely necessary to take heed of the lessons of history." Another correspondent praised the Japanese and criticized Kuropatkin specifically.[101] The newspaper published officers' admissions of military inadequacies, including a self-critical interview with General Kaulbars of the Second Manchurian Army.[102]

The government's system of communications was no better prepared than its military for the consequences of its adventurist foreign policy. On 27 February the tsar addressed representatives from the press, but without entertaining their questions. Those who hoped that this might signal the beginning of genuine communication between tsar and public, though, were destined for disappointment because the tsar did not turn to them again. Two years earlier Witte had argued unsuccessfully for the government to establish its own telegraph news agency, and this now made sense to officials who regretted having to rely heavily on the anti-Russian Reuters' reports.[103] *Pravitel'stvennyi vestnik*'s editors came out of their boring complacency and sent special correspondents to the front in an ill-begotten effort to generate support for the war.[104] The government's journalistic ineptitude fittingly reflected its lack of touch with reality; this was the only press that still viewed the Japanese as the primary enemy by the end of 1905.

The split between official and public opinion about the nature of the enemy raises an important question: Could a victory over the Japanese have restored confidence in the government by proving it correct? Given the premature surrender of Port Arthur, such a turn of events was not inconceivable. Defeating the Japanese might have offered one final splendid moment for Nicholas II to decorate his officers in full regalia, but it could not have forestalled a revolution in thought that had begun to translate into action before the Japanese surprised the inhabitants of Port Arthur. Because if the Japanese were not truly an enemy, as the newspapers were arguing, how would defeating them differ significantly from being defeated by them? Not even most Russians who opposed the war had honestly expected to lose it.

---

[101] *Pg*, 18 May 1905, no. 127.

[102] *Pg*, 7 Oct. 1905, no. 264.

[103] McReynolds, "Autocratic Journalism," 51.

[104] S. V. Smirnov, *Legal'naia pechat' v gody pervoi russkoi revoliutsii* (Leningrad: LGU, 1981), 24.

Race, Imperialism, and National Identity

Racism has always figured significantly into interpretations of this war, which marked the first time an Asian power had bested a European one in battle. But to what extent were Russians "incensed that an Asiatic people, in their minds inferior by definition, should have dared to attack the great Russian Empire"?[105] The nature of Russia's identity as an imperialist power must address this question. On the matter of race, official opinion diverged from that expressed in the mass-circulation newspapers. Kaiser Wilhelm might have written to his cousin Nicholas that Russia's "great task" in Asia was "to cultivate the Asian continent and to defend Europe from the inroads of the Great Yellow Race," but the tsar's most influential newspaper editors did not characterize the Japanese as inferior.[106] If the tsar dismissed the Japanese as "short-tailed monkeys," the popular press did not.[107] *Peterburgskii listok*'s "Secrets of the Japanese Court" had begun with the view that Asia would ultimately go to war with Europe "on strictly racist grounds," but race tantalized as sexy exotica in this espionage thriller.[108]

This is not to say that Russians were not racist, or that racial slurs could not be heard along Nevskii Prospect. Sytin's publishing house produced racist and chauvinistic pamphlets that jingoistically fed the war fever, but this must not be confused with the editorial platform of his authoritative newspaper.[109] The importance of race here lies in the direction attention to it was turned: east. The "yellow peril" had complicated interpretations because of what it implied about minorities in the empire. *Novoe vremia*'s dread of the proverbial peril sprang from its apprehensions that when the Japanese said they wanted "Asia for the Asians," they meant "Asia for Japan," which would exclude Russia as an Asian power, despite the fact that more than half of its territory lay on that continent.[110] In

---

[105] W. Bruce Lincoln argued that "feeling was deeply tinged with a racism that war with the British, the French, or even the Turks had never awakened in the breasts of the Russians. Russians were incensed that an Asiatic people, in their minds inferior by definition, should have dared to attack the great Russian Empire." *In War's Dark Shadow* (New York: Touchstone, 1983), 242. This was not the attitude expressed in the mass-circulation press, not even *Novoe vremia*, which had never minced words about Jews.

[106] Quoted in Barbara Jelavich, *St. Petersburg and Moscow: Tsarist and Soviet Foreign Policy, 1814–1974* (Bloomington: Indiana University Press, 1974), 242.

[107] Lincoln, in *In War's Dark Shadow*, wrote that the press had "seized upon Nicholas's phrase" and referred to the Japanese as *makaki* (monkeys) (243). In the hundreds of articles I read about the war in the various newspapers, I did not once find the word *makaki*.

[108] *Pl*, 2 June 1904, no. 150.

[109] Otto, *Publishing for the People*, 89.

[110] *Nv*, 31 Dec. 1904, no. 10359.

their search for a national identity, when Russians reevaluated their relations with other Slavs, they were calling into question the traditional
role of race. Moving eastward, they needed to synthesize the two halves
of the empire into one multiracial culture. If Russians were to think of
themselves as half-Asian, that meant accepting the peoples there as
equals; even *Novoe vremia* had lauded the Tatar blood flowing in Russian
veins.[111] The point is not that Nicholas II had called the Japanese "monkeys" while Doroshevich did not, but the different view of the yellow
races reflected substantive political differences: Doroshevich and the others were speaking of a cultural assimilation that went against the grain of
official nationality.

The "King of Feuilletonists" had more pity than censure for Japanese
sycophants who debased themselves to curry favor among the British
snobs they wanted to mimic. In fact, Doroshevich found in British racism
the source of his frustration with both the Japanese and their supporters.
Bragging about his friendships among Japanese won during previous
travels, he puzzled about why this people would respond to the prodding
of those who would not even permit the Japanese entry into the exclusive
social clubs established on their own territory.[112] Nor did Doroshevich
find in the white man's religion any inherent right to rule. Misunder-
standings about religion were as important to his view of Russia's place
in the Orient as the misconceptions about who the true racists were. In
the Eastern countries he visited, he found it galling that the misinformed
public accused Russia rather than England of launching a holy crusade
for Christianity. He reported, "They don't know that Russia has syna-
gogues, mosques, Buddhist temples, and that there's even a temple for
fireworshippers in Baku."[113] Merezhkovskii pointedly argued that religion formed one definition of culture, and if Orthodox Russians had trouble respecting Japanese paganism, they should keep in mind the inadequacies of their own church.[114]

The issue of race came up repeatedly in Nemirovich-Danchenko's journey to Mukden. Looking at the Oriental faces around him, the writer
who had occasionally used the word "*zhid*" in the 1880s exhibited a paternalistic attitude more subjectively racist than Doroshevich's. He observed, for example, that living in the East created the impression of
"looking at the world through a glass of tea" and thought it quaint rather
than barbaric when Chinese workers cooked a dog for dinner. Arguing
against racist behavior, he recounted the story of how a Chinese engi-
neer, treated badly by Russians, had justifiably deserted to the Japa-

[111] *Nv*, 16 Jan. 1896, no. 7142.
[112] Doroshevich, "Anglichane i iapontsy," in *Vostok i voina*, 117–31.
[113] Ibid., 30–31.
[114] *Rs*, 12 Aug. 1905, no. 217.

nese.[115] Percy Palmer also commented that "Japan is one of the most remarkable countries among world powers and I now see that the Russians have a false idea about the little brown men."[116] These observations were not used to justify Russian conquest in the name of a superior civilization.

As European Russia engorged the many nationalities along its borderlands, being a citizen of Russia equated less and less with being Slavic. In 1902 Leikin had escorted readers of *Peterburgskaia gazeta* to a large open-air market to show them the Russian melting pot: the various merchants and their customers all swore to their own Russianness, while seeing each other as ethnic minorities, here a Pole, there a Georgian, but all Russians first in their own minds.[117] Culture, not race or class, dominated in this argument for superiority, based somewhat shakily on an idealized view of multiethnic harmony. During the Russo-Japanese War, when the Eastern races figured heavily in public thinking, *Birzhevye vedomosti* ran series of feuilletons asking "What Is a Nation?" Because race constituted one definition, attention then turned to assimilation.[118]

Incorporating the East into the empire required a new perception of what it meant to be Russian, especially after the Bulgarians had made it plain that being Slavic was not enough. At base an imperialist philosophy, the new nationalism sought to synthesize both Russia's past and future and the Western and Eastern halves of its geopolitical personality. In official circles, Prince E. E. Ukhtomskii at *SPB vedomosti* became the most vocal *vostochnik*, or Easternizing antithesis of the Westernizers. This group propagated the view that Russia would find its national character where the sun rose rather than where it set. (Ukhtomskii also controlled the bank that financed the Chinese portion of the Trans-Siberian, so, like that of Rhodes, his patriotism was not pure.)[119]

At the popular level, Doroshevich translated a number of Eastern fables and legends. At times he made convenient use of the allegorical nature of these tales to discuss sensitive issues in the language of Aesop, as in the story of an Indian religious mystic who shared many of Tolstoi's political characteristics, and problems with officials.[120] It was, however, primarily the flexibility of allegory, its capacity to allow the writer to tell a good story colorfully, that made Doroshevich comfortable in this Eastern literary convention, as he was with Asian civilizations in general. All

---

[115] Nemirovich-Danchenko, *Na voinu*, 95, 163–65.
[116] Interview in *Russkoe slovo*'s Sunday supplement, *Iskra*, 9 Jan. 1905, no. 9.
[117] *Pl*, 1 April 1902, no. 89.
[118] *Bv*, 1 Nov. 1904, no. 561.
[119] Von Laue, *Sergei Witte*, 150.
[120] "Dobryi bogdykhan," in Doroshevich's *Izbrannye passkazy i ocherki* (Moscow: Moskovskii rabochii, 1962), 444–48.

Russians, from the peasant soldiers striking out for Manchuria to the merchants contemplating new markets, were captivated by the Orient. The complexities of cultural synthesis proved especially challenging to the Russian intelligentsia, who incorporated Eastern themes into their arts and were far less sanguine than Doroshevich. In Andrei Belyi's *Petersburg*, the synthesis of East and West in the Russian personality failed, and the Eastern influences made Russia violent, barbaric.[121] Doroshevich showed considerably more optimism.

Doroshevich's images of Russia's imperialistic intentions can be faulted as self-serving, brotherly beyond the point of credulity, but all imperialists had glorified excuses for their activities; their zeal gave "manifest destiny" its driving force. Russians, too, felt their destiny to be manifest, and they saw it as the need to reconcile the two halves of their empire's psychologically and geographically split personality. Significantly, they sought a treatment that would restrain the long-dominant Western half. Kipling did not believe a cultural synthesis possible between East and West, but for Doroshevich the twain met in Russia. Nemirovich-Danchenko had already expressed deep sympathy for the Filipinos denied their independence first by Spain and then by the United States.[122]

Unlike in the West, where the jingoistic press had united governments with public opinion, the substance of Russian imperialistic journalism illustrated how the new nationalism widened the gulf between autocracy and civil society. In Russia, when the autocracy had embarked upon a war that society had not wanted fought, it squandered its few remaining coins of legitimacy as the institution best able to rule Russia. When confidence in the tsarist government crumbled, the daily newspaper had already established itself as one of the most important of the alternative realms in which political discourse could be aired. Unlike the previous losses, including the Russo-Turkish War, where winning the war had lost Russia the peace, the failed battle with Japan had little bearing on Russia's sense of its self-importance in the civic imagination.

The mass-circulation newspapers would seem to suggest that Russian imperialism resembled Western imperialism in its external structure. However, the differences in contents of the newspapers of Russia and the West bespoke important variations in the formation of national character. Russia's brand of state capitalism, for example, suggested that Russia's sense of self-righteousness was based on what it did economically differently. Arguing that a state-based capitalism spread the boundless benefits

[121] Robert A. MaGuire, "Macrocosm or Microcosm: The Symbolists in Russia," *Review of National Literature* 3, no. 1 (1972): 141.

[122] Nemirovich-Danchenko wrote about meeting influential Filipino novelist José Rizal, with whom he sympathized, before the novelist's execution by the Spanish in 1896. "Tsvetok svoego naroda," reprinted in *Vechnaia pamiat'* (Petrograd: Gos. Izd., 1919–1920).

of technology without the selfishness of the profit motive so detrimental to the colonized peoples, Russia's philosophers of imperialism tried to sell the idea that their incursions were morally superior to Western ones.[123] Dissatisfaction with Western economic models then carried over to mistrust of aspects of the political system that, although acknowledged by most as preferable to tsarism, had exhibited weaknesses that Russia's antiautocratic element hoped to improve upon before applying them at home.

The nationalistic images drawn in Russia's imperialistic journalism suggested that when readers had stripped the traditional symbols of their authority to rule, public opinion would not turn unquestioningly to the West for replacements. Geyer concluded his study of Russian imperialism with the observation that educated Russians did not see their future in the East, where the "areas seemed more a kind of exotic appendage than a vital part of the Russian cause."[124] Certainly, power and prestige lay to the West. The nationalists measured Russia's accomplishments against European, not Asian, standards, because Russians wanted to redress a century of inferior status, lost wars, and diplomatic humiliations. The Russians Doroshevich spoke for sought acceptance among Europeans as equals, which meant on their own terms. These readers undoubtedly felt considerably closer to the objectionable British bourgeoisie than to the Orientals who considered household pets edible, but they still kept their cultural distance from Western militarism and selfish individualism. The closer Russia drew to the West, the more certain fundamental differences emerged, which did nothing to ease the strains of their ambivalent relationship. This would only add to the confusion of Russia's search for political direction when revolution erupted in 1905.

[123] Amfiteatrov, in *Strana razbora* (227), also argued this point.
[124] Geyer, *Russian Imperialism*, 346.

9

Russian Newspapers in Revolution, 1905–1907

IN HIS New Year's feuilleton of 1905, Doroshevich remarked ironically that "one doesn't need to be a prophet to predict that 1905 will be an unusual year."[1] Although the capitulation of Port Arthur had brought 1904 to a dramatic close, it was not the defeat that had inspired Doroshevich's comment. The war dragged on, and public opposition to the government continued to build. The civil and peasant unrest that had induced Nicholas to press for the "small victorious war" in the first place had been exacerbated rather than calmed. The circulation of news about both the dissension and the war that had turned out neither small nor victorious kept tensions high.

The importance of the Russo-Japanese War as a catalyst for the 1905 Revolution cannot be overstated, but Russian society did not need Father Gapon to lead it into direct confrontation with the autocracy; it had already started down that road. Industrialization had made educated and urban Russians keenly aware of the constraints of the autocratic form of government, and by the end of the nineteenth century more and more of them wanted deep-rooted, if not radical, changes in the political system. In his study of political change in societies undergoing rapid modernization, Samuel Huntington argued that the expansion of mass media tends to "extend political consciousness, multiply political demands, and broaden political participation." He further argued that "the political essence of revolution is the rapid expansion of political consciousness and the rapid mobilization of new groups into politics at a speed which makes it impossible for existing political institutions to assimilate them."[2] This mobilization began in earnest in Russia in 1905, and the subject of this chapter is the role of the daily newspaper in raising political consciousness and contributing to the resultant instability.

The dates that traditionally demarcate the 1905 Revolution are 9 January 1905 and 3 June 1907: the first, "Bloody Sunday," is the date that tsarist troops fired into a crowd of unarmed workers marching peacefully on the Winter Palace, and the second is the day that Prime Minister P. A. Stolypin effected a coup d'état against the protoparliamentary

---

[1] *Rs*, 1 Jan. 1905, no. 1.

[2] Samuel Huntington, *Political Order in Changing Societies* (New Haven, Conn.: Yale University Press, 1968), 5, 266.

Duma and restored a conservative order. Although this chapter ends with the coup, it begins before Bloody Sunday, with the gathering of opposition. The newspaper played a crucial role in the revolutionary process. First and foremost, the papers disseminated information. Second, the press encouraged readers to recognize that they could themselves effect change. The press, "present[ing] news as a problem demanding thought and action," helped readers to perceive of society as organized around their own interests, which they would therefore move to protect.[3]

The Russian mass-circulation press at the turn of the century, however, still functioned under censorship and could not maneuver without impunity. In addition to the assault on the tsarist government evident in the news, the press waged a specific war for its own liberation from censors. The greatly revised censorship statute of 24 November 1905 did not deliver all the promised freedoms any more than the 1865 code had lived up to the letter of its law, but they both had perceptible impacts on the development of newspaper journalism. In many respects, the battle for freedom of the press reads like a microhistory of the broader political struggle, beginning with the explosion of newspapers of all editorial leanings during the heady "Days of Liberty" at the end of 1905 through the reassertion of the government's will in June 1907.

Not only did the commercial press have the autocracy to confront, but as a result of the revolution a second institution had entered the public sphere: the State Duma. On 17 October 1905, when Nicholas II delivered the quasi-constitutional "October Manifesto," he promised the convocation of an elective representative body with limited legislative authority. Suffrage was not universal, nor was representation democratic, but political parties had to be organized to stand for election. The Russian papers did not leap backward in comparative time and align themselves with parties. Instead, the major political parties tried their hand at reaching voters by publishing newspapers intended to compete with the mass-circulation dailies.

More serious competition between the independent press and parties arose over the formulation of the political agenda, which embraced such questions as the most effective means of resisting the autocracy and the restructuring of objectives after the deliverance of the October Manifesto. However unrepresentative the Duma, it still offered a concrete realm for political activity. The "new politics," which had challenged Western parties by emphasizing the role of mass communications in establishing the contours of public debate, had come to Russia before political parties. The Proppers and the Sytins did not want to lose their influence to rival authorities; newspaper publishers, like the politicians,

[3] Hughes, *Human Interest*, 251.

"represented a new group in Russian society, a professional middle class, whose educational and social status naturally cultivated a desire to participate in the formulation and execution of public policies, to have a say in the governing of the country commensurate with their status."[4] Circulation translated not only into profits but also into influence, and the stakes of public opinion were not trivial.

Protoparties: Interest Groups and the Press

A study of the relationship between the formation of political parties and the newspapers must begin by examining the distinctive way in which these parties were organized in Russia. The history of Russia's commercial mass-circulation press paralleled more closely that of the Western press than did the history of its other political institutions. In his seminal work on the formation of parties in tsarist Russia, Leopold Haimson located the cardinal difference between the evolution of the concept of a political party in Russia and the West: Western parties had grown out of the contest for control of extant representative institutions, whereas the absence of such institutions in Russia had forced groups to seek their political identity in their relationships to the state, the source of both their rights and their obligations. Composed of intellectuals, Russia's protoparties, including populists, Marxists, and liberals, maintained the intelligentsia's tradition of isolation from the masses. However much some of them proselytized among workers and peasants, they still believed that they were holding political knowledge in trust, and they doubted their own ability to bridge the cultural chasm of peasant Russia. Not obliged to compromise with themselves, they surely did not have to make the concessions necessary to work with each other. Sytin and Propper, on the other hand, knew *compromise* as a recurrent word in their vocabularies. As Haimson continued, though, as a result of industrialization, during the 1890s the various strands of public opinion had coalesced and, accepting the legitimacy of its own aspirations, the people were willing to act against the state.[5] The concurrent development of the commercial press was not coincidental to this new attitude, but nor can it claim to have directed it.

Of the major parties to emerge from the revolution and stand for elec-

---

[4] Terrence Emmons described Kadet leaders thus in *The Formation of Political Parties and the First National Elections in Russia* (Cambridge, Mass.: Harvard University Press, 1983), 72.

[5] Leopold Haimson, "The Parties and the State: The Evolution of Political Attitudes," in Cyril E. Black, ed., *The Transformation of Russian Society* (Cambridge, Mass.: Harvard University Press, 1960), 110, 120.

tion, two would receive the most attention in the mass-circulation newspapers and from the limited voting public. The first, the Constitutional Democrats, the "Kadets," organized in 1906 around the dual principles of constitutionalism and parliamentarianism. For the most part, Kadet leaders came from professional backgrounds and, informed by the tradition of separation of the intellectual from the people, they held themselves above class and other interest groups. Western European politics provided a second, sometimes contradictory, source of influence in their ideological development.[6] Liberals united around ideals, however, could fragment under the demands of action. It was much easier to speak of a parliament as the Western-oriented leaders did, and quite another matter to institute universal male suffrage in peasant Russia. The solution to Russia's most urgent problem, its agricultural poverty, would require wrenching economic and social changes that would call into question the meaning of private property: Should land be forceably alienated from the gentry and turned over to the peasantry, and, if so, at what price? And how could the restive working class, with whom the other social estates had had unprecedented contact in the streets all year long, be quieted? The Kadets' answers could by no means satisfy all of the liberals.

The second party, the Union of October 17, or the "Octobrists," was the conservative offshoot of the original grouping that had also produced the Kadets. Monarchists and nationalists, this assembly of primarily wealthy industrialists and provincial gentry had a fundamentally paternalistic attitude toward Russia's workers, peasants, and ethnic minorities. They believed that a nationally elected legislative body could end the arbitrary exercise of power, while maintaining the tsar as the correct symbol of moral authority. This party recalled many of the old Slavophile emotions about the uniqueness of Russian culture and had a distaste for the Western roots of Kadet liberalism. Elections were held to four Dumas. In the first two, both of which were prorogued by the tsar after only a few months, the Kadets held the plurality of seats. The Octobrists would hold the plurality in the more stable, but far less democratic, Third and Fourth Dumas.

The extremist parties would ultimately have the final say in Russian politics. As Roberta Manning has demonstrated, the extreme right manipulated the reformed government after 1905, and their domination of national issues severely restricted the chances for political pluralism such as the moderates had envisioned.[7] By undermining the confidence of most Russians in the prospects of electoral representation, the rightists

---

[6] Emmons, *Formation of Political Parties*, 22.

[7] Roberta Thompson Manning, *The Crisis of the Old Order in Russia: Gentry and Government* (Princeton, N.J.: Princeton University Press, 1982).

helped to pave the way for the Bolsheviks in 1917. However, as the pages of the mass-circulation newspapers reflect, liberalism had not spent itself by October of 1917. The dialogue between the mass-circulation press and the Kadets, as with the Octobrists but less so, explicated the debates and options within the liberal camp.

For a variety of reasons, signified by such disparate incidents as Witte's fall from grace and the restructuring of two major newspapers, 1903 serves as an appropriate year to mark the point by which the autocracy had lost its authority to govern effectively. Pressure was building from a variety of sources as the nineteenth century drew to a close: workers struck factories for better conditions; peasants rebelled against landowners for more land; members of the zemstvos struggled to administer the provinces; and professional groups came together in pursuit of guarantees of civil liberties. But so long as the opposition remained disunited and held conflicting goals, the tsar could maintain his position. In 1903 Marxist-turned-liberal P. B. Struve spearheaded the coalition of oppositional forces with the creation of the underground "Union of Liberation," which gave shelter to all groups who made the overthrow of the autocracy their primary objective.

As the war with Japan continued to go badly throughout 1904, the public became increasingly animated by the government's incompetence and began to believe that it could force the autocracy to recognize the need for elected representatives to take part in running the country. The zemstvos, themselves elective institutions within a limited franchise, formed the natural center of opposition. The first confrontation was slated for November 1904 when leaders of the Union of Liberation combined with others from the zemstvos to organize a conference that month. Concurrent with the zemstvo congress in St. Petersburg, the Union of Liberation had inspired the so-called banquet campaign, recalling the Parisian movement of 1847–1848 that brought primarily the educated and liberal elements together in formal, but not yet institutionalized, settings to discuss political options.[8]

The press wanted to take part in the banquet campaign. Although the minister of internal affairs distributed one of the despised circulars to newspaper editors forbidding them from reporting openly on the banquets, the careful reader could find news reports relating to them buried in the back pages. The minister successfully limited discussion of this story, which rivaled the impending doom in Port Arthur, but could not stem the tide of popular discontent.[9] Editorials in *Russkoe slovo* caught the upbeat mood of the liberals' campaign: "We are living through a

[8] Ascher, *Revolution of 1905*, 60–70.
[9] Lemke, "V mire usmotreniia," 124.

good, reassuring revitalization of society. . . . Head and hands are getting down to business"; "There's as much disorder here as in the Far East.
. . . Everything is in disarray, and we must take part in the reconstruction"; "Liberalism has appeared always and everywhere as a necessary precondition for creative government actions."[10] Doroshevich was right; it took no special clairvoyant powers to divine that 1905 would not be a year like any other.

The boulevard press, too, wanted a say. Khudekov brought *Peterburgskaia gazeta*'s readers into national discourse by involving them in the same discussions that preoccupied those at the banquets. An interview with Professor V. I. Sergeevich reminded readers of the significant differences between Russia's past two quasi representative bodies: the *veche*, an urban assembly with slight roots in ancient Rus' that had flourished in the economically developed northeast in the fifteenth century, and the *zemskii sobor*, or "assembly of the land," the sporadic summoning by tsars of members of the populace from all around the empire when they wanted information on issues national in scope.[11] The paper also asked readers what they might draw most meaningfully from Russia's political heritage, especially that left by the intelligentsia. It stressed that the concept of state had to be mentally shifted from the bureaucracy to a representative legislature, emphasizing that public service must remain an integral part of Russian politics.[12]

9 January to 17 October 1905 in the Press

Hopes that the collapse in the Far East would compel the government to seek out liberals for advice proved premature in January 1905. The ghastly official error of firing on the unarmed workers allowed the tsar to react quickly and repressively while the public reeled from the shock. When printers joined other striking workers to protest the government's actions, they prevented the national capital from learning about the events in the newspapers. Strikes broke out all over the country in protest of the slaughter of 130 and wounding of 299 others on Bloody Sunday. Workers in the streets, shutting down industry and threatening destruction of private property, posed a profound dilemma for their employers, especially newspaper publishers who had long been sympathetic toward the rights of workers. It was important, therefore, to distinguish between rabble-rousers, such as the government had tried to paint

[10] *Rs*, 1 and 6 Oct. and 16 Nov. 1904, nos. 273, 278, 319.
[11] *Pg*, 28 Jan. 1905, no. 20.
[12] *Pg*, 25 Jan. and 10 June 1905, nos. 17, 149.

Gapon, and workers seeking the same protection of civil liberties that others wanted. All newspapers featured regular sections on "Strikes and Disorders" with factual information from their own and official sources.

In Moscow, a comparison of how *Russkoe slovo* reported the tragic day with *Moskovskii listok*'s coverage shows both the liberal/conservative gamut of attitudes and the censor's presence. Sytin's editors, obligated to print the official notice from the governor-general telling workers not to participate in the march, then tucked the official account behind a flattering biography of Gapon, "whose name one encounters often these days in the news from St. Petersburg."[13] Petrov, the priest on staff, echoed Gapon in arguing that the Church had an obligation to tend to the flesh as well as to the soul.[14]

Pastukhov was perfectly willing to uphold the autocracy's position that Gapon was an outside agitator and reported that the government had not used force against the demonstrators.[15] Pastukhov had no truck with protesters of any sort, holding up in praise the exemplary shop assistants who had refrained from striking, waiting patiently instead for the government to produce legislation that would improve their lot.[16] Following Bloody Sunday, *Moskovskii listok* ran for several weeks a special section of "Readings for Workers," religious tracts with messages quite unlike Petrov's, preaching a gospel of passivity.

In St. Petersburg, *Novoe vremia* expressed the view of the conservative element, but its editorial policy did nothing to bolster the autocracy. Suvorin's editors discussed the specific events of Bloody Sunday in two contexts: how news of disorders at the rear was distressing the boys who had sacrificed so much in the patriotic defense of Port Arthur, and how the delighted Western press was grossly exaggerating the casualties on Nevskii Prospect in their prolonged smear campaign against Russia.[17] The newspaper's only discussion of Gapon came up in May 1906 when the priest committed suicide.[18] Yet throughout that explosive January, *Novoe vremia* presented an analytical series on the worker question in which the author defended repeatedly workers' rights against exploitation by industrialists. The writer found it reasonable to assume that workers would respond to revolutionaries because government and management had demonstrated continually their insensitivity to labor.[19]

The urban press was more prone to take the matter directly to the streets. A week after Bloody Sunday, *Peterburgskaia gazeta* interviewed

13 *Rs*, 10 Jan. 1905, no. 10.
14 *Rs*, 26 June 1905, no. 170.
15 *Ml*, 11 Jan. 1905, no. 11.
16 *Ml*, 25 Feb. 1905, no. 56.
17 *Nv*, 15 and 18 Jan. 1905, nos. 10367, 10370.
18 *Nv*, 2 May 1906, no. 10823.
19 *Nv*, 19 Jan. 1905, no. 10371.

Fig. 14. Father Grigorii Gapon's suicide in *Novoe vremia*, 1906

workers protesting against their factory's administration. The story introduced thoughtful men with justifiable grievances obeying the letter of the
law going up against callous bosses.[20] In October, just as the general
strike was bringing the country to a standstill, *Peterburgskaia gazeta* began a serial novel about a sympathetic Gapon-like priest aiding exploited
workers in their struggle against "the greed of Russian capitalists, who
want dividends and nothing more."[21] *Peterburgskii listok*, too, serialized
a novel about a compassionate priest working among the exploited poor.
The alcoholic and abusive priests also found in this story contrasted
sharply to the Gapon character, and their characters could be construed
as criticism of the Church.

After the initial outburst, the strike movement quieted down for the

[20] *Pg*, 15 Jan. 1905, no. 7.
[21] *Pg*, 10 Oct. 1905, no. 267.

remainder of the winter. The war with Japan lumbered on, and public opinion increased its offensive against the autocracy. Nicholas II had hoped that by replacing Minister of Internal Affairs Sviatopolk-Mirskii with the nondescript A. G. Bulygin, he could curb the unrest by shifting blame away from the system onto an individual. The assassination on 4 February of former governor-general of Moscow Grand Duke Sergei Aleksandrovich exposed the weakness of the tsar's logic. Nicholas empowered Bulygin to form a committee to consider reforms, much as his grandfather had proceeded after the disaster in the Crimea. Two weeks later, on the anniversary of the emancipation of the serfs, editors turned all their attention to the Tsar-Liberator. As *Peterburgskaia gazeta* exalted, "This anniversary of 19 February coincides with a great historical moment, when Russian society is gripped by a thirst for rejuvenation such as it has never before experienced."[22]

The warmer weather of May brought renewed strike activity, and at the end of the month, when the Japanese sank the Russian fleet in the Tsushima Straits, the public spoke out with greater candor. Professional organizations, sprouting up spontaneously throughout the spring, coalesced in Moscow as the Union of Unions, headed by future Kadet leader P. N. Miliukov. In *Russkoe slovo*, Boborykin wrote, "We have only one enemy, and it is not in Tokyo, but much closer."[23] *Russkoe slovo* did not relieve its frontal assault, and Petrov's references to the American Bill of Rights smacked of republicanism.[24] Although the minister of internal affairs suspended street sales that summer, newsboys often wrapped a reactionary newspaper around bundles of *Russkoe slovo* for covert distribution.[25] Several provincial revolutionaries remembered *Russkoe slovo* as a primary source of news and inspiration during 1905.[26]

Peterburgskaia gazeta declared war on the bureaucracy, arguing that "in Japan, we didn't know the territory, the enemy, or our own strengths. But in our war with the bureaucracy, we know our enemy, and it is hateful to us."[27] Bulygin, trying to salvage something for the government, also turned attention to the bureaucracy: the last circular to newspaper editors, distributed 4 July 1905, sanctioned rather than prohibited a certain type of criticism: "The censorship must not forbid articles which attack the bureaucracy; for it must take into account that . . .

[22] *Pg*, 19 Feb. 1905, no. 42.

[23] *Rs*, 10 June 1905, no. 154.

[24] See, for example, Petrov's articles in *Russkoe slovo* on 14 and 26 June 1905, nos. 158, 160.

[25] TsGIA f. 776, op. 8, d. 848, ll. 25, 42, 88, 94; op. 2, d. 36; S. R. Mintslov, "14 mesiatsev 'svoboda pechati' (17 okt. 1905—1 Ian. 1907)," *Byloe*, no. 3 (1907): 131.

[26] *Trudy Imp. vol'nogo ekonimicheskogo obshchestva*, no. 3 (1905): 56.

[27] *Pg*, 10 and 14 June 1905, nos. 149, 153.

certain newspapers have accepted the concept of an autocratic government within a legal-constitutional framework."[28] Promoting rather than restricting critique, this reversal of twenty-five years of censorship policies read like the handwriting on the Old Testament wall.

As Abraham Ascher has pointed out in his history of 1905, "A casual glance at newspapers for the late summer and fall of 1905 . . . [illustrates that] . . . no meeting of Russians, regardless of its ostensible purpose, could avoid some outburst of hostility toward the government."[29] The workings of Bulygin's committee had been well publicized through orchestrated leaks to the press, and when it delivered its handiwork in August, the majority of public opinion would have none of the so-called "Bulygin Constitution."[30] The tsar, however, approved this measure, which allowed an impossibly nonrepresentative electoral body to have no more than consultative privileges in the running of the state. Support came only from the vexatious *Moskovskii listok*, which had complained in July that "liberals did not speak for all of Russia" as they claimed.[31]

The news itself had made plain to readers the breadth of the opposition and offered them the potential safety of numbers. *Russkoe slovo* added special supplements for weeks following Bloody Sunday, advertising that these sheets would contain telegraph news received until 5:00 A.M. and could only be purchased in the street editions.[32] When strikes reappeared in the south, Sytin's Odessa correspondent re-created the drama: "Right now, as I am writing these lines, circulars from the city government are being distributed everywhere—on walls, on houses, in people's hands."[33] One of the more literary accounts described Lieutenant Shmidt's ill-fated mutiny in Sevastopol; the correspondent opened with a description of a peaceful dawn over the city, then detailed the bloody riots, closing with the streetlights coming on as order was restored.[34] In Tiflis, "the streets resembled a medieval camp. There are armed people everywhere—on foot, on horseback, in phaetons, and in the most diverse clothes."[35]

The government's inability to pacify discontent through halfhearted reforms ultimately led to the general strike that brought the autocracy to its knees. The strike began on 20 September when printers in Moscow

[28] Benjamin Rigberg, "The Tsarist Press Law of 1894–1905," *Jahrbucher für Geschichte Osteuropas* 13, no. 3 (1965): 343.
[29] Ascher, *Revolution of 1905*, 193.
[30] Ibid., 178–79.
[31] *Ml*, 13 July 1905, no. 192.
[32] *Rs*, 22 Jan. 1905, no. 20.
[33] *Rs*, 24 June 1905, no. 168.
[34] *Rs*, 21 Dec. 1905, no. 326.
[35] *Rs*, 7 Dec. 1905, no. 323.

walked off the job to demand higher wages and better working conditions. From this point until after the proclamation of the October Manifesto, strikes of printers and telegraph operators sporadically interrupted the publication of newspapers in both capitals. The character of the protest movement changed when on 4 October the central bureau of the Railroad Union called for a strike over political rather than economic issues. Support grew incrementally, moving across railroad lines into other areas of society, including the newspaper publishers themselves, until it paralyzed the nation.[36] Nicholas had no choice but to bring Witte, enjoying popularity for having negotiated in August a surprisingly favorable treaty with the Japanese, back into the government as prime minister, commissioned to oversee a meaningful reform of the Russian government.

On 17 October, Witte delivered the manifesto from the tsar promising civic freedoms and electoral representation. Printers still on the picket lines kept St. Petersburg from reading details in their favorite newspapers for the next few days, but when *Peterburgskaia gazeta* returned, it advertised an upcoming novelization of that remarkable October.[37] *Russkoe slovo* received a copy of the tsar's decree in time to reprint most of it in the next day's paper, and the paper's bannerline read "18 October— The First Day of Freedom!" *Russkoe slovo* also featured the interview with Witte, who had called Russia's first important press conference to try to impress upon publishers the importance of lending him their support.[38]

On the other side of Moscow, *Moskovskii listok* dejectedly criticized the manifesto: "Now the ship of state will no longer be navigated by Imperial Will, which stood above estate [*sosloviia*] interests and was guided solely by God and conscience with the good of the nation at heart. But now [it will be navigated by] the will and the understanding of those political parties who, by accident of election, will occupy the predominant place in the State Duma."[39] Pastukhov need not have been so glum; the October Manifesto and the political parties that the public pinned its representative hopes on had a long road to travel from theory to practice.

Novoe vremia, the more eloquent voice of conservatism, took a significantly different position. In 1895 Suvorin had agreed with Pastukhov that calls for even limited democratic participation were, in the new tsar's words, "senseless dreams." But Suvorin had considerably more access to the circles of power than did Pastukhov, and he littered his diary with frustrations about the leadership of Nicholas II and his personal prefer-

---

[36] V. Portugalov, "Obedinenie pressy v dni svobody," *Tovarishch*, 17 Oct. 1906, no. 89.

[37] *Pg*, 2 Nov. 1905, no. 283.

[38] *Rs*, 19 Oct. 1905, no. 274.

[39] *Ml*, 19 Oct. 1905, no. 283.

ences for a parliamentary government.[40] Had he simply been a toady in 1895? The more reasonable explanation would be that he had objected to the fact that it was the liberal element demanding change. By 1905, when a number of forces had begun to pressure the autocracy, like the emerging Octobrist leaders, Suvorin and his editors began moving cautiously. *Novoe vremia*'s New Year's editorial had spoken dismally of "the ship of our dear Motherland [being] run aground."[41] But one of Tolstoi's sons, named for his father, began to contribute feuilletons about the moral responsibilities of undertaking the reforms that everyone scented in the offing.[42] By the issuance of the October Manifesto, *Novoe vremia* was rejoicing because "that which was yesterday a dream is today a reality; that which we talked about yesterday as the future today became our present."[43] Suvorin and his staff, too, thought the country should be run by "people like themselves."[44]

The two months that followed issuance of the manifesto showed the fragility of the document and how superficial its resemblance to a Western constitution. During these so-called Days of Liberty, society became intoxicated by its apparent victory. Political drunkenness swayed the liberals, including future leaders of both Octobrists and Kadets, to decline Witte's entreaties to participate in the government he was trying to put together. Incensed that Witte had raised archreactionary P. N. Durnovo from assistant to minister of internal affairs, they overplayed their hand when they made Durnovo's ouster the price for their participation. They also demanded an immediate convocation of a constituent assembly. But Russia's first prime minister refused to allow them to captain his ship, and they would have plenty of time later to regret their highhandedness.

The far left, too, exaggerated its strength. The radicalized soviets, or workers' councils, that had arisen spontaneously throughout 1905 continued to lead strikes, although none could compare in scope to the general strike of October. The St. Petersburg Soviet, headed by then-Menshevik Leon Trotsky, disrupted life in the national capital and urged workers to take power through an armed uprising. Witte ordered the leaders of the soviet arrested on 3 December. The next day's events in Moscow began the critical face-off between far left and far right that, in hindsight, emerged as the unavoidable consequence of the heady "Days of Liberty." As Laura Engelstein has argued in her study of Moscow in 1905, liberals "now saw the government pitted against the whole of Russian society. Its

---

[40] *Dnevnik Suvorina*, 224, 258, 339.
[41] *Nv*, 1 Jan. 1905, no. 10360.
[42] *Nv*, 21 Jan. and 25 Feb. 1905, nos. 10373, 10408.
[43] *Nv*, 22 Oct. 1905, no. 10638.
[44] Emmons, *Formation of Political Parties*, 72, referring to the Kadets.

paranoid brutality had deprived it of moral and political authority."[45] But putting down the insurrection had allowed Witte to present a stable front and to secure the French loans necessary to stabilize the government. *Novoe vremia* praised the prime minister's resolute action, calling on the state to stand tough against disorder and to move on to reform.[46] With the government steadied and the public demoralized, it remained to be seen how viable a political alternative the Duma would in fact present.

Political Parties, Politicized Press

Editors and publishers of mass-circulation newspapers had expended considerable energies to establish an institution to which readers could turn for counsel of all sorts, whether it be picking a horse at the track or voting in elections to the City Duma. The prospect of electing a State Duma, despite the fact that most editors and publishers wanted one, created a competitive political realm. Editorial pages confirmed that leading journalists had political ambitions and did not want to be writing editorials to themselves. Russians staggering under the weight of their newly won freedoms had enormously complex decisions to make about what they envisioned for Russia and how they might help to attain it. Parties and editors alike wanted to influence their decisions. Sytin's editors said as much directly when they told readers in 1906 that "the great success of our newspaper has given us new responsibilities. . . . the goal of the newspaper should be to relate to readers as a friend and companion, and also as an advisor and a leader."[47]

The logical party for editors of the liberal mass-circulation dailies to support was the Kadets, with whom they shared the most in common. The Kadets themselves appreciated the importance of communicating through periodicals. In Germany in 1902 Struve had begun *Osvobozh-denie* (Liberation), a small publication that aided the organization of the Union of Liberation. In 1904 a weekly journal published by liberal jurists, *Pravo* (*Law*), became the acknowledged organ of the still-illegal union.[48] But such aspiring politicians as Miliukov and I. V. Gessen wanted a mass-circulation paper, not a "thick" journal with narrow appeal. Recognizing the advantage of securing an established newspaper with a sizeable and generally sympathetic audience, the Kadets sought out first Sytin and then Propper. The rumor that the Kadets offered Sytin

[45] Laura Engelstein, *Moscow, 1905* (Stanford, Calif.: Stanford University Press, 1982), 221.

[46] *Nv*, 12 Dec. 1905, no. 10684.

[47] *Rs*, 1 Jan. 1906, no. 1.

[48] Smirnov, *Legal'naia pechat'*, 45–46.

a million rubles for *Russkoe slovo*, provided that the popular staff remain, probably said more about Sytin's perceived strength than party coffers. Nevertheless, they apparently approached Sytin, and Doroshevich threatened to resign should the paper be aligned to any political party.[49] Miliukov and Gessen had better luck with Propper, but only briefly.

Birzhevye vedomosti editor Kaufman recalled in his memoirs how miffed Propper became when his staff presented him with their own "constitution" in 1905. Annoyed because they had insinuated that he could not "publish his newspaper according to the new conditions of Russian life," he responded by replacing them with "the new people," the Kadets. Changing the name to *Svobodnyi narod* (*The Free People*) and breaking all the rules that had made him so successful a publisher, Propper's new editors launched a ferocious attack on his former patron, Witte, over the appointment of Durnovo. Within three weeks the censors had twice closed his paper. In a short time Propper had his fill of partisan politics; when the publisher found his authority reduced to taking orders from secretaries to have windows repaired, he tore up the agreement.[50]

In February 1906, Gessen and Miliukov founded *Rech'* (*Speech*), which combined news and party politics in the format of a mass-circulation daily and held a modest circulation through 1917. Insufficient capital funding prevented the editors from ever establishing an exclusive network of correspondents, and the newspaper often earned more from street sales than from subscriptions.[51] The Octobrists also tried their hand at publishing a daily. The party's *Golos moskvy* (*Voice of Moscow*), founded in 1906 by capital from the conservative Moscow merchantry, failed to attract readers and simply died in 1915, at a time when the Octobrists held the majority in the Fourth Duma.[52] The Progressive party, formed in 1912 by industrialists dissatisfied with the Octobrists' limitations, published a Moscow daily, *Utro Rossii* (*Russian Morning*), a newspaper founded in 1907 by party leader P. P. Riabushinskii.[53] Like *Rech'*, this newspaper offered more than dry party polemics, but even circulations as high as forty thousand were still dwarfed by the large commercial dailies.

[49] Bokhanov, *Burzhuaznaia pressa*, 119; and Dinershtein, "A Leviathan," 64.

[50] Kaufman, "Iz zhurnal'nykh vospominanii," no. 12, 1076–77. Kaufman did not say whether or not Propper surrendered to the demands of the staff's "constitution." Also, I. I. Iasnitskii, *Roman moei zhizni* (Moscow and Leningrad: Gos. Izd., 1926), 306.

[51] Iu. I. Fedinskii, "Material'nye usloviia izdaniia russkoi burzhuaznoi gazety," *Vestnik MGU*, journalism series, no. 2 (1980): 25–32; and E. G. Kostrikova, "Istochniki vneshnepoliticheskoi informatsii Russkikh burzhuaznykh gazet," *Istoricheskie zapiski* 103 (1979): 277–78.

[52] Michael C. Brainerd, "The Octobrists and the Gentry in the Russian Social Crisis of 1913–1914," *Russian Review* 38, no. 2 (1979): 169.

[53] A. N. Bokhanov, "Iz istorii burzhuaznoi pechati, 1906–1912," *Istoricheskie zapiski* 97 (1976): 263–89.

The Newspaper and the Duma

Rather than stabilizing the country, Russia's first elected representatives quickened unrest by pressing for many more demands than the autocracy had anticipated. Even though the intricate electoral system depended upon a series of indirect elections, the final 497 men who served as deputies to the First Duma represented the popular mood reasonably well. Convened on 10 May 1906, the First Duma lasted only forty sessions before its irreconcilable disagreement with the government over the land question: the Duma insisted that land be alienated, with compensation, from gentry, state, and Church alike, and made available to the peasantry. This the autocracy categorically refused to do. Stopped by a stalemate, the tsar dissolved the standing Duma and called for elections to a second.

If Russia's First Duma gave a lesson in political naiveté, the Second, convened on 5 March 1907, did not show significant maturity in parliamentary procedure. The centrist groups had lost ground to the extremes of both wings, especially to the left, which nearly doubled its representatives to 216. While the Second Duma was filled by a more vocal and less yielding faction than the First, the government, too, had strengthened its resolve. The despised Durnovo had been replaced at the Ministry of the Interior just before convocation of the First Duma by Stolypin, who had attracted favorable notice in official circles for refusing to give ground to demonstrators in Saratov in 1905, where he was governor-general. Appointed prime minister after the dissolution of the First Duma, he began the relentless "pacification" of the countryside that earned him the nickname "strongman of the autocracy," while hangmen's nooses entered the argot as "Stolypin's neckties." Prepared to work with the Second Duma, Stolypin had an agricultural reform program, but instead of redistributing land, he concentrated on breaking up the commune and creating individual farmsteads. But the demands for land that had brought the First Duma to a standstill had not diminished and pushed the Second to a similar impasse.[54]

Stolypin forced a confrontation with deputies when he ordered them to withdraw the immunity provided by the Duma to the Social Democratic members whom he wanted arrested for treason. To do so would destroy the Duma floor as a place for open political debate. At the deputies' refusal, Nicholas prorogued this Duma and Stolypin rewrote the electoral laws to ensure a conservative majority, such as would be mandatory if the government and the Duma were to accomplish anything together.

[54] Manning, *Crisis of the Old Order*, chapter 13.

To say that most Russians wanted to replace the autocracy with some form of legislative parliament in 1905 is to belabor the obvious. The crucial question was how this might be peacefully accomplished when the autocracy still held the reins of power, which neither Witte nor Stolypin hesitated to lash. General philosophical empathies about the definition of and approach to the most serious problems plaguing Russia did not translate into agreement about the best means to effect change. The commercial newspapers, with the exception of *Moskovskii listok*, during the first two Dumas had faith in the parliamentary process. All papers featured information about the campaign and profiles of leading candidates, especially Kadets and Octobrists, and provided sample ballots with information about how, when, and where electors could vote. Professions of independence meant little; the Octobrists advertised heavily in *Moskovskii listok*, party leader A. I. Guchkov held shares in *Novoe vremia*, and Kadet names appeared as often as those of some feuilletonists in *Russkoe slovo* and *Birzhevye vedomosti*.

Editorial coverage of the ill-fated First Duma in *Peterburgskaia gazeta* disclosed the intense frustrations of those who wanted this institution to work at all costs. "Why are our representatives playing such secondary, subordinate roles?" demanded one feuilletonist. "In ten weeks [Kadets] Kedrin and Petrunkevich . . . have not said one word. Literally, not a single word." But the politicians' indifference was not unlike that of too many readers: "The public is more interested in the fact that one of [Kadet] Nabokov's cufflinks cost more than [Trudovik] Zhilkin's entire suit."[55] The deadlock on the land question made dismissal of the First Duma imminent, so when it came the already prepared editors could write with conviction, "The king is dead, long live the king!" and begin plans for a second election.[56] The editors thought it especially important that readers understand that the tsar's actions here would not destroy their overall objectives, and they assured readers that there was nothing constitutionally out of the ordinary about the dismissal, that such things happened, too, in politically mature countries. Apathy posed a greater threat in the long run in *Peterburgskaia gazeta* than did the dismissal.[57]

Russkoe slovo shared misgivings about the "poison of passivity" that threatened to abort the chances for constitutional reform.[58] As *Russkoe slovo* viewed the Duma, "All thinking people, whether or not they have the right to vote, are morally obligated to spend a part of every day considering what they can contribute to the electoral campaign."[59] When the

---

[55] *Pg*, 3 July 1906, no. 179.
[56] *Pg*, 11 July 1905, no. 187.
[57] *Pg*, 11–12 July 1906, nos. 187–88.
[58] *Rs*, 19 Jan. 1906, no. 9.
[59] *Rs*, 8 Jan. 1906, no. 7.

legislative body was in session, special correspondents reported daily by telephone from St. Petersburg and stenographic accounts of meetings appeared as supplements. A "Gallery of Contemporaries" featured portraits of Duma deputies. The editorial columns entered the debates, informing and offering advice.[60]

For all the idealized imaginings of what the Duma might achieve, agrarian unrest, sporadic mutinies, and urban strife continued to plague the country. News about disorders juxtaposed to that about the Duma made plain the incapacity of the latter to govern competently. Even *Russkoe slovo*'s special correspondent to the Duma, lawyer S. V. Varshavskii, bemoaned the boring speeches; the excitement was in the halls, where everyone was talking about the pogroms in southern Russia.[61] Nonplussed by I. V. Zhilkin's sartorial negligence, Sytin hired him to write about life on the Duma floor, and he worked for years at *Russkoe slovo*. His reportage, though, did not bear out his optimisim that although the national heart was weak, its pulse was getting stronger in the Duma.[62]

Elections to the Second Duma gave *Russkoe slovo* another deputy-correspondent: Petrov represented the "Party of Peaceful-Renewalites," a small new party formed by those in general sympathetic to aspects of both Kadets' and Octobrists' platforms but not satisfied with the specifics of either. Hinting of Slavophilism, the party fell closer to the Octobrists than to the Kadets with its program to engender "cooperation between the landowning gentry and the peasants."[63] Petrov was attracted to the Slavophile elements that made this party "truly Russian" in its denial of European influences, but others at *Russkoe slovo* found the party "in desperate need of talent and energy."[64] Petrov never showed much faith in the Duma, which was for him a bureaucracy unable to protect his civil rights. This pessimism fed others at *Russkoe slovo*, who wrote the week before the Stolypin coup that "nothing can save that which history has doomed to destruction."[65]

Although *Russkoe slovo* hardly greeted the "System of the Third of June" with enthusiasm, the editors pointed out that the landowners now favored by the electoral laws had in Europe provided the foundation for the development of a liberal middle class.[66] Although *Russkoe slovo* disagreed with his agrarian reform project, the significance of which will be addressed in the next chapter, Stolypin was credited for at least trying to

[60] *Rs*, 3 June 1906, no. 144.
[61] Ibid.
[62] *Rs*, 4 June 1906, no. 145.
[63] Emmons, *Formation of Political Parties*, 358.
[64] *Rs*, 12 June 1907, no. 133.
[65] *Rs*, 26 May 1906, no. 120.
[66] *Bv*, 5 June 1907, no. 9929; *Rs*, 20 Oct. 1907, no. 241.

work with the Second Duma, which suggested a modicum of hope for the Third.[67] The Duma must be maintained, not sacrificed on principle.

The other liberal newspapers also reacted with curiously more optimism than might be expected. Although the government had promised a Third Duma, it had already been well established that the electoral laws would weight the elections heavily in favor of the landowning nobility. *Peterburgskaia gazeta* showed the most disheartened regret, saddened expressly because the Third Duma could not conceivably seat a Kadet majority.[68]

That *Birzhevye vedomosti*'s editors calmly accepted the fate of the Second Duma is more surprising, but their attitude can be explained by their anxiety that the radical left would destroy the Duma out of spite. Even before Stolypin confronted the Second Duma over the political immunity of the Social Democrats, *Birzhevye vedomosti* had become extremely annoyed with the Marxists for jeopardizing the Duma's future with their counterproductive grandstanding. *Birzhevye vedomosti* reported actively on the congress of Social Democrats being held then in London, with special attention to their discussions about the appropriate role to play in the Russian Duma.[69] As the Kadets debated a marriage of convenience with the left, Propper's editors argued vehemently against association with the extremists on the grounds that any bloc with the Marxists would prove disastrous to constitutionalism, as the latter wanted only a tribune for agitation.[70]

Like the other major papers, *Peterburgskii listok* welcomed the new election laws. Agreeing with Stolypin, the editors thought it of the utmost importance that the Duma be able to work with the government, which could not happen unless the legislative body was also conservative.[71] The electoral laws disappointed the editors when they did not allow the hardworking smaller landowners an equal say to the owners of the massive estates.[72] The newspaper appeared to be of two minds: one feuilletonist would trivialize the dismissal, while another would bemoan public apathy toward it.[73] *Peterburgskii listok* saw the Duma's potential strength in its capacity to replace the bureaucracy over time.[74]

The conservative papers, predictably, rejoiced. *Novoe vremia*, the newspaper of choice among the new majority, denied that a coup had

[67] *Rs*, 7 June 1907, no. 129.
[68] Reprinted in *Bv*, 5 June 1907, no. 9929.
[69] *Bv*, 17 May 1907, no. 9899.
[70] *Bv*, 19 June 1907, no. 9939.
[71] *Pl*, 4 June 1907, no. 151.
[72] *Pl*, 12 June 1907, no. 158.
[73] *Pl*, 7 and 20 June 1907, nos. 154, 166.
[74] *Ml*, 24 May 1907, no. 140.

been executed: "The tsar took it upon himself, fulfilling his obligation to God and history, to save the new order."[75] Throughout, *Novoe vremia* insisted that the government had taken action based on constitutional rather than arbitrary license. *Moskovskii listok* made Stolypin a hero because he challenged the Kadets.[76] When the Second Duma reached its standoff over the agrarian question, the prime minister came off better than the floundering coalitions.[77] Never a fan of political parties and threatened by the disorders that Stolypin had done much to quell, Pastukhov greeted the "System of the Third of June" with relief. In what was probably the first time he asked readers to believe in foreigners' attitudes about Russia, Pastukhov argued weakly that international public opinion sided with Stolypin, not the Duma.[78]

Russkoe slovo and the Kadets: Liberal Press, Liberal Party

That the liberal press did not intend to relinquish its role in formulating political discourse to the newly organized liberal party emerges clearly in *Russkoe slovo*, especially in Doroshevich's feuilletons. Fundamentally, however, *Russkoe slovo* and the Kadets agreed on the basics: both were nationalistic, were committed to rule of law, supported no one class at the expense of others, and wanted increased protection for workers and alienation of state and gentry lands for the peasantry.[79] *Russkoe slovo* also shared an occasional feuilletonist with *Rech'*, for example, Merzhekovskii and Kornei Chukovskii. Sytin's unwillingness, therefore, to use his newspaper as a springboard for the Kadets underscored that he and his editors did not want to forfeit their agenda-setting roles. Editorial attacks on the Kadets evidenced competition over setting the terms of liberalism.

Shortly before the Moscow uprising, *Russkoe slovo* had expressed severe disappointment with Witte's government over the conservative electoral regulations that would severely restrict the democratic potential of the Duma.[80] As workers prepared to move against the state, *Russkoe slovo* caricatured Witte as Hercules, slicing off the heads of the "hydra of revolution."[81] After the aborted Moscow uprising, the paper cautioned

[75] *Nv*, 4 June 1907, no. 11216. See also the synopsis provided by *Birzhevye vedomosti* of all major newspapers' editorial reactions, 5 June 1907, no. 9929.

[76] *Ml*, 4 Jan. 1907, no. 3.

[77] *Ml*, 31 May 1907, no. 140.

[78] Supplement to *Ml*, 4 June 1907.

[79] William Rosenberg, *Liberals in the Russian Revolution: The Constitutional Democratic Party, 1917–1921* (Princeton, N.J.: Princeton University Press, 1974), 12–46; and Emmons, *Formation of Political Parties*, 21–88.

[80] *Rs*, 2 Dec. 1905, no. 318.

[81] *Rs*, 7 Dec. 1905, no. 323.

readers not to allow the alarm generated by the violence to play into the hands of those whose commitment to the October Manifesto could be lessened once their most pressing individual needs had been met. The government, reneging on the promises made in October, had forced people into the streets to defend the manifesto.[82]

The Moscow uprising occurred just before the elections to the First Duma, and the Kadets debated boycotting them in protest. This was the first of many issues that troubled the nascent party as it organized into a formal body to represent Russian liberalism at the polls. The Kadets ended up making several compromises that shook the faith of many who saw in them the prospect of a liberal, progressive Russia. Having a plurality but not a majority in the first two Dumas, the Kadets needed to find partners to form a bloc, and members differed over whether to court from the right or from the left. Where the middle class was weak and the have-nots so inordinately outnumbered the haves, aspiring liberals were bound to have difficulties hoeing a middle ground. After having ordered Witte, for example, to call immediately for election to a constituent assembly, within a few months the Kadets had moderated their demands and were speaking of a constitutional monarchy and had stopped pushing for universal, direct, and secret balloting. In the opinion of some observers, the Kadets' shifting positions revealed a latent conservatism that suggested that they could not be depended upon to defend the workers and peasants, those Russians who needed protection most. The Kadets imagined that they could surmount their troubled relations with the leftist parties by remaining "above classes" (*nadklassnost'*), a misguided perception that would split the party in 1917 along the ideological fault line that had been present from the party's inception.[83]

Russkoe slovo presented the Kadets as having sold out their principles when action in the streets threatened their immediate gains. Before Stolypin's coup, the editors had flirted with the notion of getting the moderate populists to form a party that might be more effective than the Kadets, who vacillated between right and left. Worried that the best organized hope for liberal Russia would seek compromise with the Octobrists instead of looking to their left, *Russkoe slovo* editorialized that "the main enemy is on the right. It always has been, and always will be there."[84]

Doroshevich's barbed satires verbalized editorial policy most eloquently. In the first two months of 1906, he attacked those who had betrayed the revolution. He targeted not only Witte, but the liberal middle

[82] *Rs*, 19 Dec. 1905, no. 324.
[83] Rosenberg, *Liberals*, especially chapter 1.
[84] *Rs*, 29 and 30 Sept. 1907, nos. 223–24.

classes, whom he saw as having sacrificed the bodies of innocent Muscovite workers for the protection of their own private property. These people, among whom he included the Kadets, preferred the continuation of the autocracy as soon as they felt their individual interests threatened.[85] The French who bailed out Witte "were not the French of 14 July."[86] The prime minister was a second Napoleon, waving only an illusion of a constitution.[87]

Shortly after Stolypin's coup, Struve began to argue in the pages of *Pravo* for more conservatism in the party.[88] *Russkoe slovo* objected strenuously.[89] Doroshevich ridiculed the Kadet leader, caricaturing him as the emissary of a female landowning Kadet who, on her deathbed, had sent him to negotiate a comfortable spot in heaven. Doroshevich traced the political shifts of an egocentric Struve who, lacking the patience to wait in line at the Pearly Gates, grabbed a spot in hell for his colleague.[90] The "King of Feuilletonists" had little faith that this party would not act first out of its own self-interest, because "a bureaucracy of landowners was growing in [the Kadets] like a tapeworm."[91] In later years Sytin toyed with the idea of hiring Struve as an editor, but his staff objected.

The Censorship Reform of 1905

By any measure the daily newspaper spoke more openly after the tsar eased the censorship in November. A study of this reform must consider two factors: the legislation itself and the ability of the government to implement it. The laws revealed what the officials saw to be the problems, and the censors' application of the statute provided one yardstick by which to measure governmental authority. Comparing the circulars of forbidden topics with the contents of various newspapers confirmed that the government could not impose itself at will. Although such commands as that in 1901 "to exclude completely discussion of the worker question from the press" were unenforceable in the scope of their demands, they could make editors circumspect about what they might say.[92] On the other hand, editors never knew for certain how censors would respond,

[85] *Rs*, 11 Jan. 1906, no. 10.

[86] Bukchin, *Sud'ba fel'etonista*, 181.

[87] *Rs*, 2–4 Feb. 1906, nos. 32–34.

[88] Richard Pipes, *Struve: Liberal on the Right, 1905–1944* (Cambridge, Mass.: Harvard University Press, 1980), 3–65.

[89] *Rs*, 19 Sept. 1907, no. 213.

[90] *Rs*, 8 July 1907, no. 156.

[91] *Rs*, 6 Nov. 1906, no. 255.

[92] Lemke, "V mire Usmotreniia," 135.

so they constantly probed the ambiguous limits of the law. *Russkoe slovo*, for example, violated three circulars in 1901, but received different punishments. In two instances (undisclosed), the Moscow censorship committee simply reprimanded the editors. But when *Russkoe slovo* published a forbidden story about a trip Tolstoi took to the Crimea, the newspaper lost its street sales for a week.[93] As Suvorin observed about this circular, "We have two tsars: Nicholas II and Lev Tolstoi. Which is stronger? Nicholas can do nothing about Tolstoi . . . but Tolstoi can shake Nicholas's throne and his dynasty."[94]

Looking at censorial authority, 1903 again appears as the pivotal date of declining governmental effectiveness. *Birzhevye vedomosti*'s Kaufman remembered this year and the next as among the most tense in terms of censorship, but the record suggested that he and his colleagues were becoming more sensitive because they were also growing bolder.[95] In January the beleaguered Chief Administration of Press Affairs complained that even official periodicals were ignoring the circulars.[96] Once censors detected the crumbling of power, they hesitated to assume the responsibility for enforcing it. The Moscow committee, for example, despite orders to refer only matters of exceptional importance to the Chief Administration in St. Petersburg, began sending all questionable articles in *Russkoe slovo* to headquarters, whose overworked staff just kept kicking them back.[97] Presumably, censors were no stricter with other newspapers, and their unwillingness to punish signaled to editors that past boundaries should be tested whenever possible. Sytin found his street sales suspended again briefly in 1903, on direct orders from Assistant Minister Durnovo, for articles that the censors had ignored.[98]

The tsar had made reform of the censorship one of the matters that the Bulygin Committee was to consider. Bulygin named D. F. Kobeko, director of the Imperial Library, to chair a commission that would have two years to compose a new statute.[99] The restive populace accelerated their labor, and the first article of the October Manifesto promised freedom of speech. On 24 November 1905 the promulgation of the new censorship statute gave journalists much reason to cheer: gone were the circulars, warnings, administrative punishments, and preliminary censorship of any

[93] TsGIA f. 776, op. 8, d. 847, ll. 164, 190, 195.

[94] *Dnevnik Suvorina*, 263.

[95] Kaufman, "Iz zhurnal'nykh vospominanii," no. 12, 1073.

[96] Rigberg, "Tsarist Press Law," 340.

[97] The provisions for committees' responsibilities are in the *Ustav o tsenzure i pechati*, 1890, art. 19. Communications between the Moscow committee and the Chief Administration are in TsGIA f. 776, op. 8, d. 847, ll. 197, 199–201, 215–16.

[98] TsGIA f. 776, op. 8, d. 847, l. 228.

[99] Ruud, *Fighting Words*, 213–14, 218–19.

sort. Journalists would stand responsible only before a court of law. Qualifications for editing and publishing were relaxed, and the five thousand–ruble deposit was no longer required.[100] Before, prospective publishers had to apply to the Chief Administration of Press Affairs for permission to publish; now they only had to register with local authorities. As in 1865, the initial decree was designated "temporary," in this case until the Duma could legislate permanent regulations. Again as in 1865, later versions of the statute returned a conservative element that perverted the spirit of the reform. At least Propper no longer had to send flowers to important wives to avoid having his street sales suspended.

New periodicals materialized following the decree like mushrooms after an April shower.[101] In 1905, 118 new titles appeared, a number that grew to 608 the next year, but declined to 331 the year of Stolypin's coup.[102] Numbers alone, however, can provide only the vague contours of change. They do not tell which titles were actually the same newspaper, for example, the twice-opened Kadet *Birzhevye vedomosti*. More important, they do not reveal which periodicals died natural deaths at the hands of the disinterested public and which the censors took out of circulation.

Censors quickly found a new route to attack the press, one that turned censorship over to where the editors had long said they wanted it, the courts. The blessing of legality was mixed. Within the first two months after the reading of the new press law the government closed more than sixty periodicals for breaking not civil but criminal laws.[103] The sporadic labor unrest that followed the October Manifesto invigorated censorship committees to charge editors with "incitement to riot or to strike," article 129 of the criminal code.[104] After Propper retrieved his paper from the Kadets, Kaufman found himself on trial several times for inciting to riot, although he never served a prison sentence.[105] Notovich fled to Paris, and Sytin hired Varshavskii, his paper's legal correspondent, to keep his editor son-in-law Blagov out of jail. Between November 1905 and August 1906, Blagov was charged with, and found innocent of, violating article 129 six times.[106] Prosecution on these grounds raised more than reasonable doubts that the government would protect freedom of speech, and

[100] *Zhurnal ministerstva iustitsii*, no. 5 (1906): 1–5.

[101] The cover of the "thin" journal *Oskolki* for 24 Dec. 1905 satirized the new regulations that harvested the new newspapers like toadstools. Reproduced in Ascher, *Revolution of 1905*.

[102] Smirnov, *Legal'naia pechat'*, 12.

[103] Ruud, *Fighting Words*, 224.

[104] Ibid., 222–23.

[105] *Bv*, 5 and 21 Nov. 1906, nos. 9580, 9606.

[106] TsGIA f. 776, op. 8, d. 848, ll. 118, 134–36, 138–39, 146.

the censors wielded this statute as their replacement weapon after losing the circulars (see appendix B, table 13).

Stolypin dashed the few remaining hopes for the decree of 24 November when, one day before he prorogued the Second Duma, he gave local authorities the right to institute "obligatory decrees" for purposes of restoring order. These decrees empowered officials, without turning first to the courts, to fine newspaper editors for articles they interpreted as breaches of security, thereby returning administrative arbitrariness (see appendix B, tables 13–14).[107] For so successful a publisher as Sytin, these fines absorbed little of his operating budget: 7 percent in 1907, but less than 1 percent in 1909.[108] For the big newspapers, as one *Novoe vremia* city editor pointed out, "The new fines were like a child's toy compared to the pre-1905 suspensions of advertising or street sales."[109]

Stolypin, like Witte, also had specific ideas about the relationship between politics and information, and he accompanied his censorship with his own "Information Bureau" in the Ministry of Internal Affairs. The specific function of this news bureau was to get positive information about the government in the press, but it failed miserably.[110] Stolypin also became involved in publishing a newspaper, *Rossiia (Russia)*, which he hoped to use to sell his reforms to the reading public. The newspaper, which specialized in success stories of Russian agriculture and sometimes featured drawings by one of the tsar's sisters, drew ridicule from the independent newspapers.[111]

The question of how much influence this subjective censorship of arbitrary fines and criminal accusations could wield was essentially moot.[112] Publishers still held onto their public space, which they had widened considerably since the Japanese had aided their cause by attacking Port Arthur. Improved technology also had a political contribution; in 1906, Sytin published photographs of his destroyed factory, and *Peterburgskaia gazeta* displayed the macabre open-coffin photograph of a Jewish politician assassinated by a right-wing thug.[113] The most important lesson that the government could have learned was that it could not generate respect

---

[107] P. Tolstoi, "Obiazatel'nye postanovleniia o pechati v poriadke okhrany," in V. Nabokov, ed., *Svoboda pechati pri obnovlennom stroe* (SPB: Obshchestvennaia pol'za, 1912), 86–121.

[108] *Otchet pravleniia tovarishchestva I. D. Sytina*, 1907 and 1909.

[109] Snessarev, *Mirazh*, 17.

[110] E. V. Lentenkov, "K istorii pravitel'stvennykh informatsionnykh tsentrov v Rossii (1906–1917), *Vestnik LGU*, no. 20 (1973): 80.

[111] Doroshevich once wrote that *Rossiia* had pictured hippopotami as cows in its foolish efforts to present the land reforms as wildly successful. *Rs*, 8 Jan. 1914, no. 5.

[112] Jacob Walkin, "Government Controls over the Press in Russia, 1905–1914," *Russian Review* 13, no. 3 (1954): 203–9.

[113] Supplement to *Rs*, 1 and 8 Jan. 1906, nos. 1–2; *Pg*, 22 July 1906, no. 198.

for itself among the reading public by intimidating the communicators upon which readers relied. Authority crumbled before institutions did, a point that seemed lost on Stolypin when he tried to brace his own political program by returning the threat of administrative controls. Readers could not be punished into believing in the system, which balanced so precariously on a public opinion that still had access to news about the government's activities. Whatever the disappointments of Duma and revolution, public opinion had nonetheless gained confidence from having forced effective changes on the government. It could happen again.

Lenin described the 1905 Revolution as the "dress rehearsal" for 1917. A rehearsal, however, presumes that the stage has been set and the actors will be playing the same roles that they will play on opening night. Although Russia's mass-circulation newspapers would again in 1917 present an independent forum for political exchange, the changed circumstances of the intervening years made the press into a different character in the drama, itself revised. For one thing, the newspaper had many more lines in the new script. During the interrevolutionary era the political right would take control of the government and deflate the spirit of October, many intellectuals would retreat from past ideas of public service, the leftists would regroup and retrench, while the mass-circulation press would explode the scope of its competence.

10

The Newspaper Between Revolution and War, 1907–1914

LEOPOLD HAIMSON raised an issue in 1964 that continues to inform all discussions of the era between the Stolypin coup and the onset of World War I. Evaluating both Soviet and Western interpretations of these critical years, he focused on how the two schools offered different explanations for the role of the Great War in the events of 1917. In the West historians argued that, despite the post-1907 reaction, Russian society was evolving according to Western socioeconomic models. Although social and political conditions were strained in 1914, peaceful evolution would have allowed liberals to realize their goal of a constitutional parliament, had the war not interrupted and exacerbated the strains. Soviets, in contrast, argued that an upsurge in revolutionary labor activism, triggered by the massacre by government troops of the unarmed strikers at the Lena Goldfields in 1912, had reached a climax in July 1914. The assassination of Archduke Franz Ferdinand occurred coincidentally to the strikes, and the outbreak of war allowed the government to repress radicals and to draft workers as the hostilities diverted attention away from the revolutionary movement. By 1915, however, the radical element had resumed leadership of the working class and strikers were returning to the lines; the war had postponed a revolution on the verge of explosion.[1]

Haimson shifted attention to the nature of the social stability upon which the case for "peaceful evolution" ultimately rested. Contrasting the situation in urban Russia leading up to 1905 with that just prior to July 1914, he found a significant difference in how political interest groups responded to the circumstances that had changed in the course of the decade. He determined that *obshchestvo*, or educated and privileged society, during the interrevolutionary era was characterized by a "dual polarization," separating itself from the tsarist government on one side and the working class on the other. In 1905, the disparate social and political clusters had been able to submerge their differences and establish a set of common goals. However, the inability to override disagreements and reconstruct this coalition after 1907 led to two "separate revolution-

---

[1] Leopold Haimson, "The Problem of Social Stability in Urban Russia, 1905–1917," *Slavic Review* 23, no. 4 (1964): 619–24, and 24, no. 1 (1965): 1–22.

ary processes, each adding to the pressures against the tsarist regime but also contributing—by their separation—to the eventual disintegration of the whole fabric of national life." Because this dual polarization was already evident by 1914, and the three groups were growing farther apart, the war cannot be referenced as the catalyst for the Bolshevik Revolution.[2]

Subsequent scholarship has fleshed out in almost painful detail the failures of institutions that might have generated a firmer basis for social and political cohesion: unions were quickly rendered impotent, thereby thwarted from giving workers a voice in management or ameliorating economic grievances that would have quieted unrest; the reactionary right took control of electoral politics and did not respond to the liberal press's wishful thinking in June 1907 that they would put public above private interests; many from the intelligentsia rejected their traditional roles and retreated from political activism; and the Kadets neither resolved their internal differences nor recovered from the rewriting of the electoral laws to organize into a mass party.[3]

Haimson blamed the intelligentsia in large measure for failing to "secure the bridges" built in 1905 between classes, arguing that short-term political stability was purchased with long-term social instability.[4] Moving away from the elite groups upon which he focused, though, can provide a second reading of the situation. However clear it became after 1917 that a network of social bridges had indeed been left unattended, a reading of the mass-circulation newspapers published during these seven pivotal years indicates that editors and publishers thought either that they had strengthened alliances forged earlier or were attempting to do so. Editorial writers defended the civil rights of all groups and continued to assert themselves as spokespersons for the poor and disenfranchised, although they did not speak in one voice. Publishers could have interpreted from their rising circulation figures that readers were accepting many of their judgments. When Haimson referred to editorial attacks on the government for its violence against the strikers as "the only articulate expressions of the concern of educated society," his qualifying "only"

---

[2] Ibid., 21–22.

[3] A sampling of this literature must include: Victoria E. Bonnell, *Roots of Rebellion: Workers, Politics, and Organizations in St. Petersburg and Moscow, 1900–1914* (Berkeley and Los Angeles: University of California Press, 1983); Joseph Bradley, *Muzhik and Muscovite: Urbanization in Late Imperial Russia* (Berkeley and Los Angeles: University of California Press, 1985); Manning, *Crisis of the Old Order*; Rosenberg, *Liberals*; Robert Thurston, *Liberal City, Conservative State: Moscow and Russia's Urban Crisis, 1906–1914* (New York: Oxford University Press, 1987); Boris Shragin and Albert Todd, eds., *Landmarks*, trans. Marian Schwartz (New York: Karz Howard, 1977); and E. D. Chermenskii, *IV Duma is sverzhenie tsarizma v Rossii* (Moscow: Mysl', 1986).

[4] Haimson, "Social Stability," 21.

slighted an extremely significant public.[5] A look at the crisis brewing in
the Duma that summer supports the evidence culled from newspapers
that a variety of forces had begun to increase their demands for political
change. Where the newspapers presented signs of social instability, the
roots of the problems were fixed in the unsatisfactory political situation
and therefore could be plucked out through reforms.

During the interrevolutionary years, as Menshevik leader Fedor Dan
pointed out, "To the growing class maturity of the proletariat corresponds
a similar growing class maturity of the bourgeoisie."[6] The mass-circulation press reflected this. A casual comparison of Russia's mass-circulation
newspapers between 1907 and 1914 with their Western counterparts
would support the argument that Russia was moving down the same path
in socioeconomic development that the West had taken. Spiraling circulations, greater sensationalism, increased use of new technologies that
reproduced illustrations inexpensively, made the Russian press read very
Western indeed. A photograph in *Peterburgskaia gazeta* of members of a
St. Petersburg social club, posing in their soccer uniforms, illustrated the
medium's ability to capture the poise of the bourgeoisie without sacrificing its concern for the underprivileged, as it persevered in the exposés
of slumlords and child abuse. All newspapers' absorbing fascination with
aviation and their intensely competitive coverage of the race from Petersburg to Moscow in 1911 likewise reflected a growing sophistication of
both the medium and the society on which it reported. The appearance
of a "kopeck" press in 1908 finally gave Russia its "penny" equivalent and
integrated a whole new stratum of readers into the newspaper audience.

We turn to the kopeck press for insights into the relationship between
liberals and labor in the interrevolutionary period. The most significant
representative of the "new" journalism born of the "System of the Third
of June," the Petersburg tabloid *Gazeta kopeika* (*The Kopeck Gazette*)
promised the world, literally, every day for one kopeck. Despite a 1910
advertising boast that "*Kopeika* will satisfy the most demanding readers,
regardless of which class they belong to," the paper's contents show it
clearly marketed for the working and other lower classes. Its phenomenal
circulation of 250,000 in 1909, only its second year of publication, nearly
doubled *Russkoe slovo*'s figures and made *Kopeika* the most popular
newspaper in the empire. *Kopeika* is a particularly valuable source for
studying the polarization of the middle and the lower classes because it
offered news and entertainment of specific interest to the latter, but presented issues in such a way that the newspaper affirmed the values and
ideology of the former. If ever the liberal middle had a cultural medium

[5] Ibid., 2.
[6] Ibid., 630.

through which to reach workers, it was *Kopeika* and its kopeck imitators spreading around Russia's metropolitan areas; by 1911 twenty-nine kopeck dailies circulated in the empire.[7]

Before moving on to analyses of the individual newspapers, a brief overview of three major events will elucidate how the news itself allowed journalists to encourage the public to resist the Old Regime. The first, the dramatic death of Lev Tolstoi in November 1910, gave newspapers occasion to comment at length on all that the great man had exemplified, and his opposition to the tsarist government was legendary. The story was so big that even Stolypin's *Rossiia* deferred to Tolstoi as a moral authority.[8] Not only did the editorial page allow for interpretative comment, but reporting of the particulars of the death itself, which occurred in a railroad station outside of provincial Astapovo where Tolstoi had collapsed after having just embarked on a religious pilgrimage, showed in its best light the capabilities of Russia's communications system. The coverage itself became a genuine media event, and reporters waiting in railroad sidecars and fighting over the telegraph created a circus atmosphere, while readers waited on edge to learn the exact moment of the passing of the titan.

Two other incidents also contributed directly to the collapse of autocratic authority. In September of 1911, Stolypin, while accompanying the tsar and other high officials to Kiev, was assassinated while attending a performance of Rimskii-Korsakov's *Tale of the Tsar Saltan*. The killer confounded right and left alike by being both Jewish and a secret police agent. The mixture of politics and sensationalism appeared made-to-order for the popular press. *Kopeika*, for example, reproduced the floor plan of the opera house to show where Stolypin had been seated.[9] The more serious newspapers took the opportunity to comment on the inadequacies of Stolypin's government, using his violent death as a metaphor for the failure of the "System of the Third of June."

Stolypin's successors had far less competence than the slain prime minister to brace the foundations of the House of Romanov. The third pivotal news event also took place in Kiev and likewise involved a Jew. In March 1911, during Passover, the body of a young Christian boy was found brutally murdered. A Jewish watchman, Mendel Beilis, who worked near the cave where the body was discovered, was charged with draining the boy's blood to make his holiday matzos. In 1913, when the case finally came to court, the trial became a cause célèbre and drew international coverage. Local journalists doubled as detectives to find the truly guilty party in this contrived affair. When Minister of Justice I. G. Shcheglovi-

---

[7] *Gazetnyi mir za 1911* (SPB: n.p., 1911), 334.

[8] *Rossiia*, 7 Nov. 1910, no. 1526.

[9] *Gk*, 4 Nov. 1911, no. 1123.

tov involved the autocracy in prosecuting the watchman, even many conservatives were mortified. Evidence against the mother of one of the victim's friends and her gang of thieves was continually brushed aside in favor of the coincidence of religion, and editorial comments seemed almost superfluous next to the facts from the trial. Through its mass-circulation press, the tsarist government disgraced itself publicly.[10]

In addition to undermining both government and Duma, the newspapers offered an alternative source of political authority with whom they identified their editorial platforms, Russia's historical intelligentsia. Although a significant number of intellectuals, those whom Haimson charged with renouncing the messianic ethos of 1905, withdrew from social activism after 1907, the older generation had established its political authority by putting themselves on the line to demand increased rights for all Russians. Many of their clashes with the autocracy had landed them in prison or forced other deep sacrifices, which made them ideal figures for inspiration during these troubled times.

The historical intelligentsia found a new place in the post-1907 mass-circulation press. In the absence of sufficiently satisfying contemporary political heroes, the old intellectuals were returned as symbols, and little attention was given to the complexities of their individual thoughts. The hundredth anniversary of Gogol's birth in 1909 prompted a torrent of articles, as did the fiftieth anniversary of Slavophile Ivan Aksakov's death later that year and the tenth anniversary of populist Mikhailovskii's death in 1914. Each of these three men represented a significantly different ideal, but their dissimilarities could not be gleaned from the collective media response that stressed their love of the Russian people and contributions to its culture. In part an expression of cultural nationalism, the attention to the intelligentsia also demonstrated a search for political bearing after 1907.

It is natural to expect the press to honor national figures, but the venerable position to which the intelligentsia found themselves raised during the stagnant Duma years had political connotations. In the 1860s and 1870s, newspaper journalists were in competition with this same intelligentsia. Fifty years later, well established themselves, it was to their advantage to emphasize their connections to tradition. Literary critic Belinskii, the thorn in Kraevskii's side and one of the greatest inspirations to young revolutionaries from the 1840s, found himself a hero in *Moskovskii listok* in 1911, celebrated for his commitment to serving society.[11] Belinskii's heir, Dobroliubov, was not only remembered for his republicanism during the dark days of Nicholas I, but cynically brought into the present

[10] Hans Rogger, "The Beilis Case: Anti-Semitism and the Politics of the Reign of Nicholas II," *Slavic Review* 25, no. 4 (1966): 615–29; and Haimson, "Social Stability," 10.

[11] Sunday supplement to *Ml*, 1911, no. 20.

in *Birzhevye vedomosti* with a discussion of his pessimism about the Great Reforms.[12] In *Russkoe slovo* in 1914, Amfiteatrov interviewed the ghost of anarchist M. A. Bakunin one hundred years after his birth, mitigating the revolutionary's obsession with destructive violence behind his defense of human rights and culture.[13] N. M. Karamzin, Russia's first historian, despite his staunch defense of the autocracy under Alexander I, was praised for "intelligence and hard work" in *Birzhevye vedomosti* a week after nihilist D. I. Pisarev had been hailed in the same pages as a "Russian national genius."[14] This reverence for the old-style intellectuals, even when their activities had to be recast to dilute their thoughts, made the distaste for most Duma deputies all the more conspicuous. Aversion to the autocracy and the present Duma did not mean indifference toward politics.

The view of newspaper journalists as a new intelligentsia casts a new light on the interrevolutionary years because the retreat of many from the former corps of leaders has been used to explain the loss of unity and direction after 1905.[15] *Vekhi* (*Signposts*), a 1909 collection of self-critical essays by prominent intellectuals, has long served as the textbook example of the intelligentsia's disillusionment with political activism. Advising readers to withdraw from the public sphere and commit their energies instead to a private quest for moral absolutes, the *Vekhi* group abandoned their traditional role in Russian politics.[16] Newspaper journalists, despite their dissatisfaction with the status quo, were not so disabused of the notion of the writer's continued political responsibility.

Gazeta kopeika

The combined forces of censorship, technology, and economy had prevented the growth of a kopeck press before 1905. The censors had fretted about what the lower classes read, and the technology could not produce these papers cheaply enough without infusions from advertisers willing to invest in the poorest segment of the population. But Stolypin's reforms had helped to create a lower class with pocket money for leisure activities. The founder of the first successful *Kopeika*, M. B. Gorodetskii

---

[12] *Bv*, 17 Nov. 1911, no. 12689.

[13] *Rs*, 18 May 1914, no. 113.

[14] *Bv*, 29 Nov. and 1 Dec. 1916, nos. 15945, 15957.

[15] Haimson, in "Social Stability," argued that "it is difficult to escape the conclusion that the failure of Russia's first revolution, and the repudiation it induced among so many in the intelligentsia of their traditional revolutionary ethos, substantially contributed to the character and pattern of the second" (21).

[16] Jeffrey Brooks, "*Vekhi* and the *Vekhi* Dispute," *Survey* 86, no. 1 (1973): 21–50.

Fig. 15. The staff of *Gazeta kopeika*

(1866–1918), found himself unemployed in Petersburg when the government chased Notovich, his publisher, to Paris in 1905.

A liberal Jew who had learned his trade writing about the poor and
exploited laborers in his native southwest corner of European Russia, Gorodetskii recognized that the striking workers had many a commercial
publisher who defended their interests, but none who appealed to them
directly. With other members of *Novosti*'s defunct staff he began *Segodnia (Today)* in 1906, but it was little more than a pale imitation of the
successful boulevard fare. When *Segodnia* died a natural death, Gorodetskii teamed up with several relatives and Vladimir Anzimirov, a populist writer who had been covering the provinces for *Russkoe slovo*, to
produce a remarkably unique addition to the newspaper contingent in
the national capital, available for three rubles annually or one kopeck per
single issue beginning 19 June 1908.[17] A year later Anzimirov would
leave to inaugurate Moscow's kopeck press, which, far more radical, lived
a precarious existence under a variety of names with different editors and
publishers.[18]

Despite *Kopeika*'s conspicuous differences from the other newspapers,

[17] Obituaries of Gorodetskii in *Gk*, 14 and 16 March 1918, nos. 3304, 3306; *Nash vek*, 10
March 1918, no. 45.
[18] On the various Moscow *Kopeikas'* problems with censors, see TsGIA f. 776, op. 16g.
2, d. 515, l. 4; and f. 31, op. 5, d. 716, ll. 5, 10.

from its tabloid size to its focus on the lower classes, Gorodetskii advertised its similarities. His 1910 publicity brochure swore that "we have thousands of letters from readers thanking us for informing them on everything that is in the largest newspapers, but in a clear and comprehensible format." Furthermore, readers were assured that "the authors of these letters are not semiliterate people who could not get through a sheet from a big newspaper, but are from the intellectual professions and are highly educated." From such questionable puffery as this it was a short step to merchandising the serialized potboilers as a respectable genre: "*Kopeika* wants to divert its readers from the boring, gray sameness of daily life by offering for their reading pleasure big and stimulating novels. . . . although they are not based on actual cases from [the Pinkerton Detective Agency], they are so well written that they seem . . . artistically believable."

This pamphlet presented the editorial concept that made *Kopeika* so valuable as a cultural artifact: the paradox of integration and escapism. Gorodetskii clearly wanted his readers to feel themselves a part of the larger social order, and he saw his newspaper as a mechanism that would facilitate assimilation. When he told readers that he was intentionally supplying them with an escape hatch, he implied that just as they exited through *Kopeika*, they would return through it. Keeping the editorial page filled with liberal defenses of workers' rights, he offered his paper as a pillar of their community.

It is not my purpose here to depict Gorodetskii as an evil capitalist gleefully subverting the revolutionary movement by deflecting workers' attentions away from important political issues, but he fit the stereotype so easily that it is difficult not to notice. Gorodetskii's editorial policies raise one of the thorniest problems in dealing with newspapers, the issue of intentionality: what personal agendas did editors and publishers have, and how did they set them? *Kopeika*'s contents suggest that its staff intentionally sought to integrate its working-class audience into their liberal hopes for Russia. Gorodetskii, who grew up impoverished in the Pale, undoubtedly sympathized with his readership and, like the old-time populists, felt the responsibility of improving the lot of the less fortunate. Even if detective fiction usually overwhelmed editorial attention to both Russian belles lettres and workers' educational activities, Gorodetskii sought to raise the cultural level of his audience.[19]

Despite his early background in reporting, Gorodetskii seldom wrote for the paper himself, leaving it to two feuilletonists to set his newspaper's tone. O. Ia. Blotermants, who like Gorodetskii had started in Rostov-na-donu, wrote sometimes under his own name but more often as

---

[19] Brooks, in *When Russia Learned to Read*, discussed *Kopeika* (130–41).

"The Wanderer." He became *Kopeika*'s most prolific writer. The next leading feuilletonist was a woman, Olga Gridina, about whom the sources remain silent. The working woman's Lukhmanova, Gridina paid a surprising amount of attention to the international suffragist movement, but she also spoke to the concerns of the girl in the cotton factory trying to decide whether or not to supplement her income through prostitution. Gridina's articulate feminism, like Blotermants's defense of groups on society's periphery, enhanced *Kopeika*'s liberal credentials.

Gridina and Blotermants showed great compassion for society's underdogs, but did not dwell on pity. On the contrary, they told those left out of the mainstream to accept responsibility for their own lives, and promised them that they could turn to *Kopeika* for advice on how to reach their goals. Gridina and Blotermants differed in style from other newspapers' resident feuilletonists in ways that reflected their audience. For example, Leikin and "Sir Beach Brandy" at *Peterburgskaia gazeta* entertained with anecdotes about people and predicaments familiar to their readers, and Doroshevich's use of situated language kept him outside the action as the roving eye, but *Kopeika*'s columnists were much more prone to giving counsel. Gridina and Blotermants set themselves up as intimate companions, couching their admonitions in quasi cautionary tales about ills that had befallen people they knew or in response to letters from readers.

Gridina's reach for a previously neglected audience, the lower-class female, evidenced the presence by the end of the first revolutionary era of a number of women who, poor and badly educated, had new opportunities to pull themselves out of their straits. Attentive to their harsh realities, Gridina encouraged among them a philosophy of feminism that combined female solidarity to overcome the prejudices of society's dominant male structure with the individualism of self-help. In short, she sold a fundamentally bourgeois worldview in that she dissociated gender from class and emphasized the importance of individual efforts to raise one's status and enter the world of comfort and security. These were not, however, inspiring feuilletons that assured just rewards for hard work, as Gridina remained at heart cynical about Russia's ability to find direction.

A typical column brought Gridina into direct contact with her audience, as in her telling of a late-night meeting with a prostitute who had turned to her for guidance. Many of the incidents and friends she described may well have been fabricated, such as this back-street rendezvous with a hooker, but the feuilletonist recounted them as episodes from reality. Like *Peterburgskii listok* in the 1860s, *Kopeika* had license to move between fact and fiction because its audience was new to newspapers and coming from a literary tradition in which didacticism played a key role. In this story, the forlorn "Liza" had been a maid, beloved by the family she served, but had succumbed to the temptations of the high life of the underworld. Sorely regretting her decision, she turned to Gridina, who then asked readers how they might advise the girl. A nun suggested that Liza might find peace in the Bible, to which Gridina responded that religion alone could not solve society's social and economic problems.[20] When a widow complained to the journalist that the women for whom she sewed took advantage of her need for their money, Gridina chastised the employers and reminded all that the poor do not want charity, just the opportunity to earn an honest ruble.[21] This fed into another of her favorite themes: that women should take care of other women.[22]

Gridina's acquaintances included women in the newer professions as well as in the oldest. She eschewed the word *feminism* because it brought to mind the loud and unruly British suffragettes who, in her opinion, embarrassed women rather than furthered their causes. "A friend of mine is the first female in the export business," she told readers, "and if you were to question her about feminism she'd ask, 'how is it sold? in bags or whole wagons?' She'll do more for women's rights than all those exalted rioters in London."[23] Her attack on suffragettes did not dilute her message of economic and social equality, which interested her more than the vote. Surveying women's rights in Russia, she saw that "we now have the right to earn half as much as men do, the right to be their toys, and to take care of the kids when they abandon us."[24] Agreeing with playwright Henrik Ibsen that women allow themselves to live as dolls, she chided those who, unlike her friends the female bankers, "cling to the bedroom and are afraid that they won't be invited to waltz if they know too much about stocks and bonds."[25]

Suicide was another of her most common themes, and, again focusing on women, she presented it as the choice individuals made to escape the harshness of their circumstances. Significantly, her suicides did not take their lives because they were mentally unstable or diseased by alcoholism. The suicide pact of two girls in a provincial gymnasium gave Gridina pause to condemn the unhealthy educational system that had depressed the girls by forcing them to read books that were alien to their personal lives.[26] She then expanded this into a criticism of society as a whole, "confused and rudderless since 1905, unable to satisfy either our personal

[20] *Gk*, 17 Oct. 1910, no. 806.
[21] *Gk*, 4 Jan. 1910, no. 523.
[22] *Gk*, 10 Oct. 1909, no. 449.
[23] *Gk*, 10 June 1912, no. 1398.
[24] *Gk*, 26 March 1910, no. 604.
[25] *Gk*, 13 Jan. 1910, no. 532.
[26] *Gk*, 4 April 1910, no. 613.

or our social lives."[27] But when three young Muscovite millionaires committed suicide, men who enjoyed prospects denied her readers, she insisted that they "did not have a right to," that they were "shirking their responsibilities."[28]

The more prolific Blotermants, as "The Wanderer," used essentially the same technique to send corresponding signals. Like Gridina's, a number of his acquaintances walked on the wild side. Readers consulted him about their personal problems, and he preached the doctrine of self-help as the most satisfying approach to life's difficulties. His hopes for a better future depended upon a liberalism capable of moderating between Russia's two extreme political impulses, but in 1918 he found himself studying in a special course on Bolshevik journalism.[29] Undoubtedly, his Bolshevik editors did not appreciate his prerevolutionary style.

"The Wanderer" appeared to have a number of comrades from the countryside benefiting from Stolypin's breakup of the commune. He told, for example, about a friend who had just moved from Kiev and, in search of companions, joined one of the self-education groups that began developing in workers' circles even before 1905. This particular gathering, though, turned out to be a gang of thieves and gamblers, and Blotermants's friend began crossing the street in order to avoid the shame of having to confront the journalist.[30] Another of his many provincial buddies found himself unwittingly taken in by a gang of card sharks.[31] For all his warnings about what might happen to the uninitiated, "The Wanderer" was still not likely to take up the plight of the newly arrived. When yet another friend came to town and asked for his help in finding a job, the feuilletonist denied this request because "people must make their own careers, they don't get others to do it for them."[32]

Blotermants criticized existing institutions when they failed to protect his readers; arguing for improved health care for prostitutes and better salaries for clowns, he spoke out for society's most marginal elements.[33] He attacked the city government for not dealing effectively with the dilemma of infant mortality, just as he faulted the national government for its hypocritical attitude toward alcoholism, reaping the profits in the state stores, which he suggested should at least be removed from the poorer sections of town.[34] Befitting his sympathies for individualism, "The Wan-

---

[27] *Gk*, 11 April 1910, no. 6201.
[28] *Gk*, 3 Nov. 1910, no. 823, and 20 Nov. 1911, no. 1200.
[29] *Gk*, 14 March 1918, no. 3304.
[30] *Gk*, 15 Nov. 1911, no. 1195.
[31] *Gk*, 1 April 1910, no. 610.
[32] *Gk*, 17 April 1910, no. 626.
[33] *Gk*, 30 March and 24 Oct. 1910, nos. 607, 813.
[34] *Gk*, 5 April 1910, no. 614, and 10 May 1912, no. 1368.

derer" could accept the market as a mediating force. When the City
Duma raised the issue of whether or not utilities should be held publicly
or privately, he argued that private firms had proven more responsive to
public needs than had government-managed services, although he
stopped one step short of urging private ownership.[35] He also applauded
a charitable organization that decided, while remaining nonprofit, to run
its affairs on the basis of commercial management techniques.[36]

Kopeika fostered values associated with the middle classes, especially
those of personal choice and honest work, but the reality that many readers toiled in difficult and demeaning jobs forced its feuilletonists to temper faith in individualism with the fantasies of a liberating fluke of fortune. "The Wanderer" told, for example, of a group of industrious
workers whose labors had been rewarded when the owner willed them
his factory.[37] The newspaper's writers sought to integrate their lower-
class readers into their vision of social reality, not segregate them according to their place in the labor force. One story told of a factory owner
who paid for exploiting his workers with debilitating family problems: he
had had to toss out his good-for-nothing sons, his wife was in an asylum,
and he was in court trying to recover money stolen by his brother. Observations that the fellow had only his millions, "which can neither warm
nor lighten his life," served up morality as the great equalizer.[38] Murders
committed to acquire inheritances were used for editorial commentary
on money being the root of all evil.[39]

Kopeika's writers painted a picture of a modern world in that they encouraged readers to assume greater individual responsibility. But society
was changing so fast that most readers would need a familiar setting to
which they could return if they made the wrong selection from among
the new opportunities. Ideas about mobility, social and geographical, in
the interrevolutionary era were expressed most clearly in the serial novels that adorned *Kopeika's* front page. The contradiction inherent in the
competing notions of individual choice and institutional security surfaced
as these novels' dominant theme. In his analysis of *Kopeika's* serials, Jeffrey Brooks argued that they allowed readers "to resolve in fantasy the
tension between the promising individual and the collective, between
the dream of personal success and social harmony." The recurring plot of
the novels called for a hero (the protagonists were always male) to leave
his community and find adventure, happiness, and success when freed
from constraints, but ultimately choose to retake his place in the society

[35] *Gk*, 24 Nov. 1912, no. 1565.
[36] *Gk*, 15 May 1912, no. 1372.
[37] *Gk*, 26 May 1912, no. 1383.
[38] *Gk*, 22 Nov. 1912, no. 1563.
[39] *Gk*, 28 Aug. 1911, no. 1116, and 6 May 1912, no. 1134.

he had forsaken. Self-assertion was rewarded, but was not in and of itself the hero's ambition.[40] Like Blotermants's steady stream of friends in from the provinces, the heroes could indulge briefly in wine, women, and song, but then had to either assume the obligations of the modern world or be consumed by it. The fiction combined the escapism of fantasy with the return to the familiar, and it reproduced the underlying editorial pitch that it might behoove readers to relinquish their fates to those with a better understanding of the situation. *Kopeika* offered sanctuary to a goodly number of displaced and ambitious lower-class Petersburgers.

The newspaper also intensified their need to seek refuge. *Kopeika* was as yellow as any newspaper Russia ever produced, and violent crimes were as staple to the newspaper as its serial fiction. Editorially, crime in *Kopeika* represented a social disease contracted from the government's uncoordinated and dislocating policies of industrialization. Criminals were often described as victims, and the conditions of modern life more villainous than the individuals. Watching the collapse of the social order, *Kopeika*'s editors questioned the ability of the state to govern. One editorial, for example, argued that alcohol-related crimes should be separated from others, and the punishment for the former should include medical treatment.[41] A woman was taken to court for peddling her young daughter to a lecher in order to afford vodka, for which the editors took society to task: "Did this happen among the Hottentots in Central Africa? No, here in Petersburg. Not only are the mother and the old man guilty, but so is everyone who let this happen."[42] When a twelve-year-old boy stabbed his mother when she forbade him to attend a party, editors queried, "Who is guilty? The street that destroyed his soul, the mother who brought hatred, not love, to his heart, or the conditions of life?"[43]

Gorodetskii's first hire, Vladimir Trofimov, like Bennett's for the "penny" *Herald*, was a police reporter. Also writing feuilletons as "The Nutcracker," Trofimov remained one of *Kopeika*'s most productive writers until, in a burst of patriotism, he joined the army in 1916 at age forty-three and died from an infection contracted working with a dental unit.[44] His highly personalized accounts from a back bench in the courthouse made him one of *Kopeika*'s most ideologically influential writers because he interpreted the functioning of law and the establishment of order for his audience. Trofimov described the entire judicial system, not just the details of specific crimes, and he maintained the principle of objectivity

---

[40] Jeffrey Brooks, "The Kopeck Novels of Early Twentieth Century Russia," *Journal of Popular Culture* 13, no. 1 (1977): 85–97.

[41] *Gk*, 9 Jan. 1909, no. 174.

[42] *Gk*, 29 July 1908, no. 35.

[43] *Gk*, 2 Jan. 1909, no. 168.

[44] Obituaries in *Gk*, 24 Jan. 1916, no. 2706, and *Pg*, 24 Jan. 1906, no. 23.

Fig. 16. Front-page illustrations in *Gazeta kopeika*. *Left*: "The house in Old Village where 3 people were brutally murdered 3 days ago." *Right*: "An attack on the cashier at a city pawnshop, on the staircase of a house on Sadovaia Street."

that recalled Chekhov's dictum that readers did not need to be told that stealing horses was wrong. His reports carried the weight of Chibnall's argument that reportage on the justice system helped a community to define its moral perimeters.[45]

On one occasion, Trofimov followed a peasant woman wandering help-lessly around the circuit court in a futile search for justice after having been swindled out of the money for a new roof. The reader might wonder why Trofimov did not intervene on her behalf, but his recounting of the apathetic treatment that her shabby dress and ungrammatical language met with from clerks made his point.[46] He spoke once with parents in from a village who were suing their daughter for disrespect because after she had married well, she snubbed them.[47] Trofimov also mixed genres, at times making fact indistinguishable from fiction, as when he began one story with a description of a man embracing his sick wife and children as he set out for the day. Instead of work, today the man went to court, where "the secretary read the accusation in a steady, metallic voice," the droning voice sending the man to prison for embezzling funds to pay his wife's medical bills.[48] Society and the state appeared to be at odds on distinguishing right from wrong, and *Kopeika*'s Petersburg could be a depressing place in which to live.

It could also be an extraordinarily exciting one. As Elizabeth Butler wrote in her 1909 study of why the drudgery of factory work sends labor-

[45] Chibnall, *Law-and-Order News*, xi.
[46] *Gk*, 12 Nov. 1909, no. 472.
[47] *Gk*, 8 Nov. 1909, no. 468.
[48] *Gk*, 31 Jan. 1909, no. 193.

ers to seek sensational entertainment, "Dulled senses demand powerful stimuli; exhaustion of the vital forces leads to a desire for the crude, for violent excitation."[49] Any issue of *Kopeika* lent credence to this philosophy. One day the police found a corpse at 80 Fontanka Street, whose "head had been sliced off and set on top of the torso. . . . when they raised the blinds, they saw that the head had been scalped and the eyelids, nose, and lips cut off."[50] The rest of Butler's quote is more problematic with regard to *Kopeika*: "In such circumstances, culture of hand or brain seems unattainable, and the sharing of our general heritage a remote dream." This was a primary issue for Gorodetskii and his staff: could *Kopeika* incorporate the working class into their vision of Russia? *Kopeika* relied on sensationalism to grab the workers' attention. The rapes and intrafamilial slayings that prompted editorial comments made for piquant drama in the news pages, and woodcut illustrations brought readers to the site where the deeds were done. Again, the color of journalism covered over the political implications of the connection between sensationalism and class-based readership.

J. W. Freiberg argued succinctly that the bias intrinsic to sensational journalism favors the middle at the expense of the lower classes: "In the sensationalist press, natural disasters, social and political conflicts and shifts in the careers of the famous and infamous are all covered in precisely the same tone, rendering the sensationalist press incapable of distinguishing social and political crises from natural disasters. The ideological implication is clear: the contradictions and conflicts of class relations that bring about *social* turmoil are confounded with fires and floods that bring about natural turmoil. . . . There are no social classes in this worldview and no class conflict."[51]

Historical coincidence provided an excellent opportunity to apply Freiberg's reasoning to *Kopeika*'s editorial policies: on 3 April 1912 (15 April in the West), the luxury liner *Titanic* struck an iceberg in the North Atlantic and took more than one thousand passengers to a watery grave; two days later, Russian government troops fired into a crowd of striking miners at the Lena goldfields in Siberia, killing 107. The root of the first disaster was in nature, the second, in politics.

Kopeika's editors reacted as Freiberg's thesis implied they would, reinforcing the view that the causes of both disasters were equally beyond readers' control. Comparing the amount of total news space for both stories for the two weeks after they occurred, the 6 percent for the *Titanic* nearly equalled the 7 percent for the Lena massacre, which made the

---

[49] Quoted in Czitrom, *Mass Media*, 48.

[50] *Gk*, 5 Oct. 1909, no. 434.

[51] J. W. Freiberg, *The French Press: Class, State, and Ideology* (New York: Praeger, 1981), 225–26.

events of proportionally identical significance. Nor was there a discernible difference in orientation of news reportage.[52] A particularly disgusting account of miners weaving around the barracks, vomiting up meat described as "not only inedible and indigestable, but unknowable as well," diverted focus away from the politics: improve the food and you improve the situation.[53]

A look at the other newspapers' coverage of these two events shows that the censors did not mute the public outrage about Lena, and that in the serious press Lena pushed the *Titanic* to the back columns. *Russkoe slovo*, for example, never had more than a column on the ocean liner, and on the massacre at Lena the paper brooded that "this is the most serious event in Russia since 1905. It illustrates that our government still does not understand its basic obligations."[54] *Novoe vremia* showed that its conservatism did not stretch to state brutality, and although the Jewish directors of the mining corporation were blamed in part, so was the Russian government, which had failed to work seriously to find a peaceful solution to the strike.[55]

In the long run, the most potentially serious challenge to *Kopeika* came from the Bolsheviks, who began *Pravda* on 22 April 1912 with a promise that all income from the two-kopeck first issue would go to the families of the slain workers. The Bolsheviks had voted in 1907 against working on the staffs of bourgeois newspapers, and *Pravda*'s inaugural edition also featured a short morality tale on the dual evils of drinking vodka and reading *Kopeika*.[56] Market competition in workers' circles between these two papers would have helped to elucidate the polarization of workers and liberals, but the government never let *Pravda* publish long enough for that.

The information about workers, their social activities and organizations, and the features of special interest to them, from Blotermants's advice to the adventure serials they devoured, sustained the notion that workers were part of a unified society, and editorials advised readers to act within the accepted structural norms. *Kopeika*, for example, commended workers in Ekaterinaslav for asking forgiveness for their participation in the seizure of the railroad in 1905.[57] Workers were praised when they filed petitions for reforms through official channels instead of

---

[52] This is based on a quantitative analysis of *Kopeika* in April 1912, nos. 1329–49.

[53] *Gk*, 19 April 1912, no. 1347.

[54] *Rs*, 10 April 1912, no. 83.

[55] *Rs*, 8 April 1912, no. 81, reprinted a *Novoe vremia* editorial on Lena to show that even conservatives were upset with the government.

[56] G. Zinoviev, "Protiv uchastiia v burzhuaznoi pechati," *Prosveshchenie*, no. 4 (1914): 77–81.

[57] *Gk*, 2 Jan. 1909, no. 168.

by striking.[58] Reacting to the radical strikes in July 1914, *Kopeika's* editors praised those workers who had "put aside class interests" and returned to work, "displaying that intelligence that makes Russia great."[59]

The war began a few days later, and *Kopeika's* circulation began to slide. It would be marvelously convenient to look back on that editorial from the perspective of 1917 and cite it to explain *Kopeika's* suddenly declining fortunes. Social observer L. M. Kleinbort, who wrote for the Menshevik-oriented journal *Sovremennyi mir* (*The Contemporary World*), found dissatisfaction with *Kopeika* in his research on the factory floor. "*Kopeika* poisons the soul," complained one worker. Its readers were suspected to be doormen, cabbies, and prostitutes, not yet culturally sophisticated but nonetheless drawn to the printed word.[60] Someone else recommended that the paper be called *Strikebreakers' kopeika* because it advertised companies whose workers were on strike.[61]

Kopeika cultivated assimilation rather than separation, but looking at what it did not do begs the question of how many workers in 1914 would have settled for the ideology it offered. In 1913, when St. Petersburg had a factory-worker population of 216,000, *Kopeika's* circulation was 220,000.[62] Undoubtedly many cabbies and prostitutes read *Kopeika*, but so too did a large number of workers. Gorodetskii's newspaper exemplified how the liberals tried to use the mass-circulation press to encourage the workers to share their political vision, and its popularity must have contributed to the liberals' sense that workers stood behind them.

Russkoe slovo

Despite a precipitous drop in circulation from 150,000 to 100,000 in 1906, Sytin's newspaper recovered in the following year and held its steady pace to the benchmark of one million in 1917. Sytin and his journalists continued to conduct the new politics associated with collecting and distributing information, and when the Duma faded as a representative body capable of legislating reforms, *Russkoe slovo* set with determination and clarity its own oppositional agenda. There was more than a grain of truth in the editorial comment that Russia was the only country

[58] *Gk*, 5 May 1909, no. 283

[59] *Gk*, 18 July 1914, no. 2156.

[60] L. M. Kleinbort, "Ocherki rabochei demokratii," *Sovremennyi mir*, no. 2 (1913): 114–15.

[61] L. M. Kleinbort, *Ocherki rabochei intelligentsii*, 2 vols. (Petrograd: n.p., 1923), 20.

[62] *Ocherki istorii Leningrada*, 4 vols. (Moscow and Leningrad: Akademiia Nauk, 1956), 3, 12.

in the world where politicians looked to the mass-circulation press and then did the opposite of what they read.[63]

To reach his objectives, Sytin borrowed from Russia's traditional source of political opposition, the educated elite. Many of Russia's foremost progressive minds offered solutions to national dilemmas in the pages of Russkoe slovo. Boris Veselovskii, whose four-volume history of the zemstvos argued for increased decentralization in self-government, wrote articles along the same lines for Russkoe slovo. In addition to Petrov, A. V. Kartashev, director of the Petersburg Religious Philosophical Society and one of the leading proponents of the separation of church and state, wrote regularly on religion.[64] Another member of the young modernist crowd that had gathered at the Merezhkovskiis' salon in the 1890s, and intimate friend to ballet impresario Sergei Diaghilev, Dmitrii Filosofov, wrote feuilletons regularly. Future Nobel laureate Ivan Bunin published his classic Sukhodol first in Russkoe slovo, and Gorky allowed Sytin to serialize excerpts from his memoirs there. The list went on to include symbolist poets Konstantin Bal'mont, Viachaslav Ivanov, Anna Akhmatova, and even a hesitant Alexander Blok.[65] Sytin paid these writers as much as one thousand rubles per contribution.[66]

Selling poetry or feuilletons to the empire's most widely circulated newspaper did not equate with self-sacrifice to take a political stand, but Russkoe slovo constructed a cultural bridge and invited the intelligentsia to use it to communicate. Stalwarts Doroshevich and Nemirovich-Danchenko remained on hand as the personal links between the new intelligentsia and the old. Cultural conservative A. I. Izmailov sat as Russkoe slovo's resident literary critic, and he had little patience with modernism or what he deemed "the social irresponsibility of individualism" of some of those who published alongside him.[67] The newspaper specifically connected culture with politics, expressed in an editorial that emphasized culture over party affiliation as the basis of political science in Russia.[68]

Prominent Moscow University economist Professor I. Kh. Ozerov joined Russkoe slovo's constellation of influential contributors, setting the paper's economic position. Ozerov accepted on principle Witte's demand

[63] Rs, 14 March 1909, no. 60.

[64] Rs, 7 Feb. 1913, no. 31. See also Merezhkovskii's review of Kartashev's Reforma, reformatsiia, i ispol'nenie tserkvi in Rs, 24 Dec. 1916, no. 297.

[65] Aleksandr Blok, Sobranie sochineniia, 8 vols. (Moscow: Gos. Izd. Khud. Lit., 1960–1963), 7:115.

[66] When Leonid Andreev accepted five thousand rubles for promising five contributions in 1912, he found himself losing a lawsuit for submitting a play of his currently being produced in Moscow. TsGALI f. 1694, op. 1, d. 78, ll. 1–6; f. 595, op. 2, d. 2, l. 1 and d. 3, ll. 1–2.

[67] Rs, 1 Jan. 1912, no. 1.

[68] Rs, 8 Jan. 1908, no. 6.

that Russia become industrialized, but he hesitated to follow Western blueprints to reach that goal. For example, he objected to Stolypin's "wager on the sober and the strong," the prime minister's plan to allow for the development of independent farmsteads in the countryside, because the Russian peasantry was not prepared to emulate Western agrarian conventions by the stroke of a pen. *Russkoe slovo*'s attitude toward Stolypin's agrarian reforms showed that on the critical peasant question, the newspaper stood with the peasantry against the land-owning gentry. When the first portion of the legislation appeared in November 1906, *Birzhevye vedomosti* praised it as the fulfillment of Witte's aspirations, arguing that Stolypin's plan to break up the commune represented a major step toward making peasants equal citizens in the empire.[69] Like the urban press, Propper's paper had mocked those who idealized the *muzhiki* because he saw the peasantry as potentially skilled producers, not the mythical soul of Russia.[70] *Russkoe slovo*, however, saw the reforms as fundamentally political, not economic, and registered severe misgivings about a plan that was "too West European" and that would not protect the poor from the wealthier peasants.[71] Ozerov and the others who wrote on national economics for *Russkoe slovo*, including his university colleague Mikhail Bernatskii, saw disaster in Stolypin's plans because they did not address the essential problems of the provinces.

Russkoe slovo's economists did not agree with the prime minister's logic that independent farmsteads were the key to a modern agricultural Russia, arguing instead that the country's large landowners were characteristically a backward lot and that the communes gave the peasantry its cultural foundations because schools and health care were organized communally.[72] Private property, like competitive capitalism, lost its legitimacy when it permitted exploitation; land belonging to the gentry simply had to be made available to the peasantry.[73] Instead of overturning the peasants' way of life, the government should be actively incorporating them into its future by extending credits that would weave them into the economy and by giving them significantly greater say in local government.[74] When "friends of the people" argued against sending justices of the peace into the village because peasants had their own traditions of justice, *Russkoe slovo* exploded against this opposition to assimilation.[75]

[69] *Bv*, 14 Nov. 1906, no. 9594.

[70] *Bv*, 1 May 1903, no. 213.

[71] *Rs*, 14 Nov. 1906, no. 277, and 13 May 1907, no. 109.

[72] *Rs*, 13 May and 5 July 1907, nos. 109, 153, and 7 Oct. 1910, no. 230.

[73] *Rs*, 4 May 1907, no. 101, and 8 March 1909, no. 55.

[74] *Rs*, 10 Jan. 1908, no. 8, and 21 April 1909, no. 90.

[75] *Rs*, 21 Feb. 1912, no. 42.

Modernizing the national economy required working with existing institutions, and the capital investment needed to industrialize Russia would have to come substantially more from the state than from private individuals. As the economists saw it, the fundamental flaw was not with state capitalism per se, but with the way in which this particular state managed its money. Echoing two of Witte's most constant refrains, Ozerov saw the potential strength of the country in a consumer-oriented economic infrastructure, and the state monopoly on alcohol was one of the gravest evils of the tsarist regime. He drew the two together when he pointed out that money workers spent on booze could have gone for other consumer products, and because alcohol diminished productivity, society had to pay double for drink.[76] Arguing, with Witte, that the economy made a better measure of national strength than the military, he favored investment in consumer-oriented industries, such as cloth factories.[77] But should Russia, short of investment capital, borrow from the West? Yes, but only so long as money came without the strings of foreign management.[78] In *Russkoe slovo*, the proper development of the national economy depended upon the combination of individual efforts and state investments for the public good; the trusts and monopolies of the West were poison to Russia, whose natural resources were too scarce to be entrusted to those whose personal dividends mattered more than public interest.[79]

On the worker question, editorial support for the right to unionize, for insurance on the job, and even to strike, held firm.[80] To prevent a radicalization of the workers, their living and working conditions must be improved so that radicals' slogans would not attract them.[81] When the strikes started up again after the tragedy at the Lena goldfields, Bernatskii told the government to pay attention to Western use of legal arbitration in resolving conflicts between management and workers.[82] The economic writers also chastised shortsighted factory owners who refused to recognize that satisfied workers would improve their productivity.[83]

The lower classes were not the only groups *Russkoe slovo* sought to integrate into a new national whole. The staff had very specific ideas

[76] *Rs*, 8 Jan. 1908, no. 6.

[77] *Rs*, 27 March and 3 April 1909, nos. 70, 75.

[78] *Rs*, 25 March 1909, no. 69.

[79] *Rs*, 16 Jan. 1913, no. 13. In 1916, however, when Russia's mounting war debts had begun to cripple the national economy, Ozerov turned to the United States with an offer of land grants in exchange for investing in the railroad. Ozerov, "The Economic Situation in Russia," *Russian Review* 2, nos. 1–2 (1916): 7–13.

[80] *Rs*, 4 Sept. 1907, no. 203, and 5 Jan. 1908, no. 4.

[81] *Rs*, 18 Sept. 1907, no. 213.

[82] *Rs*, 13 Feb. 1913, no. 36.

[83] *Rs*, 13 Jan. 1913, no. 11.

about Russia's identity as a nation, and the overtures toward tolerance of differences struck up during the Russo-Japanese War now played to a nationalistic house listening for strains of assimilation. The editors appealed for a great Russia held together by geographical boundaries and culture rather than race or religion, although the Great Russian ethnic bias was unmistakable. Numerous travelogues acquainted readers with the expansive empire. In 1907 V. Varvarin (the pseudonym conservative critic V. V. Rozanov used when he wrote for *Russkoe slovo*) sailed down the Volga, "the Russian Nile," and found unity between river and urban populations in their "Russian souls," a concept found frequently in Sytin's "truly Russian" paper.[84] Petrov, dispatched to Central Asia in 1913 to assess the cultural wants of "our property" there, called for primary education and social services, but wanted them conducted in Russian.[85]

Still, the new Russian was not necessarily Slavic. When Austria annexed the South Slavic provinces of Bosnia and Herzegovina in 1908, *Russkoe slovo* waxed indignant not on the basis of Pan-Slavic emotions, but because Austria had humiliated the Russian government with its unilateral action.[86] The incident was interpreted as confirmation of the need for a secure national identity.[87] Five years later a series of skirmishes erupted among the various Balkan states, and the Slavic territories appealed to Russia for backing against the non-Slavs in the border disputes. Doroshevich satirized the Slavs in the Balkans (especially the Serbs) as children looking to Russia as their mother, and admonished that the time had come for the kids to grow up.[88] He echoed Witte's notion that "nobody here, no serious thinker, is interested in these vain and restless Balkan peoples who are not really Slavs but badly baptized Turks."[89]

If other Russians felt more fraternal toward the Balkans than Witte and Doroshevich, the concept of what "Russia" meant had nonetheless changed. In the opinions of *Russkoe slovo*'s writers, Russia was neither an empire nor a race, but a more closely circumscribed political unit awaiting suitable government. When *Novoe vremia* complained that the ethnic mix of the Russian Army would undermine its effectiveness because nationalities would fight for different causes, *Russkoe slovo* responded that all Russian soldiers would fight for what they believed in most, civil rights.[90]

[84] *Rs*, 17 July 1907, no. 163. This series on the "Russian Nile" was followed by one on the "Sleeping Tsarevna," a tour of southern Russia and the Caucasus.

[85] *Rs*, 16 Jan. 1913, no. 13.

[86] *Rs*, 4 March 1909, no. 51.

[87] *Rs*, 20 March 1909, no. 65.

[88] *Rs*, 6, 8, and 10 Jan. 1913, nos. 5, 6, 8.

[89] Quoted in Hans Kohn, *Pan-Slavism: Its History and Ideology* (South Bend, Ind.: University of Notre Dame Press, 1953), 205.

[90] *Rs*, 15 July 1907, no. 162.

But would soldiers fight for the Duma? As constituted, it did not provide the proper government. In the first months after the Stolypin coup there was still hope because "every civilized country knows that there are problems with a constitution, just as there are problems with railroads, but you wouldn't travel without an engine."[91] Optimism soured quickly. On the fifth anniversary of the October Manifesto, the Third Duma was "the gravedigger of everything that happened 17 October."[92] The Octobrists were denounced as garden slugs who had left their slime all over the chairs in the Duma, creating a sleazy zone between the opposition and the reactionary forces.[93] However, as Filosofov gently chided, it had become fashionable to call the Fourth Duma boring, and though boring it certainly was, he questioned that sensationalism should divert attention away from the only alternative to autocracy.[94] Despite its constituents, the Duma still had possibilities as an institution.

The Other Liberal Newspapers

Harold Williams, a London *Times* correspondent to St. Petersburg, described *Birzhevye vedomosti* as "resembl[ing] the *Russkoe slovo* in many respects. It is non-party, opposed to the Government, sensational and gossipy. Its provincial edition is widely read by country priests and village school teachers."[95] The paper's contents show that Williams was not far off the mark. During the cholera epidemic of 1909, for example, a series of feuilletons "From the Nightmares of Cholera" gave frighteningly gruesome details of the disease contracted by members of the village intelligentsia, forewarning of "what can happen to you, reader, if you haven't taken precautions."[96] The author of a correspondence course on journalism advised students that to publish with *Birzhevye vedomosti* they must collect details on "huge fires, brutal murders, and scandals in the [provincial] dumas."[97] Propper settled for supplying a largely liberal readership with what Sytin refused to give them, lowbrow reading material alongside serious matter.

Birzhevye vedomosti "resembled" *Russkoe slovo* because they shared a number of correspondents and feuilletonists. Ozerov set editorial poli-

[91] Ibid.
[92] *Rs*, 17 Oct. 1910, no. 239.
[93] *Rs*, 13 Feb. 1913, no. 36.
[94] *Rs*, 6 Feb. 1913, no. 30.
[95] Harold Williams, *Russia of the Russians* (New York: Charles Scribner's Sons, 1916), 113.
[96] *Bv*, 11 July 1909, no. 11204.
[97] *Kak korrespondirovat'*, part 10, 292.

cies on economics at both papers. Izmailov wrote literary reviews also for the two, and corresponded from Kiev on the Beilis trial for *Birzhevye vedomosti*; this paper was more vocal than others in its defense of Russian Jews against the anti-Semitism made so appalling by this case.[98] Merezhkovskii's wife, the eccentric modernist Zinaida Gippius, sold short stories sparingly to *Birzhevye vedomosti*. Kuprin also sold pieces occasionally to both papers. Still in the Kadets' camp, *Birzhevye vedomosti* induced leading party member N. A. Gredeskul to write commentaries periodically.[99]

An obvious difference between *Birzhevye vedomosti* and *Russkoe slovo* came in the standard entertainment features. The "Memoirs of the Crown Princess of Saxony" complemented a regular feature on "Social Life Abroad."[100] *Birzhevye vedomosti* also gave readers science fiction, "A Story from Life in 3911."[101] In other respects, too, *Birzhevye vedomosti* was more entertaining; the paper published enough pictures to hire a staff photographer by 1913. It appeared that Propper had conceded to Sytin as the most politically influential publisher, and balanced his liberal editorial message with the escapism that Sytin eschewed.

Peterburgskaia gazeta remained the most cordial daily, giving more attention to personalities than political issues. Where *Russkoe slovo* interviewed Octobrist leader Guchkov to inform about his party's platform, *Peterburgskaia gazeta* solicited his wishes to readers on New Year's Day.[102] *Russkoe slovo* generated public agendas, *Peterburgskaia gazeta* public personas. More visually stimulating after 1907 did not also mean more scandalous, although the novels below the fold of the front page still tantalized. News on local issues kept civic consciousness attuned to such issues as the inadequacies of transportation, housing, and the plight of the poor. National politics and the Duma received adequate but unenthusiastic coverage, and editors remained frustrated that what deputies wore to the Duma still seemed to matter more than what they discussed.[103]

This paper's readers met the rich, famous, and powerful as private individuals, and its editors used interviews considerably more than any other. Although *Birzhevye vedomosti* and *Kopeika* might also publish New Year's greetings from national figures, *Peterburgskaia gazeta* went well beyond that.[104] Correspondents surveyed public leaders in politics,

[98] *Bv*, 3 Sept. and 30 Nov. 1911, nos. 12510, 12660.

[99] *Bv*, 1 Nov. 1911, no. 12611.

[100] The serial ran in *Birzhevye vedamasti* in the autumn of 1912.

[101] *Bv*, 12 Nov. 1911, no. 12631.

[102] *Pg*, 1 Jan. 1908, no. 1. Guchkov wanted "peace and enlightenment for the fatherland."

[103] *Pg*, 20 Jan. 1908, no. 19.

[104] *Gk*, 1 Jan. 1909, no. 167.

Fig. 17. "Secrets of Magic." This woodcut illustration
for a booklet on how to perform magic tricks was typical for all of the boulevard newspapers.

the arts, and science to bring personal opinions, both trivial and profound, to readers. Topics covered in these questionnaires included "The
Worst Day in My Life," which gave readers familiarity with the private
lives of such celebrities as Miliukov, Gorky, and dancer Isadora Dun-
can.[105] Artists and art experts were queried on "Art and Shamelessness,"
an issue of great interest during the Silver Age's self-absorbed flirtations
with decadence and pornography.[106] Another poll among artists, who included Nemirovich-Danchenko and the fashionable painter Ilya Repin,
asked whether or not liquor stimulated their creative juices; they all condemned alcohol as a source of inspiration.[107]

Interviews with specialists and readership polls during the interrevolutionary era showed that *Peterburgskaia gazeta* stayed on top of contem-

[105] *Pg*, 11 Jan. 1908, no. 10.
[106] *Pg*, 12 Jan. 1908, no. 11.
[107] *Pg*, 6 Jan. 1908, no. 5.

porary concerns, ranging from whether or not surgeons should be held criminally responsible in the event of disaster on the operating table, to questioning if women were physically capable of being jockeys.[108] Science, psychiatry, and information from experts continued as important features, giving the newspaper the patina of an expert witness itself. Halftone technology made it possible, for example, to reproduce handwriting on newsprint; the signature of a murderous student replicated in *Peterburgskaia gazeta* permitted readers to search for signs of psychological instability in his handwriting.[109] Readers could also gaze into drawings of the eyes, the "mirrors of the soul," of local notables, from members of the City Duma to actresses.[110] The new technology allowed the paper to publish the photograph of a grain merchant to help the police in a missing persons case.[111]

Peterburgskaia gazeta appeared to be "taking the politics out of politics," the complaint lodged by politicians against the mass-circulation newspapers that balanced their news on national political issues with equal or greater attention to sports, fashion, and other such trivia in the minds of polemicists. *Peterburgskaia gazeta* could make an appropriate illustration of the anomie that had beset so many after the Stolypin coup, who, after having lost their bid for a genuinely representative government, settled back into their own amusements. What did it mean when editors filled news space describing how the Stolypin family spent its summer vacation instead of dissecting the prime minister's proposals for agrarian reform?[112]

Peterburgskaia gazeta's editors were as depressed as those of any other about the Duma, which "would probably devote its next session to discussing repairs to the laundry at Dorpat University," in reference to the infamous legislation submitted by the Council of Ministers to the First Duma for the construction of said laundry.[113] However, the polls and interviews actively engaged readers in matters of contemporary interest. By 1911, many Russians probably were more interested in the Stolypins' summer plans than in the endless debate about the commune; the topic was not so much *apolitical* as it was *differently* political. When *Peterburgskaia gazeta* presented to readers the private lives of public officials, it reconstituted the definition of *public*. The implications of this, though, would soon be aborted.

Peterburgskii listok, too, took advantage of the new technology, in this

[108] *Pg*, 7 March 1908, no. 65, and 3 July 1911, no. 179.
[109] *Pg*, 3 and 7 Jan. 1906, nos. 2, 6.
[110] *Pg*, 20 Jan. 1908, no. 19.
[111] *Pg*, 6 Jan. 1908, no. 5.
[112] *Pg*, 14 July 1911, no. 190.
[113] *Pg*, 1 Jan. 1908, no. 1.

case to turn even yellower. Alternately arousing and repellent, the paper's stories provided an escape from monotony into a very scary world. A drawing of a female customer being shot at point-blank range during the robbery of a post office, even though the story reported that the victim had been a male clerk, created thrills as well as trepidation.[114] The brutal murders of a tailor and his family in their beds one evening in 1910 inspired a pictorial description: "He lay on the bed, still dressed, his face to the window, legs spread and arms akimbo. [His wife's] head was saturated with coagulated blood and brains, beaten in with some kind of heavy object."[115] However, by 1907 *Peterburgskii listok*'s sensationalism also sought a few of the underlying sociopolitical implications of crime.

Hooligans, the "uncivilized" youths turned loose in the streets by uncoordinated urbanization, posed a greater danger to the cultural than to the legal system, and their activities received particular notice in *Peterburgskii listok*. In her study of hooliganism in St. Petersburg, Joan Neuberger argued that after the 1905 Revolution *Peterburgskii listok* changed its perspective on these young toughs. Whereas earlier the editors had viewed them as random and impudent individuals, their greater numbers and increasingly aggressive behavior after 1907 made hooligans now appear as symptoms of a worsening social malaise. News about hooligans' behavior increased in *Peterburgskii listok* in proportion to their effrontery, so the paper's coverage of this topic had insight into its views on attitudes toward social integration.[116]

Neuberger draws from a variety of sources other than this boulevard paper, and her conclusion that changed perceptions of hooligans by 1914 reflected a loss of faith by much of society that the lower classes could be assimilated into one culturally cohesive Russia emphasizes how even the slightly better heeled elements were pulling away from the lower.[117] Concentrating on the press, however, *Peterburgskii listok*'s petty bourgeois readers would count among the most likely targets of these thugs, and the paper's attention to hooliganism can also be viewed as an editorial campaign calling attention to the inability of the state to ensure the basic right to walk freely down Nevskii Prospect. The newspaper with possibly the most immediate stake in hooliganism and its victims, *Kopeika*, did not distinguish them meaningfully from the other unfortunates. Readers who favored corporal punishment for these miscreants

[114] *Pl*, 24 May 1907, no. 140.

[115] *Pl*, 1 Nov. 1910, no. 300.

[116] Neuberger, "Crime and Culture," especially chapter 2, and "Stories of the Street: Hooliganism in the St. Petersburg Popular Press," *Slavic Review* 48, no. 2 (1989): 177–94.

[117] Neuberger, in "Crime and Culture" (289), and Bradley, in *Muscovite and Muzhik* (351–52), argued that the upper and middle classes were conflating workers with the urban poor.

were criticized as "uncultured,"[118] and like other social problems, the causes of hooliganism contained the seeds of its solution.[119] Gorodetskii's staff worried primarily about the distance widening between state and society, not among social strata.

The Conservative Newspapers

Just as the editorial policies of the liberal press divided between national and urban, so too did those of the conservative. *Moskovskii listok* expressed the greatest alarm of any major daily about the social chaos. During the 1905–1907 period of unrest, when other newspapers featured special sections on "Strikes and Disorders," *Moskovskii listok* billed the same incidents as "Disorders, Murders, and Robberies," suggesting a very different political interpretation. The use of severe headlines continued after the 3 June coup, making Pastukhov's the major law-and-order newspaper; in contrast, for example, *Birzhevye vedomosti* had a regular section entitled "Arrests and Illegal Searches." The correspondents who formerly recorded the gossip from the "Streets and Alleyways" now found only "Brutal Murders" along Moscow's boulevards. Like the other urban newspapers, *Moskovskii listok* was visibly more sensational after 1907, and crimes of passion became an especially captivating news topic.

Politically, the newspaper held a predictable course. Stolypin remained the newspaper's hero and editors supported his brutal pacification of the countryside, although they paid little attention to agrarian matters.[120] The royal family and the Octobrists also turned up regularly and becomingly in *Moskovskii listok*. The serial novels alternated criminal with historical types. Where Petersburg's boulevard papers fictionalized contemporary events, Moscow's still looked nostalgically to the past but through modern eyes; for example, a serial on the reform project of Mikhail Speranskii, undertaken just prior to the Napoleonic Wars in an attempt to preserve the autocracy while establishing an efficient system of rule by law, sounded suspiciously contemporary in 1909.

Pastukhov died in 1911, and the new publisher moved away from the right toward the center; unfortunately, circulation figures were not available to measure his success. On one litmus test of conservatism, anti-Semitism, *Moskovskii listok* became muted after 1911. Covering the case against Beilis in 1913, *Moskovskii listok* reported the facts of the trial without editorial comment. Suvorin passed away in 1912, but under

---

[118] *Gk*, 15 Nov. 1911, no. 1195.
[119] *Gk*, 28 Nov. 1912, no. 1569.
[120] *Ml*, 4 Oct. 1909, no. 227.

Menshikov *Novoe vremia*'s editorial position stayed the same. When *Novoe vremia* joined the tsarist government in prosecuting the watchman, the paper embarrassed even many conservative Russians with its uncompromising stand.[121] But the Jewish question was one of the few points on which this newspaper and government could agree by 1913.

Novoe vremia, by virtue of its powerful readership and its access to government circles, stands out for its value as a source to analyze relations between a key segment of educated society and the state. In his analysis of *Novoe vremia*'s contents during the years from Stolypin's assassination to the strikes of July 1914, David Costello argued that as long as Stolypin reigned, *Novoe vremia* had believed the state capable of reforming itself to allow for public opinion to play a role in government. But when it became apparent that the autocracy had no wish to accommodate even the conservative reformers, the newspaper withdrew its support and by 1913 had moved with the Octobrists into a parliamentary-style "loyal opposition." The government under Stolypin's successors had interfered with elections to the Fourth Duma in 1912, trying to assure a reactionary, not even Octobrist, majority. When the government alienated the moderate conservatives, it lost touch with the last group that harbored even vague hopes of communicating between public and autocracy.[122]

Novoe vremia's reformist bent put it in the mainstream of the mass-circulation press. It brought no less attention than *Russkoe slovo* to the government's incompetence to deal with the most serious national concerns, agrarian backwardness, alcoholism, hooliganism, and other consequences of industrialization. Throughout the spring of 1914, Duma members began forming loose blocs to defy the government's high-handed and arbitrary treatment of it as a legislative body. An editorial in *Novoe vremia* on 31 May 1914 summed up the paper's position on the future: "Cooperation between the regime and the Duma, which represent[s] society, [has] become impossible."[123] The sympathy for strikers at Lena reappeared as incriminations of the autocracy for having squandered its authority. If *Peterburgskii listok* conflated at times the "dangerous" and the "working" poor, *Novoe vremia* did not; hooligans belonged in work camps, but the strikers that July brought deserved legal redress for their "monstrous despair."[124]

---

[121] Snessarev, in *Mirazh* (124–27), told how appalled many *Novoe vremia* correspondents were at being told to report Beilis's guilt.

[122] David Costello, "*Novoe vremia* and the Conservative Dilemma, 1911–1914," *Russian Review* 37, no. 1 (1978): 41, 48. See also A. V. Avrekh, *Tsarizm i IV duma, 1912–1914 gg.* (Moscow: Nauka, 1981).

[123] Costello, "*Novoe vremia*," 50.

[124] Costello, "*Novoe vremia*," 46; and Haimson, "Social Stability," 21.

In her study of revolutionary Moscow in 1905, Engelstein argued that the "real triumph of the working class [was] its ability to take part in the political process along with the larger community."[125] From *Novoe vremia* to *Russkoe slovo*, newspaper readers saw the same thing, which led them to believe that the working class shared many of their ideas. In 1907 Izmailov wrote in *Russkoe slovo* that a separate literature "for the people" was unnecessary because such social distinctions no longer existed in Russia.[126] Even if *Moskovskii listok* and *Peterburgskii listok* tended to report more of a division than the others, recent research by Daniel Orlovsky has suggested that a significant component of the targeted audience for these street sheets, the lower-middle social strata, joined with workers in 1917 and aided the Bolshevik regime in reconstructing the institutions necessary to administer the country.[127] The presumption of the middle to speak for the lower classes, hardly unique to Russia, pointed to optimism about solidarity rather than a feeling of separation.[128] The larger issue for those in the middle was whether or not the fissures between those represented by the liberal *Russkoe slovo* and the conservative *Novoe vremia* could be patched over. When the autocracy toppled in 1917, the newspapers' unanimous support for the Provisional Government indicated at least their willingness to try.

This study of newspapers cannot address, much less resolve, all the questions Haimson raised about the implications of the two revolutionary processes simmering just prior to the World War. In the first place, except for *Kopeika*'s readers, the workers themselves are primarily the straw men of editorials. But the argument that the major commercial newspapers did not discern political distances between the various social groups had implications for how they reported national issues. One criticism lodged against Haimson when his essay first appeared was that he had examined Russia in isolation from the rest of Europe, thereby minimizing the international crisis building to a climax throughout those same seven years.[129] News from the Balkans overwhelmed that from the streets of Petersburg in July 1914, and it is not illogical to assume that the average Russian cared more about the Austrian archduke than sporadic and

[125] Engelstein, *Moscow 1905*, 225.

[126] *Rs*, 15 June 1907, no. 136.

[127] Daniel T. Orlovsky, "State Building in the Civil War Era: the Role of the Lower-Middle Strata," in Diane P. Koenker, William G. Rosenberg, and Ronald Grigor Suny, eds., *Party, State, and Society in the Russian Civil War* (Bloomington: Indiana University Press, 1989), 180–209; and "The Lower Middle Strata in Revolutionary Russia," in Samuel D. Kassow, James L. West, and Edith Clowes, eds., *Between Tsar and People: Civic Culture in Late Imperial Russia* (Princeton, N.J.: Princeton University Press, 1991).

[128] Nord, "Paradox of Municipal Reform," 142.

[129] Theodore Von Laue, "The Chances for Liberal Constitutionalism," *Slavic Review* 24, no. 1 (1965): 34–46.

localized skirmishes in the national capital. The Russian press had already proved its political mettle twice in war; the approaching conflagration could be expected to serve journalists' purposes once again. Sensitive to only one polarization under way, that of public opinion from the autocracy, Russian reporters could be presumed to recognize that the story about to break would have significant political utility. How war correspondence once again furthered broader objectives is the subject of the next and final chapter.

11

The Newspaper in World War and Revolution, 1914–1917

WORLD WAR I brought down the House of Romanov, but Russians did not replace the dynasty with the constitutional government anticipated by their mass-circulation press. The war and revolutions of February and October 1917 are intertwined so closely that to view each independently would affect the interpretations of both. The newspapers tightened this connection, as editors consciously orchestrated news from the front to complement their demands for political reforms. Public opinion played an unprecedented role, and prominent leaders of all political persuasions began turning more often to members of the press to present information about the series of crises brought on by the unending combat. The daily newspaper's significance as an indispensable source of information and an essential arena for political discourse became so pronounced during the Great War that editors and publishers took for granted an enhanced political role in postwar Russia.

My purpose in this chapter is to increase our understanding of why those in the middle failed to secure their objectives in 1917 rather than explain why the lower classes succeeded in theirs. Editorial promises to workers and peasants to incorporate their needs in all postwar resolutions had been given in good faith, which led journalists to assume that they were speaking on behalf of all Russians. The newspapers suggest that the liberal bourgeoisie became embroiled in class war because it viewed serious social conflict as the antiwar ravings of unpatriotic, even treasonous, Bolsheviks.

From July 1914, changes in the personnel and institutions administering the war kindled hopes that political reforms would follow it. Staggering losses on the battlefield and mounting difficulties in trying to supply basic commodities to both front and rear had prompted local organizations to take charge of matters previously left to the government's bureaucracy. The movement originated in zemstvo and urban agencies of self-government, and industrialists began to form war-industries committees in the summer of 1915. The concurrent formation of the Progressive Bloc by members of both Duma and State Council, led by Miliukov and composed of leaders from the moderate middle, added institutional legitimacy. Although these groups were not formally joined under so spacious an umbrella as the Union of Unions, and in fact often worked at cross-purposes when competing over jurisdictions, combined they reflected a politically maturing constituency. The newspapers presented an image of civic-minded organizations making policies that were national in scope, forming a potential united front against the autocracy. This image suggests that those participating in this front would have better success effecting a revolution based on their political ambitions than that which transpired in 1917.

Not only who administered the war, but also how it was fought influenced how it was reported. Stalemates on all fronts led to unprecedented carnage, accelerated by the new weapons designed for mass destruction, and the airplane and the submarine extended the fighting physically into new realms. At first, the popular newspapers of the respective belligerent nations had the responsibility of justifying the war to readers, an uncomplicated task in the enthusiastic August of 1914. As the fighting dragged on, however, it fell to the lot of the press to lift readers' morale. Militaries had been falsifying news from the battlefields from their first contacts with reporters, but what happened in World War I greatly expanded the enterprise of generating politicized information about the combat. Propaganda, or "control of opinion by significant symbols . . . by stories, rumours, reports, pictures and other forms of social communications,"[1] entered the war as a newly designed political weapon. The French, German, English, and U.S. governments all organized official bureaus to work with the press to supply uplifting propaganda.[2] It bears emphasizing that although military censors screened information first, and supplied questionable data on their own, the overall news strategy was not forced by the censorship. Governments and journalists, despite certain frictions, worked together because they both believed in victory and appreciated the deepened significance of public opinion. Nemirovich-Danchenko could just as easily have made these remarks as the London *Daily Telegraph*'s Sir Philip Gibbs: "We wiped out of our minds all thought of personal scoops and all temptation to write one word which would make the task of the officers and men more difficult or dangerous. . . . We were our own censors."[3]

[1] Harold Lasswell, *Propaganda Technique in the World War* (New York: Knopf, 1927), 9.

[2] Lasswell, *Propaganda Technique*, was the first and best study of propaganda during the Great War. See also George Bruntz, *Allied Propaganda and the Collapse of the German Empire in 1918* (New York: Arno Press, 1972). Knightley, in *First Casualty* (79–112), discussed the British propagandistic coverage of World War I.

[3] Knightley, *First Casualty*, 97. Ilya Ehrenburg, who reported the French front for *Birzhevye vedomosti*, waited until after the hostilities to comment candidly on the brutality he had witnessed. W. Bruce Lincoln, *Passage Through Armageddon: The Russians in War and Revolution* (New York: Simon and Schuster, 1986), 269.

Gibbs, Nemirovich-Danchenko, and the other war correspondents put the principle of journalistic objectivity to a decisive test, and abused it badly for political reasons. Coverage of this war made politically clear that news had become a commodity, something manufactured and marketed. Critics after the war, from Lippmann to the Frankfurt School, looked back on the cooperation between journalists and governments and saw in it a cynical manipulation of the masses, their reaction brought on in part by the shock of the slaughter and the unsatisfactory peace settlement.[4] As Karl Kraus noted shortly after the bloodshed had begun, "the press is not the messenger, it's the deed."[5] During the war itself, though, the use of propaganda was considered to be progressive, liberal, and moral because that was how its practitioners viewed their actions. Postwar studies that emphasize the untruths told by newspapers during World War I tend to judge the pre-1918 press according to standards set after journalistic objectivity had been called into question. This study of Russian newspapers will help to reestablish the focus firmly in the war years, because in Russia there would be no postwar liberalism about which to read in a commercial press.

Although World War I was of greater lasting significance to Russian history than either the Russo-Turkish or Russo-Japanese Wars, it was of comparatively less importance to structural developments in newspaper journalism. The earlier wars had set the role of technology in transmitting and structuring news, and had authenticated the daily paper as a medium capable of mobilizing public opinion. War correspondence still boosted a young writer's career, and several future important Soviet writers, including Alexei Tolstoi, Konstantin Trenev, Ilya Ehrenburg, and Nikolai Gumilev established themselves through reporting on World War I for the popular press.

Yet the difference between the coverages of the two wars separated by less than a decade is astonishing, prompting the immediate question, why? I argue here that Russia's journalists hesitated to report the World War accurately because the domestic political situation had changed in their favor, and their coverage of the war with Japan had been instrumental to that change. Many Russian editors had opposed the Russo-Japanese War before it had begun and had celebrated military defeats for the political victories they portended. Even conservative communicators,

---

[4] Schudson, *Discovering the News*, chapter 4; Habermas, *Structural Transformation*, 196–98; Sidney Kaplan, "Social Engineers as Saviours: Effects of World War One on Some American Liberals," *Journal of the History of Ideas* 17, no. 2 (1956): 347–69; and Cecil Eby, *The Road to Armageddon: The Martial Spirit in English Popular Literature, 1870–1914* (Durham, N.C.: Duke University Press, 1987), chapter 11.

[5] Quoted in Suzanne Ruta's review of Karl Kraus's *Die Dritte Walpurgisnacht*, in *The Village Voice Literary Supplement*, February 1990, 12.

such as the official Russian news agency and *Novoe vremia*, openly reported the bad news of defeats in the war against Japan. The big story of
1915, the critical shortage of armaments that forced retreat and sent millions of Russian foot soldiers into battle underprepared, went unreported
in the daily press. The scandals exposed during the Russo-Turkish and
Russo-Japanese Wars lay in stark contrast to the new quiet in editorial
offices.

Newspaper coverage of the Great War gave the impression that for
many, the defeat of Germany promised more than the long-sought-after
equal status as a European power, itself something worth winning.[6] Editors connected propagandistic coverage with political change, and they
believed that a victory would result in the end of Russian absolutism. The
social revolution simmering in July was not simply postponed by the outbreak of hostilities, it was coopted by reformists who believed that discontent could be channeled into support for a war that they anticipated
from the outset would produce liberal reforms. It appeared that editors
were propagating for a "short, victorious war" on the same grounds as the
tsar had in 1904: they foresaw political and military success occurring
simultaneously.

Russkoe slovo dominated Russian journalism after 1914; Sytin so far
outdistanced the competition that circulation climbed swiftly from over
six hundred thousand to one million, almost ten times that of the nearest
competitor. Doroshevich's guess that each issue had seven readers might
have erred on the side of underestimation, as peasant communes had
begun subscribing to newspapers in greater numbers and *Russkoe slovo*
was most often the paper of choice.[7] The combination of an excellent
news service, access to the most important people in both the government and the independent organizations, and its editorial orientation toward constitutionalism gave Sytin's paper the trappings of an institution
of public opinion in and of itself. Two of the paper's regular analysts
found themselves members of the Provisional Government in the summer of 1917: Kartashev, a Kadet, served briefly as the first minister of
religion, and Bernatskii held the post of assistant minister of finance. Alexander Kerenskii, socialist deputy to the Third and Fourth Dumas and
second prime minister of the Provisional Government, mixed in intellec-

---

[6] Rosenberg, in *Liberals*, argued that for the Kadets, "there was no question in [the war]
that Russia's own international position had to be protected . . . [moreover] the war
brought new hopes that the government would finally recognize the Kadet party's potential
government role" (38–39).

[7] Doroshevich *Polveka dlia knigi*, 422; Vl. Murinov, "Gazetnyi golod v derevne," *Vestnik
vospitaniia*, no. 4 (1916): 177–89; and *Statisticheskii ezhegodnik Moskovskoi gubernii za
1915*, part 2 (Moscow: n.p., 1916): 100–101.

tual circles with Kartashev and Merezhkovskii.[8] Those at *Russkoe slovo* had valid reason to feel optimistic about the future.

Russkoe slovo's towering presence during the war years makes it almost a misnomer to refer to the other newspapers as its "competition," but they mirrored the variety in the Russian audience. *Birzhevye vedomosti* underwent editorial changes during the war. Propper made his paper esoteric competition for the "professors' newspaper," *Russkie vedomosti*; in addition to the modernist writers, his staff included the renowned psychiatrist V. M. Bekhterev, artist N. K. Rerikh, literary critic Boris Eikhenbaum, man of letters Maxim Kovalevskii, influential lawyer A. F. Koni, and outspoken Kadet V. A. Maklakov. Two members of the *Vekhi* group, Doroshevich's nemesis Struve and religious philosopher Nikolai Berdiaev, also wrote occasionally, as did prophet of the Apocalypse Vladimir Solovev. So successful was the new formula that Propper added a separate Moscow edition in 1916.

In the national capital, renamed *Petrograd* to erase the German-sounding *Petersburg*, the rechristened *Petrogradskii listok* and *Petrogradskaia gazeta* fit espionage and other war themes into their serial novels, fictionalizing more love at the rear than death at the front. Photographs and other illustrations brought the war graphically to readers. *Petrogradskaia gazeta* even adapted its "Sports Journal" to the war by featuring photos of sportsmen now in officers' uniforms.

Handicapped by the sibling rivalry of Suvorin's less talented sons, *Novoe vremia*'s position had slipped. The exposé written by a discharged city editor in 1914 prematurely consigned the paper to its grave, but two years later when one of the paper's correspondents, Ivan Manasevich-Manuilov, was found to be using his connections at the Ministry of Internal Affairs to sell influence, he contributed to the paper's decline; Suvorin's faults had not included corruption.[9] Throughout the war, *Novoe vremia* continued the same reformist editorial line taken when it became evident after Stolypin's assassination that the government would not even share power with society's better elements.

In the final months of the Old Regime, the attitude of a few officials toward *Novoe vremia* indicated that they finally saw the value of courting public opinion. In 1916 Minister of Internal Affairs A. N. Khvostov had begun considering arrangements for the government to buy controlling interest in *Novoe vremia*, but Minister of Finance P. L. Bark, a stockholder in the newspaper, opposed the acquisition.[10] It would have been

---

[8] Richard Abraham, *Alexander Kerensky: The First Love of the Revolution* (New York: Columbia University Press, 1987), 44.

[9] Snessarev, *Mirazh*, 134.

[10] Iu. Oksman, "*Russkaia volia*, banki i burzhuaznaia literatura," *Literaturnoe nasledstvo*, no. 2 (1932): 165–67.

attendant upon government, not editorial policy, to change if the newspaper was to both serve an independent audience and express official will.

Some officials were contemplating such a change. Khvostov's deliberations about *Novoe vremia* point to an axiomatic shift in the government's attitude toward the press, an important move that registered how the daily newspaper had at last penetrated the uppermost official circles as a competitive political institution. They began turning to representatives from the press to explain their policies. Only the tsar shied completely away from any publicity, other than releasing stilted family portraits for the various illustrated supplements. It is doubtful that candid interviews about his son's hemophilia, his own authoritarianism, or his wife's relationship with the mesmerizing Siberian monk Rasputin could have produced a climate favorable to saving his throne, but Nicholas II's longstanding aversion to publicity mirrored his personal view that the absolutist monarch personified the public.[11] Most readers, on the other hand, were better prepared to accept him as an article of popular consumption, as the British were coming to regard their royalty, generations before the House of Windsor became the *pièce de résistance* of tabloid journalism.[12]

The relationship between the mass-circulation newspapers and the successive Provisional Governments, composed of shifting coalitions of socialist and liberal ministers, emphasized the extent to which publishers held political ambitions. Support for the new government in all its political configurations was unswerving. Editorially, newspapers pressed whatever political line the prime ministers adopted, despite the fact that the information in the news pages often contradicted the proclaimed popularity of certain positions. The question of collusion between journalists and officials arises from the extraordinary harmony between the two, although the sources allow for no more than informed speculation that this occurred. When the autocracy collapsed, Russia's government and its commercial press at last joined forces in the space created by the latter. Having contributed to the transformation of power, the newspapers wanted to participate in the structuring of the new order.

Setting victory over Germany as the principal issue on the political agenda, publishers proved no better able than tsarist officials to interpret the news that disputed public support for a number of their policies. Reading Russia's commercial newspapers in 1917 and watching the hapless Kerenskii fail again and again to mobilize public opinion, one calls into question the sources of his intelligence. Although it is by no means

[11] Wortman, in "Moscow and Petersburg," argued that Nicholas II believed in a seventeenth-century ideal of political communion between tsar and people.

[12] Tom Nairn, *The Enchanted Glass: Britain and Its Monarchy* (London: Hutchinson Radius, 1988).

clear that a victory or armistice early in 1917 would have secured the Provisional Government, that Kerenskii waited until the eve of the Bolshevik Revolution to consider responding to popular demands showed how distanced he was from the mood of the populace. Some of the prime minister's judgments must be attributed to selfish advice and bad information. Russia's journalists must bear part of the responsibility for their political failure.

Russkoe slovo Covers the Great War

The Great War affected the mass-circulation press in two especially important ways, both of which can be seen most clearly in *Russkoe slovo*. My analysis of war correspondence makes a case study of *Russkoe slovo* because not only did the other papers reprint from Sytin's, but every example cited below had numerous analogs in all of the other papers. The editors welcomed the outbreak of war with a gush of cultural messianism: "We must fight for the radiant future of humanity, for the destruction of the dreadful nest of militarism. . . . If at any time the light of peace is to shine from the East it is now or never!"[13] Assassin Gavrilo Princip was described as as much a victim as the slain archduke.[14] The military, however, did not always appreciate that the press was holding up a new line of defense in the age of mass communications, the propaganda front. Despite the paper's unflinching prowar temper, the military high command more than once accused *Russkoe slovo* of "playing into the hands of German propagandists."[15] But the few times military censors brought *Russkoe slovo*'s editors to court, charges were dropped.[16]

In his seminal investigation into the development of propaganda techniques during World War I, a study undertaken in 1927 in the atmosphere of postwar pessimism, Harold Lasswell fixed on specific ways in which news generates symbols most effectively: contrasting war guilt with war aims; coloring and fabricating atrocities by enemy troops; drawing an illusion of victory; portraying allies as trusted friends, despite in some cases negative prewar relations; and attempting either to demoralize the enemy or to present the image of an adversary who has lost the will to fight.[17] Lasswell analyzed how Western newspapers had at-

[13] *Rs*, 20 July 1914, no. 166.

[14] *Rs*, 18 June 1914, no. 139.

[15] TsGIA f. 776, op. 8, d. 854, l. 9; and A. F. Berezhnoi, *Russkaia legal'naia pechat' v gody pervoi mirovoi voiny* (Leningrad: LGU, 1975), 19–22.

[16] TsGIA f. 776, op. 8, d. 853, ll. 210–13, and d. 854, ll. 9, 103–4.

[17] Lasswell organized chapters 3–7 of *Propaganda Technique* around these specific themes.

tempted to control opinion, demonstrating the production of propaganda to be a considerably more sophisticated enterprise than the moral outrage at the Bulgarian horrors or the jingoism of imperialistic journalism. A content analysis of *Russkoe slovo* shows Sytin's newspaper to fit Lasswell's frame like a textbook example.

Although Germany was in a coalition that included Austria-Hungary, Turkey, and revanchist Bulgaria, in the Allies' press the Kaiser was the foe and his confederates mere dupes. Because the Germans attacked first, and through neutral Belgium, establishing war guilt was straightforward. Published interviews with German emigrants in Switzerland who blamed their country solely for the war substantiated the accusation.[18] In addition to the civilizing mission of stamping out German barbarism, territorial annexation constituted a primary war aim. In November 1916, when Russia's domestic crises threatened the disintegration of its fighting capabilities, the Allies made public the secret treaties' promise of the Turkish Straits as Russia's booty in the postwar settlements. Hailed as a "cherished goal" in *Russkoe slovo*,[19] the newspaper further argued that any future peace for Europe depended upon Russian acquisition of the straits because "without them we will continue to suffocate, feeling the need to open the window."[20]

Petrov, who wrote on many different aspects of the war, emerged as *Russkoe slovo*'s chief propagandist and avidly supported annexation of the straits. When President Woodrow Wilson began 1917 with a note to European countries to cease fighting and settle scores without annexations, Petrov grew livid and used the occasion to defend Russia precisely because of the promised territorial spoils. Invoking Tolstoi's name where it was unlikely that the moral philosopher would have appreciated it, Petrov cursed the profiteering United States and argued that peace-loving Russians deserved the straits to mitigate the suffering Germany had caused them.[21]

The historical stereotype of Germany as the barbarian military culture of Wagnerian operas made for quick copy. Germany had provided ample negative public relations when it misread Belgian public opinion and went to battle with innocent citizens protesting against the violation of their territory, although *La Liberté*'s use of numerology to identify the Kaiser as St. John's Beast of the Apocalypse stretched the imagination.[22] Although the urban press at first wallowed in the atrocities, *Russkoe slovo*'s preferred tack was to concentrate on alleged German mistreatment

[18] *Rs*, 27 Nov. 1916, no. 274.
[19] *Rs*, 24 Nov. 1916, no. 271.
[20] *Rs*, 23 Nov. 1916, no. 270.
[21] *Rs*, 11 and 14 Jan. 1917, nos. 8, 11.
[22] Lasswell, *Propaganda Technique*, 90.

of Russian prisoners of war, and reporters especially liked to contrast Hun brutality to Slavic benevolence on that score.

In 1916 Petrov penned a series, "Over There," about the rough handling of Russian prisoners of war by Germans. "Let's leave German customs to the Germans, and not allow them to defile Russian land or the Russian soul with new German obscenities," he wrote. Furthermore, he told readers, "the situation of our POWs is much worse than it is for French or British troops."[23] This complemented an earlier story on German POWs surprised by the decent treatment they received at Russian hands; supposedly, German troops were under orders to kill the wounded and mutilate their bodies.[24] Austrian troops in Russian camps, *Russkoe slovo* reported, did not require guards because they had no desire to escape the good life of bringing in the harvest in the Ukraine.[25]

The newspaper's perpetuation of an illusion of victory astonishes in the face of a reality that claimed almost two million Russian lives, approximately twice that many wounded, and more than two million taken prisoner. Reportage of the first major defeat, the rout of General A. V. Samsonov's Second Army at Tannenberg in August 1914, established a pattern that editors would adhere to until the summer of 1917: following a list of the day's victories on other fronts, readers learned that "while we were in the process of strengthening our fortifications, two of our units were attacked by German heavy artillery. According to our reports, our troops fought gallantly. Generals Samsonov, Pestich, Martov, and several other members of the staff were killed."[26] Veteran war horse Nemirovich-Danchenko returned from the pasture of travelogues to write the obituary for his comrade Samsonov, but did not inform readers that the despondent commander had died by his own hand.[27] No need to bring public morale down as low as the general's.

Despite Tannenberg, Russia enjoyed early successes against the Austrian troops in Galicia. Nemirovich-Danchenko, on hand to follow the Russian advances, fairly glowed from occupied Poland that "they love us here, and want nothing better than for us to stay here after the war."[28] The Austrian Poles would not see this rather dubious wish granted, and Russian fortunes had spoiled by June 1915 when German reinforcements spelled the less capable Austrian troops and the tsar's poorly prepared forces began to feel the crippling shortage of war materials. Watching the

[23] *Rs*, 3 April 1916, no. 77.
[24] *Rs*, 17 June 1915, no. 138.
[25] *Rs*, 14 July 1915, no. 189.
[26] *Rs*, 19 Aug. 1914, no. 189. Nor did the allied press receive the truth about Tannenberg. Knightley, *First Casualty*, 93.
[27] *Rs*, 20 Aug. 1914, no. 190.
[28] *Rs*, 23 Oct. 1914, no. 244.

evacuation of L'vov, Nemirovich-Danchenko echoed the General High Command that this was a "strategic retreat" and concentrated on the valor of the fighting men.[29] But when he reported that the Russian soul could stand up to German technology, he overstepped the bounds of credulity for all but the willfully naive.[30] A far cry from his antiwar stance in 1905, when he could not justify the expense of precious youth, Nemirovich-Danchenko had apparently decided that young men were not too high a price to pay for this victory.

Another of *Russkoe slovo*'s many war correspondents, A. Pankratov, interviewed soldiers in retreat. He found them consistently relaxed and ready to charge again upon command.[31] Any victory, however slight, was headlined, whereas defeats were downplayed, in the style of the following: "There was heavy fighting today in the south. Our troops counterattacked bravely. However, the enemy was able to occupy some of our trenches."[32] *Russkoe slovo* also charged that the German press had resorted to describing their defeats as victories, hinting that *they* needed to falsify information but *we* did not.[33]

When victory was not an illusion, as in the spring of 1916 when General Alexei Brusilov led a major offensive in the southeast, Sytin's correspondent described the terrified Austrians scrambling away from Russians, bayonets fixed in hot pursuit.[34] He affirmed the paper's institutional importance when he told readers, "Your correspondent had the privilege today to meet with General Brusilov and extend the congratulations of *Russkoe slovo*."[35] The boon of Brusilov's successes proved ephemeral, and by the fall of 1916 Russian troops found themselves again on the defensive.

Nemirovich-Danchenko was also enlisted to sell readers on the notion that France and England, "cultural cowards" in his words before 1914, were trustworthy allies.[36] He toured both countries to tell how the Western powers were contributing meaningfully to the war effort. He commented on how France's successful industrialization had given it the capacity to prosecute the war, and his exchanges with soldiers in the trenches showed their zeal for keeping Germany's Western front

[29] *Rs*, 15 June 1915, no. 136.
[30] *Rs*, 29 July 1915, no. 174.
[31] *Rs*, 27 June 1915, no. 147.
[32] *Rs*, 23 Oct. 1916, no. 245.
[33] *Rs*, 24 Jan. 1917, no. 19.
[34] *Rs*, 29 May 1916, no. 123.
[35] *Rs*, 26 May 1916, no. 120.
[36] Nemirovich-Danchenko, reviewing an exhibition of Western artists, concluded that "they lack our courage." *Rs*, 12 Aug. 1907, no. 191. Knightley, in *First Casualty* (138–41), discussed similar projects undertaken by the British to present Russia as a trustworthy ally.

strong.[37] He also took his skills in the vivid depiction of battle with him, describing an exciting dogfight in the air above Verdun, where French "falcons" hunted down German "pirates." His calculation that the Germans lost twenty-three planes that day but the French only three was probably exaggerated in the interest of building confidence.[38]

The purposefulness of France and England contrasted sharply with the degeneracy of Germany. Portrayals of Germany on the brink of domestic collapse complemented descriptions of its exhausted troops, not quite defeated by the Russians but depleted by combat with them.[39] After the February Revolution, when the debate about Russia's continued participation in the war sharpened considerably, the mass-circulation press painted a picture of a desperate Germany on the verge of surrender, not unlike the Russia in which readers lived. The interminable war had induced serious internal crises in Germany as in all the Continental belligerents, and in Copenhagen *Russkoe slovo*'s correspondent scoured German papers for reports of domestic shortages of foodstuffs and stories about striking workers.[40] The newspapers evoked the sense that Russia need only hang on for a short while longer to gain that for which so many lives had already been spent.

The Newspapers and the Crisis of Authority in 1915

The underlying agenda set by war coverage called for a transfer of authority from autocratic to public institutions. The editorial decision to pump up optimism about the war cast a purely political eye to the future; *Russkoe slovo*, like the Progressive Bloc, war-industries committees, and city and zemstvo organizations, wanted to demonstrate that it could administer the war successfully. No longer content to solicit only Christmas gifts for soldiers' families, newspapers now collected and distributed supplies to the troops. When pessimism crept into war correspondence, the reporter used it to link military defeat to the inadequacies of the government to fight it without public input. One of the few realistic accounts by Petrov during the retreat from Galicia in 1915, in which he described the battlefield as "bloody porridge," preluded his critique that "our biggest mistake is that we have been unable to separate ourselves from the 'war

[37] *Rs*, 22 July and 8 Dec. 1916, nos. 169, 283.

[38] *Rs*, 28 Sept. 1916, no. 223.

[39] *Rs*, 30 July and 12 Aug. 1915, nos. 175, 185. Petrov wrote that the Germans were going mad from the ferocity of Russian attacks at a time when the Russians were madly retreating. *Rs*, 7 July 1915, no. 155.

[40] *Rs*, 7 April 1917, no. 76.

book' written in the chancellories."[41] He made clear that it was not the
fighting men who had caused his loss of faith.[42]

Returning to Haimson's thesis that social revolution was about to explode in July 1914, the groundswell of patriotism that met the declaration
of war seemed to wash away many of the differences dividing Russians;
only the Bolsheviks in the State Duma voted against credits to fund the
fighting. But the heralded *edinstvo* (unity) between tsar and people only
papered over the impression created a few weeks earlier of Russia on the
edge of social and political ruin, and the two sides coming together differed significantly in how they interpreted *edinstvo*. The tsar had accepted it as the mandate he had lost in 1905 and therefore felt no need
to share authority of any sort, if one discounts the counterproductive
counsel from his hysterical wife and her spiritual advisor. In stark contrast to a confirmation of absolutism, constitutionalists, including newspaper editors, read in the notion of unity between government and public an endorsement that now the two stood on equal footing.[43]

The long and torturous summer of 1915 made plain how unprepared
the government was to pursue the war beyond the first few months. The
shortage of shells that pitted the Russian foot soldier with little more than
his Slavic soul to defend himself was a political godsend for the constitutional elements. Even before the debilitating scarcity of weaponry became manifest, liberals and regional organizations wanted to share in running the war. Therefore, when the tsar's government began losing battles
at a terrible cost of lives, the span from socialists to conservatives began
brewing for action. V. S. Diakin argued that after the summer defeats the
liberal constitutionalists saw the autocracy, not Germany, as the primary
enemy.[44] Analysis of the newspapers indicates that this conclusion overstated the situation, but the attack on tsardom picked up steam as the
military lost it on the Galician front. In August, the Progressive Bloc began meeting to discuss how to form a government that, without forcing
the tsar off the throne, would enjoy "popular confidence." *Russkoe slovo*
asserted itself in the fray, speaking out against the regime, "with its organic denial of public participation."[45] Later the newspaper conducted a
nationwide survey of local officials asking whether or not the central authorities were handling the grain crisis satisfactorily; the unanimous "no"
circulated by *Russkoe slovo* could only increase the competition for authority.[46]

[41] *Rs*, 22 and 27 July 1915, nos. 168, 174.
[42] *Rs*, 22 Aug. 1915, no. 193.
[43] *Rs*, 21 Aug. 1915, no. 192.
[44] V. S. Diakin, *Russkaia burzhuaziia i tsarizm v gody pervoi mirovoi voiny, 1914–1917*
(Leningrad: LGU, 1967), 102.
[45] *Rs*, 20 Aug. 1915, no. 191.
[46] *Rs*, 20 Oct. 1916, no. 242.

If, as argued earlier, a Russian victory in the war with Japan would not have prevented a political revolt, it stands to reason here that an early victory over the Germans would not have suppressed the revolution impending in the summer of 1914. The position newspapers took in both conflicts underscored how these wars fit into larger political objectives, which were influenced by but not dependent upon battle. The manner in which *Russkoe slovo* treated the Duma during World War I showed how the press was redrawing the political landscape in light of its own aspirations and expectations. The composition of the state legislature had not changed in 1914, but the uninitiated reader would not have realized that by reading *Russkoe slovo*. The majoritarian Octobrists were not suddenly welcomed as democratic representatives, although they were no longer depicted as covering their chairs with slime. Duma in essence meant Progressive Bloc, which in turn connoted liberal leadership. An editorial in June 1915 called for the convocation of the state legislature and the settling of effective administrative power on the war-industries committees and zemstvos.[47]

Edinstvo, the dominant theme of public spiritedness, became further charged with political innuendo as an editorial topic during the pivotal August of 1915. *Russkoe slovo* called for interclass and interparty harmony, telling readers to put aside personal interests: speculators, merchants refusing to accept paper rubles in inflationary times, and the wealthy who displayed conspicuous consumption were all rebuked.[48] Still writing on behalf of local self-government, Veselovskii counseled zemstvo leaders to stand up to the ultraconservative minister of internal affairs N. A. Maklakov and to stretch beyond the frame of their 1864 charter as much as they thought necessary to supply the country's needs.[49] *Russkoe slovo's* editors fairly demanded to be allowed to shoulder their load for the Motherland, pointing out that to do so they must receive information kept behind closed chancellory doors.[50] When defeats mounted in 1915, despite the careful wording in reporting them, *Russkoe slovo* attributed losses to restrictions levied in 1910 on the freedom to discuss military affairs in the press, restrictions that had prevented newspapers from serving the public's interest.[51]

Public figures began to respond through the newspaper to the issues it addressed. The willingness to grant interviews is an appropriate measure of how political leaders perceive the press. The first American president to respond publicly through journalists, for example, was the nearly im-

---

[47] *Rs*, 19 June 1915, no. 140.
[48] For example, two articles in *Rs*, 20 Aug. 1915, no. 191.
[49] *Rs*, 30 July 1915, no. 175.
[50] *Rs*, 12 Aug. 1915, no. 185.
[51] *Rs*, 18 Aug. 1915, no. 189.

peached Andrew Johnson, and the first British prime minister to make shrewd use of interviews was the redoubtable Gladstone during the Midlothian Campaign that returned him to office in 1880. *Peterburgskaia gazeta* had been soliciting personal opinions since the 1890s, but Witte's press conference in 1905 marked the first major move by a Russian official toward the public represented by newspapers. Thereafter other ministers spoke occasionally to reporters, and the political party press and Duma deputies who gave interviews further connected the idea of government to public opinion.

The showdown begun in the summer of 1915 between autocracy and the groups who wanted decision-making turned over to them was reflected in interviews of leading tsarist officials. The two ministers of internal affairs that Nicholas named that summer, the respected Prince Nikolai Shcherbatov and the sycophantic Khvostov, both met immediately with members of the press and promised increased cooperation with public bodies.[52] Although they did not adjust their programs to recommendations made in editorials, when Minister of Transportation A. F. Trepov, of Agriculture A. A. Bobrinskii, and of Finance Bark spoke to readers through *Russkoe slovo* about the serious crises that their respective ministries were working to resolve, they were consciously using a forum sanctioned by the public.[53] Whether or not readers accepted Trepov's promises of an adequate winter fuel supply or Bobrinskii's assurances that people standing in endless lines simply wanted white bread when plenty of black was available is beside the point that the ministers thought it expedient to give the public an explanation. Even the decrepit, ineffectual prime minister Prince N. K. Golitsyn felt it necessary to respond publicly to the rumors about whether or not the Duma would be reconvened in February 1917.[54]

The tsarist government could not have saved itself by simply presenting a likeable face to newspaper readers, but the fact that important officials were changing their methods with regard to public opinion intimates that other concessions were in the offing. Moreover, when officials expressed themselves to and through newspapers, they augmented the editors' confidence about the postwar future. The fight between tsarist government and constitutionalists began in earnest on 1 November 1916 when Miliukov, speaking from the floor of the Duma, asked thunderously whether the government was treasonous or merely stupid in its manifest failure at war. Censors overstepped their legal bounds and blocked reprinting this speech and others that echoed support. Editors responded

[52] *Rs*, 12 June and 29 Sept. 1915, nos. 131, 227.
[53] *Rs*, 20 May, 10 Nov., and 30 Dec. 1916, nos. 116, 260, 301.
[54] *Rs*, 24 Jan. 1917, no. 19.

by leaving blank spots in news columns, an expensive waste of space to make a point to readers about the return of oppression. *Russkoe slovo*, though not defying the ban on the speech itself, reported openly on the censorship of it, telling readers that Prime Minister Boris Sturmer had ordered Duma President Mikhail Rodzianko to suppress the steno-graphic account.[55] Menshikov at *Novoe vremia* protested that "the dan-ger is not in public thought or public feelings, but in that which . . . reminds us of those deathly terrible lessons already learned from forced silencings of press and society."[56] The Kadets' *Rech'* published a circular, which was itself illegal after 1905, forbidding publication of information on the movements of ministers during the "leapfrogging" of hirings and firings that autumn.[57] Given that ministers were granting interviews any-way, the censors would have been hard-pressed to enforce this.

The most sophisticated effort on the government's part to use the pop-ular press to influence public opinion was initiated by Khvostov's succes-sor, A. D. Protopopov. As vice-president of the Duma and a Petrograd industrialist, Protopopov's appointment had raised hopes that Nicholas was signaling that he wanted a link to public institutions. The new min-ister failed his colleagues outside the government when he showed that his penchant for palace intrigue outweighed any commitment to reform, but in his entry into the arena of newspaper journalism he showed the greatest sophistication since Witte. Hoping to conserve what he could of the autocracy, Protopopov undertook an ambitious project to publish the daily *Russkaia volia* (The Russian Will), staffed by members of the liberal intelligentsia who opposed the autocracy but supported the war. An en-thusiastic Leonid Andreev headed the literary section and Vl. Azov, for years a regular at *Russkoe slovo*, wrote editorials. The quixotic Amfitea-trov, who five years earlier had criticized Sytin for not standing far enough to the left, wrote feuilletons. Sologub also contributed, as did Kadet Gredeskul. Korolenko, on the other hand, was mortified at being approached to participate and demanded retractions when his name was mentioned in connection with the paper.[58]

Protopopov's use of opposition writers, whom the public trusted more than it did his bureaucrats, indicated that he had accepted that following the victory, political institutions would incorporate public opinion much more than previously. Symbolically important but never a particularly

---

[55] *Rs*, 5 Nov. 1916, no. 256. In 1907 Stolypin had modified the censorship to allow the president of the Duma to withhold reports from the floor, although the November actions were not Rodzianko's.

[56] Reprinted in *Rv*, 6 Nov. 1916, no. 257.

[57] ROBL f. 358, k. 148, ed. khran. 10, l. 158.

[58] Oksman, "*Russkaia volia*," 174–86; and James Woodward, "Leonid Andreev and *Russ-kaia volia*," *Slavic and East European Studies* 10, parts 1–2 (1965): 26–35.

well read newspaper, *Russkaia volia* made headlines when the anarchists briefly commandeered its editorial offices. In an ironic epilogue, the Bolsheviks took over its presses for *Pravda* on the eve of their revolution, 24 October 1917.[59]

February–October 1917 in the Mass-Circulation Press

The demonstrations that toppled Russia's Old Regime began on 23 February 1917, International Women's Day. By the end of the week, the tsar had abdicated, he and his family had been placed under house arrest, and the liberal constitutionalist groups had organized a Provisional Government to orchestrate the transfer of political power. The composition of the Provisional Government reproduced the moderate and liberal consensus such as that found in the newspapers' editorial policies, not the elected majority in the Duma. Headed by Prince G. E. L'vov, the nonparty director of the Union of Zemstvos, Kadet leader Miliukov took over the Ministry of Foreign Affairs, Left Octobrist and director of the Central War-Industries Committee A. I. Guchkov was minister of war, and Kerenskii, the brilliant young lawyer who had defended the miners after the Lena massacre, sat at Justice as the only socialist minister.

Printers had joined other strikers during the turbulence, but the Society of Journalists in Petrograd combined energies and published handbills of information, so the national capital was not bereft of information. When regular newspaper publication resumed, all of the major newspapers greeted the Provisional Government as the sole legitimate ruling institution, in place until an elective Constituent Assembly could be convened after the war. It would have been astonishing had editorial policies recommended otherwise. The Provisional Government demonstrated that the admiration was mutual when it declared an end to censorship and convened an All-Russian Congress of Newspaper Editors, empowered to dismantle the Chief Administration of Press Affairs.[60]

In other parts of Petrograd, Moscow, and throughout the country, a different kind of political exercise was also under way. Drawing from their experiences in 1905, soldiers, workers, and peasants were electing soviets from among themselves. A central organization in the national capital, the Petrograd Soviet, provided the locus, just as the Provisional Government gave theoretical aegis to the public executive committees being formed around the empire by local leaders, primarily liberals and

[59] E. A. Vechtomova, *Zdes' pechatalas' "Pravda,"* Essays on the history of typography, no. 4 (Leningrad: Lenizdat, 1969), 80–105.

[60] TsGIA f. 1358, op. 1, d. 4 contains numerous press clippings about the congress.

moderate socialists. The juxtaposition of the Provisional Government and the Petrograd Soviet created a situation of "dual power" in which the first institution presumed authority on the basis of liberal ideology, but the other had authority conferred upon it by the masses. Members of the Provisional Government believed that they held power because they held the best interests of all citizens at heart and had the political experience necessary to effect substantial reform. Russian socialists by and large accepted the February Revolution as the correct bourgeois stage of Marx's historical dialectic, and the Petrograd Soviet deferred to the Provisional Government on those grounds.

The nature of dual power lies at the heart of any discussion of the politics of 1917 because it focuses on who could wield real power and on what basis. Provisional Governments collapsed one after another, proving no better able than the tsarist regime to prosecute the war or to supply the rear. Yet not until the Second Congress of Soviets, convened on 25 October, would power be taken in the name of a Soviet government, and it would happen under Bolshevik command. Between March and October the successive Provisional Governments tried to exert their authority, but could not expend what they did not hold. The Soviet, in contrast, refused even when pressed to exercise its power.

In his study of 1917 in provincial Saratov, Donald Raleigh emphasized the significance of both political contests unfolding that year, the first between liberalism and socialism, represented by dual power, and the second between moderate and radical socialism.[61] "Dual power" as such was conspicuously absent as an issue of editorial debate; the Provisional Government, in whatever political configuration, had sole power to make decisions. Instead of the growing contestation over authority, the commercial mass-circulation newspapers kept the war as the dominant issue on the political agenda. This ultimately proved to be both an ideological and a tactical error, and it is difficult to read the newspapers of this year without wanting to write a letter to the editor with the sound advice of hindsight. Ideologically, the commercial publishers left themselves wide open to charges of exhibiting exploitative bourgeois behavior, accusations that would sharpen as working-class consciousness grew out of the unwillingness of the government and its supporters to respond to strikers' demands.[62] Tactically, the uncompromising support for prosecution of the war led editors to identify the Bolsheviks immediately as enemies of the people because of their opposition to the fighting. This occurred even before Lenin had returned to present his provocative April Theses calling

[61] Donald J. Raleigh, *Revolution on the Volga: 1917 in Saratov* (Ithaca, N.Y.: Cornell University Press, 1986), 323.

[62] William Rosenberg and Diane Koenker, *Strikes and Revolution in Russia, 1917* (Princeton, N.J.: Princeton University Press, 1989).

for an end to the war and the transfer of power from the Provisional Government to the soviets.[63]

Those editors who saw February as the realization of unity between government and people failed to assess the deepening rifts among social groups. This became evident in the way in which they allowed the Bolsheviks to set several important terms of political discourse. In March the Bolshevik party held such meager positions in the soviets that several leaders contemplated reconciliation with the Mensheviks.[64] For the newspapers, however, "Bolshevik" meant anyone who professed to a radical antiwar ideology, stirring up trouble in the factory and at the front. When editors began employing Bolshevik vocabulary to discuss class warfare, they did so because the subject itself seemed laughable. It was suddenly forgotten that Doroshevich had made *burzhui* a synonym for what was contemptible about the West; when the Bolsheviks began using it to signify the Russian middle-class enemy, it became admissible to be a member of this group because the Bolsheviks opposed them.[65] All newspapers made a fetish of *burzhuaziia*, from *Novoe vremia* to *Kopeika*.[66] In April a feuilletonist at *Birzhevye vedomosti* was denying vehemently that Russia's independent press had ever been *burzhui*, using the word as Doroshevich had, but by July Sologub was defining *burzhui* as "respect for order and patriotism."[67] Editors incorporated *burzhui* into the vocabulary of the war in such a way as to subvert its cultural and class connotations.[68]

As convenient symbols upon which to peg the reasons for Russia's problems at the front, the Bolsheviks shared news space with the German-born Tsarevna Alexandra and her fancied lover, Rasputin. The censors had not been able to contain news of the lascivious monk's murder by prominent right-winger Vladimir Pureshkevich and Prince Felix Iusupov in December 1916. Graphic stories detailing the discovery of a mysterious corpse in the Moika Canal turned into an editorial celebration in *Russkoe slovo* about the removal of the "red flag waved before our European friends whenever anyone wanted to humiliate us."[69] Newspapers wisely avoided mention of the royal family at this time, but such editorials as the one cited here, which presupposed knowledge of Rasputin's

[63] *Rs*, 22 and 25 March 1917, nos. 65, 68.

[64] Alexander Rabinowitch, *The Bolsheviks Come to Power: The Revolution of 1917 in Petrograd* (New York: W. W. Norton, 1976), xvii–xxiii.

[65] *Rs*, 22 March 1917, no. 65.

[66] *Nv*, 29 April 1917, no. 14764; *Gk*, 13 June 1917, no. 3181.

[67] *Bv*, 23 April and 25 July 1917, nos. 16198, 16352.

[68] Rosenberg and Koenker reached a similar conclusion: "The language of class was increasingly the language of both management and workers in 1917." *Strikes and Revolution*, 328.

[69] *Rs*, 21 Dec. 1916, no. 294.

influence, revealed how effectively the rumor mill ground. The colorful monk had enjoyed a certain notoriety in the popular press before becoming firmly ensconced in the Winter Palace, but was last mentioned in print when, just before the assassination in Sarajevo, a religious fanatic had made an attempt on his life. The body pulled from the canal made too good a story for any paper to pass up.[70]

After the abdication, the empress's dalliance with the monk made for delicious gossip. Alexandra's own sister spoke to *Russkoe slovo* about the tsarevna's relationship with the Siberian mystic, but without disclosing the reason for Alexandra's psychological dependency, his ability to soothe the pains of her son's hemophilia.[71] The Rasputin story attributed the military losses to personalities that made for cheap scapegoats, which implied that once the reason for defeats was removed the democratic replacement could turn the tide and win. Like Lenin, Alexandra was suspected of German espionage. Lumping the Bolsheviks loosely with the Romanovs would not wear well strategically, however, because the profound distinction between Bolshevik opposition and Rasputin's interventions quickly surfaced. Rasputin quietly faded while the Bolsheviks grew stronger.

The way in which the newspapers coupled the Bolsheviks' position on class war with their protests against the Great War raises the question of how Russia's commercial press regarded the increasingly socialist cast in the Provisional Government. Notably, no newspaper commited itself to a Kadet position. The papers evidenced the possibilities for cooperation between liberalism and moderate socialism, one found to a lesser degree among the other belligerents. In England, France, and Germany, when the respective socialist parties voted to support a nationalist over a class war, they were welcomed by liberal governments; France's *union sacrée* had brought socialist ministers into the government. Just as Protopopov had recognized that the future of the tsarist government would soon depend upon compromise with constitutionalists when he needed their backing to sustain the war effort, the liberal editors quickly found common cause with the moderate socialists. Not only had the latter accepted the February Revolution as legitimately bourgeois, but they supported the war. Differences between liberals and moderate socialists did not disappear from *Russkoe slovo*; Kartashev resigned from the Second Provisional Government because he objected to the socialists' influence,[72] and Bernatskii did not support outright socialization of the land, although he

---

[70] Although A. Vershanin at *Birzhevye vedomosti* lambasted the press for its irresponsibly lurid coverage, his own newspaper interviewed doctors and attendants about the remains at the morgue. *Bv*, 21 Dec. 1916, no. 15997.

[71] *Rs*, 8 March 1917, no. 53.

[72] *Rs*, 14 July 1917, no. 210.

wanted much more of it available to the peasantry.[73] But on the controversial demand for the straits, *Russkoe slovo* at first admonished workers that they needed access to the Mediterranean to improve trade, but then quietly gave into peace without annexations.[74]

Listening to the voices on the left was not simply a case of expedient editorial policy. Russia's liberals had realized from their first experiences organizing political parties that to advocate universal suffrage meant to incorporate the overwhelming peasant majority into the electorate, and attracting these voters would require a socialist plank on land reform. Nor had Russia's state capitalism fostered a Westernized economic liberalism. Moreover, Russia's political tradition of opposition to autocracy had evolved from the ideas of an intelligentsia who had repudiated several Western political as well as economic concepts, and the newspaper journalists saw themselves as heirs to this legacy. In the despondency brought on by the "System of the Third of June," Russian editors had turned back to the historical intelligentsia for inspiration. Like the intelligentsia of old, they found encouragement in the Russian tradition of commitment to the cultural whole. When socialist correspondent Zhilkin wrote in *Russkoe slovo* in 1917 that "the Russian press is the natural child of Russian literature," he specifically dissociated it from Western commercial values and placed it under Tolstoi's shadow.[75]

The fall of the autocracy allowed Russians to applaud the deeds of those people who had at tremendous personal sacrifice made February possible. The figures most celebrated in the newspapers following the abdication were Russia's leading socialists: Georgii Plekhanov, the "Father of Russian Marxism," Ekaterina Breshko-Breshkovskaia, the Socialist Revolutionary (SR) "grandmother of the revolution," and Prince Peter Kropotkin, the internationally renowned theorist of nonviolent anarchism. Although the compromise ultimately proved ineffective, the newspapers indicate that many of the possibilities for the alliance found in 1917 had been present in 1914, before the disastrous war had made radical solutions all the more attractive.

The possibilities for negotiation between liberalism and socialism surfaced most clearly in *Birzhevye vedomosti*. Executive editor I. I. Iasinskii joined the Bolsheviks in December 1917, an indication of his longtime leftist sympathies. "Legal" Marxist-turned-liberal economist M. Tugan-Baranovskii, who also contributed to *Russkoe slovo*, wrote a series explaining how the political inclinations of Russia's peasantry would affect Russia's constitutional future. As if to allay readers' misgivings, he

---

[73] *Rs*, 17 May 1917, no. 109.
[74] *Rs*, 11 and 16 May 1917, nos. 105, 108.
[75] *Rs*, 14 April 1917, no. 82.

stressed that those who wanted to own and work their land shared most readers' fundamental values.[76] Such religiocentric feuilletonists as Sologub and Berdiaev sent readers in the midst of a political crisis off to ponder the meaning of life. In January 1917 Sologub mused, "What will be tomorrow? or next week? No one knows, and no one can know this . . . ," meandering off into a treatise on the current loss of faith.[77] This turn to the soul, decidedly un-Western, typified the neo-Slavophilism that favored socialism.

Birzhevye vedomosti's most prominent reporter was SR Vladimir Burtsev, a former populist who had lived in Siberian exile but spent the interrevolutionary years in Paris exposing tsarist double agents, the infamous *okhranki*.[78] Burtsev, like Plekhanov and many other important socialists, had greeted the war with patriotic enthusiasm. This had made it possible for him to return to Russia, where he took up his pen against the autocracy. In December 1916 Burtsev applied his investigative skills to freeing a peasant deputy to the Second Duma and his son, jailed seven years earlier on charges of murdering a local provocateur. The exposé played widely in all the papers, and Burtsev became a reportorial celebrity, contributing also to *Petrogradskaia gazeta* and *Kopeika*.

Burtsev's well-established opposition to the tsar was probably more important than his socialist credentials. Like Kerenskii, who was a member of the labor branch of Burtsev's party, the reporter exemplified how the policy of continuing the war separated the moderate from the radical socialists, just as it brought the moderates together with the liberals on the issue that took precedence over all others. Burtsev accentuated his position on the war in a story about how even the unjustly imprisoned peasant deputy had sent a son to the front.[79] He showed his patriotic mettle when he went into editorial battle with Gorky following the stormy "July Days," when workers and soldiers had clashed violently with cossack forces over the issue of transferring power to the soviets. Gorky had resurrected his socialist daily *Novaia zhizn'* (*New Life*) from 1905 and held the radical position, and Burtsev accused him of "serving German interests."[80]

Bolshevism, presented in *Birzhevye vedomosti* as the incipient threat of civil war, hovered in the background of all questions about war and

[76] *Bv*, 14 April 1917, no. 16182.

[77] *Bv*, 1 Jan. 1917, no. 1.

[78] Vl. Burtsev, *Bor'ba svbodnuiu Rossiiu: Moi vospominaniia (1882–1922 gg.)* (Berlin: Gamaiun, 1923).

[79] *Bv*, 27 Jan. 1917, no. 16064.

[80] *Bv*, 12 July 1917, no. 16330, contained an open letter from Gorky to Burtsev defending himself. Burtsev also appealed through *Kopeika* for information on German spies, which he equated with the antiwar Bolsheviks. *Gk*, 9 June 1917, no. 3178.

politics. Propper's editors, the most sensitive to anti-Semitism, stretched
their fear of Lenin's party into an emotional denunciation of Vera Cher-
ebniak, the unaccused but widely recognized guilty ringleader in the
murder for which Beilis had stood trial, as a Bolshevik.[81] They left unstated Bolshevik leaders Trotsky's and Kamenev's Jewishness.

Editorial outbursts against the Bolsheviks could only deflect attention
for so long away from the Provisional Government's incompetence at
war. Kerenskii's disastrous June Offensive, a last-ditch effort to affirm the
newly democratic Russia as a reliable ally, had provoked street demonstrations in July. Burtsev and others read this incorrectly as evidence of
Bolshevik manipulation of the gullible masses. Kerenskii responded to
the crisis by reneging on two of the most happily received policies of the
First Provisional Government: he reinstituted a censorship of the radical
press and reinstated the death penalty as punishment for desertion. His
decisions gave pause to many about the credibility of the Provisional
Government. Studies of workers have established that the severity of the
government's actions generated serious misgivings, and that animosities
against the Bolsheviks began to evaporate as the dust cleared from the
streets in July.[82] Every newspaper in this study jubilated in March at
these political expressions of the government's good will, yet accepted
these reversals of policy as unfortunate but necessary. Only *Kopeika*
spoke out against the death penalty, but in the same breath it urged readers not to take their protests to the streets.[83]

The street fare touched up editorial positions with sensory appeals.
Peterburgskaia gazeta used halftone technology to tell through illustrations first the Rasputin story and then about the Bolsheviks' treason. *Kopeika* and *Peterburgskaia gazeta* both broke stories that Bolsheviks were
often millionaires, whose leaders maintained "in various banks sums of
money that are a far cry from proletarian."[84] *Peterburgskii listok*, which
had initially welcomed Lenin much as it had the other returning leftist
exiles, soon recognized how significantly he differed; its writers, like
those at other papers, changed their tone after April from ridicule to apprehension.[85]

Moskovskii listok read much like its counterparts in Petrograd, adding
Pazukhin's "Far from Life," a serial about workers going out on strike,
falling in love, and being duped by Bolshevik rabble-rousers. Another
novel, "The Bloody Fog," recalled the successes of workers and educated

[81] *Bv*, 12 Oct. 1917, no. 16480.
[82] Rabinowitch, *Bolsheviks Come to Power*, chapter 5; and Diane Koenker, "The Evolution of Party Consciousness in 1917: The Case of the Moscow Workers," *Soviet Studies* 30,
no. 1 (January, 1978): 38–62.
[83] *Gk*, 19 Aug. 1917, no. 3232.
[84] *Pg*, 9 July 1917, no. 158; *Gk*, 13 July 1917, no. 3207.
[85] *Pl*, 4 and 7 April and 5 May 1917, nos. 80, 83, 108.

society when they joined forces in 1905. More significant, by the summer of 1917 this newspaper, formerly the most conservative of the commercial dailies, was noticeably sympathetic to the SRs. It featured biographies of party leaders prominently and gave special play to speeches from SR ministers in the coalition government.[86] One of the most revealing anecdotes of the problem of dual power told of a demonstrator grabbing SR Minister of Agriculture Viktor Chernov in July and demanding, "Take the power, you son of a bitch, when it's being offered to you." *Moskovskii listok* editorialized in much the same tone that "power belongs to those who can wield it. The democracy [as opposed to the Provisional Government] has it, but its representatives consistently refuse to take the responsibility on their shoulders."[87]

Kopeika continued its efforts to pull worker-readers into the liberal mainline. Gorodetskii put the Soviet on the front page when it published entreaties to workers not to follow Bolshevik strike leaders. Kerenskii was the hero here; photos of him could consume an entire page, and the paper also peddled a poster of him suitable for framing.[88] At a time when class differences were intensifying, *Kopeika* showed itself to stand firmly in the middle. As the number of deserters climbed, *Kopeika* turned to officers instead of foot soldiers for commentary. Reminding readers that Russia's first revolutionaries, the Decembrists, were officers, this paper, which surely held greater interest for enlisted men, now referred to the latter as the "dark people," the benighted Russian peasantry.[89] Bolsheviks were rowdies, the rough street element, again, the "dark people."[90] In August, when the Provisional Government attempted to bring together a sampling of interest groups to Moscow at the State Conference called in anticipation of the Constituent Assembly, the resultant gathering found themselves stuck in a city ground to a standstill by a Bolshevik-led general strike. Despite workers on the picket lines, *Kopeika* extolled this conference as proof of class unity in Russia.[91] The tabloid's last serial novel, "The Price of Revolution," featured a villainous Bolshevik who, working undercover for the Germans, penetrated a decent, pro-war workers' circle.

Kopeika's fortunes had begun to dwindle since the war began; a num-

[86] For example, *Ml* had a series on "Heroes of the Revolution" that featured biographies of Breshko-Breshkovskaia, Viktor Chernov, and Boris Savinkov. *Ml*, 20 July and 1 and 13 Aug. 1917, nos. 163, 173, 183.

[87] *Ml*, 16 July 1917, no. 160.

[88] Daniel Orlovsky argued for the importance of Kerenskii as a new kind of 'tsar figure' in "The Provisional Government and Its Cultural Work," in Abbott Gleason, Peter Kenez, and Richard Stites, eds., *Bolshevik Culture* (Bloomington: Indiana University Press, 1985), 44.

[89] *Gk*, 13 Sept. 1917, no. 3261.

[90] *Gk*, 11 Aug. and 4 Oct. 1917, nos. 3232, 3279.

[91] *Gk*, 11 Aug. 1917, no. 3232.

ber of factors can explain its waning popularity. Its price had climbed
steadily to reach eight kopecks. *Kopeika* had no correspondents at the
front, which made it less newsworthy than other papers. Moreover, it
was not the *Kopeika* of old. War stories had by and large replaced the
lurid local news. The serial novels now took place at the front and offered
more patriotic propaganda than excitement. Gorodetskii's newspaper circulated at 120,000 in June 1917, but that figure was halved in October.
The Petrograd Soviet "borrowed" *Kopeika*'s high-speed presses to produce *Izvestiia* (News), which undoubtedly cut into material supplies and
time on the machinery, thereby reducing the number of papers
printed.[92] But studies of the development of working-class consciousness
throughout 1917 show workers rejecting the politics found in *Kopeika*'s
all-class editorial policies.[93]

Kopeika's decline raises the question of the success of its new and immediate competition, the socialist press permitted by the end of censorship. The contents of these newspapers lie beyond the purview of the
present study. Available figures for the socialist publications refer to what
parties printed rather than what readers registered their subscriptions
for, but there remains little doubt that the Bolsheviks' *Pravda, Soldatskaia pravda* (*The Soldier's Truth*), or *Derevenskaia bednota* (*Village
Poverty*) had ready-made audiences, as did the Mensheviks' *Vpered* (*Forward*) or Gorky's *Novaia zhizn'*.[94] Evidence does not show conclusively
that workers switched their newspapers to follow their votes, but many
moved in that direction.[95] Gorky, educating in the difference between
the bourgeois and socialist press, produced a brochure explaining how to
subscribe to the right newspapers.[96] Compared to the paper's initial success, *Kopeika*'s declining circulation made plain its inability to satisfy the
lower-class readership it sought.

[92] E. N. Burdzhalov, *Russia's Second Revolution: The February 1917 Uprising in Petrograd*, ed. and trans. Donald J. Raleigh (Bloomington: Indiana University Press, 1987), 192.

[93] In addition to Raleigh, Rabinowitch, and Koenker, see S. A. Smith, *Red Petrograd:
Revolution in the Factories, 1917–1918* (New York: Cambridge University Press, 1983).

[94] M. S. Cherepakhov gave the circulation for *Vpered* at forty thousand, *Derevenskaia
bednota* at forty thousand, and *Soldatskaia pravda* at fifty thousand. *Russkaia periodicheskaia pechat' 1895–oktiabr' 1917. (Spravochnik)* (Moscow: Gos. izd. polit. lit., 1957), 238,
242.

[95] Raleigh, in *Revolution on the Volga* (70), showed more enthusiasm for the socialist than
the bourgeois press in Saratov; Diane Koenker, *Moscow Workers and the 1917 Revolution*
(Princeton, N.J.: Princeton University Press, 1981) (62), cited a survey of worker-readers
demonstrating some of them turning away from *Russkoe slovo* in favor of socialist papers in
1917; and *Russkoe slovo*'s Zhilkin, a member of Kerenskii's branch of the SRs, wrote that
many soviets were organizing boycotts of bourgeois newspapers, including his. *Rs*, 14 April
1917, no. 82.

[96] N. M. Fedorovskii, "Kakuiu mne vypisat' gazetu? (Obzor sovremennoi pressy). Politi-
cheskoe chtenie dlia derevni" (Ardatov: Izd. *Novaia zhizn'*, 1917).

The Provisional Government's Official Media

In addition to the censorship, the Provisional Government inherited the official media, the most important of which included the official telegraph agency and the lackluster *Pravitel'stvennyi vestnik*, renamed *Vestnik vremennogo pravitel'stva* (*Herald of the Provisional Government*). The commission of editors organized to liquidate the Chief Administration of Press Affairs was also empowered to oversee the operations of the official publications, with the idea that it would keep official accounts to turn over to the new government created by the Constituent Assembly.[97] At neither institution was there a wholesale reshuffling of personnel because the staffs were composed more of journalists with notions of providing factual information than of apologists for the autocracy. The government's handling of the official media demonstrated the difficulties of coordinating liberal ideals with the practical demands brought on by revolution.

Finances generated a fundamental problem that the best political intentions could not resolve. It was decided, for example, that the PTA would become self-supportive, doubling and then tripling the rates for its bulletins. Publishers paid the higher prices, and the PTA collected its first profits during the first few months it communicated for the new regime.[98] The newspaper proved more problematic because it faced less demand but more competition. The government could hardly hope for subsidies from commercial advertisements; the collapse of the economy had so tightened the advertising ruble that even such impressive sellers as *Russkoe slovo* had been forced to inflate subscription prices to cover costs from the loss of ads. Adopting the tsarist government's tactics of raising revenues, the new one obligated official agencies to advertise in and bureaucrats to subscribe to *Vestnik*. When printers struck for higher wages, the government simply generated income by compelling thousands more provincial functionaries to subscribe.[99]

Yet the Provisional Government was quite keen to the propagandistic possibilities of circulating information on a mass scale. Most of the independent publishers made a few copies of their newspapers available gratis as a charitable gesture to army hospitals and also collected back issues for distribution by the Red Cross. For the first few months the new government distributed twenty thousand copies of *Pravitel'stvennyi vestnik* free to the military, which quickly proved cost prohibitive and had no perceptible impact on the mounting desertions.[100] Moreover, the

[97] Both archival fonds are in TsGIA; that for the telegraph agency is f. 1358, and that for the newspaper is f. 785.

[98] TsGIA f. 1358, d. 4, ll. 84–85, and d. 5, ll. 95, 117.

[99] TsGIA f. 785, op. 1, dd. 215–16.

[100] TsGIA f. 785, op. 1, d. 184, l. 97, 102–7.

Ministry of Foreign Affairs instructed the telegraph agency's director to send only favorable stories to the Allies, even when that meant suppressing the truth.[101] To be sure, as Lasswell made clear, the Allies had similar thoughts, and considerable American funds were expended on propaganda into and about Russia to prop up its image as a strong and reliable ally.[102] The Provisional Government behaved in character, which kept it out of step with the growing number of men and women taking to the streets.

The Press and the Collapse of the Provisional Government

The failure of the June Offensive and the resultant "July Days" had prompted the government to intensify its disciplinary measures as it attempted to gain control of the increasingly chaotic country. As Allan Wildman has shown, the military high command broadcast false information about desertions and panic at the front because it sought to justify its increasingly repressive actions.[103] Changes in coverage of the army in the field indicated that editors, if not working in collusion with the Provisional Government, continued their support in the news pages as well as in editorials. *Russkoe slovo*'s man at the front, for example, bluntly described in August the "disorganized masses of soldiers, rushing away in an uncontrollable stream."[104] In September, when General Mikhail Alexeev resigned as commander-in-chief, he gave reporters a frank interview about decline of discipline and morale.[105] These were hardly the first such problems the military had faced in the past three years, but they appeared in print only when this news corresponded to other political and editorial objectives.

Even before its fatal confrontation with the Bolsheviks, the Provisional Government had to defend itself against the right. The State Conference held in Moscow in August had prompted a right-wing coup attempt by General Lavr Kornilov. The press did not support the attempt, but undoubtedly some editors harbored sympathies quietly. When Kornilov went on trial that October, *Novoe vremia* covered the story under the headline "Was This a Mutiny [*miatezh*]?", intimating that the general had been taking a politically correct measure. *Russkoe slovo*, on the other

---

[101] TsGIA f. 1358, op. 1, d. 4, ll. 3–4, 50–51, 73–80.

[102] Lasswell, *Propaganda Technique*, 119–20.

[103] Allan Wildman, *The End of the Russian Imperial Army: The Road to Soviet Power and Peace* (Princeton, N.J.: Princeton University Press, 1987), chapter 4.

[104] *Rs*, 23 Aug. 1917, no. 192; and Wildman, *End of the Imperial Army*, 190.

[105] *Rs*, 20 Sept. 1917, no. 214.

hand, condemned Kornilov and intensified its support for Kerenskii's government.

The Provisional Government's decision to continue the war must figure prominently into any discussion of the nature of the Bolshevik Revolution. Reading the newspapers for 1917 restores images of patriotic enthusiasm for the war effort seldom found in social histories that chronicle the politicization of the lower classes. Photographs remind that throngs cheered in the street, and editorials promised that victory was in sight, especially after the Americans joined the Allies that April. The legitimacy of the Provisional Government rested on its ability to function as a European Great Power, and the independent publishers did what they could to support this test of authority. But being both Great and European meant being victorious over the Germans. Ironically, this study began with *Golos* protesting that newspapers could not create public opinion, but ends with *Russkoe slovo* attempting to do precisely that.

The newspapers of 1917 also stimulate an eerie feeling of the Bolsheviks' predestination. Identified as the principal menace to the revolution, they threatened as the realization of the liberals' worst fears: the ignorant dark masses had been brought under the control of demagogues. When the Bolsheviks captured the majority in the Moscow City Duma at the end of September, *Russkoe slovo* accepted with regret that "Moscow is the heart of the country and this seems to be what the country wants."[106] By the middle of October the commercial newspapers carried a front-page section called "Toward the Bolshevik Uprising," which both informed and tried to invigorate readers to prepare to take a stand when the Bolsheviks made their move. Any theory of the October Revolution that rests on the notion of a Bolshevik conspiracy must take into account that even if readers did not know exactly what was happening behind the closed doors at party headquarters, they could anticipate armed uprising.[107] As *Kopeika* editorialized, the Bolsheviks came to power "in plain sight of everyone."[108]

This raises the question of why the millions of newspaper readers did not respond and stand up to the Bolsheviks, which in turn asks who was reading these newspapers and why. As Orlovsky has argued, many from the middle and lower-middle social strata, as well as a number of profes-

[106] *Rs*, 29 Sept. 1917, no. 222.

[107] Robert Daniels's argument that before the Military Revolutionary Committee began securing the bridges on 24 October "the average citizen had no idea that violent revolutionary clashes were in the offing" was drawn from a diarist's entry that "judging by the morning papers, I didn't expect anything special." *Red October: The Bolshevik Revolution of 1917* (New York: Charles Scribner's Sons, 1967), 140. *Birzhevye vedomosti* headlined that day "The Uprising Has Begun."

[108] *Gk*, 14 Nov. 1917, no. 3300.

sionals, had given up on the Provisional Government.[109] The same papers that promised victory and republicanism reported the strikes, the peasant unrest, and the unwillingness of the soldiers to fight. Attention on the Bolsheviks had included a number of interviews with their supporters, although not with party leaders. What readers knew best about the Bolsheviks was that this party wanted to end the war, and with the Germans in Riga this probably did not sound like a bad idea to many readers, who could hear the approaching enemy artillery.

Many Russians undoubtedly met the actual events of 25 October with either boredom or measured relief that the confrontation had finally begun. Like the Mensheviks and SRs who stormed out of the Congress of Soviets in defiance of the Bolsheviks' unilateral move, many readers would not expect the Bolsheviks to secure and maintain power. Nor would they realize that the newspapers which supplied their information would tomorrow be lost to them forever.[110] Past experience with revolution had taught readers that newspaper publication would be interrupted by striking printers; not even Leninist policy in October 1917 called for a one-party press. By December, however, the tsarist government's circulars seemed pale in comparison to the quickly organized revolutionary tribunals, radical bands exercising a summary justice that held editors and journalists criminally accountable for their opposition to the new regime. The extremities of censorship created dissension even among Bolshevik leaders.[111]

Questions about political blunders by all parties continue to nag because decisions regarding the war figured so heavily into the Bolshevik Revolution. Newspaper coverage of the hostilities must be counted among the miscalculations. But would reporting considered objective by post-Vietnam journalists have significantly altered the situation by disillusioning those whom Petrov was courting? Information influences opinions; those going to the Bolsheviks were not simply spellbound by Trotsky's oratorical gifts. But to ask for skeptical war correspondents to set the record straight as Neil Sheehan and David Halberstam did in Vietnam is to remove news reporting from the context that did not differentiate between propaganda and objectivity, which during World War I were part of the same liberal ideology. Nor should Russia be withdrawn from the wider European context; by the end of 1917 the governments

[109] Orlovsky, "State Building" and "The Lower Middle Strata."

[110] A. Z. Okorokov, in *Oktiabr' i krakh russkoi burzhuaznoi pressy* (Moscow: Mysl', 1970), chronicled the closing of the commercial papers and their sporadic reopenings under different names.

[111] Albert Reiss, "Lenin on Freedom of the Press," *Russian Review* 36, no. 3 (1977): 274–96. See also Peter Kenez, *The Birth of the Propaganda State: Soviet Methods of Mass Mobilization, 1917–1929* (Cambridge: Cambridge University Press, 1985), 29–49.

of all the belligerents were struggling with striking workers, populaces were losing the will to fight, and the crisis of liberalism originating in newspaper propaganda had already begun.[112]

Russia's newspapers had constructed a place in Russia's semifeudal political and economic structure in which the emerging civil society could form a rudimentary public opinion on a variety of social and political matters. The commercial basis to this press made it liberal because newspapers depended upon and sold ideas about individualism and choice. The ability to supply information gave newspapers value as a sphere open to the public, and the function of the press was to mediate between state and society in order to help overcome the separation between the two. Both the Provisional Government and the editors and publishers of the mass-circulation newspapers believed that with the February Revolution they had successfully navigated the divide. They considered that the Russian population at last was at one with its government, and that by providing factual information to reasoning minds they would supply the basis for an equitable and constitutional legal system. For whatever their ultimate failure to achieve their political aims, the mass-circulation newspapers had contributed decisively to the transformation of power that ended Russia's Old Regime.

[112] Marc Bloch remembered from his experiences in battle: "The prevailing opinion in the trenches was that anything might be true, except what was printed." Quoted in Paul Fussell, *The Great War and Modern Memory* (New York: Oxford University Press, 1975), 115. Fussell argued, "A lifelong suspicion of the press was one lasting result of the ordinary man's experience of the war" (316). See also Knightley, *First Casualty*, 99.

Conclusion _____

To M. N. POKROVSKII, future dean of Marxist historians, fell the honor of officially closing *Russkoe slovo*, a sign of the paper's recognized stature.[1] As for a number of the large dailies, pale imitations of *Russkoe slovo* reopened under several mnemonic titles only to be closed by the tribunals for spreading "lies."[2] Legal correspondent Varshavskii tried to explain the new system, but a less patient feuilletonist for *Nashe slovo (Our Word)* damned the Bolsheviks for behaving as grandparents trying to give birth to the grandchild with the intermediate step of parents.[3] After pleading with the new leaders to include other parties and social estates in their new government, *Kopeika* avoided confrontation and reappeared with the escapist novels that had both made it popular and earned it the scorn of serious revolutionaries. But none of the old papers could survive Fannie Kaplan's attempt on Lenin's life in July 1918. Reversing the Western pattern, political journalism supplanted the commercial.

The mass-circulation press had served a vital function under the Russian autocracy. It established an institution between private individuals and the state in which a public opinion could take shape and find expression. In the West, commercial journalism developed only after the writing of constitutions and the formation of representative parliaments, and its political utility has traditionally been viewed from its relationship to the expanding electorate. Russians, however, had to depend more heavily upon commercial print communications to develop an opposition to the autocratic form of government. Their popular dailies proved instrumental in depriving the tsar of his status as the referential embodiment of politics, the only "public person," long before Duma president Rodzianko pleaded with Nicholas II to tender his abdication.[4] The papers created a public, one which has heretofore been no more than a shadowy figure in the historical picture of prerevolutionary Russia. The persistence of a censorship to the end of Russia's Old Regime has clouded past assessments of the efficacy of newspapers to mobilize public opinion; this study has given weight and features to that public.

The daily newspaper played an integral role in the evolution of Russian

[1] *Nash vek*, 3 Dec. 1917, no. 4.

[2] Okorokov, in *Oktiabr'* (343–76), included a supplement of the openings and closings of the papers into 1918.

[3] *Nashe slovo*, 17 April 1918, no. 4.

[4] Habermas, in *Structural Transformation* (7–11), discusses monarchical "publicness" under European absolutism.

society after the Great Reforms as both a part of and a voice for the new opportunities, and it also represented the social changes resulting from industrialization. The first independent daily, *Golos*, reflected the interests of a gentry in search of new ideas that would help them adjust to their changing world, just as the last newspaper presented here, *Kopeika*, was read by the lower social orders coming to share certain values and ideas that reform and industrialization had made accessible to them. The boulevard press, *Peterburgskii listok*, *Peterburgskaia gazeta*, and *Moskovskii listok*, integrated the merchantry, artisans, and petty bureaucrats into the newspaper audience. The nationally circulated newspapers that followed *Golos*, especially *Novoe vremia*, *Birzhevye vedomosti*, and *Novosti*, significantly expanded the base of readership from the educated middle groups. Sytin's *Russkoe slovo*, attracting readers from all social strata after the turn of the century, created Russia's most potentially influential medium of communications.

This array of papers available from street sellers in tsarist Russia's two capitals reflected the plurality of the newspaper audience, and it offered a place for a relative degree of social and cultural integration. Readers shared access to much of the same information, but they had dissimilar ideas about what was most important or how events should be interpreted. Readers from the boulevard craved their pulp serials, just as those who subscribed to the national press wanted their commentaries on international events, but common concerns about national and civic issues bound all readers together. The newspapers gave these various groups a common frame of reference for their experiences, however different these might be. To someone scanning the front pages at a kiosk in 1914, a picture would emerge of a country on the brink of political revolution, but not one that would reverse the social order of those who would hold power.

The newspapers had been crucial to bringing readers to that brink. They had offered modern alternatives to Russian traditions, and their circulations evidenced the enthusiasm for change. Communications technology overcame geographical obstacles and made it possible for the press to foster an identity based on territory rather than ethnicity. Newspapers' contents encouraged ideas about participatory citizenship. Whether reading about the Great Reforms in *Golos* or answering one of *Peterburgskaia gazeta*'s surveys, audiences enjoyed unprecedented opportunities to take part in the world that began outside their front doors. Newspapers also accelerated the secularization of culture. From the serial novels of the urban papers to the glossy Sunday supplements, the dailies made available choices from a system of values that extolled Christianity but did not require adherence to the dogma of Orthodoxy. The importance of the emerging marketplace as a mechanism for regulating culture and society was evident in all facets of newspaper publishing; the attraction of consumerism could be found in the news as well as on the advertising pages.

News itself was a fundamentally modern concept. Objectivity and facticity reordered reality on what the nineteenth century deemed a scientific basis, and when readers could master the data of the news they increased their ability to understand and manage their own lives. The Russo-Turkish War of 1877, the first issue of national consequence that the reformed press could partake in, allowed the press to generate public opinion as so formidable a political force that it drove Alexander II to take action against his own better judgment. As a result, coverage of this war taught readers to expect that they had a right to information about issues that affected them. The increased importance of newspapers gave reporters a sense of professional obligation, and they believed that they had a duty to provide objective news as a public service. Their notion of objectivity, however, which presumed an idealized neutrality, one free of class or political bias, proved to be a self-deluding philosophy. Coverage of World War I and the revolutions of 1917 laid bare the misconceptions about neutral reportage.

By the time of the Great War, Russian paralleled Western journalism in many significant ways. The Russian newspaper played essentially the same role in modernization as did its Western counterparts: it provided information, interpretations, and space for advertisers to grease the wheels of commerce. On the other hand, the Russian press operated within an environment that differed in so many basic respects that contrasting it to the Western one has allowed us to expand established arguments about the role of the commercial press in the evolution of liberal democratic politics.[5] The tsarist empire's economic structure, reliant on gentry domination of peasant agriculture and state capitalism, had determined that attitudes toward the economy would develop differently. In Russia, responding to the consumer market did not require buying into the same notions of capitalism that characterized that market in the West. Editorial hostility to predatory capitalism can be read in part as a sign of Russia's chronic ambivalence about its relationship to the West. However, the sarcasm of such popular writers as Doroshevich, when he sniffed that for Americans "the dollar is everything," underlay distinctively Russian attitudes that grew from the empire's unique historical development.

The prerevolutionary press made evident the willingness with which readers would explore solutions to Russian problems that were not sim-

[5] Reinhard Bendix, "Tradition and Modernity Reconsidered," *Comparative Studies in Society and History* 9, no. 2 (1967): 329–35.

ply derived from Western responses to analogous situations. For example, Russia's commercial journalism left ajar the door to moderate socialism because many observant men and women distrusted laissez-faire capitalism, fearful that unrestrained individualism would subject the many to exploitation by the few. The national political idols appearing in Russia's mass-circulation press were consistently those who argued most vociferously against uncritical adoption of Western economic and political models. In 1917 the independent papers recognized the benefits of a political settlement between liberals and moderate socialists, having accepted that universal suffrage would send a peasant majority to the Constituent Assembly. Astute readers knew that private property, one of the inalienable rights assured by liberal Western governments, could not simply be transplanted into Russia without the modifications that would address the centuries of inequality in land ownership. Prominent SR Breshko-Breshkovskaia addressed this issue in the popular press, just as Tugan-Baronovskii tried to reassure readers that consensus could be found with the peasantry on the question of property rights in postwar Russia. The comparison of Russian to Western journalism underscores how similarities in editorial function could lead nonetheless to differences in editorial positions.

Looking at Russian journalism from the vantage point of previous studies of the Western press has also shifted attention to the historiographical debate about the nature of who comprised Russia's middle classes and why they proved unable to effect political reform. This emerging social group supplied the bulk of readers, reporters, publishers, and advertisers. Past studies of the growth of political conciousness among those who fall most readily into the bourgeoisie, the merchantry and the industrialists, have helped to explain the failure to secure a constitutional regime in February 1917. None were sanguine about the prospects for a united and politically powerful bourgeoisie, even when excluding the Bolshevik factor. Russia's business element lacked the ties to the professional world that had been so instrumental in Western developments, working instead from connections to the tsarist bureaucracy that prevented them from recognizing the importance of a constitution to protect their interests.[6] The other group most closely connected to the middle, the professional intelligentsia, exemplified organizationally by the Kadet party, had the best chance to effect liberal change. Once again, deficiencies become apparent without references to Bolshevik strengths. The Kadets assumed a paternalistic posture toward the lower classes for whom they claimed to

---

[6] Owen, *Capitalism and Politics*; Rieber, *Merchants and Entrepreneurs*; Jo Ann Ruckman, *The Moscow Business Elite* (DeKalb: Northern Illinois University Press, 1984); and V. Ia. Laverychev, *Krupnoe burzhuaziia v poreformennoi Rossii (1861–1900 gg.)* (Moscow: Mysl', 1974).

speak, but, fearful of the uncultured masses, they kept their political as well as social distance.[7] Lenin's charge to Kadet A. S. Izgoev that liberals did not have the nerve to take power was reflected time and again in their unwillingness to convert rhetoric into action.[8]

If, however, as I have argued, the newspapers reflected greater cultural cohesion and a wider basis of support for reformist sentiments than separate studies of either the protobourgeoisie or the Kadets, what happened to their readers in 1917? In February Sytin would have agreed with Lenin that 1905 had been a "dress rehearsal," but for the publisher it turned out to be only the first act. The alliance between white and blue collars forged during the first revolutionary crisis was interpreted by Sytin and other publishers to be a reliable indicator of joint aspirations. They believed that once the autocracy had fallen, a constitutional, elective parliament would replace it and class differences would dissolve with universal suffrage. After all, they wanted for workers and peasants what those perennially alienated groups wanted for themselves: fair contracts, arable land, and civil liberties. The liberal element insisted upon waiting until after the anticipated victory over the Germans to realize the opportunities made possible by the end of tsardom, but it was a war they could not win once they lost the support of the soldiers fighting it in 1917.

The most pressing question, therefore, is why journalists were willing to accept the illusion of victory they had created on front pages when many knew the facts to be otherwise. It would be too facile to argue that they simply misread their own propaganda, although their eagerness to prove themselves correct contributed substantially to their problems. Newspaper editors had many reasons to believe that they had a majority behind them. The Petrograd Soviet deferred to the Provisional Government, which indicated that those sending deputies to soviets also accepted the legitimacy of the ruling institution recognized by the press. Like the socialist ministers who joined the coalition governments, though, the Petrograd Soviet was considerably more cautious than the rank and file. This allowed journalists to present a myopic view of interclass unity, one that overlooked the elements of social revolution in favor of a strictly political interpretation of events, even after the collapse of the first Provisional Government over its annexationist war policy. News coverage of 1917 emphasizes the importance of the World War leading to the denouement that October because the press continued to advance the platform of those who had proved woefully inept at solving the country's urgent problems.

[7] Rosenberg, *Liberals*, 90; and Chermenskii, *IV Gosudarstvennaia duma*, 309–11.

[8] E. D. Chermenskii, *Burzhuaziia i tsarizm v pervoi russkoi revoliutsii*, 2d ed. (Moscow: Mysl', 1970), 417.

The failure of liberalism, historically connected to both the middle class and the mass-circulation press, raises the question of what this political philosophy meant to Russia's middle classes. Max Weber's insight that "Russian liberalism was a movement not of socioeconomic interest but of ideas"[9] underscored the distinctive roles of state capitalism and the intelligentsia in Russia's historical evolution. Also, as Michael Karpovich argued, the defeat of the Kadets makes an inadequate gauge to measure the potential of Russian liberalism.[10] He also observed that the weakness of the middle class "has been assumed rather than investigated," doubting in any case "the organic connection between liberalism and middle classes."[11] Russia's newspapers reinforce Karpovich's doubts insofar as liberalism has been defined according to criteria established by Western political evolution.

Andrzej Walicki analyzed the legal philosophies of Russian liberalism and, drawing from the long historical ties between liberal and socialist thought, argued that Russian liberalism evolved into a "rule-of-law socialism."[12] Generations of intellectuals, dismayed by the inequalities seemingly inherent in Western individualism, hoped to develop from uniquely Russian circumstances a philosophy that would guarantee equality in a largely peasant society, where formal electoral rights meant little if the underclasses had so little effective control over their daily lives.[13] This perspective appeared again and again in editorial positions across the sweep of the Russian press, from *Moskovskii listok*'s distaste for parliamentarianism to *Russkoe slovo*'s use of the symbolic Tolstoi. The socialist slant to liberalism characteristic of Russia's commercial journalism compares to the classical liberal editorial policies of the Western press which inspired the initial interpretative link between the commercial press and the expansion of democracy.[14] Once again, newspapers performing similar functions produced dissimilar results.

The connection Weber drew between politics and ideas in the Russian setting referred to the importance of journalists in mounting opposition to the autocracy. Newspaper reporters had mixed reactions to the Bolshevik Revolution. Unlike the Kadet leaders who lived their remaining

[9] Quoted from Richard Pipes, *Struve: Liberal on the Left, 1870–1905* (Cambridge, Mass.: Harvard University Press, 1970), 285.

[10] Michael Karpovich, "Two Types of Russian Liberalism: Maklakov and Miliukov," in Ernest J. Simmons, ed., *Continuity and Change in Russian and Soviet Thought* (Cambridge, Mass.: Harvard University Press, 1955), 142.

[11] Ibid., 129.

[12] Walicki, *Legal Philosophies*, especially chapter 7.

[13] Ibid., 59.

[14] Dan Schiller, for example, argued that the early commercial press "owed much of its success in its new role to the acceptance of natural rights—in particular, the right to property." *Objectivity and the News*, 179.

years in Parisian exile planning the evanescent counterrevolution, many of the prominent reporters remained to work under the new regime. Where the Kadets approximated Antonio Gramsci's "traditional" intellectuals, newspaper journalists paralleled the "organic," or those produced by the social changes to which they also contributed.[15] Doroshevich and Giliarovskii, among the first graduates of Pastukhov's "school" at *Moskovskii listok*, welcomed the fact that Russians at last had control of their country after 1917; Doroshevich's daughter succeeded him as a popular Soviet feuilletonist. *Birzhevye vedomosti* editor Iasinskii created a stir when he volunteered for service to the Bolsheviks,[16] but he was one among a number, including Svirskii and Blotermants, who enjoyed a career in Soviet journalism. Nemirovich-Danchenko, on the other hand, appointed professor of Russian geography from his background in travelogues, left Moscow in 1922 to conduct archival research in Berlin and did not return, but nor did he involve himself in oppositional émigré circles.[17] Sytin, the most successful commercial publisher, perhaps exemplified best the attitudes of many who remained behind and continued in their former occupations: never a Bolshevik, he was a nationalist above all else and saw no viable alternatives among the conservative rivals to the new regime.[18]

It must be remembered that the future of Russia's middle classes was not decided in October 1917. Although, like all moderate groups, they disappeared when polarization destroyed the center during the civil war,[19] the Bolsheviks had to compromise their own hard line and depended upon the skills of many from the middle when they inaugurated the New Economic Policy (NEP) to put the country back on the road to economic recovery. Much about NEP would be attractive to prerevolutionary moderates. But just as NEP did not allow political interest groups other than the Bolsheviks to formulate policy, neither did it permit the circulation of a nonparty press. This prevented newspapers from assuming their prerevolutionary capacity to institutionalize a space in which state and society could confront one another; as Habermas argued, "the occupation of the political public sphere by the unpropertied masses led to an interlocking of state and society which removed from the public

[15] Chibnall, in *Law-and-Order News*, discusses Gramsci's theory of two types of intellectuals, the "organic" and the "traditional professional" (211).

[16] *Delo naroda*, 5 Dec. 1917, no. 224.

[17] TsGALI f. 355, op. 2, d. 276, ll. 1–2.

[18] Kugel', "Sytin," 16–19. Revered primarily for his contributions to publications for the masses, a street in Moscow now bears Sytin's name. See also Charles A. Ruud, *Russian Entrepreneur: Publisher Ivan Sytin of Moscow, 1851–1934* (Montreal: McGill-Queen's University Press, 1990), chapter 10.

[19] Karpovich, "Two Types," 142–43.

sphere its basis without supplying a new one."[20] It bears emphasizing that newspapers provide a source of ideology, and the first attempts to use the daily press to inculcate Soviet norms disappointed its prospective audience, many of whom remembered *Kopeika* fondly after having lost it.[21]

Walter Lippmann, the journalistic scholar who opened this study, will appropriately conclude it as well. A member of the official U.S. Creel Commission for propaganda during World War I, he had no less pause than Nemirovich-Danchenko to reconsider the response of human nature to mass communications after his own performance in selling the war. Lippmann produced one of the first major studies that challenged the notion of political neutrality in objective reporting with his investigation of how the American press had misinformed about the Russian Revolution.[22] Never mind that Lippmann succeeded where Nemirovich-Danchenko failed. The differences between Russia and its allies in their respective postwar political situations underscored the deeper socioeconomic disparities that the press could report but not resolve. If this ultimately meant that the approaching end to tsardom would not have resulted in a Western-style liberal government, it still did not foreordain that values associated with freedom of the individual and elective representation, not to mention the personal choice intrinsic to consumerism, would so soon be lost to Russia's political future.

[20] Habermas, *Structural Transformation*, 177.

[21] Jeffrey Brooks, "Public and Private Values in the Soviet Press, 1921–1928," *Slavic Review* 48, no. 1 (1989): 16–35.

[22] Walter Lippmann and Charles Merz, "A Test of the News," *New Republic* 23 (supplement to issue of 4 Aug. 1920): 1–42.

APPENDIXES

A

Numbers, Circulations, and Street Sales of Newspapers

TABLE 1
Numbers of Newspapers in the Two Capitals

	St. Petersburg		Moscow	
	Dailies	*Non-Dailies*	*Dailies*	*Non-Dailies*
1860	5	24	2	9
1870	17	30	4	8
1880	22	43	7	11
1891	17	61	11	32

Source: *Ocherki po istorii Russkoi zhurnalistiki i kritiki* (Leningrad: LGU, 1965), 2:449.

TABLE 2
Periodicals in Russia in 1908 and 1909

1908		1909	
Number of Publications	*Years of Existence*	*Number of Publications*	*Years of Existence*
684	1	682	1
350	2	316	2
36	5	49	5
154	10	18	10
96	30	12	20
15	100	12	30
3	150	7	40
		8	50
		2	60
		3	150

Source: *Vystavka proizvedenii pechati za 1908, za 1909* (St. Petersburg: n.p., 1911), 18, 28.

Note: In 1908, Russia had 433 daily newspapers, and 7 published twice daily; these numbers the next year were 684 and 5, respectively. In 1909, 89 newspapers appeared, some briefly, in St. Petersburg, and 63 in Moscow.

TABLE 3
Number of Russian-Language Newspapers

	Empire	St. Petersburg (Daily)	Moscow (Daily)	Twice Daily
1908	602	—	—	7
1909	662	89[a]	63[a]	5
1910	680	63	56	6
1911	773	—	—	—
1912	876	92	70	6
1913	874	103	56	11
1914	972	106	61	12
1915	715	78	39	10

Sources: *Statistika proizvedenii pechati vyshedshikh v Rossii za 1910–12, 1913, 1914, 1915* (St. Petersburg: n.p., 1916); *Vystavka proizvedenii pechati za 1909* (St. Petersburg; n.p., 1911).

[a] Includes non-dailies.

TABLE 4
Daily Street Sales, St. Petersburg, 1867–1880

	SPB vedomsti	Golos	Novoe vremia	Peter. listok	Peter. gazeta	Russkii invalid	Novosti	Birzhevye vedomosti	Totals
1867	1,000	2,700	—	1,000	390	300	—	400	—
1876	700	2,007	3,200	—	—	—	550	420	12,716
1877	390	3,870	3,825	—	—	—	225	—	—
1880	—	4,500	4,000	2,200	—	—	370	—	23,980

Source: B. I. Esin, "Materialy k istorii gazetnogo dela v Rossii," *Vestnik MGU*, journalism series, no. 4 (1967): 85–86.

TABLE 5

Annual Street Sales, St. Petersburg, 1905–1915

	Novoe vremia	Grazhdanin	Birzhevye vedomosti.a.m.	Birzhevye vedomosti.p.m.	Peter. listok	Peter. gazeta
1905	5,162,603	6,271	—	6,522,774	9,814,261	3,580,090
1906	5,459,627	4,555	1,861,579	8,658,774	10,815,690	5,341,023
1908	4,690,446	1,635	1,130,371	7,385,494	11,131,116	6,654,696
1909	4,632,610	—	945,207	9,459,495	13,266,490	7,718,235
1910	3,877,369	2,147	881,125	8,945,663	11,948,190	6,924,562
1911	5,045,338	2,188	819,235	8,556,233	17,204,028	5,808,722
1912	4,894,497	—	719,822	9,543,101	18,803,907	9,455,502
1914	3,924,136	—	2,584,099	18,301,114	16,457,418	7,955,995
1915	6,212,252	—	5,383,439	24,460,985	23,984,368	11,811,494

	Gazeta kopeika	Pravit. vestnik	Rech'	Russkoe slovo	Sovrem. slovo	Ruskii invalid	Vecher. vremia
1905	—	282,765	—	—	—	—	—
1906	—	23,719	1,747,510	—	—	—	—
1908	2,233,167	16,670	2,044,522	7,986	1,026,564	27,283	—
1909	10,229,268	—	1,633,067	29,595	—	—	—
1910	9,264,763	16,803	2,495,383	39,439	166,722	18,928	—
1911	17,308,717	—	3,153,711	79,327	3,701,326	—	—
1912	17,172,315	—	2,839,094	81,626	3,950,297	—	3,077,224
1914	9,404,760	—	2,166,339	108,986	2,621,507	—	6,875,422
1915	5,514,156	55,996	2,974,160	—	5,073,787	6,429	15,914,570

	Pravda	Den'	Malenkaia gazeta
1912	1,792,693	—	—
1914	—	888,555	—
1915	—	1,069,447	3,706,910

Source: TsGIA f. 776, op. 29, dd. 29–37.

TABLE 6

Circulations of St. Petersburg Newspapers

	Birzhevye[a] vedomosti	Molva	Nedelia	Golos	Sev. pchela
1860s	—	—	—	10,000	4,000
1870	8,000	—	2,000	14,000	—
1870s	—	—	7,500	22,000	—
1880	—	4,000	—	23,000	—
1882	—	—	8,500	25,000	—
1890	—	—	15,000	—	—
1892	—	—	11,000	—	—

	Novosti	Syn otechestva	Russkii invalid
1860s	—	20,000[b]	—
1870	1,900	—	—
1880	15,000	—	—
1882	17,000	14,000	5,000
1890	—	—	—
1905	35,000	—	7,000

	Novoe vremia	Peter. gazeta	Peter. listok	Birzh. vedomosti I[c]
1870	—	—	9,000	—
1880	20,000	—	12,000	—
1882	20,000	20,000	10,000	—
1880s	25,000	22,000	10,200	—
1890	—	—	13,000	—
1895	30,000	30,000	24,000	30,000
1900	60,000	—	30,000	—
1905	71,500	—	—	—
After				
1905	60,000	20,000	80,000	—
1915	80,000	50,000	88,500	52,000
1916	76,000	50,000	128,500	57,000

	Birzh. vedomosti II[c]	Gazeta kopeika	Rech'	Narodn. Svoboda[d]
1905	130,000	—	—	24,000
After			17,000	35,000
1905	80,000	—	40,000	—
1909	—	250,000	—	—
1912	—	—	35,000	—
1913	—	220,000	—	—

TABLE 6 (*cont.*)

	Birzhevye[a] vedomosti	Molva	Nedelia	Golos	Sev. pchela
1915	228,000	170,000	45,000	—	
1916	157,000	135,000	40,000	—	
1917	—	120,000 (June) 60,000 (October)	—	—	

	Den'	Verchern. vremia	Malenk. gazeta	Sovrem. slovo
After 1905	23,000	—	—	—
1915	40,000	135,000	—	75,000
1916	30,000	120,000	60,000	56,000

Source: See sources for table 8.

[a] This edition was published by K. V. Trubnikov.

[b] More than half of these were distributed in the provinces.

[c] "I" refers to the St. Petersburg edition of the paper and "II" refers to the second edition, which was distributed in Moscow and the provinces.

[d] This also refers to *Svobodnyi narod*, the newspaper's other name. These were Kadet publications, published by S. M. Propper in the winter of 1905 in place of the first edition of *Birzhevye vedomosti*.

TABLE 7

Circulations of Other St. Petersburg Newspapers in 1905 Only

Nasha zhizn'	40,000
Novaia zhizn'	20–50,000
Rossiia	10,000
SPB vedomosti	7,000
Slovo	20–30,000
Grazhdanin	3,000

Source: TsGIA f. 776, op. 29, d. 29.

TABLE 8
Circulations of Moscow Newspapers

	Russkie vedomosti	Mosk. listok	Utro rossii	Russkoe slovo	Mosk. kopeika
1880s	—	30–35,000	—	—	
1890	25,000	—	—	—	—
1895	23,000	30,000	—	—	
1898	—	—	—	13,200	—
1899	—	—	—	18,700	—
1900	—	40,000	—	28,400	—
1901	—	—	—	30,600	—
1902	—	—	—	30,100	—
1903	—	—	—	43,700	—
1904	—	—	—	117,000	—
1905	50,000	—	—	157,700	—
1906	—	—	—	98,100	—
1907	—	—	—	126,500	—
1908	—	—	—	127,360	—
1909	—	—	10,000	146,500	100,000
1910	—	45,000	25,000	198,100	150,000
1911	—	—	—	219,600	—
1912	—	—	—	287,500	—
1913	—	—	40,000	325,700	—
1914	—	—	—	619,500	—
1915	—	—	—	655,300	—
1916	50,000	—	—	739,000	—
1917	—	—	—	1,013,000	—

Sources: Figures for tables 5, 8 were culled from a variety of sources, often contradictory. Wherever possible, I have used archival sources or secondary sources which I know to be based on archival data. For unsubstantiated secondary literature, if figures differed dramatically from archival sources from about the same time period, I did not use it. The sources are: TsGIA f. 776, op. 29, d. 29, ll. 8–27; TsGIA f. 776, op. 29, d. 15, ll. 20–30; TsGIA f. 777, op. 19, d. 40, l. 2; GIALO f. 706, op. 1, d. 1137; TsGALI f. 358, k. 148, ed. khran. 10, l. 133; TsGALI f. 595, op. 1, d. 40, l. 84; Balmuth, *Censorship*, 95, 113; Esin, "Materialy," 84–86; *Ocherki po istorii zhurnalistiki*, vol. 2; *Polveka*, 419; Skrobotov, *"Peterburgskii listok" za 35 let*; S. Sredinskii, *Gazetno-izdatel'skoe delo* (Moscow: n.p., 1924), 10–13.

B

Statistics on Punishment by the Censorship

TABLE 9
Government Closings of Periodicals, 1865–1904

	Closed for Ignoring Warnings	Closed for Violating Circulars
1865–1869	10	—
1870–1874	13	1
1875–1879	18	9
1880–1884	8	6
1885–1889	4	4
1890–1894	1	—
1895–1899	7	—
1900–1904	3	3

Source: V. Rozenberg and V. Iakushkin, *Russkaia pechat' i tsenzura v proshlom i nastoiashchem* (Moscow: Izd. M. i S. Sabashnikovykh, 1905), 140.

TABLE 10
Number of Administrative Fines and Warnings Against Newspapers, 1865–1904

	Fines	Warnings
1865–1869	60	46
1870–1874	103	58
1875–1879	164	26
1880–1884	94	41
1885–1889	60	13
1890–1894	48	8
1895–1899	101	27
1900–1904	82	20

Source: Rozenberg and Iakushkin, *Russkaia pechat' i tsenzura*, 136–37.

TABLE 11
Commerce-Related Punishments by Censors, 1870–1904

	Prohibition of Advertising	*Prohibition of Street Sales*
1870–1874	0	34
1875–1879	1	58
1880–1884	3	26
1885–1889	6	21
1890–1894	6	22
1895–1899	10	31
1900–1904	5	26

Source: Rozenberg and Iakushkin, *Russkaia pechat' i tsenzura*, 138, 141.

TABLE 12
Percentages of Types of Punishment, 1865–1904

	Warnings	*Street Sales Prohibited*	*Temporary Suspension*	*Advert. Suspended*	*Closing*
1865–1869	76.6	—	16.7	—	6.7
1870–1874	52.4	33.0	13.6	—	—
1875–1879	43.3	35.3	18.3	0.6	2.5
1880–1884	43.6	27.7	20.2	3.2	5.3
1885–1889	21.6	35.0	25.0	10.0	8.4
1890–1894	16.6	45.8	20.8	12.5	—
1895–1899	26.7	30.7	28.7	9.9	4.0
1900–1904	24.1	31.3	31.3	6.6	6.7

Source: Rozenberg and Iakushkin, *Russkaia pechat' i tsenzura*, 144.

Note: Rows do not always total 100 percent because there were occasional punishments administered by special decree.

TABLE 13

Court Trials of Censorship Cases, According to Articles 1008–22, 1024–38, and 1041–48 of the Criminal Code

	Accused	Found Innocent	Found Guilty	Sentenced to Jail	Arrested	Fined
1890	35	15	19	—	10	9
1891	48	25	22	—	2	20
1892	59	7	52	—	6	46
1893	53	16	37	—	5	32
1894	20	3	17	—	—	17
1895[a]	2	—	—	—	—	—
1896[a]	2	1	—	—	—	—
1898	13	6	7	—	1	6
1899	31	8	23	—	6	17
1900	28	19	8	—	3	6
1901	30	14	16	—	2	4
1902	29	8	21	—	6	15
1903	24	4	20	—	3	16
1904	16	7	7	—	2	5
1905	7	—	7	—	—	7
1906	223	148	175	—	12	58
1907	246	89	157	—	30	116
1908	146	39	63	7	17	83
1909	132	58	83	4	20	59
1910	136	36	100	2	22	47
1911[a]	198	57	142	2	65	74
1912	172	58	94	2	22	70
1913[a]	95	26	53	6	9	38

Source: Svod statisticheskikh svedenii o podsudimykh opravdannykh i osuzhdennikh po obshchikh su-debnykh mest (St. Petersburg: Izd. Min. Iiust., 1892–1916).

Note: These include all press crimes except defamation of character. The figures in columns 2 and 3 do not always total those in column 1, but they are never so different as to create a serious discrepancy. Figures for 1897 were not available.

[a] Some of the accused in these years fall into a special category, in which the accused were declared innocent by special decree: 2 in 1895, 1 in 1896, 20 in 1911, and 16 in 1913.

TABLE 14
Aggregate Punishments, 1905–1910

	Imposed by Administration	Imposed by Courts
Number of fines	903	155
Amount, in rubles	474,870	21,538
Newspapers closed	1,046	224

Source: A. B. Ventin, "Piatiletnye itogi," *Sovremennyi mir*, no. 12 (1910): 89.

Note: These figures were collected from newspaper articles and wire service reports. They include the whole country, but Moscow and St. Petersburg account for the overwhelming majority.

TABLE 15
The Administration, the Courts, and Censorship, 1907–1909

	Editors Tried	Editors Jailed or Arrested	Newspapers Closed by Courts	Newspapers Closed by Admin.	Fines[a] by Courts	Fines[a] by Admin.
1907	507	180	81	333	26 (5,378)	270 (169,175)
1908	95	101	9	63	27 (3,410)	175 (117,550)
1909	60	69	9	25	24 (2,790)	216 (94,125)

Source: A. B. Ventin, "K statistike repressii v Rossii," *Sovremennyi mir*, no. 4 (1910): 69–72.

Note: These figures were collected from news stories and wire service reports. The reactionary press is also included here, although it constitutes a fraction of the total figures.

[a] Numbers in parentheses indicate the ruble amount of the fines.

C

Content Analyses of Major Newspapers

The following tables are based on analysis of the contents of the newspapers during one week in the given year. The categories were modified from Paul Deutschmann's 1959 study, *News-Page Content Analysis of Twelve Metropolitan Dailies*. Numbers indicate percentage of news space dedicated to each category. Editorials and feuilletons, like hard news, were considered according to topic. The percentage of advertising space was tabulated separately. Columns do not always total 100 due to rounding error.

TABLE 16
Content Analysis of *Golos*

	1876	1882
National politics	19	22
National news	16	17
Local news and government	4	7
International news and government	14	12
War, rebellion, and defense	5	4
Economics and transportation	16	15
Crime	4	3
Public welfare and education	3	3
Accidents and disasters	1	0
Science and inventions	2	1
Entertainment	4	3
Literature and theater reviews	3	4
General interest	9	8
(Total percentage of advertising)	(39)	(38)

Note: Cost, with delivery, was 16 rubles.

TABLE 17

Content Analysis of *Peterburgskii listok*

	1864	1870	1893	1910
National politics	0	2	4	12
National news	5	7	12	9
Local news and government	31	33	21	18
International news and government	0	4	3	5
War, rebellion, and defense	0	2	1	0
Economics and transportation	0	3	7	5
Crime	13	14	9	13
Public welfare and education	26	8	12	14
Accidents and disasters	0	0	2	3
Science and inventions	0	0	0	0
Entertainment	8	18	18	14
Literature and theater reviews	4	0	2	2
General interest	12	8	8	6
(Total percentage of advertising)	(45)	(30)	(34)	(38)

Note: Cost rose within the first years from 3 to 5½ rubles, an extra ruble or more with delivery. By 1910 the price had risen to 9 rubles.

TABLE 18

Content Analysis of *Peterburgskaia gazeta*

	1868	1886	1908
National politics	8	2	13
National news	11	9	7
Local news and government	19	23	16
International news and government	8	4	6
War, rebellion, and defense	3	1	1
Economics and transportation	1	3	3
Crime	9	7	10
Public welfare and education	17	12	11
Accidents and disasters	2	1	2
Science and inventions	0	1	3
Entertainment	8	14	11
Literature and theater reviews	6	10	10
General interest	7	13	8
(Total percentage of advertising)	(28)	(32)	(33)

Note: Cost rose from 4 to 7½ rubles, with and extra ruble or more for delivery. The cost in 1908 was 9 rubles.

TABLE 19

Content Analysis of *Novoe vremia*

	1900	1907	1912
National politics	24	23	24
National news	11	8	7
Local news and government	8	6	4
International news and government	14	12	11
War, rebellion, and defense	6	5	7
Economics and transportation	9	11	10
Crime	2	3	4
Public welfare and education	4	7	7
Accidents and disasters	1	1	4[a]
Science and inventions	0	3	2
Entertainment	3	2	2
Literature and theater reviews	2	5	4
General interest	15	13	15
(Total percentage of advertising)	(46)	(44)	(47)

Note: Cost with delivery, rose from 14 to 17 rubles between 1900 and 1912.

[a] The *Titanic* sank during the week under review.

TABLE 20

Content Analysis of *Birzhevye vedomosti*

	1864	1870	1893	1910
National politics	2	8	9	18
National news	17	11	14	13
Local news and government	4	6	8	10
International news and government	7	8	11	9
War, rebellion, and defense	0	3	3	2
Economics and transportation	64	42	19	12
Crime	0	9	5	6
Public welfare and education	1	5	12	9
Accidents and disasters	0	0	2	1
Science and inventions	3	1	1	0
Entertainment	0	1	3	8
Literature and theater reviews	0	0	5	4
General interest	2	5	6	9
(Total percentage of advertising)	(29)	(17)	(23)	(31)

Note: Cost fluctuated from 8 to 16 to 12 to 10 rubles, depending on whether Trubnikov or Propper was publishing, and at what time.

TABLE 21

Content Analysis of *Moskovskii listok*

	1881	1892	1907
National politics	5	7	19
National news	9	11	12
Local news and government	16	14	11
International news and government	6	6	5
War, rebellion, and defense	3	1	1
Economics and transportation	4	6	8
Crime	10	9	7
Public welfare and education	13	14	10
Accidents and disasters	2	3	2
Science and inventions	2	1	0
Entertainment	9	13	12
Literature and theater reviews	7	8	5
General interest	12	7	6
(Total percentage of advertising)	(27)	(37)	(37)

Note: Cost rose from 7½ to 9 rubles, extra with delivery.

TABLE 22

Content Analysis of *Russkoe slovo*

	1895	1898	1904	1907	1912
National politics	15	13	16	32	23
National news	12	11	12	15	12
Local news and government	10	12	10	7	7
International news and government	15	9	7	5	8
War, rebellion, and defense	2	3	14	2	9
Economics and transportation	8	7	6	6	5
Crime	3	4	6	4	7
Public welfare and education	8[a]	6	5	7	7
Accidents and disasters	2	2	1	2	1
Science and inventions	1	2	0	1	1
Entertainment	8	9	6	7	8
Literature and theater reviews	2	6	3	4	4
General interest	13	15	13	7	8
(Total percentage of advertising)	(13)	(31)	(48)	(54)	(47)

Note: Cost, with delivery, rose from 5 to 8 rubles between 1895 and 1912.

[a] This was dominated by religious themes.

TABLE 23

Content Analysis of *Gazeta kopeika*

	1909	1912
National politics	13	14
National news	6	7
Local news and government	8	7
International news and government	8	9
War, rebellion, and defense	2	5
Economics and transportation	3	2
Crime	9	8
Public welfare and education	12	9
Accidents and disasters	9	9
Science and inventions	1	3
Entertainment	18	16
Literature and theater reviews	1	2
General interest	10	10
(Total percentage of advertising)	(27)	(41)

Note: Cost, with delivery, was 3 rubles. Delivery outside the city cost an extra 50 kopecks, and selected illustrated supplements could also be purchased with the annual subscription.

Index ─────────────────────────────

advertising, 17, 25, 27, 50, 98, 151

agenda-setting function of press, 28, 124, 199

Alexander II, 4, 18, 23, 40, 83, 206; assassination of, 94–96

Alexander III, 96, 98, 107, 125, 190

Amfiteatrov, A. V., 133–34, 181–83, 228, 267

Barnum, P. T., 115–16

Beilis, Mendel, 226–27, 249–50

Belinskii, Vissarion, 33–34, 55, 59, 117–18, 120, 227

Bennett, James Gordon, 15, 36–37, 61, 119, 148, 154

Bernhardt, Sarah, 98–99, 104

Birzhevye vedomosti, 3, 53, 126–30, 158–59, 175, 185, 244–45, 257, 272–74, 283; circulation of, 298–99; content analysis of, 310; street sales of, 296–97

Bliuvshtein, Sofia ("The Golden Arm"), 113, 139, 164–65

Blotermants, O. Ia., 153, 230, 231, 233–34, 288

Bolsheviks, 253, 264, 269–76, 278–79, 288

bourgeoisie. *See* middle classes

British press, 15–16, 28, 58, 80–81, 114, 119, 121–22, 124–25

Carey, James, 4n, 8n, 116

Catherine the Great, 19, 22

censorship, 21–24, 27, 41, 54, 63, 96, 100, 102, 106, 112, 124, 127, 149, 173; under the Bolsheviks, 280; military, in World War I, 254, 259; and 1905 Revolution, 199, 218–21, 266–67; under the Provisional Government, 274; statistics on punishment, 302–6

Chartier, Roger, 116

Chekhov, Alexander, 100, 163

Chekhov, Anton, 64, 100, 118, 162–64

commercialism, 5, 12, 26, 30, 97, 99, 109, 131, 139, 147, 157, 284

conservatism, 5, 74, 103, 181, 249–50

consumerism. *See* commercialism

corruption in journalism, 17, 156–59

crime news, 41–42, 60–61, 235–36; and murders at Ligovo (1886), 137–38; and Palem case (1895), 141–43

Custer, General G. A., 86

Doroshevich, V. M., 54, 103–4, 110–11, 133–34, 145, 148, 156, 163–65, 168–69, 174–75, 179–80, 188, 195, 217, 243, 288

Duma, 199, 210, 215; First, 212–13; Second, 212, 214; Third, 244, 247; Fourth, 244, 250

Dupuy, Jean, 16, 148

facticity and fact-mindedness in journalism, 14, 24, 68, 112, 117, 119, 146

feuilletonists, 26, 66–70, 230–34

French press, 16–17, 28, 119, 121, 124, 145, 162, 260

Gazeta kopeika, 225, 229–39, 283; circulation of, 298; street sales of, 297; content analysis of, 311

Giliarovskii, V. A., 89, 102, 151, 155, 173, 288

Girardin, Emile, 16, 36–37, 128n

Goldkin, E. L., 17, 80, 145

Golos, 30–51, 54–56, 67, 96, 113, 126, 279, 283; circulation of, 298; content analysis of, 308; street sales of, 296

Gorky, Maxim, 150, 246, 273

Gorodetskii, M. B., 153, 228–29

Gradovskii, G. K., 89–91, 93, 131, 156

Grazhdanin, 100, 128

Greeley, Horace, 99, 129n

Gridina, Olga, 231–32

Habermas, Jürgen, 3, 12, 29, 288

Haimson, Leopold, 7, 200, 223–24, 228n, 251

Harmsworth, Alfred (Lord Northcliffe), 16, 122, 125, 128n, 148

Hearst, William Randolph, 79, 114, 129n, 171, 173, 173n

Herzen, Alexander, 23, 117

imperialism, reflected in journalism, 169–
71, 179–85, 193–97
intelligentsia, 30, 34, 71, 99–100, 113–14,
117, 160–62, 196, 224, 227–28
investigative reporting, 58–59, 65, 164, 273

"journalese," 52, 59, 68, 91, 164

Kadets (Constitutional Democrats), 201,
210–11, 213, 216–18, 256n, 285, 287
Katkov, M. N., 34–35, 39, 93, 128, 131.
See also Moskovskie vedomosti
Kaufman, A. E., 153, 158, 211, 219–20
Kerenskii, Alexander, 256, 258–59, 268,
274, 275n
Khudekov, S. N. *See Peterburgskaia gazeta*
Korolenko, V. G., 132, 166, 267
Korsh, Baron V. F., 34–35, 75, 131
Kraevskii, A. A., 31–34, 38–39, 74, 113,
131, 148. *See also Golos*
Krestovskii, V. V., 59–61, 71, 89
Krizis verkhov (crisis of authority, 1915–
1917), 263–68
Kuprin, Alexander, 149–50, 245

language. *See* "journalese"
Leikin, Nikolai, 68–70, 98, 148, 195
Lena goldfields massacre, 237–38
Leskov, Nikolai, 77, 131, 148
liberalism, as reflected in the Russian
press, 5, 11–12, 216–18, 230–31, 244–48,
269, 271, 280, 284, 287
Lippmann, Walter, 11, 29, 289
Lukhmanova, N. A., 191, 231

MacGahan, Januarius Aloysius, 81–82, 89,
90
Menshikov, M. O., 149, 158, 180, 267
Merezhkovskii, D. S., 176, 194, 257
Miakotin, V. A., 8, 99–100, 114
Miasnitskii, I. I., 104, 148, 173
middle classes, 5–7, 53, 97, 109, 119, 147,
169, 170n, 200, 217, 225, 231, 234, 237,
248, 251, 253, 270, 285, 287–88
Miliukov, P. N., 206, 211, 246, 253, 268
Moskovskie vedomosti, 19–20, 25, 35, 72,
102
Moskovskii listok, 102–6, 109–13, 249, 283;
circulation of, 300; content analysis of,
310

national identity. *See* nationalism, expressed in journalism
nationalism, expressed in journalism, 44–
46, 62, 64–65, 86, 110, 179–85, 243, 283
Nechaev Affair, 40–41, 63, 71, 92, 107
Nemirovich-Danchenko, V. I., 87–92, 120,
133, 145, 148, 186–87, 194, 196, 246,
261–63
Nicholas I, 20, 22, 59
Nicholas II, 74, 125, 199, 206, 208, 212,
219
Nord, David Paul, 44, 124
Notovich, O. K., 160. *See also Novosti*
Novoe vremia, 25, 79, 83, 133, 158, 243,
250, 257, 283; circulation of, 298; content analysis of, 309; street sales of, 296–
97
Novosti, 131–32, 150, 152

objectivity in reporting, 8, 36–37, 59, 92,
118, 155, 165, 187
Octobrists, 201, 211, 213, 244; A. I. Guchkov and, 245, 268
Orthodox church, 46, 66, 107, 176, 194,
204–5, 240, 283
Otechestvennye zapiski, 33, 59, 66, 96,
113, 117

Park, Robert, 56, 145n
Pastukhov, N. I., 101–2, 148, 159, 249
peasant question, 134, 178, 241, 285
Peterburgskaia gazeta, 63–71, 105, 138,
203, 245–46, 257, 283; circulation of,
298; content analysis of, 309; street sales
of, 296–97
Peterburgskii listok, 52–63, 248–49, 257,
283; circulation of, 298; content analysis
of, 308; street sales of, 296–97
Petit Prisian, Le. *See* Dupuy, Jean
Petrov, G. S., 176, 204, 206, 214, 243,
260, 263
Pravda. *See* Bolsheviks
Pravitel'stvennyi vestnik, 21, 40, 63, 89,
107, 277
Press, La. *See* Girardin, Emile
professionalization of journalists, 147, 153–
61
propaganda, 254–55, 259–60, 278, 280, 289
Propper, S. M., 126–30, 181. *See also Birzhevye vedomosti*

Provisional Government, 268–69, 274–75, 277–80

public sphere, 3, 12, 13n; Russian press as representative of, 27, 29, 50, 54, 73, 97, 130, 135, 147, 155, 175, 185, 247, 281, 289

Pulitzer, Joseph, 114–15, 120–21, 126, 160

Pushkin, Alexander, 20, 32; and Pushkin Celebration of 1880, 36; and Pushkin Celebration of 1887, 139–41

Rasputin, 258, 270–71

Rech'. See Kadets (Constitutional Democrats)

Revolution of 1905, 203–10

Revolution of 1917, 268–76

revolutionary movement, 49, 63, 76–77, 92–93

Rossiia (Doroshevich's edition), 133–34

Rossiia (Stolypin's edition), 221, 226

Russkaia volia, 267

Russkie vedomosti, 102, 117–18, 133

Russkoe slovo, 168, 173–79, 202–3, 216–18, 239–44, 256, 272, 277, 283; circulation of, 300; content analysis of, 311

Saltykov-Shchedrin, M. E., 66, 117, 167

Schudson, Michael, 5, 15, 159n

Sel'skii vestnik, 107

sensationalism, 60, 97, 106, 112, 119, 237, 248; and "yellow" journalism, 114–15, 115n

Severnaia pchela, 20–21, 25, 77

Shreier, Iulii, 89, 131, 149, 153, 155–56

Slavophilism, 30, 35, 110; and Pan-Slavism, 82–83, 85

socialism, as reflected in the Russian press, 5, 269, 271–72, 280, 285, 287

Sokolova, Alexandra, 77–78, 103, 148

Soviet: St. Petersburg (1905), 132, 209; Petrograd (1917), 268–69, 276, 286

SPB vedomosti, 19, 33, 75, 77, 195

Stead, William, 58, 114

Stolypin, P. A., 198, 212, 215–16, 221, 226, 247

street sales, 3, 25–27, 206, 296–97; and railroad delivery, 136

Struve, P. B., 202, 210, 218

Suvorin, A. S., 74–77, 113, 129, 131–32, 136, 148, 159, 249. See also Novoe vremia

Svirskii, A. I., 151–52, 288

Sytin, I. D., 168, 171–72, 218, 288. See also Russkoe slovo

technology, 13, 22, 28, 73, 83, 97, 113, 221, 247; and telegraph, 47–48, 186, 192, 277

"thick" journals, 30, 32–33, 49, 68, 76, 78, 99, 114, 117, 166

"thin" journals, 100, 114

Times (London), 15, 37, 79

Tolstoi, Dmitrii, 35, 96, 107, 126

Tolstoi, Lev, 172–73, 175–76, 185, 195, 219, 226, 260, 272

Trubnikov, K. V., 47, 126, 135, 151

Turgenev, I. S., 23, 33, 67, 83

U.S. press, 14–15, 28, 44, 46, 79, 99, 115, 119, 124–25, 156, 159–60

war correspondence, 79–80, 255; Russo-Japanese War, 185–92; Russo-Turkish War, 81–91; World War I, 259–63

Westernizers, 30, 35, 76, 110, 195

Witte, S. Iu., 126–30, 192, 209, 243

worker question, 43–44, 66, 111, 177, 234, 238–39, 242

Zarudnye, A. A. and N. A. See Peterburgskii listok

Zasulich, Vera, 92–93, 143